Employee Rights and Employer Wrongs

How To Identify Employee Abuse

And How To Stand Up For Yourself

Suzanne Kleinberg and

Michael Kreimeh

U.S. Version

Other Books by Suzanne Kleinberg

From Playstation® to Workstation: A Career Guide for Generation Text Surviving in a Baby Boomer World.

Keeping Up With The Jacksons: A Financial Management Guide for the American Teen

Employee Rights and Employer Wrongs:

How To Identify Employee Abuse

And How To Stand Up For Yourself

U.S. Edition

Suzanne Kleinberg and Michael Kreimeh

Potential To Soar Publishing

Toronto, Canada

Canadian Cataloguing in Publication Data

Library and Archives Canada Cataloguing in Publication

Kleinberg, Suzanne, 1963-
    Employee Rights and Employer Wrongs: How to Identify Employee Abuse and How to Stand Up For Yourself / Suzanne Kleinberg; Michael Kreimeh, illustrator.

Includes index.
ISBN 978-0-9866684-8-7

1. Employee rights. 2. Labor laws and legislation.
3. Bullying in the workplace--Law and legislation. 4. Work environment--Canada.
I. Kreimeh, Michael, 1970- II. Title.

HF5549.5.E428K54 2011   331.01'10971   C2011-901281-2

Potential To Soar Publishing
Thornhill, Ontario

Dedication

This book is dedicated to all the hard working Americans trying to earn an honest living in such diverse, complex and always changing work environments.

Disclaimer

The materials available in this book are for informational purposes only and not for the purpose of providing legal advice. You should contact an attorney to obtain advice with respect to any particular issue or problem. The opinions expressed in this book are the opinions of the individual authors and may not reflect the opinions of any individual attorney.

Every reasonable effort has been made to ensure that the information presented in this book is current and accurate. At any time, some details may not yet reflect recent changes in laws, statutes or rulings.

Links within this book to websites are provided for the convenience of readers. Neither the authors nor publisher of this book creates or maintains these websites and does not accept any responsibility for their content and accuracy.

Neither the authors nor the publisher will be liable for any loss or damages of any nature, either direct or indirect, arising from use of the information provided in this book.

Table of Contents

Employee Rights _____ 1

America Against the World _____ 3

What is an Employee? _____ 3

Human Resources – Whose Side Are They On? _____ 5

Basic Employee Rights _____ 7

Fair Labor Standards Act (FLSA) _____ 7

Current Minimum Wage _____ 7

Hours of Work, Overtime, Meal and Other Breaks _____ 13

Equal Pay Legislation _____ 17

Legal and Public Holidays _____ 17

Vacation Time/Pay_____ 19

Right to Refuse Work_____ 23

Civic Duty _____ 25

Family and Medical Leave Act (FMLA) _____ 28

Expanding the Definition of Family_____ 28

Maternity, Parental and Adoption Leave _____ 29

American with Disabilities Act (ADA) _____ 49

Whistleblower Protection _____ 52

Employer's Rights _____ 65

Paycheck Deductions_____ 65

Reimbursements _____ 79

*Workplace Privacy*_____ 80

*Common Employer Wrongs*_____ 104

Dismissals_____ 104

Discrimination _____ 123

How to Tell You are Being Terminated _____ 138

What To Do If You Are Targeted For Termination._____ 141

Collecting Your Evidence _____ 145

Common Mistakes Employers Make_____ 147

Common Mistakes Employers Make _____ 147

Disciplinary Action _____ 149

Handling a Termination Meeting _____ 151

Should I Sign a Release? _____ 153

Post – Termination Emotions _____ 154

What Happens if the Business files for Bankruptcy? _____ 158

What Happens if a Business is Sold? _____ 159

Resignation _____ 160

Termination Law _____ 165

Legal Advice _____ 173

Hiring an Attorney _____ 173

The Court Process _____ 186

Negotiating a Package _____ 188

Preparing For Severance Negotiation _____ 195

Tips For Lawyer-Assisted Negotiations _____ 200

How Much Should I Ask For? _____ 202

Appendix A: Termination Laws by State _____ 205

Appendix B: Complaint Process _____ 291

Appendix C: Sample Letters _____ 351

Sample Demand Letter For Unpaid Wages _____ 353

Sample Letter To Retract Spontaneous Resignation _____ 354

Sample Discrimination Complaint Letter _____ 355

Sample Sexual Harassment Complaint _____ 357

Sample Racial Discrimination Letter _____ 360

Sample Letter Notice of Default _____ 362

Sample Non-Acceptance Letter _____ 363

Sample Reprimand Protest Memo _____ 366

Sample Tip Reduction Complaint Letter _____ 369

Sample Pregnancy Discrimination Complaint Letter _____ 371

Appendix D: Case Studies _____ 377

Allegation: Racial Discrimination _____ 377

Allegation: Sexual Harassment by a Superior _____ 379

Allegation: Attempted Dismissal Using Harassment _____ 381

Allegation: Creating / Sustaining a Hostile Work Environment _____ 386

Allegation: Discrimination for Disability/Racial & Retaliation _____ 390

Allegation: Retaliation in the form of Constructive Dismissal _____ 393

Allegation: Retaliation for Verbal Complaint_____ 397

Glossary _____ 399

Index _____ 405

Introduction

Have you ever wondered if your boss is treating you within your legal rights? Many employees put up with unwarranted stress, excessive workloads, and violation of rights because they are either in fear of losing their jobs, unsure of their legal rights or a combination of both.

During times of economic uncertainty, many employers knowingly (and sometimes unknowingly) take advantage of this fear by pushing employees to the limit. Just because an employer does not overtly threaten your job does not mean that you haven't been bullied. Unethical actions can be equally interpreted as menacing and exploitative. And unless you have a few hundred dollars handy, you cannot even get a consultation with an employment lawyer to understand your rights.

For many, the workplace has become a stressful, self-esteem crushing and frightening place that impacts health, relationships and emotional balance. As employees, we all need a little guidance and hope to cope with the daily grind. This book will cover what the basic employee rights are in the U.S. for full-time permanent and non-union employees.

Over the past several decades, American employees have been slowly stripped of their rights as workers and as humans. Compared to the rest of the industrialized world (and many non-industrialized countries), the U.S. has fallen far behind in protecting its hard-working labor force, the backbone of the country's economic strength, from retaining basic workplace rights. Unions and labor rights groups have been defanged. And when groups start to stand up for these well-deserved rights, the elite label them as "socialists" to scare everyone back to their seats.

The first step to moving forward is understanding your rights, exercising them and protecting them. All of this can be done calmly, professionally and legally.

This book is in no way a substitute for the advice of an experienced labor lawyer. It is more of a guide to help you decide if it is worth pursuing legal or government assistance. It is **NOT** to be taken as legal advice for individual cases, as each case always has unique circumstances.

Preface

Nearly half (49%) of North American employees have been affected by workplace bullying, either being a target themselves or having witnessed abusive behavior against a co-worker. 65% of people in the U.S. say they have experienced discrimination of some type. A large majority of those who feel they have been discriminated against did nothing about it and most were unhappy with the outcome. Less than 5% of the wrongful dismissal cases actually go to court due to quick settlements. This small percentage reflects only the cases that have actually been pursued which are a small fraction of potential cases of unfair termination.

Americans who suffer from workplace hostility experience stress-related health problems, including anxiety, panic attacks, sleep disorders and depression, just to name a few. Prolonged exposure to stress in the workplace can lead to other serious health concerns, such as problems related to cardiovascular, neurological and immune system health. Also, victims often decide to quit their jobs and end up trading the stress of bullying for the stress of being unemployed.

Too many people tolerate unfair, and in some cases abusive, workplace environments because they do not feel that they have any options. This book was developed with those people in mind. When you are unsure of your rights but unsure whether you need a lawyer, this book is designed to fill that gap and help you understand what your rights are and what your first steps may be. We have also included some sample letters that you may want to use to address your employer.

Hopefully, this book will guide you to a better work environment and happier, more balanced, life.

Employee Rights

America Against the World

Are you aware that the U.S. is well *behind* the rest of the world in many areas of workplace protection? For example, in parental leave policy, a 2012 Human Rights Watch report declares that the U.S., along with Papua New Guinea, Swaziland, Liberia and Lesotho are the only countries in the entire world that provide no mandated financial support for paid maternity leave. (Even Afghanistan offers 90 days at 100% pay.) Only two U.S. states -- California and New Jersey -- have public paid leave insurance programs.

America also stands out, and not in a positive way, regarding its approach to guaranteeing paid vacations. While U.S. employers are not legally required to provide full-time employees with any vacation pay, the rest of the world approaches this issue differently. Canada guarantees 10 days paid per year, Mexico 7 days, Vietnam 10 days, Brazil 30 days, Norway 25 days, Denmark 6 weeks and so on.

And the U.S. does not protect its employees who are terminated without cause with any legal minimum termination/severance pay. Many countries have a range depending on length of service. Canada guarantees its terminated employees a minimum of up to 8 weeks, Chile 30 days, Germany 1-7 months, Mexico 1 month, Sweden up to 6 months, Thailand up to 300 days, and so on.

If you have these benefits, then it is because your company provides them as an incentive to attract talent. Not because the government mandates them to do so.

These facts are not meant to depress you. However, they do put into perspective the current state of the American worker and that it is crucial to exercise every legal right afforded to you. It is also important to recognize the imbalance in the workplace, stay aware of proposed changes that will impact you and fight to not only retain your rights but also stop further erosion of these rights. It is up to you to take the initiative.

What is an Employee?

Before we get into the rights afforded to employees in the U.S., let's start off by looking at the legal definition of what an employee is. There are a lot of words that are used to describe a person who provides services to an employer: employee, contractor, consultant, worker, staff, and so on.

When we refer to an "employee", we are limiting the discussion to a person who is employed for an indeterminate period to regularly work the standard number of hours fixed by the employer and is not held by a collective bargaining agreement (union) or temporary contract. In other words, an employee, for the purposes of this book, is someone who works directly for a company in return for financial compensation without the benefit of union membership or contract limiting length of employment.

You can go to your state government's website and see a variation of this definition in "legalese". Each state's definition of an employee differs slightly so it is easy to get confused. However, to be consistent, we will use the above consistent definition as it is easy to understand.

Employee's Responsibilities

In order to determine whether you are being treated unfairly, you need to ensure that you are living up to your end of the employment contract. It is essential that you fulfill your responsibilities as an employee. Aside from the job description, an employee's responsibilities generally include (but not limited to):

• Showing up on time for work.
• Putting in the required hours.
• Behaving honestly.
• Following the employer's instructions (unless safety or the law would be breached).
• Keeping trade secrets.
• Doing the job to the best of one's ability.
• Contributing to a positive work environment.

Employer's Responsibilities

What's more challenging, however, are the employers' responsibilities. In the absence of a detailed written employment contract, both employers and employees often find that there are grey areas that may cause confusion or problems in the employment relationship further in the future.

Once individuals are in an employment relationship, they are protected by federal and state laws. Each state, for example, legislates basic working conditions, such as minimum wages, hours of work, rest periods, eating periods, overtime pay, paid public holidays, vacation with pay, pregnancy or parental leave, and termination or severance notice and pay. Many of these are minimums and an employee may be entitled to additional protection.

Other laws affecting the workplace govern health and safety, human rights, retirement, benefits, workers' compensation, and employment insurance, just to name a few. With variations in the laws across the U.S., it is strongly recommended that specific employment situations should be referred to an experienced labor lawyer for clarification.

Human Resources – Whose Side Are They On?

It is easy to think that your company's Human Resources ("HR") department is in place to protect the employee and stand up for the "little guy". This assumption could not be more wrong. One of the key reasons why HR is in place is to protect the company. Sure, they have policies and procedures that appear to address the employee's needs for fairness and respect and HR must act on them, however, their true goal is to warn the company's executive team of impending lawsuits or potential bad publicity.

HR reps are highly trained in how to get you to weaken your own potential case and help the employer build its defenses against your complaint. HR departments might actually try to help you fix your problem, but at the same time they are going to be helping their employer prepare its defense. Everything you do or say will be used against you later, if the need arises.

However, you still have to go through the HR process. If you have a harassment or discrimination claim, you <u>must</u> follow HR procedures, otherwise it will appear that your claim lacks validity and will negatively impact you in any future lawsuit or complaint.

If you do file a harassment claim with HR, please be sure that you have all the information to provide for them at your initial meeting to show that this is a serious offense. As well, be sure that this is something that you want to do and follow through with completely. Ask yourself the following:

- Is this a first or repeated offense?
- Were there any witnesses to corroborate your side?
- Is there any other way to verify the occurrence (documents, emails, etc.)?
- What was the impact of the offense (to you, your team, etc.)?
- What would happen if you did not report the offense? You need to consider this before you go to HR along with what you feel is the seriousness of the offense.
- Does the manager have a past record of similar offenses?
- How difficult is the situation to cope with? In other words, how close are you to going to a third party (government labor board or lawyer) in order to resolve the problem?
- How well do you trust your HR department and/or representative to conduct the investigation fairly, objectively and thoroughly? If the HR department is weak, then retaliation is a possibility from your manager. If this is the case, you will need to record any perceived retaliation.
- How important is confidentiality? While it is promised, it is rare as the HR rep will need to discuss the situation with various management personnel in order to provide a status or investigate.

This list is not to deter you. It is to ensure that when you file a complaint, you are fully prepared so that you will be taken seriously and that you understand what is expected of you.

Keeping this in mind and your continuing willingness to move forward, make an appointment with HR to discuss your situation. Make sure that the HR personnel take copious notes and give you a copy to review before the investigation proceeds. As well, make certain that s/he explains the process thoroughly.

For example, in many corporations, when HR receives a complaint, they complete a standard grievance form and give it to you to sign. Part of their investigation usually includes notifying the person that your complaint is about. Then they put the complaint in a file until another similar complaint is filed. If your boss harasses you and, for whatever reason, does not harass anyone else, then your complaint may sit in that file and s/he would not be reprimanded. And if there is no other manager to transfer you to (e.g. there is only on accounting department in the company), then it may lead to an awkward situation for you.

As well, if you file a legitimate complaint against a manager that is perceived as a "good guy", then you may get a cold shoulder from co-workers if word gets out. Remember, if you experience retaliation or the conduct continuing, you must report it.

However, there are also certain protections afforded you when you report a complaint. Some of these positives include:

- You may establish a form of protection from further harassment or wrongful dismissal.
- You may inspire other people to come forward that could reinforce your claim.
- Your complaint establishes a basis for future complaints/lawsuits.
- Your complaint will put your "victimizer" on notice and will be added to his/her personnel file.

This is not to discourage you but to enlighten you of the possible situations you may find yourself in and to prepare for them. Harassment or discrimination should not be tolerated whether there is only one victim or 100 victims. But sometimes, you need to stand up for yourself by yourself.

Basic Employee Rights

While many specifications in regard to pay, vacation time, overtime and other entitlements may vary from state to state, many of the concepts are the same. Please be sure to check your state or federal specific website for details.

Fair Labor Standards Act (FLSA)

In terms of labor regulations, the FLSA is a federal statute that outlines the basics regulations as it relates to minimum wages, overtime and child labor standards. In general, most labor laws are governed by the Fair Labor Standards Act (FLSA). The FLSA outlines the standards for employers to follow to ensure that all workers are treated fairly and equitably. States must comply with the Act if their own laws are insufficient or non-existent.

Keep in mind, that the FLSA outlines exceptions to their regulations so be sure to check out their website (www.dol.gov/whd/flsa/) to ensure that you understand how these exemptions affect your rights.

Some exemptions include independent contractors, volunteers, commissioned workers, some auto dealership employees, some executive, administrative and professional roles and seasonal employees. For a more detailed list, a list is provided at this website: www.dol.gov/elaws/esa/flsa/screen75.asp or search for "Exemptions" at the FLSA website.

Current Minimum Wage

Almost every state has its own minimum wage. Any increases in the minimum wage are regulated by the state or FLSA. Therefore, one state government's increase to the minimum wage is no guarantee that other states will follow accordingly.

When a state is not listed, then the state's minimum wage follows the FLSA standard.

Jurisdiction	Minimum Wage (2012)
FLSA	$7.25
Alabama	None**
Alaska	$7.75
Arizona	$7.65
Arkansas	$6.25*
California	$8.00
Colorado	$7.64
Connecticut	$8.25
District of Columbia	$8.25
Florida	$7.67
Georgia	$5.15*
Illinois	$8.25
Louisiana	None**
Massachusetts	$8.00
Maine	$7.50

Michigan	$7.40
Minnesota	$6.15*
Mississippi	None**
Montana	$7.65
Nevada	$8.25
New Mexico	$7.50
Ohio	$7.70
Oregon	$8.80
Rhode Island	$7.40
South Carolina	None**
Tennessee	None**
Vermont	$8.46
Washington	$9.04
Wyoming	$5.15*

*Where the state minimum wage is below the FLSA rate, the FLSA rate applies.

**Where the state has no legislated minimum wage, the FLSA rate applies.

Note: Where the state minimum wage exceeds the FLSA, the state rate applies.

Exemptions:

Workers who provide "companion" services for the care, fellowship, and protection of persons who because of old age or physical or mental infirmity cannot care for themselves, may be exempt from minimum wage application. Such services include household work for aged or infirm persons, including meal preparation, bed making, clothing washing and other similar personal services. General household work is also included, as long as it does not exceed 20% of the total weekly hours worked by the companion. Where the 20% limitation is exceeded, the employee must be paid the minimum wage. The term companionship services do not include services performed by trained personnel such as registered or practical nurses. Covered domestic service employees who reside in the household are entitled to minimum wage.

The following are examples of employees exempt from both the minimum wage requirements:

- Executive, administrative, and professional employees (including teachers and academic administrative personnel in elementary and secondary schools), outside sales employees, and certain skilled computer professionals (as defined in the Department of Labor's regulations)
- Employees of certain seasonal amusement or recreational establishments
- Employees of certain small newspapers and switchboard operators of small telephone companies
- Seamen employed on foreign vessels
- Employees engaged in fishing operations
- Employees engaged in newspaper delivery
- Farm workers employed on small farms (i.e., those that used less than 500 "man-days" of farm labor in any calendar quarter of the preceding calendar year)
- Casual babysitters and persons employed as companions to the elderly or infirm

Younger Workers

Many states have regulations that stipulate that if you are under 20 years of age, you may be paid as little as $4.25 per hour during your first 90 consecutive calendar days of employment. Check your state labor board if this applies to you and/or for specific guidelines.

Apprenticeship

An employer is exempt from the paying minimum wage for employees who are being trained on the job under special certificates from the Department of Labor. Many of these programs are better known as internships or co-ops. Check your state labor board for specific guidelines.

Tipped Workers

Employers of tipped employees (i.e., those who customarily and regularly receive more than $30 a month in tips) may consider tips as part of their wages, but employers must pay a direct wage of at least $2.13 per hour if they claim a tip credit.

Tips are the property of the employee. The employer is prohibited from using an employee's tips for any reason other than as a credit against its minimum wage obligation to the employee ("tip credit") or in furtherance of a valid tip pool. Only tips actually received by the employee may be counted in determining whether the employee is a tipped employee and in applying the tip credit.

Tip Credit: The FLSA permits an employer to take a tip credit toward its minimum wage obligation for tipped employees equal to the difference between the required cash wage (which must be at least $2.13) and the federal minimum wage. Thus, the maximum tip credit that an employer can currently claim under the FLSA is $5.12 per hour (the minimum wage of $7.25 minus the minimum required cash wage of $2.13).

Tip Pool: The requirement that an employee must retain all tips does not prevent a valid tip sharing arrangement among employees who customarily and regularly receive tips, such as waiters, waitresses, bellhops, counter personnel (who serve customers), bussers, and service bartenders. A valid tip pool may not include employees who do not customarily and regularly received tips, such as dishwashers, managers, and janitors. Check your state's website to see if your state allows tip pooling.

Requirements

The employer must provide the following information to a tipped employee before the employer may use the tip credit:

1) the amount of cash wage the employer is paying a tipped employee, which must be at least $2.13 per hour;

2) the additional amount claimed by the employer as a tip credit, which cannot exceed $5.12 (the difference between the minimum required cash wage of $2.13 and the current minimum wage of $7.25);

3) that the tip credit claimed by the employer cannot exceed the amount of tips actually received by the tipped employee;

4) that all tips received by the tipped employee are to be retained by the employee except for a valid tip pooling arrangement limited to employees who customarily and regularly receive tips; and

5) that the tip credit will not apply to any tipped employee unless the employee has been informed of these tip credit provisions

An employer who fails to provide the required information cannot use the tip credit provisions and therefore must pay the tipped employee at least $7.25 per hour in wages and allow the tipped employee to keep all tips received

<u>Retention of Tips</u>: A tip is the sole property of the tipped employee regardless of whether the employer takes a tip credit. The FLSA prohibits any arrangement between the employer and the tipped employee whereby any part of the tip received becomes the property of the employer. For example, even where a tipped employee receives at least $7.25 per hour in wages directly from the employer, the employee may not be required to turn over his or her tips to the employer.

<u>Service Charges</u>: A compulsory charge for service, for example, 15% of the bill, is not a tip. Such charges are part of the employer's gross receipts. Sums distributed to employees from service charges cannot be counted as tips received, but may be used to satisfy the employer's <u>minimum wage</u> and overtime obligations under the FLSA. If an employee receives tips in addition to the compulsory service charge, those tips may be considered in determining whether the employee is a tipped employee and in the application of the tip credit.

<u>Credit Cards</u>: Where tips are charged on a credit card and the employer must pay the credit card company a percentage on each sale, the employer may pay the employee the tip, less that percentage. For example, where a credit card company charges an employer 3 % on all sales charged to its credit service, the employer may pay the tipped employee 97 % of the tips without violating the FLSA. However, this charge on the tip may not reduce the employee's wage below the required <u>minimum wage</u>. The amount due the employee must be paid no later than the regular pay day and may not be held while the employer is awaiting reimbursement from the credit card company.

<u>Minimum Wage Issues</u>:

- Where an employee receives tips only and is paid no cash wage, the full <u>minimum wage</u> is owed.

- Where deductions for walk-outs, breakage, or cash register shortages reduce the employee's wages below the minimum wage, such deductions are illegal. Where a tipped employee is paid $2.13 per hour in direct (or cash) wages and the employer claims the maximum tip credit of $5.12 per hour, no such deductions can be made without reducing the employee below the minimum wage (even where the employee receives more than $5.12 per hour in tips).

- Where a tipped employee is required to contribute to a tip pool that includes employees who do not customarily and regularly receive tips, the employee is owed all tips he or she contributed to the pool and the full $7.25 minimum wage.

- Where the employer takes the tip credit, overtime is calculated on the full minimum wage, **not** the lower direct (or cash) wage payment. The employer may not take a larger tip credit for an overtime hour than for a straight time hour (*i.e.*, $4.00 tip credit per hour for the non-overtime hours and $5.12 tip credit per hour for overtime hours).

Hours of Work, Overtime, Meal and Other Breaks

Legislation across the country varies from state to state. While some jurisdictions are thoroughly legislated in regard to work hours, breaks, overtime or days worked, most leave some of the details up to the discretion of the employee/employer relationship under the guidance of the FLSA.

It is important to understand what your rights are in this area because many employees don't realize that they may be entitled to breaks and overtime pay.

The table below outlines the basics in each area for each jurisdiction. If your jurisdiction is not listed, then it follows the FLSA. Remember, some exemptions may apply under the FLSA.

Some of the common exemptions include:

- Executive, administrative, and professional employees (including teachers and academic administrative personnel), outside sales employees and certain skilled computer professionals.
- Employees of certain seasonal amusement or recreational establishments.
- Employees of certain small newspapers and switchboard operators or small telephone companies.
- Employees engaged in fishing operations, newspaper delivery, seamen on foreign vessels, babysitters, companions to the elderly or infirm or some farm workers.
- Certain commissioned employees, vehicle salespersons, parts clerks and mechanics, taxi drivers, announcers, news editors and chief engineers in certain non-metropolitan broadcasting stations and movie theater employees.
- Domestic service workers who reside in their employer's residence.

However, California overtime rules applies to all people who have an "employment" relationship.

Please check the applicable government website or call your state labor board for details or any updates.

Jurisdiction	Standard Hours	Overtime (OT) Rate	Right to Refuse OT	Time Off in Lieu of OT Wages	Meal and Other Breaks
FLSA	8 in a day; 40 in a week	1 ½ times reg. rate	No unless under 16 years old.	Not in private sector	No
Alaska			Yes for nurses only		
California	8 in a day; 40 in a week.	1 ½ times reg. rate. For first 8 hours 2 times for over 12 hour day. On the 7th day, the first 8 hours are at 1 ½ rate and over 8 on the 7th day at double time.	Yes only if employee has already worked over 72 hours in a week *and* is employed is specific roles.		Meal Periods: ½ hour during each shift in excess of 5 consecutive hours of work. Second meal period required for work over 10 hours in a day. Rest Period: paid 10-minute rest for each 4 hours worked.
Colorado	12 in a day; 40 in a week				Meal Periods: ½ hour after each 5 consecutive hours of work. Rest Period: paid 10-minute rest for each 4 hours worked.
Connecticut	8 in a day; 40 in a week[10]				Meal Periods: ½ hour after first 2 hours and before last 2 hours for employees who work 7 ½ consecutive hours or more.
Delaware	40 in a week				Meal Periods: ½ hour after first 2 hours and before last 2 hours for employees who work 7 ½ consecutive hours or more.
Illinois	40 in a week				Meal Periods: Hotel room attendants receive a minimum of one paid 30-minute meal period for each workday of seven hours or more. Rest Period: Hotel room attendants receive a minimum of two 15-minute paid rest breaks for each workday of seven hours or more.
Kansas	46 in a week.				
Kentucky	8 in a day; 40 in a week				Meal Period: Reasonable unpaid usually ½ hour between 3rd and 5th hour of work.. Rest Period: Paid 10-minute rest period for each 4-hour work period.
Maine	40 in a week		Yes only if you have worked 80 hours of OT in a 2-week period.		Meal Period: ½ hour after 6 consecutive hours.
Massachusetts	40 in a week				Meal Period: ½ hour if work is more than 6 hours.

Minnesota	48 in a week				Meal Period: Sufficient unpaid time for 8 consecutive hours or more. Rest Period: Paid adequate rest period within each 4 consecutive hours to utilize restroom.
Nebraska					Meal Period: ½ hour off premises between 12pm and 1pm or at other suitable lunch time.
Nevada	8 in a day; 40 in a week				Meal Period: ½ hour for every 8 consecutive hours of work. Rest Period: Paid 10-minute rest period for each 4 hours worked.
New Hampshire	40 in a week[33]				Meal Period: ½ hour after 5 consecutive hours of unless feasible for employee to eat while working and is permitted to do so.
New Jersey			No unless employed in specific healthcare worker role.		
New York	40 hours in a week		No except for nurses.		Meal Period: ½ hour noonday period for shifts of more than 6 hours. An additional 20 minutes between 5pm – 7pm for shifts starting before 11am until after 7pm. 1 hour in factories.
North Dakota	40 hours in a week				Meal Period: ½ hour on each shift exceeding 5 hours.
Oregon	40 hours in a week				Meal Period: ½ with relief from all duty, for each 6-8 hours, between 2nd and 5th hour for work period of 7 hours or less and between 3rd and 6th hour for work period over 7 hours. If relief of all duty is not feasible then meal break will be with pay. Rest Period: Paid 10-minute rest for every 4-hour segment..
Rhode Island	40 hours in a week		No except for nurses		Meal Period: 20-minute mealtime within a six hour work shift and a ½ hour mealtime within an eight hour work shift.
Tennessee					Meal Period: ½ hour for work shift of 6 consecutive hours or more.
Texas			No except for nurses		
Vermont	40 hours in a week				Meal Period: Reasonable opportunity during work periods to eat. Rest Period: Reasonable opportunity during work periods to use restrooms.
Washington	40 hours in a week				Meal Period: ½ hour for shifts over 5 hours between 2 hours – 5 hours from start of shift. Paid if employee is required to remain on duty.

| | | | | | An addition ½ during overtime for employees working 3+ hours beyond regular workday.

Rest Period: Paid 10-minute rest for each 4-hour shift scheduled as near as possible to midpoint of each work period. |
|---|---|---|---|---|---|
| **West Virginia** | 40 hours in a week | | | | Meal Period: 20 minutes for 6 consecutive hours of work or more. |

Notes :

[1] States not listed do not require rest periods.

[2] Not displayed in table are exemptions for executive, administrative and professional employees, outside salespersons, union workers and farm workers.

[3] California overtime rules apply to <u>all</u> people who have an "employment" relationship.

[4] If overtime (OT) rate is not specified, then it follows the FLSA guidelines.

[5] In California, "comp time" schemes, where employers tell employees that since they worked 10 hours on Monday they can work 6 hours on Tuesday, are illegal because even though the employees are not working more than 40 hours for the purposes of overtime compensation under federal law, they are working more than 8 hours for purposes of California overtime law and rounding the 6 and 10 hour workdays to two 8 hour workdays would cheat the employee out of two hours of overtime pay.

Equal Pay Legislation

Equal pay means that an employer can't pay you less based solely on your gender. In general, if you are doing the same work with the same responsibility, skill level, effort and working conditions, then you should be paid the same as anyone else doing this job regardless of whether the other person is a man or a woman. Under the Equal Pay Act, an employer cannot deny women equal pay for equal work; deny women transfers, promotions, or wage increases; manipulate job evaluations to relegate women's pay; or intentionally segregate men and women into jobs according to their gender. All forms of pay are covered by this law, including salary, overtime pay, bonuses, stock options, profit sharing and bonus plans, life insurance, vacation and holiday pay, cleaning or gasoline allowances, hotel accommodations, reimbursement for travel expenses, and benefits. If there is an inequality in wages between men and women, employers may not reduce the wages of either sex to equalize their pay.

Similar legislation prohibits compensation discrimination on the basis of race, color, religion, national origin, age, or disability. Unlike the Equal Pay Act, there is no requirement that the jobs must be substantially equal.

Legal and Public Holidays

The U.S. does not have national holidays in which all employees in the country receive a mandatory day free from work and all business is closed by law. The federal government only recognizes national holidays that pertain to its own employees; it is at the discretion of each state or local jurisdiction to determine official holiday schedules.

The Fair Labor Standards Act (FLSA) does not require payment for time not worked, such as holidays that fall on non-work days, for example, weekends for office personnel. These benefits are generally a matter of agreement between an employer and an employee. As well, it does not demand premium pay for holidays worked.

If employers voluntarily pay their employees for holidays they do not work, then the employers do not have to pay their employees overtime compensation for those holiday hours, even if the total hours for that week exceed 40 hours. For example, an employee who works a 40-hour regular workweek could receive holiday pay for eight hours on Christmas Day. If they did not work on that holiday then they will receive 48 hours at their regular pay rate. However, if an employee works the same amount of hours that week and works on Christmas Day, the employee will be entitled to overtime compensation after 40 hours.

An employer has the right to demand that an employee work on a holiday if the operation of the business requires it. For example, in a tourist business, it is not unusual for the business to run on Independence Day. Therefore, the employer is allowed to require the employee to work on that holiday.

Federal employees have it a little better. They are paid for the holiday if they don't have to work it. If they do, then they can receive holiday premium pay (which is equivalent to regular pay) on top of their regular pay which totals twice their regular pay.

The following statutory holidays are recognized by the labor boards of the various jurisdictions:

Holiday	Jurisdiction Observed
New Year's Day	All
Martin Luther King Day	All except for Rhode Island
Rosa Parks Day	CA, OH
Lincoln's Birthday	CT, IL IN*, IA, MO, MT NJ, NY
Washington's Birthday	AL, AK, AZ, AR, CA CO, CT DC GA*, HI, ID, IL, IN*, MN, MD, MA, MI, MO,MN, MS, MT, NE, NV, NH, NJ, NM*, NY, ND, OH, OK, OR, PA, SC, SD, TN, TX, UT, VT, VA, WA, WV, WY
Susan B. Anthony Day	FL, WV, WI
César Chávez Day	CA, TX (optional), CO (optional)
Good Friday	CT, DE, FL, HI, IN, KY, LA, NJ, NC, ND, TN, TX
Emancipation Day	DC
Patriot's Day	MN, MA
Confederate Memorial Day	AL, GA, MI, SC, TX
Memorial Day	All
Jefferson Davis Day	AL, MS
Independence Day	All
Labor Day	All
Columbus Day	AL, AZ, CO, CT, DC, GA, ID, IL, IN , MN, MD, MA, MO, MT, NE, NJ, NM, NY, OH, PA, RI, SD, UT, VT, VA, WV, WI

General Election Day	HI, IL, IN,KY, LA, MD, MI, MT, NJ, NY, WI
Veteran's Day	All
Thanksgiving	All
Day after Thanksgiving	DE, FL, GA, IN,IA, KY, MN, MD, MI, MO, NE, NV, NH, NM, OK, PA, TX, WA WV
Christmas Eve	AK, GA, IN, KY, MI, NC, OK, TN, TX, VA, WY
Christmas	All
Day after Christmas	AL, NC, TX
New Year's Eve	AL, KY, MI WV, WI

* May celebrate the holiday on a different day that the common day.

Vacation Time/Pay

Similar to public holidays, the Fair Labor Standards Act (FLSA) does not require compensation for time not worked, such as vacations. Continuation of salary while an employee is on vacation is considered a benefit and is a matter of agreement between an employer and an employee. Some states have supported a "use it or lose it" policy in which if you do not use your allotted vacation time within the specified year, you will lose your right to that vacation time or the wages to compensate for it. Other states allow you to carry over the unused vacation time to the next year.

The legality of the use-it-or-lose-it policy has been brought into question in some states. In California, this policy is illegal under the California Vacation Law. In California, businesses must allow their employees to take their earned vacation time when it is convenient for them, instead of removing it after a set period.

In contrast to use-it-or-lose-it policies, policies that establish "caps" on vacation pay accruals are permissible in California. Caps occur when an employee has accrued a specified amount or more in days of vacation. An employer may choose to cap the amount at a certain level to limit how many days that an employee can carry over into the next year. This policy will not only have an impact on the number of days of vacation to carry over, but it will have an impact on the number of vacation days that you will receive in payment if you should separate from the company.

If your company has a vacation policy, it should state how it is accrued, when it can be taken, if you can carry days over or get them paid out and what happens to this time when you leave the company. If there is a use-it-or-lose-it policy, vacation usually is not paid out. In New York, for example, vacation that is accrued must be paid in wages if the employee leaves. Only a written policy in New York would require that vacations be paid out at year end.

Here is a list by state of vacation laws. For more details or updates, please check with the labor board of your state.

Jurisdiction	Vacation Time Req.	Cap Vacation Days	Payout on Termination	Use it or Lose it Policy Allowed
Alabama	No	Yes	No unless company policy requires it	Yes
Alaska	No	Yes	No unless company policy requires it	Yes
Arizona	No	Yes	No unless company policy requires it	Yes
Arkansas	No	Yes	No unless company policy requires it	Yes
California	No	Yes	Yes	No
Colorado	No	Yes	No unless company policy requires it	Yes
Connecticut	No	Yes	No unless company policy requires it	Yes
Delaware	No	Yes	No unless company policy requires it	Yes
Florida	No	Yes	No unless company policy requires it	Yes
Georgia	No	Yes	No unless company policy requires it	Yes
Hawaii	No	Yes	No unless company policy requires it	Yes
Idaho	No	Yes	No unless company policy requires it	Yes
Illinois	No	Yes	Yes	Yes (must be reasonable timeframe)
Indiana	No	Yes	No unless company policy requires it	Yes
Iowa	No	Yes	No unless company policy requires it	Yes
Kansas	No	Yes	No unless company policy requires it	Yes
Kentucky	No	Yes	No unless company policy requires it	Yes
Louisiana	No	Yes	Yes	Yes
Maine	No	Yes	No unless company policy requires it	Yes

Maryland	No	Yes	Yes unless employees notified in writing	Yes
Massachusetts	No	Yes (must be reasonable)	Yes	Yes (employee must be given reasonable timeframe
Michigan	No	Yes if employee signed an agreement	No unless company policy requires it and employee signed an agreement	Yes if employee signed an agreement
Minnesota	No	Yes if employee agrees in writing	No unless company policy requires it	Yes if employee agrees in writing
Mississippi	No	Yes	No	Yes
Missouri	No	Yes	No	Yes
Montana	No	Yes (must be reasonable timeframe)	Yes	No
Nebraska	No	Yes	Yes	No
Nevada	No	Yes	No unless company policy requires it	Yes
New Hampshire	No	Yes	No unless company policy requires it	Yes
New Jersey	No	Yes	No unless company policy requires it	Yes
New Mexico	No	Yes	No unless company policy requires it	Yes
New York	No	Yes (as long as employees are notified of policy in writing	No unless company policy requires it	Yes (as long as employees are notified of policy in writing)
North Carolina	No	Yes (as long as employees are notified of policy in writing	No unless company policy requires it	Yes (as long as employees are notified of policy in writing)
North Dakota	No	Yes	Yes	Yes (as long as employees are notified in writing and are given a reasonable timeframe)
Ohio	No	Yes (as long as employees properly notified)	No as long as employees are aware of the policy	Yes as long as employees are notified of policy
Oklahoma	No	Yes	No unless company policy requires it	Yes as long as employees are notified
Oregon	No	Yes	Yes if company policy is silent or ambiguous on the issue	Yes (as long as employees are notified and are given a reasonable timeframe)
Pennsylvania	No	Yes	No unless company policy requires it	Yes
Rhode Island	No	Yes	Yes after one year of service	Yes

South Carolina	No	Yes	No unless company policy requires it.	Yes
South Dakota	No	Yes	No	Yes
Tennessee	No	Yes	No unless company policy requires it	Yes
Texas	No	Yes	No unless company policy requires it	Yes
Utah	No	Yes	No unless company policy requires it	Yes
Vermont	No	Yes	No unless company policy requires it	Yes
Virginia	No	Yes	No unless company policy requires it	Yes
Washington	No	Yes	No unless company policy requires it	Yes
West Virginia	No	Yes	No unless company policy requires it	Yes
Wisconsin	No	Yes	Yes	Yes

How does the vacation policies in the U.S. compare to other industrialized nations. Unfortunately, not very well. Compare the differences in this table (Mercer 2011).

Country	Paid Vacation
United Kingdom	28
Poland	26
Austria	25
Bolivia	25
Denmark	25
Finland	25
France	25
Greece	25
Sweden	25
Venezuela	24
Brazil	22
Spain	22
United Arab Emirates	22
Australia	20
Croatia	20
Japan	20
Russia	20
Mexico	16
Hong Kong	14
India	12
Canada	10
China	10
United States	0

Right to Refuse Work

There are occasions where it may be unreasonable for an employer to insist that an employee perform his/her duties. While you don't have the right to refuse work for minor changes in the workplace, you do have the right in situations where your health or human rights are at risk.

Here are the most common issues.

Religious Holidays

Workers whose religious beliefs are infringed upon by a shift change, such as one that requires them to work on a holy day, have the right to request a different shift. Workers also have the right to arrange a substitute to work in their place.

Employers must take all reasonable steps to accommodate any employee who requires a particular day or time off for religious reasons. But if such accommodations prove overly difficult or impose a considerable hardship on the business, the employer has the right to make the employee choose between working or receiving a discharge.

Shift Changes

Employees have the right to be notified in advance of a shift change. The required amount of notice varies from state to state. An employee has the right to refuse a shift change if it interferes with the ability to perform their job, such as lack of childcare. However, workers have the obligation to report conflicts. If the employer cannot accommodate the shift change request, workers can take the time off with vacation pay or without pay. If the conflict cannot be resolved, an employee may be laid off for their inability to perform the job.

Illness

The circumstances under which employees have a right to refuse to work are very limited. You would have to feel that the conditions reflect an imminent danger under the OSHA standards. You may be able to call in sick but it is up to the company's policy as to whether your sick day is paid or unpaid. Plus many employers will require written verification from a medical professional if you take a sick leave over two days consecutively.

In rare cases, you may be able to justify that the illness of others may create a danger for you such as in cancer patients undergoing chemotherapy who must avoid others with influenza. But you would need to provide sufficient medical documentation to support your claim. And there would be no guarantee that the time you take off would be paid.

For more information, go to the subsection in this book on "Sick Leave".

Added Responsibilities

As of 2011, every state has "employment at will" laws in place except for Montana. This law allows employers to terminate employees at any time. At-will employment also permits employers to alter employee job descriptions as they see fit with proper notice to workers of changing expectations and job requirements.

An at-will employee refusing to take on larger responsibilities as required when an employer changes employee job descriptions, may give the employer justifiable grounds to terminate the worker. Such terminations are based on the grounds of employee fault and may result in the terminated employee being ineligible for unemployment benefits.

Overtime

As mentioned in the "Hours of Work, Overtime, Meal and Other Breaks" section above, in general, employees do not have the right to refuse overtime. While a few states may have stipulations for nurses or a cap on overtime hours, most states do not provide an employee with such protection.

Unsafe Workplace

You do not have the right to walk off the job because of unsafe conditions. When you believe working conditions are unsafe or unhealthful, you should call your employer's attention to the problem. If your employer does not correct the hazard or disagrees with you about the extent of the hazard, you also may file a complaint with OSHA (Occupational Safety and Health Administration).

Per OSHA, your right to refuse to do a task is protected if **all** of the following conditions are met:

- Where possible, you have asked the employer to eliminate the danger, and the employer failed to do so; **and**

- You refused to work in "good faith." This means that you must genuinely believe that an imminent danger exists. Your refusal cannot be a disguised attempt to harass your employer or disrupt business; **and**

- A reasonable person would agree that there is a real danger of death or serious injury; **and**

- There isn't enough time, due to the urgency of the hazard, to get it corrected through regular enforcement channels, such as requesting an OSHA inspection.

For more information, please check your state labor board for more detailed information.

Civic Duty

Jury Duty

Employers must give employees time off to attend jury selection and to serve as jurors or as witnesses. A juror is considered to be on unpaid leave for the period of jury duty. Only a few states, including Connecticut, Massachusetts, and New York, require compensation for a limited time for employees who serve on jury or witness duty. Although the employers are not legally obligated to pay employees for lost wages while on jury duty, the employee is considered to be in continuous employment for the purposes of calculating annual vacation, termination entitlements, as well as for pension, medical or other employee benefit plans. The employee is also entitled to all increases in wages and benefits which he or she would have received if not on jury duty.

An employer cannot dismiss, suspend or reassign an employee who has been summoned or who has served as a juror, take discriminatory measures or reprisals against the employee or impose any other penalty. It is an offence for an employer to directly or indirectly threaten to cause or causes an employee loss of position or employment or to impose any monetary or other penalty because of the employee being summoned for jury service.

As soon as jury duty ends, an employee must be returned to his or her former position or comparable position. An employee who is penalized solely for performing jury duty may file a complaint with their state labor board.

Reservist Leave

USERRA (Uniformed Services Employment and Reemployment Rights Act) provides that returning service members are to be reemployed in the job that they would have maintained had they not been absent for military service, with the same seniority, status and pay, as well as other rights and benefits determined by seniority. USERRA also requires that reasonable efforts (such as training or retraining) be made to enable returning service members to qualify for reemployment.

If the returning service member cannot qualify for the revised position, s/he must be reemployed, if qualified, in any other position that is the nearest approximation to this position. USERRA also provides that while an individual is performing military service, s/he is deemed to be on a leave of absence and is entitled to the non-seniority rights accorded other similarly-situated individuals on non-military leaves of absence. There are time limits for returning to work. Check out the website www.dol.gov/vets for more details.

If you leave your job to perform military service, you have the right to elect to continue your existing employer-based health plan coverage for you and your dependents for up to 24 months while in the military. Even if you don't elect to continue coverage during your military service, you have the right to be reinstated in your employer's health plan when you are reemployed, generally without any waiting periods or exclusions (e.g., pre-existing condition exclusions) except for service-connected illnesses or injuries.

Voting

While federal law does give eligible individuals the right to vote, it does not require employers to give employees time off from work to cast their ballots. However, the laws of over half the states do require employers to allow time off to vote. In addition, many of these states also require employers to provide the voting time off with pay.

Some states that require both time off for voting and pay include:

California: An employer must allow up to two hours with pay either at the beginning or end of the employee's regular shift, if the employee does not have sufficient time outside working hours to vote at a statewide election. Employees must give their employer a minimum of two days notice of their need to take time off to vote.

Colorado: An employer must provide employees up to two paid hours when polls are open to vote. However, the time is not required if the employee has at least three hours off when polls are open.

Illinois: An employer must allow up to two hours off from work to vote between the time of opening and closing the polls and may not take any disciplinary action against the employee for doing so. The law specifically prohibits a penalty such as a reduction in compensation for the absence.

New York: An employer must give up to two paid hours off from work to vote if the employee does not have sufficient time outside working hours to vote. "Sufficient time" is defined as four consecutive hours either between the opening of the polls and the beginning of the employee's working shift, or between the end of his working shift and the closing of the polls. Employees must give their employer a minimum of two days notice of their need to take time off to vote.

Some states that require time off for voting, but without pay include:

Kentucky: Employees may take reasonable time off to vote, but may be disciplined if they do not actually vote.

Massachusetts: Employees who work in manufacturing, mechanical, or mercantile establishments must be allowed to take time-off during the first two hours after the polls open, if the employees apply for this voting leave.

Ohio: An employer may not terminate or threaten to terminate an employee for taking a reasonable amount of time to vote on Election Day.

Wisconsin: Employees may take up to three hours unpaid leave to vote and the employer may designate the time of day for the absence.

Many states, such as California and New York, also require employees to give notice to their employers that they need time off to vote and allow employers to specify when the time may be taken.

Some of the states that do not have any voting leave requirements include Connecticut, Delaware, Florida, New Hampshire, New Jersey, North Carolina, Oregon, Pennsylvania, and South Carolina.

Family and Medical Leave Act (FMLA)

The FMLA provides certain employees with up to 12 weeks of unpaid, job-protected leave per year. It also requires that their group health benefits be maintained during the leave.

FMLA is designed to help employees balance their work and family responsibilities by allowing them to take reasonable unpaid leave for certain family and medical reasons. It also seeks to accommodate the legitimate interests of employers and promote equal employment opportunity for men and women.

Employers must provide an eligible employee with up to 12 weeks of unpaid leave each year for any of the following reasons:

- for the birth and care of the newborn child of an employee;
- for placement with the employee of a child for adoption or foster care;
- to care for an immediate family member (spouse, child, or parent) with a serious health condition; or
- to take medical leave when the employee is unable to work because of a serious health condition.

Employees are eligible for leave if they have worked for their employer at least 12 months, at least 1,250 hours over the past 12 months, and work at a location where the company employs 50 or more employees within 75 miles. Whether an employee has worked the minimum 1,250 hours of service is determined according to FLSA principles for determining compensable hours or work.

Time taken off work due to pregnancy complications can be counted against the 12 weeks of family and medical leave.

Under the FMLA statute, "family member" is defined as spouse, parent, or child under 18 (unless an adult child has a disability and cannot provide self-care). Wounded service members may also be cared for by "next of kin."

In 2010, the U.S. Department of Labor clarified that non-biological or adoptive parent caregivers may take FMLA leave to care for or bond with a child if the caregiver has provided or will provide day-to-day care or assumes financial responsibility for the child.

Expanding the Definition of Family

The federal FMLA allows a worker to take leave to care for a new child or to care for a parent, a spouse, or a child under the age of 18 (or older if the child qualifies as a person with a disability) with a serious health condition. In 2008, the FMLA was amended to allow for 26 weeks of leave for military family members caring for wounded service members. For this military family expansion, the definition of "family" has been increased to include next of kin.12 State FMLA laws have also expanded the definition of family to include a wider range of family members.

State	Definition of family (Beyond child, parent, and spouse)
California	Domestic partner and domestic partner's child
Connecticut	Civil union partner14, parent-in-law
Hawaii	Grandparent, parent-in-law, grandparent-in-law or an employee's reciprocal beneficiary
Maine	Domestic partner and domestic partner's child, siblings
New Jersey	Civil union partner and child of civil union partner, parent-in-law, step parent
Oregon	Domestic partner, grandparent, grandchild or parent-in-law
Rhode Island	Domestic partners of state employees, parent-in-law
Vermont	Civil union partner, parent-in-law
Wisconsin	Parent-in-law
District of Columbia	Related to the worker by blood, legal custody, or marriage; person with whom the employee lives and has a committed relationship; child who lives with employee and for whom employee permanently assumes and discharges parental responsibility

Source: www.nationalpartnership.org

The following sections break down various aspects of the FMLA.

Maternity, Parental and Adoption Leave

Having a baby, whether it is your first or fourth pregnancy or whether you are adopting or using a surrogate, has its own set of challenges and concerns. One worry should not be your job or income. However, the reality is, in many states, this is the case.

Firstly, the U.S. is behind the rest of the world in parental leave policy, per a recent Human Rights Watch report (2012). The U.S., along with Papua New Guinea, Swaziland, Liberia and Lesotho are the only countries in the world that provide no type of financial support for mothers, according to a study done by McGill University. (Even Afghanistan offers 90 days at 100% pay.) Americans are covered by the federal Family and Medical Leave Act (FMLA), which allows employees with newborn children to take up to 12 weeks of *unpaid* leave. Only two U.S. states -- California and New Jersey -- have public paid leave insurance programs.

However, most states do have basic protection laws to protect a women's right to not be penalized for taking maternity leave. In general, employers are not allowed to retaliate against or interfere with workers who exercise their right to take legally protected maternity leave. Nor can they assign them to the "mommy track" jobs -- lower pay, inferior hours or assignments and little possibility for promotion.

However, there are still far too many employers who attempt such tactics. In the five years from 1997 to 2001, the EEOC received 20,809 pregnancy discrimination complaints. Between 2007 and 2011, they received 29,088, a 40% increase.

Here are a few examples from the U.S. Courts:

Teresa was an assistant manager at a department store for approximately 10 years. Despite her manager's assurances that she was among the leading candidates for a promotion, she was constantly passed over. Five store manager positions were awarded to less-experienced and less-qualified men within a two-month period, as well as to women with no children or who assured their boss that they would not have any more children. On occasion, one of Teresa's managers asked her, "You're not going to get pregnant again, are you?" "Did you get your tubes tied?" and "Are you breastfeeding?" Teresa alleged that the store's failure to promote her was punishment for her becoming pregnant and taking maternity leave. The jury agreed and awarded her $2.1 million.

In 2009, Darlene filed a lawsuit against her employer after he threatened to fire her. She said "My boss told me that I could take as long as I wanted on my maternity leave because I wouldn't be needed back. Of course I took mat leave and I told them that firing me was against the California labor code so I returned to work, but it was part time: they took away all of my duties except payroll." Darlene knew her rights so she was able to get her job back after four months on maternity leave. By threatening not to reinstate Darlene after she returned, then offering part-time without benefits and eliminating her responsibilities, her employer violated at least three California labor laws.

In 2012, a bookkeeper was awarded $148,000 including back pay, interest and damages for being illegally fired by a medical staffing company in Milwaukee after she became pregnant and went on maternity leave. Charges were filed against the bookkeeper's employer after she was accused by the employer of "using pre-natal doctor appointments as an excuse to play hooky from work." Adding insult to injury, she was in the hospital recuperating after a Caesarean section when she was notified of her termination—by mail.

Even with countless pregnancy discrimination settlements, women are still illegally fired or penalized for having a baby. And, surprisingly studies show that female-dominated industries do not do a better job of not discriminating against pregnant women.

Each jurisdiction has its own set of laws so it is vital that you learn what is permissible in your area. If you feel that you are being discriminated against, contact your local government labor office to understand your rights and how you can protect them. It is up to you to know your rights and take a stand to defend them.

For more information, go to http://www.eeoc.gov/laws/types/pregnancy.cfm.

Here is a small snapshot for comparison.

Country	Paid Maternity Leave	Paid Paternity Leave	Unpaid Maternity Leave	Unpaid Paternity Leave
Algeria	14 weeks @ 100%	3 days		
Australia	18 weeks @ federal min. wage	18 weeks @ fed. Min. wage	Up to 52 weeks shared between parents	Up to 3 weeks
Brazil	120 days @ 100%	5 days		
Bulgaria	1 year @ 100%, 2nd year at min. salary	father or a grandparent can take the maternity leave instead of the mother	6 months to be used until the child turns 8	6 months to be used until the child turns 8
Canada	50 weeks @ 55-70% (depending on province). The last 35 weeks can be shared with father.	35 weeks (shared with mother) @ 55-70% (depending on province)	2 weeks	
China	90 days @100%			
Denmark	52 weeks @ 100%. 18 to be taken by the mother, 2 weeks by the father, the rest as they see fit.	2 weeks of the 52 weeks paid leave is reserved for the father		
Ethiopia	12 weeks @ 100%		5 days	
India	12 weeks @ 100%			
Israel	14 weeks @ 100%. Weeks 6-14 can be taken by father.	Can take paid leave instead of mother between weeks 6-14		
Norway	56 weeks (13 months) (80%) or 46 weeks (10.5 months) (100%) - mother must take at least 3 weeks immediately before birth and 6 weeks immediately after birth, father must take at least 12	12 weeks of the 56/46 weeks paid leave is reserved for the father. If he does not take these 12 weeks, they will be lost as they can not be transferred to the mother.	The mother can also take an extra full year of unpaid leave after the paid period ends.	The father can also take an extra full year of unpaid leave after the paid period ends. In addition, the father is entitled to take two weeks unpaid leave directly before or after birth (many fathers are

	weeks - the rest can be shared between mother and father.			paid for these weeks by their employers).
Portugal	120 days 100%, 150 days 80% or 180 days 83% (if both parents share at least 30 days, not simultaneously). A 3 month extension can be requested, at 25%.	20 days 100% (10 days are mandatory)		
Sweden	480 days (16 months) (77.6% (80% of 97%) up to a ceiling the first 390 days, 90 days at flat rate) - shared with father (dedicated 60 days)	480 days (16 months) (77.6% (80% of 97%) up to a ceiling the first 390 days, 90 days at flat rate) - shared with mother (dedicated 60 days) + 10 working days in connection with the child's birth	The first 18 months (at maximum) individually, by postponing the shared paid period.	The first 18 months (at maximum) individually, by postponing the shared paid period.
United Kingdom	Currently 39 weeks paid, due to rise to 52 weeks paid from April 2010, although delayed indefinitely @ 90%	2 weeks at a fixed amount	13 weeks unpaid (maternity or adoption) for total a of 52 weeks (paid and non-paid)	
United States	0 weeks (CA: 6 weeks 55%, NJ 6 weeks 66%, WA 5 weeks $250/week possibly starting 10/2015; pregnancy treated as disability: HI 58%, NY 50%, RI formula.)	0 weeks (CA: 6 weeks 55%, NJ 6 weeks 66%, WA 5 weeks $250/week possibly starting 10/2015	12 weeks	12 weeks
Venezuela	26 weeks @ 100%	2 weeks		

Maternity Leave

The purpose of this type of leave is to allow mothers to take time off work following the birth of a child.

As mentioned above, FMLA allows up to 12 weeks unpaid leave. However, there are some states that have enacted more generous policies.

The following states -- plus the District of Columbia and Puerto Rico -- have laws that are in some ways more generous than the FMLA. What follows is a state-by-state guide to those benefits.

California

Length: Up to a maximum of 4 months.

Compensation: Women may collect state temporary disability payments of about 2/3 of their wages -- up to $490 a week -- for the time while they're physically disabled due to pregnancy and childbirth (6-8 weeks). If a company continues health insurance for employees on other kinds of leave, it must do so for women designated as disabled due to pregnancy and childbirth. **Private sector workers who earn sick leave are entitled to use up to half of their allotted leave each year for the care of a sick child or other family member, including a spouse or domestic partner with a pregnancy related disability.** Unlike similar laws in some other states, the California law does not require that employer-provided sick time be available to care for a healthy newborn or newly adopted child.

Restrictions: Women in workplaces with at least 5 employees. California include unique provisions in their antidiscrimination laws that make it unlawful for an employer to refuse a pregnant employee's request to transfer to a less strenuous or less hazardous job for the duration of her pregnancy. The employer cannot refuse the request if the request can be reasonably accommodated.

Connecticut

Length: The period of time during which the employee is physically disabled due to pregnancy and childbirth (usually 6-8 weeks). As of January 2012, many workers in service industries and in other occupations requiring public contact, who work in businesses with 50 or more employees, will be able to earn paid sick time that can be used to care for a child or spouse who is ill or needs to seek medical care. Workers may earn up to 40 hours per year. The law entitles pregnant women to use paid sick leave to seek prenatal or postnatal care.

Restrictions: Women at workplaces with at least 3 employees. In addition, because same-sex marriage is now legal in Connecticut, the state law defines family more broadly than the federal FMLA to include same-sex spouses caring for a new child or a spouse disabled by pregnancy.

District of Columbia

Length: Up to 16 weeks of leave every two years to care for a newborn or newly adopted child.

Restrictions: Workplaces with at least 20 employees; the employee must have worked at least 1,000 hours in the past 12 months. In addition, District law provides a broader definition of "family member" than the federal FMLA so that a worker in a "committed relationship" may take leave to care for a partner with a serious health condition, including a pregnancy-related disability.

Hawaii

Length: The period of time during which the employee is physically disabled due to pregnancy and childbirth (usually 6-8 weeks). Under the state family leave law, private sector workers in firms with 100 or more employees who earn sick leave or other forms of paid leave are entitled to use up to 10 days for the care of a new child or to assist an ill family member.

Compensation: Women may collect 58 percent of their average weekly wages from the state while they're physically disabled due to pregnancy and childbirth, up to a maximum of 26 weeks. The state defines family more broadly than the federal FMLA to include care giving for a designated "reciprocal beneficiary," which may include a same-sex partner.

Iowa

Length: Up to 8 weeks for disability due to pregnancy and childbirth.

Restrictions: Women at workplaces with at least 4 employees. The law is silent as to whether a woman is entitled to return to the same or a similar position after returning from leave.

Kansas

Length: The period of time during which the employee is physically disabled due to pregnancy and childbirth (usually 6-8 weeks).

Restrictions: Women at workplaces with at least 4 employees.

Kentucky

Leave: 6 weeks of family leave.

Restrictions: All employees adopting a child under age 7 are eligible.

Louisiana

Length: The period of time during which the employee is considered physically disabled due to pregnancy and childbirth (usually 6-8 weeks, up to a maximum of 4 months). Employers are not required to continue health coverage.

Restrictions: Women at workplaces with at least 26 employees. The law is silent as to whether a woman is entitled to return to the same or a similar position after returning from leave.

Maine

Length: Up to 10 weeks of leave over a two-year period for birth or adoption. Health insurance must be continued during leave; however, the employer may require that the employee pay for it. Private sector workers who earn paid leave and are employed by a firm with 25 or more employees are entitled to use at least 40 hours of paid leave per year for the care of an ill child, spouse or parent. Unlike similar laws in some other states, the law does not require that leave be available to care for a healthy newborn or newly adopted child.

Restrictions: Workplaces with at least 25 employees at a permanent work site; the employee needs to have worked for 12 consecutive months. The Maine law also defines family more broadly than the federal FMLA to include domestic partners, the children of domestic partners and cohabiting siblings.

Massachusetts

Coverage: Workplaces with at least six employees; you need to have completed your employer's initial probationary period or, if there's no probationary period, three consecutive months as a full-time employee.

Leave: Eight weeks of leave for birth or adoption of a child under age 18, or adoption of a child under age 23 if the child has a disability. Employers are not required to continue health insurance.

Minnesota

Length: Up to 6 weeks of leave for the birth or adoption of a child. Health insurance must be continued during leave; however, the employer may require that the employee pay for it.

Restrictions: Workplaces with at least 21 employees; you need to have worked for 12 consecutive months at least half time.

Montana

Length: Up to 6 weeks of leave for disability due to pregnancy and childbirth; adopting parents may take 15 days for family leave.

New Hampshire

Length: The period of time during which the employee is physically disabled due to pregnancy and childbirth (usually 6-8 weeks). If a company continues health insurance for employees on other kinds of leave, it must do so for women disabled due to pregnancy and childbirth.

Restrictions: Women at workplaces with at least 6 employees are eligible. Nonprofit, religious, educational, fraternal, and charitable corporations are exempt.

New Jersey

Compensation: All women may collect state payments for 4 weeks leave before the birth and 6 weeks afterward for a vaginal delivery; eight weeks for a cesarean section. Payments are approximately two-thirds of your weekly wages, up to $401 per week. It's possible to collect payments but still lose the job if you don't qualify for the FMLA.

Restrictions: Those eligible for the FMLA -- which New Jersey grants to workers who have worked 1,000 hours in the past year -- are secure in their job for 12 weeks. The New Jersey law also defines family more broadly than the federal FMLA to include civil union partners. However, unlike most other state laws and the federal FMLA, the New Jersey Family Leave Act does not include leave for a worker's own illness; therefore, a birth mother does not have job-protected leave to recover from pregnancy, childbirth or related medical conditions.

New York

Restrictions: Those eligible for the FMLA are secure in their job for 12 weeks.

Pay: All women who work in the private sector can collect 50 % of their average weekly wages -- up to $170 a week -- while they're physically disabled due to pregnancy and childbirth (usually 6-8 weeks, up to a maximum of 26 weeks). It's possible to collect payments but still lose the job if you don't qualify for the FMLA.

Oregon

Length: 12 weeks for birth or adoption of a child up to age 6. Birth mothers are eligible for 12 weeks of pregnancy disability leave and an additional 12 weeks of family leave to care for a new child.

Restrictions: Workplaces with at least 25 employees provided that the employee has worked at least 90 consecutive days. Temporary workers hired for less than 6 months are not covered.

Puerto Rico

Length: The time during which the employee is considered physically disabled due to pregnancy and childbirth (usually 8 weeks, though the employee may add an additional 12 weeks if there are complications).

Pay: Women may apply to collect half their pay for eight weeks.

Rhode Island

Length: Rhode Island's Temporary Disability Insurance (TDI) program provides partial wage replacement to eligible workers who are temporarily disabled, including women with pregnancy or childbirth related disabilities, or other related medical conditions.220 The TDI program is funded through workers' payroll contributions. Workers are eligible for up to 30 weeks of TDI payments up to a maximum payment cap. Under the Rhode Island family and medical leave law, workers with one year of tenure who work an average of 30 hours or more per week are eligible for up to 13 weeks of leave in a two-year period for parental or family care.

Restrictions: Those eligible for the FMLA are secure in their job for 12 weeks.

Compensation: All women may qualify to receive about 60 % of their average weekly wages from the state -- up to $504 a week -- for the duration of disability (usually 6-8 weeks, up to a maximum of 30 weeks). Women with other children may qualify for an additional benefit of up to $10 for each dependent, up to a maximum of 5 dependents. It's possible to collect payments but still lose the job if the employee doesn't qualify for the FMLA.

Tennessee

Length: Up to four months of leave "for adoption, pregnancy, childbirth and nursing an infant.

Restrictions: Full-time workers in firms with more than 100 employees and who have at least one year of tenure.

Vermont

Length: 12 weeks for birth or adoption of a child age 16 or younger. Health insurance must be continued during leave; however, the employer may require that the employee pay for it.

Restrictions: Workplaces with at least 10 employees; the employee needs to have worked at least 30 hours a week for at least one year. Under Vermont's civil union law, a civil union partner has the same rights as a married "spouse" to take family leave.

Washington

Length: The period of time during which the employee is physically disabled due to pregnancy and childbirth (usually 6-8 weeks). If a company continues health insurance for employees on other leaves, it must do so for women disabled due to pregnancy and childbirth. Women may take job-protected leave for the entire period of a pregnancy-related disability, and this period of leave does not count against a worker's parental leave rights under the state family and medical leave law.256 This means that a woman with a normal pregnancy who meets FMLA eligibility requirements and works for an employer covered by the FMLA may generally take up to 18 weeks of leave, six weeks of pregnancy-related disability leave and 12 weeks of family leave to care for her child.

Restrictions: Women at workplaces with at least eight employees.

Nursing Mothers Workplace Rights

Some states are explicit in the rights of nursing mothers in terms of break time and locations to express breast milk. Here are the ones currently outlined.

Arkansas

All nursing mothers are entitled to reasonable break time and a place other than a toilet stall to express breast milk at work, for an unspecified time after childbirth.

California

All nursing mothers are entitled to reasonable break time and a private place other than a toilet stall to express breast milk at work while their children are infants.

Colorado

All nursing mothers are entitled to reasonable break time and a place other than a toilet stall to express breast milk at work for up to two years after giving birth.

Connecticut

Employers of any size must provide all female workers a place other than a toilet stall to express breast milk at work, for an unspecified period of time after giving birth.

District of Columbia

All nursing mothers are entitled to reasonable break time and a place other than a bathroom to express breast milk at work for an unspecified period of time after childbirth.

Illinois

Nursing mothers employed by private employers with more than five employees are entitled to reasonable break time and a private place other than a toilet stall to express breast milk at work while their children are infants.

Indiana

All nursing mothers who work for larger employers in Indiana (25 or more employees) must be provided a private place other than a toilet stall to express breast milk. Unlike most other states,

Indiana's law does not require that workers also be provided reasonable break time to express breast milk.

Maine

All nursing mothers are entitled to adequate break time and a place other than a bathroom to express breast milk at work, for up to three years after childbirth.

Minnesota

All nursing mothers are entitled to reasonable break time and a place other than a toilet stall to express breast milk at work while their children are infants.

Montana

Women employed by the state are entitled to reasonable break time and a place other than a toilet stall to express breast milk at work for an unspecified period of time after giving birth. All public employers must have a written policy supporting women who want to continue breastfeeding after returning from maternity leave.

New Mexico

All nursing mothers who work for employers with four or more workers are entitled to "flexible" break times and a place other than a bathroom to express breast milk at work for an unspecified period of time after childbirth.

New York

All nursing mothers are entitled to reasonable break time and a room or other location close to their work area to express breast milk at work for up to three years after childbirth.

Oregon

All nursing mothers who work for employers with 25 or more workers are entitled to reasonable break time and a place other than a bathroom to express breast milk at work for up to 18 months after childbirth.

Rhode Island

All nursing mothers are entitled to a place other than a bathroom to express breast milk at work while their children are infants. Unlike most other state laws, the Rhode Island law permits, but does not require, employers to provide reasonable break time.

Tennessee

All nursing mothers are entitled to reasonable break time and a place other than a toilet stall to express breast milk at work while their children are infants.

Vermont

All nursing mothers are entitled to reasonable break time and a place other than a bathroom stall to express breast milk at work for up to three years after childbirth.

Paternity Leave

Paternity leave is the time a father takes off work at the birth or adoption or foster care placement of a child. This kind of leave is rarely paid. Most states use the federal Family and Medical Leave (FMLA) Act which allows an employee up to 12 weeks of unpaid leave. At the end of your leave, your employer must allow you to return to your job or a similar job with the same salary, benefits, working conditions, and seniority.

You're eligible if you meet both of the following conditions:

- You work for the federal government, a state or local government, or any company that has 50 or more employees working within 75 miles of your workplace.
- You've worked for your employer for at least 12 months and for at least 1,250 hours during the previous year (which comes out to 25 hours per week for 50 weeks).

There are a few exceptions: Your employer can deny you this leave if you're in the highest paid 10 percent of wage earners at your company and can show that your absence would cause substantial economic harm to the organization. In this case, your employer isn't required to keep your job open for you.

Another exception is if you and your partner both work for the same company. In this case, you're only entitled to a combined 12 weeks of parental leave between the two of you.

Even if you're not eligible under the FMLA, you may still be eligible for leave under your state's provisions, which are usually more generous than the FMLA, or under your company's policy.

A few companies offer new dads paid time off, ranging from a few days to a few weeks. And in 2004, California became the first state to offer paid family leave. (If you work in that state, you may be able to take up to six weeks at partial pay.)

Washington and New Jersey have also passed paid family leave laws, and other states have considered similar bills. In the meantime, though, most fathers take vacation time or sick days when their children are born, and a growing number of new dads are taking unpaid family leave from their jobs to spend more time with their newborns.

You can use your unpaid leave in any way you want during the first year after your child is born or placed with you. That means you can take it all at once or, as long as your employer agrees, spread it out over your child's first year by taking it in chunks or reducing your normal weekly or daily work schedule.

According to the FMLA, your employer must continue to keep you on their health insurance plan while you're on leave. Most typically, a company will pay your premiums for you but ask you to reimburse them for your share (the amount that's usually taken out of your paycheck).

If your job is terminated while you're on leave or you tell your company you don't intend to return to work, your employer may stop paying your premiums and put you on COBRA, a program in which you continue to be covered under the same plan but pay the entire premium yourself. Your employer may even require you to pay back the money spent to maintain your health insurance while you were on leave.

The FMLA doesn't require employers to allow you to accrue benefits or time toward seniority when you're out on leave. That means that the time on leave may not count towards time accrued towards vacation accrual and the amount of time you can say you've been with the company in order to qualify for things like:

- raises based on seniority or length of service

- additional vacation days per year

- participation in your company's 401k plan or vesting of your company's matching investment

- vesting of stock options

Finally, you won't be able to contribute to your 401(k) or flexible spending account while you're on leave since you're not receiving a paycheck and thus can't contribute pre-tax dollars.

Leave for adoptive parents or birth fathers continues to be less generous than for birth mothers, with only 32 percent of companies offering more than four weeks of paid leave to adoptive parents (up from 16 percent in 2006) and only 12 percent of companies offering paid leave of more than four weeks to birth fathers.

The United States' failure to provide access to paid parental leave means that many new mothers and fathers can only take time away from work when their employers voluntarily offer some form of paid time off for parental leave. Many employers do not provide this. In fact, employers have decreased or eliminated paid parental leave benefits in recent. According to government data, just 11% of private sector workers have access to paid family leave that can be used by fathers or adoptive mothers.

Access to paid family leave encourages fathers to take leave. Among fathers in lower-quality jobs in California, access to paid family leave has greatly impacted the average length of leave, nearly tripling the amount of time fathers reported taking off work after the birth of a child, from an average of three weeks to an average of eight weeks.

Countries vary in terms of providing individual entitlements of leave for fathers. Iceland has the most egalitarian system in the world, giving each parent the right to three months each of paid leave plus an additional three months that may be shared between the couple at their discretion, while single parents get the full entitlement. More than 50 nations, including most Western countries, also guarantee paid leave for new fathers. In the European Union, paid parental leave varies from 12 weeks in Norway to 16 months in Sweden, which reserves at least two months of its leave exclusively for fathers. Most EU countries have maintained the provisions of their programs despite the recession.

In New Jersey, men make up about 12 percent of the parents seeking paid leave to bond with a new child. In California, men's share of the leave has risen from 17 % to 26 % since 2004. As fathers who participate in parental leave increase, the greater chance of more states adopting more progressive policies to increase paid benefits.

Adoption Leave

You may take FMLA leave, vacation time, or possibly accrued sick leave if you're adopting or taking in a foster child. Generally, leave begins once the child arrives at your home (or when you leave to get the child if adopting from another country.) You may also be eligible to take time off during the adoption process to meet with lawyers or attend home visits.

The United States is one of the few industrialized nations that do not provide paid family leave for new parents. Some parents can take time off under the Family and Medical Leave Act of 1993, which guarantees eligible employees at companies with more than 50 employees 12 weeks of unpaid, job-guaranteed leave for the birth of a child or care of a newborn, adoption of a child, to care for an immediate family member with a serious health condition, or to take medical leave for a serious health condition. Similar statutes exist in Washington D.C. and some states: California, Connecticut, Hawaii, Maine, Minnesota, New Jersey, Oregon, Rhode Island, Vermont, Washington, and Wisconsin. California became the first state to enact a paid family leave act in 2002, allowing employees to take 6 weeks leave up to 55% of their weekly wages (with a benefit cap) to care for a newborn, newly adopted child and every employee who contributes to the State Disability Insurance is covered, not just those in companies with 50 employees or more.

A 2011 benefits survey of companies that are members of the Society for Human Resource Management found that 16.0% offered paid adoption leave, the same as in 2010.

Adoption Leave Policies	
Australia	18 weeks paid at national minimum wage by government. Can be taken anytime within the first year after adoption. Can be transferred to either parent.
Germany	There is no adoptive leave, but parents can utilize three years parental leave (at 67% usual salary).
Italy	Once the child is placed, three months of leave may be taken, if the child is not yet six years old.
Japan	Adoption leave does not exist in Japan, but new adoptive parents can utilize child-care leave, which lasts until a child's first birthday.
Netherlands	Four weeks leave for each new parent. In addition, parents can also receive an additional 13 weeks full-time leave or six months part-time leave before the child's eighth birthday.

New Zealand	Adoptive parents receive maternity and partner's leave, and parents can choose which partner will be the primary caregiver (who will receive 14 weeks of paid leave) and which parent will use one to two weeks leave. Parents can also share extended 52 weeks of leave.
Norway	Adoptive parents receive the same paid maternity and paternity leaves as birth parents, but the total time available is reduced by three weeks. Adoptive parents have six weeks each, and can also utilize the unpaid year-long parental leave.
Spain	In couples, one adoptive parent will receive 16 weeks leave and the other receives 13 days of leave. Adoption leave typically begins with the first day the child is with their new family.
Sweden	Eighteen months upon arrival of child.
UK	Adoptees who meet conditions can take up to 26 weeks of Ordinary Adoption Leave, as well as 26 weeks of Additional Adoption Leave. Begins on the day the child becomes a resident of the household or up to fourteen days prior.

Source: Society for Human Resource Management

Family & Medical Leave

There is no detailed list of what kind of conditions qualify. Instead, a serious health condition is defined by its effect on the individual. A serious health condition must involve either inpatient care at a hospital or medical facility, or continuing treatment by a health care provider. "Continuing treatment by a health care provider" covers many varied situations including:

- Pregnancy or prenatal care;

- Chronic conditions that extend over a long period of time and require periodic visits to a health care provider and may create periods of incapacity (asthma, diabetes);

- A permanent, long term condition for which treatment may be ineffective (e.g. Alzheimer's, a severe stroke, terminal cancer);

- Restorative surgery or treatment for a condition which, if left untreated, would likely result in a period of incapacity of more than three days (e.g. chemotherapy or radiation

- treatments for cancer, dialysis); or

- Any health condition that causes a period of three consecutive days of incapacity and is accompanied by at least two visits to a health care provider or one visit and continued monitoring by the health care provider.

Generally, things like cosmetic surgery, colds, headaches, and routine medical and dental care are not included.

You can take FMLA family leave to care for your spouse, your son or daughter under the age of 18, or your parent. Your family member must have a qualifying serious health condition. You cannot take leave to care for a child who is over the age of 18 unless the child is unable to care for himself or herself due to a physical or mental disability. You cannot use FMLA leave to care for a father-in-law or mother-in-law or a sibling.

However, if you require regular intervals in order to take an immediate family member to physical therapy or treatment, family leave may be taken intermittently when medically necessary. You may take leave in blocks of time—such as several hours, a half day, a day, a week, four weeks or 12 weeks—to care for a family member with a serious health condition. If you are going to need intermittent leave regularly, your employer may require you to transfer temporarily to another position that has the same pay and benefits but is better suited to recurring periods of leave.

Similarly the same would apply if you needed to attend treatment such as chemotherapy which would likely impact your ability to work for hours or days after treatment. You may take leave in blocks of time—such as several hours, a half day, a day, a week, four weeks or 12 weeks. And your employer has the right to transfer you temporarily to another position that can accommodate your schedule and medical needs. Depression or other doctor diagnoses psychological issues are covered in the same manner.

If you know in advance you will need to use leave, such as for a scheduled surgery, you must give at least 30 days notice to your employer, or as soon as you can if you find out you will need to take leave in less than 30 days. If the need to use leave is unplanned, such as in the case of a sudden illness, you need to follow your employer's rules about giving notice. Your failure to follow such rules could lead to you being denied leave, unless there are unusual circumstances.

Your employer can require that you or the family member you are caring for obtain certification of the serious health condition from your health care provider. Your employer can require a second opinion, but your employer must pay for the second opinion. If both opinions conflict, you and your employer must agree to a provider for a third opinion, paid for by your employer, whose determination will be final.

If your employer provides health care benefits, it must maintain those benefits at the same level and under the same conditions as if you had not taken leave. You will still have to pay your share of the premium, if you do so normally.

Your employer cannot fire you, deny you a promotion, or take other disciplinary actions against you for using FMLA leave. Your employer also cannot fire or otherwise discipline you for complaining about a violation of the FMLA.

You may use your accrued paid vacation pay towards your medical leave if you do not want to use your 12 week unpaid medical leave so that you are paid for part or all of your leave. Even if your employer doesn't want to pay you during this leave, you may insist that your accrued paid sick and annual leave be used. But you should realize that the paid leave also will count against the 12 weeks of unpaid leave you get under FMLA.

You may be entitled to paid leave under your employer's short term disability program. You may also be able to use your sick time or vacation time while you are on FMLA leave. Five states—California, Hawaii, New Jersey, New York, and Rhode Island—and Puerto Rico have Temporary Disability Insurance programs to provide some pay when a worker is out of work due to her own serious health condition, including pregnancy. California and New Jersey provide a more comprehensive paid family leave program allowing for payment when workers need time off to care for a family member or to bond with a new child. Washington State has a paid parental leave program that is expected go into effect soon.

Here are a couple of examples

Example 1: If you had a serious car accident and needed healing and rehabilitation time at home for 12 weeks, and had accrued 3 weeks of paid sick leave and 2 weeks of paid annual leave, you could use your sick and annual leave to cover 5 of the 12 weeks. The remaining 7 weeks of leave would be unpaid. In that case, you would not be entitled to 12 weeks of unpaid leave under FMLA followed by the 5 weeks of accrued leave.

Example 2: Your 85-year old mother, who lives out of town, has recently suffered a heart attack and is in the hospital. You need to take a week's vacation to care for her, organize her financial affairs, and find her a home health care provider so that she may recuperate at home. You are concerned that she may have more health issues in the coming months. You feel that you don't want to use any of your 12 weeks of family medical leave now. But if you tell your employer why you need this vacation week, he'll count it against your 12 weeks of FMLA leave. What are your options?

You don't have any legal obligation to disclose the reason of your vacation. But if your employer finds out that you used your vacation for family leave, he can retroactively designate it as such and count it against your 12-week total as long as he does it within a couple of days of finding out. There are advantages to designating this vacation time as family medical leave. As long as you provide the notice required under the FMLA, your employer will not be able to cancel your vacation. And using FMLA time will protect you if your mother's condition worsens, and you end up having to stay more than one week—your employer will not be able to argue that you are not entitled to that additional leave because you failed to give adequate notice under the FMLA.

Sick Leave

Sick leave enables employees to take time off work when ill. The U.S. does not currently require that employees have access to paid sick days to address their own short-term illnesses or the short-term illness of a family member. The U.S. does guarantee unpaid leave for serious illnesses through the FMLA. This law covers employers with more than 50 workers and, within those businesses, covers employees who have worked for their employer for at least 12 months prior to taking the leave.[1]

Four jurisdictions in the United States have passed local paid sick time laws:

In November 2006, San Francisco voters made the city the first in the country to guarantee paid sick days to all workers. Under San Francisco's law, workers earn one hour of paid sick time for every 30 hours worked. Workers in businesses with 10 or fewer employees earn up to five days per year, while workers at larger businesses earn nine days per year. Workers use paid sick time to recover from illness, attend doctor visits or care for a sick child, partner, or designated loved one.

In March 2008, the Washington, D.C. Council voted unanimously to pass legislation guaranteeing workers paid sick time. Under the Accrued Sick and Safe Leave Act, workers in businesses with 100 or more workers earn up to seven days of paid sick leave each year, workers in businesses with 25-99 workers earn five days, and workers in businesses with 24 or fewer workers earn three days. This paid time off can be used to recover from illnesses, care for sick family members, seek routine or preventative medical care, or obtain assistance related to domestic violence or sexual assault. The law exempts tipped restaurant workers as well as workers in the first year of employment. The D.C. law was also the first in the United States to include paid "safe" days for victims of domestic violence, sexual assault, or stalking.

In November 2008, paid sick days were voted in overwhelmingly by Milwaukee voters enacting a law that guarantees paid sick and safe days for all workers in the city. Unfortunately, a Milwaukee County Circuit Court judge ruled it invalid under a Wisconsin state law that bans local paid sick leave ordinances.

On July 1, 2011, Connecticut became the first state to mandate paid sick leave. The Act requires employers to allow their "service workers" to earn one hour of paid sick leave for every 40 hours worked, capped at a maximum of 40 hours per year. The Act applies to the "service workers" of employers with 50 or more employees in Connecticut during any single quarter in the previous year.

Advocates for paid sick leave point to the case of Hilda Pizarro. Pizzaro says she was suspended from her job cleaning houses for Merry Maids — which does not offer paid sick days — because she had to take her 2-year-old son to the hospital for emergency asthma treatment. While she was on suspension, she says, she was terminated.

Supporters of paid sick leave also argue that everyone benefits when sick people do not show up for work. Requiring paid sick leave "is good public policy and specifically good public health," Governor Dan Malloy said when he signed Connecticut's law last July. "Why would you want to eat food from a sick restaurant cook? Or have your children taken care of by a sick day-care worker? The simple answer is — you wouldn't."

In 2012, active paid sick days campaigns or legislation exist in Arizona, California, Colorado, District of Columbia, Hawaii, Illinois, Iowa, Maine, Massachusetts, Miami, Michigan, New Jersey, New York City, New York, North Carolina, Orange County (Florida), Oregon, Pennsylvania, Philadelphia, Vermont, Washington and Wisconsin. Check your local government website to view the status of such legislation.

If your employer does provide paid sick leave benefits, they are not obligated to pay for that time if you quit your job before using all of your allotted sick leave.

American with Disabilities Act (ADA)

The ADA is a federal law that protects the rights of people with disabilities by eliminating barriers to their participation in many aspects of working and living in America. In particular, the

ADA prohibits discrimination against people with disabilities in the full range of employment-related activities, from recruitment to advancement to pay and benefits.

The ADA does not specifically require employers to provide medical or disability-related leave. However, it does require employers to make reasonable accommodations for qualified employees with disabilities if necessary to perform essential job functions or to benefit from the same opportunities and rights afforded employees without disabilities. Accommodations can include modifications to work schedules, such as leave. There is no set leave period mandated because accommodations depend on individual circumstances and should generally be granted unless doing so would result in "undue hardship" to the employer.

Funeral & Bereavement Leave

The Fair Labor Standards Act (FLSA) does not require payment for time not worked, including attending a funeral or period of mourning. This type of benefit is generally a matter of agreement between an employer and an employee. There are no state laws requiring that any benefits be given and there are no bereavement leave federal laws.

Most companies in the U.S. do grant bereavement leave. However, there are some companies that do not grant any time off for their employees bereaved by the death of an immediate family member or a close relative. If time is allowed, this means that employees are usually given three days off with pay. A few places of work might give five days as time off with pay. Some companies may allow for a person to take additional time off without pay or want them to arrange to use personal days or vacation time. It is encouraged for an employee to find out what their company's bereavement leave policies are.

Some companies hold a very narrow definition of who a family member is. Only if one of the following dies can an employee consider time off with pay.

- Spouse
- Child
- Parent
- Grandparent
- Brother
- Sister

Some companies have expanded the list to include: domestic partner, grandchild, step-parent, stepchild, father or mother-in-law or brother or sister-in-law. Some places of employment may require that you show verification, or proof, that your loved one has died. A copy of an obituary or death certificate should suffice.

Extended Uses of FMLA

States with their own FMLAs have expanded how workers can use FMLA leave. Here are the current states with statutes in place.

State	Uses of FMLA Leave
California	Give parents unpaid leave to attend their child's school or educational activities
Colorado	Give workers unpaid leave to address the effects of domestic violence, stalking, or sexual assault
Connecticut	Organ or bone marrow donor
Florida	Give workers unpaid leave to address the effects of domestic violence, stalking, or sexual assault
Hawaii	Give workers unpaid leave to address the effects of domestic violence, stalking, or sexual assault
Illinois	Give workers unpaid leave to address the effects of domestic violence, stalking, or sexual assault
Maine	Organ donor; death of employee's family member if that family member is a service member killed while on active duty
Massachusetts	Give parents unpaid leave to attend their child's school or educational activities, take family members to routine medical visits
Minnesota	Give parents unpaid leave to attend their child's school or educational activities
Oregon	Care of for the non-serious injury or illness of a child that requires home care
Rhode Island	Give parents unpaid leave to attend their child's school or educational activities
Vermont	Give parents unpaid leave to attend their child's school or educational activities, take family members to routine medical visits
District of Columbia	Give parents unpaid leave to attend their child's school or educational activities

Whistleblower Protection

OSHA's Whistleblower Protection Program enforces the whistleblower provisions of twenty-one whistleblower statutes protecting employees who report violations of various workplace safety, airline, commercial motor carrier, consumer product, environmental, financial reform, food safety, health care reform, nuclear, pipeline, public transportation agency, railroad, maritime, and securities laws. Rights afforded by these whistleblower acts include, but are not limited to, worker participation in safety and health activities, reporting a work related injury, illness or fatality, or reporting a violation of the statutes.

Protection from discrimination means that an employer cannot retaliate by taking "adverse action" against workers, such as:

- Firing or laying off
- Blacklisting
- Demoting
- Denying overtime or promotion
- Disciplining
- Denial of benefits
- Failure to hire or rehire
- Intimidation
- Making threats
- Reassignment affecting prospects for promotion
- Reducing pay or hours

If you have been punished or discriminated against for exercising your rights under the OSH Act, you must file a complaint with OSHA **within 30 days of the alleged reprisal**. In states with approved state plans, employees may file a complaint under the OSH Act with both the State and Federal OSHA. To file a complaint with OSHA, go to this website: www.whistleblowers.gov/complaint_page.html.

Here is a list of states with whistleblower laws in place.

State	Covers	Provisions
Alabama	state employees	State Employees Protection Act
Alaska	public employees	Prohibits public employers from discharging, threatening, or otherwise discriminating against a public employee who reports to a public body or participates in a court action or inquiry on a matter of public concern. Employers are liable for compensatory and punitive damages and civil fines of up to $10,000.

Arizona	none	none
Arkansas	none	none
California	all employers	It is unlawful for an employer to make or enforce a rule or policy or to retaliate against an employee for disclosing information to a government or law enforcement agency if the employee reasonably believes the information involves a violation of state or federal law. Claims must be reported to the State Division of Labor Standards Enforcement within 90 days of the alleged retaliatory act.
Colorado	state employees and health care workers	State employees are protected from retaliation, including discharge, by their supervisor or agency for disclosing information about the actions of a state agency that are not in the public interest, such as waste of public funds, abuse of authority or mismanagement of the agency. Health care workers are protected for reporting patient safety violations. Contractors of state agencies are protected.
Connecticut	public and private employers	It is unlawful for a public or private employer to discriminate against an employee, including discharge, discipline or penalty, for reporting to a public body a violation or suspected violation of any state, federal or local law. Employees knowingly making a false report are not protected and can be discharged. An aggrieved employee can bring a civil suit for reinstatement, back-pay and benefits, after exhausting administrative remedies. Suites must be filed within 90 days of the alleged discriminatory treatment or final administrative action, whichever is later. Prevailing employees can recover costs and attorney fees. Any person can report to the state Attorney General alleged corruption, unethical practices, violation of state law, waste of funds, mismanagement, abuse of authority, or danger of public safety. Disclosure of the name of the employee is prohibited as is retaliation against such person. Persons knowingly making false reports can be dismissed.
Delaware	public employees	Public employees cannot be discharged, threatened or discriminated against for reporting a violation or suspected violation of a state or federal law to the Office of the Auditor of Accounts, unless the employee knew the report to be false. Aggrieved employees can bring a civil suit for damages within 90 days of the alleged discrimination.
DC	none	none
Florida	public and private employers	An employer may not take retaliatory personnel action against an employee because the employee has disclosed or threatened

		to disclose to a government agency an activity, policy or practice that is in violation of a law; or testified before an entity conducting an investigation into possible violations; or refused to participate in an activity, policy or practice that is in violation of a law, rule or regulation. Public employees cannot be discharged, disciplined, or subjected to adverse personnel action for making disclosures involving a violation of state or federal law that creates a substantial and specific danger to the public's health, safety or welfare.
Georgia	health workers	Provides whistleblower protection for health care workers who report Medicaid false claims.
Hawaii	private and public employers	Under the Hawaii Whistleblowers Protection Act, private and public employers cannot discharge, threaten or discriminate against an employee regarding compensation, terms, conditions, location or privileges of employment because the employee reports a violation or suspected violation of a state, federal or local law, unless the employee knows the report to be false. Greater protections provided for by collective bargaining agreements take precedence. Aggrieved employees may bring a civil suit within 90 days. Courts may order reinstatement, back-pay, and court costs, along with attorney's fees. An employer may be fined up to $500 for each violation.
Idaho	none	none
Illinois	public employees	Public employees cannot be disciplined for disclosing information that they reasonably believe shows a violation of any rule or law, or mismanagement, waste of funds, abuse of authority, or specific and substantial danger to public health or safety. The reporting employee's name cannot be disclosed without their consent.
Indiana	state employees	It is unlawful to discharge, deny salary or benefits, demote, transfer or reassign a state employee for reporting a violation of state or federal laws, agency regulation or misuse of public resources. Reports must be filed first with the employee's supervisor. If no action is taken in a reasonable time, the employee can "go public" with the information or report it to another agency or organization. The employee is not protected if the information is false.
Iowa	state employees	It is unlawful to discharge or take personnel action against a state employee in reprisal for a disclosure of a violation of a law or rule, mismanagement, abuse of fund, abuse of authority, or substantial and specific danger to public health or safety, unless such disclosure is specifically prohibited by law. Employees of a

		state political subdivision cannot be discharged or retaliated against for disclosing similar information to a member of the General Assembly or an official of the state or a political subdivision.
Kansas	state employees	State employees cannot be disciplined for discussing the operations of the agencies with a member or the legislature or for reporting a violation of state or federal law. They are not required to inform their supervisors before reporting the violation but they are required to inform their supervisors of legislative requests and the nature of the testimony they will provide. State employees may be disciplined for providing false testimony or disclosing confidential information. Aggrieved state employees can seek relief in court or before the state civil service board.
Kentucky	state employees	The state and political subdivisions cannot retaliate, threaten or discriminate against an employee who in good faith reports to state officials or agencies, the General Assembly, the Legislative Research Commission, judicial branch or law enforcement agencies a violation or suspected violation of state, federal or local law or regulation, or mismanagement, waste, fraud or endangerment of the public health. Employees are not required to give notice prior to making such a report but can be required to inform their employer of any official request to the agency for information and the substance of the testimony to be provided. Employees may be disciplined for providing false or confidential information. An aggrieved employee may file suit within 90 days for damages, reinstatement and back-pay.
Louisiana	all employers	It is unlawful for employers to retaliate against any employee who in good faith reports or complains about possible violations of federal, state, or local environmental protection laws. Aggrieved employees can bring suit in district court for triple damages, costs and attorney fees. Employers cannot discharge or discriminate against an employee for furnishing information or testifying in an investigation of a violation of state labor laws. Criminal penalties apply, with fines up to $250 and up to 90 days imprisonment. The assistant secretary of labor can also institute civil proceedings, with fines up to $500, attorney's fees and court costs to the prevailing party.
Maine	public or private employers	It is unlawful for public or private employers of one or more employees to discharge, threaten or discriminate against an employee who in good faith reports a violation or suspected violation of a state, federal or local law or regulation or a practice that endangers the health or safety of the employee,

		others or a public body; or who is asked to participate in an investigation, court proceeding or inquiry; or who in good faith refuses to carry out an order that puts the employee or others at risk. Employees must first bring the violation to the attention of a supervisor and allow reasonable time for correction. Aggrieved employees may file a complaint with the Maine Human Rights Commission for violations and retain remedies available under common law.
Maryland	public	Cannot take or refuse to take any personnel action as reprisal if employee discloses abuse of authority, gross mismanagement or waste of money, violation of law or substantial and specific danger to public health or safety and seeks a remedy
Massachusetts	any employer	An employer may not retaliate against employees who report violation of law or risks to public health, safety or the environment. Retaliation includes discharge, suspension, demotion, or other adverse action taken in terms or conditions of employment.
Michigan	all employers	Employers cannot discharge or cause the constructive discharge or discriminate against an employee because the employee or a person acting on behalf of the employee reports or is about to report a violation of local, state or federal law to a public body or is requested by a public body to take part in an investigation, hearing, inquiry or court action. Protections do not apply if the employee knows the report to be false.
Minnesota	public and private employers	Public and private employers cannot discharge, discipline, threaten, discriminate against or penalize an employee regarding compensation, terms, conditions, location or privileges of employment because the employee in good faith reports a violation or suspected violation of a state or federal law or rule or refuses to participate in any activity that the employee in good faith believes to be a violation of a state or federal law or rule. Remedies include civil action for damages, costs and attorneys fees. Employees are not protected for knowingly making a false statement. A discharged employee must request within five days a written explanation of the reason for their discharge. An employer that fails to notify a discharged employee of the true reason for their discharge within five working days of the employees request will be fined $25 per day, up to $750 per injured employee. Any notice provided to an employee cannot be the subject of an action for libel, slander or defamation brought by the employee against the employer.
Mississippi	none	none

Missouri	state employees	State agencies cannot take disciplinary action against an employee for disclosing alleged prohibited activity under investigation or for disclosing information which the employee reasonably believes to be a violation of law or rule, mismanagement, waste of funds, abuse of authority or a specific and substantial danger to public health or safety. Protections do not apply if the employees know the disclosure to be false or if it was made in reckless disregard for the truth.
Montana	none	none
Nebraska	private employers, state employees and unions	It is unlawful for an employer with 15 or more employees, or a union or employment agency to discriminate against a person who has opposed any practice or refused to carry out an action that is a violation of state or federal law.
Nevada	none	none
New Hampshire	public and private employers	Employers cannot discharge, threaten or discriminate against an employee regarding compensation, terms, conditions, location or privileges of employment because the employee in good faith reports what they believe to be a violation or state, federal or local law or rule, or if the employee participates in an investigation, hearing or inquiry conducted by a governmental agency, or for refusing to execute a directive which is a violation of rule or law. The employee is only protected if they first report the allegation to a supervisor and allow time for correction, unless the employee has reason to believe the violation will not be corrected promptly. An aggrieved employee must use available grievance procedures and then may obtain a hearing with the commissioner of labor who may order reinstatement, back-pay and benefits and injunctive relief. Aggrieved employees may also pursue relief through union procedures or at common law.
New Jersey	public and private employers	The Conscientious Employee Protection Act (CEPA) prohibits a public or private employer from taking retaliatory action against an employee who discloses or threatens to disclose to a supervisor or public body an activity, policy or practice that the employee reasonably believes is in violation of a law or rule; or provides information or testimony to a public body investigating a violation; or objects to or refuses to participate in an activity, policy or practice that the employee reasonably believes is a violation of law, fraudulent or criminal, or is incompatible with a clear mandate of public policy related to health, safety, welfare or protection of the environment. The protection does not apply unless the employee has given written

		notice of the violation to a supervisor and has given reasonable time for correction, except if the employee is reasonably certain the supervisor already knows about the violation or if the employee reasonably fears physical harm and the situation is an emergency. An employee asserting a CEPA claim must establish that they had an objectively reasonable belief that the employer's conduct was illegal or violated public policy, rather than errors in judgment by the employer.
New Mexico	none	none
New York	public and private employers	Public and private employers cannot discipline or take retaliatory action against employees who disclose or threaten to disclose activities, policies or practices that violate laws or regulations or threaten public health or safety. The protections extend to public employees who disclose to a governmental body information that they reasonably believe to be an improper governmental action. Aggrieved employees can sue for reinstatement, back-pay and benefits and may be entitled to courts costs and attorney fees. A prevailing employer may recover court costs and attorney fees if the suit is not based on law or fact.
North Carolina	none	none
North Dakota	private employers	A private employer may not discharge, discipline, threaten, discriminate or penalize an employee with regards to compensation, work conditions, location or privileges of employment because the person, or a person acting on their behalf, in good faith reported a violation or suspected violation of a state or federal rule or law, or refused an order to perform an act that the employee believes to be illegal. Within 90 days of alleged discrimination, an aggrieved employee may bring a civil suit against the employer and may recover injunctive relief, actual damages and attorneys fees. A willful violation of this law is a criminal infraction punishable by a maximum $500 fine.
Ohio	private and public employers	An employer cannot discipline or retaliate against an employee making a report of a violation of state, federal or local law or rule. The employee must notify their supervisor by written report with sufficient detail to describe the violation. The employer must make a good faith effort to correct the violation within 24 hours or the employee may notify the prosecuting authority, a peace officer or an appropriate public agency or official. Employees can be disciplined for failure to make a good faith effort to ascertain the accuracy of information reported. A separate law provides that state employees cannot

		be disciplined or retaliated against for reporting a violation of state or federal statute or rule or a misuse of public resources. Employees may be disciplined for reporting false information. An aggrieved employee's sole and exclusive remedy is to file an appeal with the state personnel board of review within 30 days after alleged discriminatory action.
Oklahoma	state employees	State employees are protected from discipline when they disclose public information or for reporting violations of state or federal law or policy, mismanagement, gross waste of public funds, danger to public health or safety; or discuss operations and functions of government agencies with the governor or the legislature. Employees are not protected if they knowingly or recklessly disseminate false or confidential information.
Oregon	private and public employees	Public employers cannot prohibit employees from reporting or punish employees who reasonably report criminal activity or gross waste of public funds. It is unlawful for any employer to demote, suspend or discharge an employee who in good faith reported criminal activity, aided in a criminal investigation or has brought a civil suit against the employer.
Pennsylvania	public employers	A public employer cannot discharge, threaten, discriminate or retaliate against an employee who makes a good faith report to the employer or appropriate agency of waste or wrongdoing, including a violation of a federal, state or local law or regulation, or codes of conduct or ethics designed to protect the public interest; or for participating in an investigation, hearing or court action. An aggrieved employee may file a civil action for injunctive relief and damages within 180 days of the alleged discrimination. Employers may be fined up to $500 for violations.
Rhode Island	public and private employers	Public and private employers cannot discharge, threaten or discriminate against an employee for reporting to a public body a violation of law or regulation or for participating in an investigation, hearing, inquiry or court action. An aggrieved employee has three years after an alleged violation to file an action for relief or damages.
South Carolina	government employers	Government employers cannot discharge, suspend, demote, decrease the compensation, discipline or threaten employees who report violation or state or federal laws or rules; or expose criminal activity, corruption, waste, fraud or gross negligence; or who testify in a trial or hearing regarding those matters. Employees who make an unfounded allegation without good faith may be discharged. If an employee's actions in reporting

		results in a saving of public funds, the reporting employee is entitled to 25% of the estimated savings up to $2,000. If an employee is dismissed within one year after having reported alleged wrongdoing, the employee may file suit after having exhausted all administrative remedies. Recoverable damages include lost wages, court costs and reasonable attorney fees, along with reinstatement.
South Dakota	none	none
Tennessee	public and private employees	Public and private employers and those paid under federal contracts may bring a civil cause of action for the retaliatory discharge of an employee for reporting illegal activities. Applies to state employees, private employees, and certain persons paid by the federal government.
Texas	none	none
Utah	public employees	Employees of the state or political subdivisions cannot be discharged, threatened, disciplined or discriminated against for reporting to a public body the existence or suspected existence of waste of public funds, property or manpower; or for a violation or suspected violation of state or federal law; or for refusing to comply with a directive the employee reasonably believes to be illegal. Employees are not protected if they fail to give written notice of the violation to the employer, unless they reasonably believe notice to be futile; fail to comply with administrative reporting procedures; or make the report knowing that it is malicious, false or frivolous. Aggrieved employees may file suit within 180 days after the alleged discriminatory action and can seek reinstatement, back-pay, benefits, court costs and attorney fees. Violating employers can be fined up to $500.
Vermont	health care employees	No employer shall take retaliatory action against any employee because the employee does any of the following: Discloses or threatens to disclose any activity, policy, practice, procedure, action, or failure to act of the employer that the employee reasonably believes is a violation of any law or that the employee reasonably believes constitutes improper quality of patient care; or provides information or testimony that the employer has violated any law or has engaged in behavior constituting improper quality of patient care. An employee aggrieved by a violation of this subdivision may: utilize any available internal process, grievance procedure, or similar process available to the employee to maintain or restore any loss of employment rights with the employer or bring an action

		in the superior court. If the court finds that the employer has violated subsection 507(b) of this title, the court shall order, as appropriate: reinstatement of the employee, including employment benefits, seniority, and same or equivalent position; payment of back pay, lost wages, benefits, and other remuneration; any appropriate injunctive relief; compensatory damages; punitive damages; attorney fees; or any other appropriate relief.
Virginia	public employees	Establishes the Fraud and Abuse Whistle Blower Protection Act to protect public employee whistle blowers from certain adverse employment actions; prohibits employers from discharging or retaliating against a whistle blower; provides a civil cause of action for the whistle blower; establishes the Fraud and Abuse Whistle Blower Reward Fund to provide a monetary reward to any person who has disclosed information of wrongdoing or abuse.
Washington	state employees	State governmental employees who provide information to state auditors about improper governmental action and suffer retaliation as a result can appeal to the superior court for a review of the alleged retaliation, without first exhausting administrative remedies. Employees must act in good faith and try to first give the information to the agency head before reporting it. State officials who retaliate can be held personally liable, with a fine of up to $3,000, a suspension of up to 30 days and at a minimum have a letter of reprimand placed in their personnel file.
West Virginia	state employers	State government employers are prohibited from discharging, threatening, discriminating or retaliating against employees by changing an employee's compensation, terms, conditions, location, or privileges because of an actual or planned good faith report of wrongdoing made to the employer or to a public body; or against employees who participate in investigations, hearings, inquiries or trials involving wrongdoing or waste. Aggrieved employees may within 180 days of the alleged discrimination sue their employer for injunctive relief and damages, including reinstatement, back-pay and benefits, court costs, witness fees and attorney fees. Employers and public officials who violate this law will be punished by a civil fine of up to $500. Unelected officials may be suspended from public service for up to six months.
Wisconsin	none	none
Wyoming	none	none

Employer Wrongs

Employer's Rights

It goes without saying that when two parties enter into a binding agreement, both parties have rights so that each can be protected. This, too, is the case in the employer/employee agreement/relationship. So, naturally, an employer has rights as well but, just what are they? Sadly, an astounding number of employees throughout the United States have an insufficient understanding of their own rights let alone the right of their employers. It is imperative that we understand just what are within an employer's rights with regards to its business practices towards its employees. Can an employer use secret surveillance devices to monitor employees? Can it access your credit report?

The following are some of the most common issues that are often confused in the American workplace today.

Paycheck Deductions

What is an employer allowed to deduct from your pay check other than taxes? Employees may deduct your 401k deductions that you designate, any legal deductions such as garnishments and family support deductions, company compulsory deductions such as union dues and your portion of benefit plan premiums, recovery of pay advances, corrections of payroll errors and voluntary deductions such as charitable donations, medical insurance, stock purchase or pension plans. As well, an employer may deduct proven shortages due to theft by the employee.

Some employers deduct the cost of uniforms and other supplies necessary for the job from employees' paychecks. And some deduct costs to an employee breaks or damages on the job.

Not all of these paycheck deductions are legal. Each state is different. Some states don't allow employers to pass certain costs on to employees. Even in states that allow employers to make these types of deductions, employers have to follow certain rules. Most (but not all) states are very clear that any deductions taken cannot push an employee below the minimum wage.

Here are some highlights for each state:

State	Deductions not allowed
Alabama	None specified
Alaska	Employers may not deduct for: • Customer NSF checks • nonpayment of goods/services due to theft or credit default • cash or cash register shortages unless employee admits wrongdoing

	in writing; lost, • missing or stolen property unless employee admits wrongdoing in writing; • breakage or damage unless caused by willful misconduct by employee and employee admits it in writing
Arizona	An employer may deduct wages from an employee's paycheck <u>only</u> with written consent by the employee for the following: - cash shortages - breakage, damage, or loss of the employer's property - dishonored or returned checks An employee must consent in writing to any deduction from wages to pay for a uniform.
Arkansas	None specified
California	An employer <u>may not</u> deduct any of the following from an employee's wages: 1. any portion of an employee's gratuities.; 2. the cost of any photograph of an applicant or employee required by the employer. 3. the cost of a bond required of an applicant or employee by an employer. 4. the cost of a uniform required to be worn by the employee, unless the employee has consented in writing to have the cost of the uniform deducted from their last paycheck if not returned to the employer. The term "uniform" includes wearing apparel and accessories of distinctive design and color. 5. the cost of tools or equipment required to be used by an employee, except employees who earn two time (2X) the minimum wage may be required to purchase hand tools and equipment customarily used in a particular industry. 6. expenses or losses incurred in the direct consequence of the discharge of the employee's work duties 7. the cost of any pre-employment medical or physical examination taken as a condition of employment or any medical or physical examination required by any federal or state law or regulation, or local ordinance. 8. An employer may not deduct amounts from an employee's wages due to a cash shortage, breakage or loss of property, or a dishonored check, unless it can be shown that the shortage, breakage, or loss is caused by a dishonest or willful act, or by the gross negligence of the employee.

Colorado	An employer <u>may not</u> make any deductions from an employee's for: - cash shortages, - damaged or lost property, - the cost of uniforms or necessary equipment, - dishonored or bad checks, or - any similar deductions. An employer may require a reasonable deposit (up to one-half of actual cost) as security for the return of each uniform furnished to employees upon issuance of a receipt to the employee for such deposit. The employer must return the entire deposit to the employee when the uniform is returned. The cost of ordinary wear and tear of a uniform or special apparel may not be deducted from the employee's wages or deposit. An employer is not required to pay for clothing accepted as ordinary street wear or for an ordinary white or any light colored plain and washable uniform unless a special color, make, pattern, logo or material is required. An employer may not require an applicant or employee to pay the cost of a medical examination or the cost of furnishing any records required by the employer as a condition of employment, except records necessary to support the applicant's statements in the application for employment.
Connecticut	An employer may not deduct the following from an employee's wages, unless the employee has signed a form approved by the Connecticut Department of Labor: - cash shortages, - damaged or lost property, - the cost of uniforms or necessary equipment, - dishonored or bad checks, - uniforms, - tools or other necessary equipment, or - any similar deductions
Delaware	An employer <u>may not</u> make any deductions from an employee's for: - cash shortages - damage or lost property, - uniforms, tools, or other necessary equipment - dishonored or bad checks, or - any similar deductions

Florida	None specified
Georgia	None specified
Hawaii	An employer cannot deduct from an employee's paycheck the following items, even with written consent from the employee: 1) fines; 2) cash shortages from a common money till, cash box or register used by two or more people; 3) cash shortages from a money till, cash box, or register under control of a single employee if the employee is not given an opportunity to account for all money received at the start of a shift and all money turned in at the end of a shift; 4) cost for breakage; 5) losses due to accepting a bad check if the employee is given discretion to accept or reject checks; 6) losses due to: - faulty workmanship, - lost or stolen property, - damage to property, - default of customer credit, - nonpayment for goods or services received by customers if such losses are not attributable to the employee's willful or intentional disregard of employer's interests; 7) medical or physical examination or medical report expenses of an employee or prospective employee required by the employer or by law.
Idaho	The employer, with the written consent of an employee, may deduct from an employee's wages: - cash shortages, - damage or lost property, - the cost of uniforms or necessary equipment, - dishonored or bad checks, or - any similar deductions
Illinois	Without an employee's express written consent given freely at the time the deduction is made, an employer may not make a deduction from an employee's wages for: - cash shortages,

	- inventory shortages, - failure to follow proper credit card, check cashing or accounts receivable procedures, - damaged property, - required uniforms, - necessary equipment, or - deposits on loaned equipment or other items.
Indiana	An employer cannot deduct wages from an employee's paycheck or fine an employee for any of the following: - cash shortages - breakage, damage, or loss of the employer's property - required uniforms - required tools - other items necessary for employment
Iowa	An employer cannot deduct or withhold wages from an employee's pay check for any of the following: - a cash shortage in a common money till, cash box, or register operated by two or more employees or by an employee and an employer. ; - any losses due to dishonored checks received by an employee if the employee has been given the discretion to accept or reject such checks and the employee does not abuse the discretion given; - any losses due to breakage, damage to property, default of customer credit, or nonpayment for goods or services rendered so long as such losses are not attributable to the employee's willful or intentional disregard of the employer's interests; - lost or stolen property, unless the property is equipment specifically assigned to an employee and the employee acknowledged receipt of the item in writing; - gratuities received by an employee from customers of the employer; - costs of personal protective equipment needed to protect an employee from employment-related hazards, unless provided otherwise in a collective bargaining agreement. This does not apply to items of clothing or footwear which may be used by an employee during nonworking hours; - costs of more than twenty dollars for an employee's return to the place of employment.
Kansas	An employer cannot deduct wages from an employee's paycheck or fine an employee for any of the following: - cash shortages - breakage, damage, or loss of the employer's property

	- required uniforms - required tools - other items necessary for employment
Kentucky	An employer may not withhold or deduct any wages from an employee's paycheck for: - fines, - cash shortages in a common money till, cash box or register used by two or more persons, - breakage, - losses due to acceptance of a bad check - losses due to defective or faulty workmanship, - lost or stolen property, - damage to property, - default of customer credit, or - nonpayment for goods or services received by the customer if such losses are not attributable to employee's intentional or willful disregard of the employer's interest, - uniforms, - tools, or - other items necessary for employment.
Louisiana	an employer may not deduct from an employee's wages, except when the specific conditions are met: - cash shortages - breakage, damage, or loss of the employer's property - required uniforms - required tools - other items necessary for employment
Maine	An employer may not withhold or deduct wages from an employee's wages for: - cash shortages, - inventory shortages, - dishonored checks, - dishonored credit cards, - damages to the employer's property in any form or - any merchandise purchased by a customer.
Maryland	An employer may not deduct the following from an employee's wages, unless the employee has given separate and distinct written consent (the written consent must only address the particular deduction to be made and nothing more): - cash shortages,

	- inventory shortages, - dishonored checks, - dishonored credit cards, - damages to the employer's property in any form or - any merchandise purchased by a customer.
Massachusetts	None specified
Michigan	An employee must consent in writing each time an employer makes a deduction from his or her wages if the deduction is for the benefit of the employer. These type of deductions include: - cash shortages - breakage, damage, or loss of the employer's property - required uniforms - required tools - other items necessary for employment
Minnesota	An employer may not deduct or withhold any part of an employee's wages for the following reasons, unless the employee has voluntarily consented to the deduction after the following events have occurred or has been held liable in court for the loss or indebtedness: - cash shortages, - lost or stolen property, - damage to property, - any other claimed indebtedness running from employee to employer.
Mississippi	None specified
Missouri	None specified
Montana	An employer may not deduct or withhold any part of an employee's wages for the following reasons: - cash shortages, - lost or stolen property, - damage to property, - any other claimed indebtedness running from employee to employer
Nebraska	An employer can only deduct the following items from an employee's pay check if the employee has consented to the deduction in writing: - cash shortages - breakage, damage, or loss of the employer's property - required uniforms - required tools - other items necessary for employment

Nevada	An employer may not make any other deductions from an employee's wages, unless: (a) The employer has a reasonable basis to believe the employee is responsible for the amount being deducted by the employer, including - cash shortages - breakage, damage, or loss of the employer's property - required uniforms - required tools - other items necessary for employment (b) The deduction is for a specific purpose, pay period and amount; and the wages. An employer may not use a blanket authorization that was made in advance by the employee to withhold any amount from the wages due the employee.
New Hampshire	An employer may not deduct any of the following from an employee's wages: - cash shortages - breakage, damage, or loss of the employer's property - dishonored or returned checks - required uniforms, as defined as a garment with a logo or distinctive design.
New Jersey	An employer may not withhold, deduct, or divert any portion of an employee's wages for: - cash shortages - breakage, damage, or loss of the employer's property - purchase of required uniforms or clothing (employers may deduct, with the employee's consent, for the rental and cleaning of required uniforms or clothing) - required tools - other items necessary for employment
New Mexico	An employer can deduct the following from an employee's paycheck only if the employee has consented in writing: - cash shortages - breakage, damage, or loss of the employer's property - uniforms - required tools - other items necessary for employment
New York	New York law does not permit employers to deduct: - cash shortages,

	- inventory shortages,
	- loss of or damage to their property,
	- required uniforms
	- required tools
	- other items necessary for employment
North Carolina	An employer may withhold or deduct a portion of an employee's wages for any of the following only after giving the employee written notice of the amount to be deducted seven days prior to date of the deduction. An employer does not have to give an employee who has been separated from employment the seven day notice.
	- cash shortages,
	- inventory shortages, or
	- loss or damage to property
North Dakota	An employer may not deduct any of the following from an employee's wages, unless the employee has specifically consented to the deduction in writing:
	- cash shortages
	- breakage, damage, or loss of the employer's property
	- required uniforms
	- required tools
	- other items necessary for employment
Ohio	An employer may not deduct from an employee's wages, unless the employee has consented to the deduction in writing, damage or loss of wares, tools, or machinery destroyed or damaged by the employee.
Oklahoma	An employer may not withhold or deduct any portion of an employee's wages unless the employee has agreed to the deduction in writing, signed by both the employee and the employer and limited to the following categories of deductions:
	- repay a loan or advance or to recover a payroll overpayment,
	- for the cost of merchandise purchased by the employee,
	- uniforms,
	- insurance premiums,
	- retirement or other investment plans,
	- for breakage or loss of merchandise, inventory shortage, or cash shortage so long as the employee was the sole party responsible for the cash shortage or item damaged or lost.
Oregon	An employer may not deduct or withhold any part of an employee's wages for the following reasons:
	- cash shortages

	- breakage, damage, or loss of the employer's property - dishonored or returned checks - required uniforms - required tools - other items necessary for employment
Pennsylvania	None specified
Rhode Island	An employer may not withhold or deduct any portion of an employee's wages for: - cash shortages, - breakage, damage, or loss of employer's property, - uniforms, - tools, or - other necessary items
South Carolina	An employer may not withhold, deduct, or divert any portion of an employee's wages unless - the employer has given the employee written notice of the withholding or deduction at the time of hire, or the employer has given the employee at least seven (7) days written notice of the withholding or deduction.
South Dakota	None specified
Tennessee	An employer may only deduct or withdraw wages from an employee's pay if the employee have given written consent.
Texas	An employer may deduct the following items only if the employee has consented to it in writing: - cash shortages - breakage, damage, or loss of the employer's property - required uniforms - required tools or other items necessary for employment - loans
Utah	An employer may deduct from an employee's wages the following so long as the deduction is agreed to by employee in writing or wrongdoing, where applicable, has been proven: - cash shortages - breakage, damage, or loss of the employer's property - purchase of required uniforms or clothing (The employer may request an amount, not to exceed the actual cost of the uniform or $20, whichever is less, as a deposit on each uniform required by the employer. The deposit must be refunded to the employee at the time uniform is returned.)

	- required tools - other items necessary for employment . An employer may not require an employee or applicant to pay for any physical examination required as a condition of employment
Vermont	An employer may not withhold or deduct wages from an employee's pay check for: - cash shortages - breakage, damage, or loss of the employer's property
Virginia	An employer may not deduct any of the following from an employee's wages unless the employee has consented in writing: - shortages, - damages, - rent, - uniforms, - tools, or - any other necessary item.
Washington	An employer may make the following deductions only from an employee's final paycheck and they only may be applied to incidents in the final pay period and may not be saved up from previous pay periods to be deducted from final check. Also, they may not reduce the employee's final check below the applicable minimum wage, even if the business makes such an agreement with the worker. The business has the burden of proving that workers were informed of company policies regarding these deductions. - Cash shortage in the till only if the business has established policies regarding cash acceptance, and if the worker has counted money in the till before and after shift and has sole access to the till during his/her shift. - Breakage, loss or damage of equipment if it can be shown to have been caused by the worker's dishonest or willful act. - "Bad checks" (NSF) or credit cards purchases accepted by the worker if the business has established check and credit card acceptance policies before the event. - Worker theft only if the business can show that the worker's act was dishonest or willful, and if the business filed a police report.

	- Other agreements made orally or in writing between the worker and business at the time of termination. An employer may make the following deduction from an employee's wages at any time during employment. These deductions may reduce the employee's wage below the minimum wage in effect at the time of the deductions. During ongoing employment, the worker and employer must agree to the deduction in advance and in writing. Deductions from a final paycheck require an oral or written agreement: - When worker agrees in advance to a deduction that is to his/her benefit. Examples: personal loans, personal purchases of business's food, equipment, services, or purchase of items the business sells to the public, for the amount to bail worker out of jail, for worker health and dental insurance payments or co-payments, etc. The deduction may not cause the business to benefit financially other than reasonable interest included in the agreement. - Medical, surgical, or hospital care or service when the business pays for the worker's medical, surgical, or hospital care or service and the worker agrees to deductions from wages to repay those costs to the business. For Example: An employer and employee agree that the employer will pay hospital costs for an employee who has no insurance and the employee agrees to specific deductions from wages to repay the employer until the debt is repaid.
West Virginia	An employer may not deduct any of the following from an employee's wages unless the employee has consented: - shortages, - damages, - rent, - uniforms, - tools, or - any other necessary item.
Wisconsin	An employer may not make any deduction from the wages of an employee for defective or faulty workmanship, lost or stolen property (presumably this would include a cash shortage), or damage to property, unless: - the employee authorizes the employer to do so in writing (The employee's written permission must be obtained after each occurrence of a problem; a blanket consent form will not work) - the employer and a representative designated by the employee (e.g.,

	union) determine the defective or faulty workmanship, loss, theft or damage is due to the employee's negligence, carelessness, or willful and intentional conduct, or - the employee is found guilty or held liable in a court of competent jurisdiction by reason of that negligence, carelessness, or willful and intentional conduct.

Wyoming	An employer may deduct from an employee's wages the following so long as the deduction meet the specified criteria listed below:
	- cash shortages
	- breakage, damage, or loss of the employer's property
	- purchase of required uniforms or clothing
	- required tools
	- other items necessary for employment
	
	An employer may withhold or deduct wages from an employee's paycheck if it is deducted:
	- for damages suffered by the employer due to the employee's negligence, provided:
	
	    - the employee's negligence is determined by a judicial proceeding;
	    - the amount of the damage suffered by the employer is determined by a judicial proceeding;
	    - the negligence and damages arise in the course of the employment; and
	    - the employer has not received payments, compensation, or any form of restitution from any insurer, assurer, surety or guaranty to cover any of the damages. Where the employer has received payments, compensation, or any form of restitution from any insurer, assurer, surety or guaranty to cover any of the damages caused by the employee's negligence, the sum of the offset shall not exceed the amount of any applicable deductible or two hundred fifty dollars ($250.00) whichever is less.
	
	- resulting from cash shortages, provided:
	
	    - the employee gives written acknowledgement upon beginning employment that he or she shall be responsible for any such shortages;
	    - the employer and employee verify in writing the amount of cash that is in the register or cash box at the beginning of the employee's work period;
	    - the employer and employee verify in writing the amount of cash

that is in the register or cash box immediately at the end of the employee's work period; and

- the employee is the sole and absolute user and had sole access to the register or cash box from the time they checked in until the time they checked out;

- as payment for any purchase of tools, equipment, uniforms, or other items required for the employment of the employee, provided:

> - the employee has actual or constructive possession of the items; and
> - the employee's purchase and receipt of the item is evidenced by written acknowledgement.

- as payment for tools, equipment, uniforms, or other items assigned to the employee by the employer, provided:

> - the item was assigned to the employee to be used within the scope of the employee's employment.
> - the employee gave written acknowledgement of the receipt of such items; and
>
> - the items have not been returned to the employer upon termination.

- as payment for any purchase of goods or services by the employee from the employer, provided:

> - the goods or services sold by the employer are sold in the ordinary course of his or her business;
> - the employee has actual or constructive possession of the goods or services purchased; and
> - the employee's purchase is evidenced by the employee's written acknowledgement.

as repayment to the employer by the employee of any cash advances, loans or payments of expenses for optional benefits such as tuition assistance, relocation and training, made to the employee by such employer, provided:

> - the cash advance, loan or payment of expenses to the employee occurred while
> said employee was in the employ of such employer; and
> - the employee's receipt of such cash advance, loan or payment of expenses is
> evidenced by the employee's written acknowledgement.

An employer may require an employee to pay for required uniforms, tools, or other necessary equipment and can deduct the cost of the items from an employee's wages so long as the employer takes the deduction:
- as payment for any purchase of tools, equipment, uniforms, or other items required for the employment of the employee, provided:

- the employee has actual or constructive possession of the items; and
- the employee's purchase and receipt of the item is evidenced by written acknowledgement.

- as payment for tools, equipment, uniforms, or other items assigned to the employee by the employer, provided:

- the item was assigned to the employee to be used within the scope of the employee's employment.
- the employee gave written acknowledgement of the receipt of such items; and
- the items have not been returned to the employer upon termination

Make sure you verify with your State Labor Board for specifics on the above.

Reimbursements

Many employees expect that the employer is obligated to reimburse them for expenses incurred by doing business on the employer's behalf. That is not necessarily the case unless the employer has a company policy stating otherwise or the state has mandated such a law. Therefore, you should not assume that your employer is required to reimburse you for mileage for business use of your car, providing your own equipment, or laundering your uniform.

For example, California has an Expense Reimbursement Law that states that "employers must reimburse employees for all expenses reasonably and necessarily related to work. If the employer requires the employee to drive, such as a courier driver, an outside sales person, the employer must cover the employee's mileage. If the employer requires the employee to have a cell phone and make calls on that phone, the employer must cover the cost of the business related calls (private calls are not eligible for reimbursement). If the employer requires the employee to have a home office, the employer must cover certain expenses reasonably and necessarily related to that office. The part that is not so simple, however, is *how* the employer calculates the employee's reimbursement amount and how the reimbursement is paid."

Before you incur such expenses, check with your state labor office and your employer.

Workplace Privacy

Drug and Alcohol Testing

There is no comprehensive federal law that regulates drug testing in the private sector. The Drug-Free Workplace Act does impose certain employee education requirements on companies that do business with the government, but it does not require testing, nor does it restrict testing in any way. Drug testing is allowed under the Americans with Disabilities Act (ADA) because the ADA does not consider drug abuse a disability -- but the law does not regulate or prohibit testing. Instead of a comprehensive regulatory system, federal law provides for specific agencies to adopt drug testing regulations for employers under their jurisdiction.

The Department of Defense requires defense contractors to set up procedures for identifying drug users, including random testing. The Department of Transportation requires the industries it regulates to conduct random drug and alcohol testing for workers in safety sensitive jobs, as well as testing after accidents and when there is "reasonable suspicion" of employee substance abuse. The federal Omnibus Transportation Employee Testing Act (OTETA) requires tests for all operators of aircraft, railroad equipment, mass transportation vehicles, and commercial motor vehicles.

Since there is no comprehensive federal drug testing law, this leaves the field open to state regulation. Many states have enacted provisions imposing drug testing restrictions of various kinds. Some limit testing to "reasonable suspicion" or "probable cause" situations. Some explicitly authorize random testing under certain circumstances. Some impose restrictions on public sector employers but not on private companies. Many prescribe specific methods for handling of specimens and he use of test results.

As a general rule, testing is presumed to be lawful unless there is a specific restriction in state or federal law. However, the law on employee privacy and related issues continues to evolve, and any testing program that is not explicitly authorized by law should be considered open to legal challenge.

For example, a California court reinstated a railroad employee who was fired for refusing to take a random drug test. The court noted that an employee's right to privacy in refusing a drug test is not absolute under the state constitution but must be weighed against the employer's operational interests. Conceding that the employer had a compelling interest in maintaining a safe workplace, the court noted that the discharged employee was simply a clerk who had no direct involvement with the railway operations. As a result, the court determined that the employee's privacy interests were more substantial than the employer's interests.

State	Drug/Alcohol Testing Restrictions for Employee Testing
Alabama	Testing authorized, including random testing and testing on reasonable suspicion, as part of fitness-for-duty exam, after on- the-

	job injury, or as follow-up to a rehabilitation program. Employees must receive 60 days' advance notice of testing policy, which must be conspicuously posted.
Alaska	Testing authorized, including random testing, for job-related purpose, consistent with business necessity. Thirty days' notice and a written policy statement must be given to employees. Discipline or discharge for positive test or refusal to submit to test. School bus drivers subject to random testing and discipline under separate provisions.
Arizona	Testing authorized, including random testing, for any job-related purpose consistent with business necessity. Written drug-testing policy must be distributed to all employees. Discipline or discharge authorized for employees who test positive or refuse to submit to test. School district transportation employees must submit to testing in the event of accident or if based on probable cause.
Arkansas	No restrictions enacted
California	Testing authorized of state employees in positions of "sensitivity." Employees who test positive may be referred for treatment or may be suspended or removed from job. Private sector and public employers of 25 or more must "reasonably accommodate" employees who want to enter drug treatment programs.
Colorado	No restrictions enacted
Connecticut	Testing authorized on reasonable suspicion of substance abuse; random testing authorized of employees in safety-sensitive jobs. Testing required for intrastate truck drivers after a reportable accident, upon reasonable cause, or at random under federal law. Discipline or discharge authorized for employees who test positive.
Delaware	Employee testing is not subject to restriction.
Florida	Testing authorized on reasonable suspicion of substance abuse, as part of routine fitness-for-duty exam, or as follow-up to employee's participation in counseling or rehabilitation. Written notice of testing program must be given 60 days in advance. Testing confers eligibility for certain discounts and other benefits under state's workers' compensation law. Discipline or discharge authorized for employees who test positive.
Georgia	Testing authorized, including random testing, on reasonable suspicion, as part of routine fitness-for-duty exam, after an on-the-

	job injury, and as part of follow-up to rehabilitation. Policy must be distributed to employees and posted. Testing confers eligibility for certain discounts and other benefits under the state's workers' compensation law. Random testing of "high risk" state government and public school employees including school bus drivers is authorized under separate provisions.
Hawaii	Testing authorized if employee receives advance notice in writing of substances to be tested for and has opportunity to disclose current prescription and nonprescription medications.
Idaho	Testing authorized, including random testing, after notice to employees. Policy must list types of tests and state that violation is grounds for misconduct discharge. Unemployment benefits may be denied for discharge because of positive result, refusal to be tested, or altering results.
Illinois	No restrictions enacted
Indiana	No restrictions enacted
Iowa	Testing authorized when there is probable cause to suspect substance abuse and employee holds job in which impairment would pose a danger, or during annual employee physical, if employee is given 30 days' notice. Random testing permitted so long as specific procedure in the law is followed using a computer-based random number generator that matches employee's social security number or payroll identification number (selection from entire employee pool, full time employee pool or safety sensitive employee pool). Substance abuse evaluation and opportunity for treatment required for first positive test result. Discipline or discharge authorized for subsequent positive result or failure to complete treatment.
Kansas	Testing authorized of state employees holding safety-sensitive jobs and individuals taking office as governor, lieutenant governor, or attorney general, but only if there is reasonable suspicion of substance abuse, as evidenced by a workplace accident or medical emergency that could be attributed to drug use, by direct observation of impaired performance, by information that the employee is using drugs, or by physical signs of on-the-job drug use. Employee testing positive for the first time must have opportunity to undergo drug evaluation and recommended treatment.
Kentucky	No restrictions enacted

Louisiana	Employee testing authorized, but employer may not discharge an employee on the basis of first-time positive test findings. Employees who are discharged for drug use, on or off the job, may be disqualified from receiving unemployment compensation. Employees of state contractors subject to random testing.
Maine	Employee testing authorized if there is probable cause for suspicion of substance abuse that is not based solely on the occurrence of an accident. Random testing authorized of employee returning to work after positive test, of employees in safety-sensitive jobs, and pursuant to a collective bargaining agreement. Employee who tests positive may be referred for counseling or treatment. Discipline or discharge authorized for refusal to submit to test, for subsequent positive result, or for failure to complete treatment.
Maryland	Employee testing authorized if supported by legitimate business reason.
Massachusetts	No restrictions enacted
Michigan	No restrictions enacted
Minnesota	Employee testing authorized after an accident, as part of an employee assistance program, when there is reasonable suspicion of substance abuse, or part of annual physical exam, provided employee has two weeks' advance notice. Random testing authorized of employees in safety-sensitive jobs. Employer may suspend or transfer employee testing positive pending outcome of confirming test. Discharge authorized only if employee refuses or fails to complete treatment.
Mississippi	Employee testing authorized on reasonable suspicion of substance abuse, in connection with rehabilitation or treatment, as part of routine physical exam, or if collective bargaining agreement authorizes random testing. Discharge authorized if employee tests positive or refuses test.
Missouri	No restrictions enacted
Montana	Employee testing authorized, including random testing, on reasonable belief of job impairment, after work-related accident causing injury or damage of $1,500 or more, or as part of regular physical exam for employees of intrastate motor carriers. Disciplinary action authorized if employee presents no reasonable explanation for positive findings.

Nebraska	Employee testing authorized without restriction. Discipline or discharge authorized after a confirming positive test or refusal to submit to test.
Nevada	Employee testing authorized for jobs involving public safety. Referral for counseling or treatment authorized for employee testing positive. Discipline or discharge authorized for subsequent positive findings, for workplace use, or for working under the influence.
New Hampshire	No restrictions enacted
New Jersey	No restrictions enacted
New Mexico	No restrictions enacted
New York	No restrictions enacted
North Carolina	Employee testing not subject to restriction.
North Dakota	No restrictions enacted
Ohio	Employee testing authorized on reasonable suspicion of substance abuse, for new hires, after an accident, and as follow-up to a treatment program.
Oklahoma	Employees testing authorized on 30 days' advance notice to employees of policy describing the potential discipline for positive test result.
Oregon	Employees testing authorized on 30 days' advance notice to employees of policy describing the potential discipline for positive test result.
Pennsylvania	No laws enacted
Rhode Island	Employee testing authorized on reasonable suspicion of substance abuse and in conjunction with rehabilitation program. Random testing prohibited.
South Carolina	Testing authorized, including random testing, with follow-up tests within 30 minutes of initial test.
South Dakota	Testing authorized of state employees holding safety-sensitive jobs if there is reasonable suspicion of substance abuse.
Tennessee	Testing of Corrections Department employees authorized if there is reasonable suspicion of substance abuse. Employees who test positive subject to appropriate disciplinary action, but counseling and rehabilitation must be offered.

Texas	No restrictions enacted
Utah	Employee testing authorized pursuant to employer's written policy, distributed to all employees, in cases of possible employee impairment, workplace accidents or theft, safety maintenance, or productivity/quality/security maintenance. Employees who test positive or refuse to be tested are subject to referral for rehabilitation or disciplinary action, including discharge.
Vermont	Employee testing authorized as part of an employee assistance program or when there is probable cause for suspicion of substance abuse. Random testing prohibited. Employer may suspend employee who tests positive for period of rehabilitation, but may not discharge an employee who agrees to rehabilitation after first positive test.
Virginia	No restrictions enacted
Washington	Testing authorized for private employers on 60 days' notice to employees, in cases of workplace accidents, as part of an employee assistance program, on reasonable suspicion of substance abuse, or at random. Employers' written substance abuse policy must be posted and distributed to employees. State agencies can test on reasonable suspicion—stated in writing—for safety-sensitive positions pursuant to a written testing policy.
West Virginia	No restrictions enacted
Wisconsin	No restrictions enacted
Wyoming	No restrictions enacted

Technology

Employees wrongly assume that the equipment and resources provided by an employer is subject to the employee's eyes only. Nothing could be further from the truth. Because the company owns the computer, email, internet access, phone, notebooks, etc. they have the right to access what you use your business tools for. And they do. You have no right to privacy even if you use the company laptop at home. They can track everything you do so be mindful because it can be used against you.

Your employer might be spying on you in several ways, such as:

- Recording your office phone conversations

- Videotaping your every move throughout your workplace

- Searching through your office computer files

- Monitoring your office computer keystrokes

- Reading your incoming and outgoing email

- Monitoring the websites you visit

- Tracking your location through your company cell phone, security badge or both

Employee workplace privacy rights laws are few and weak. If your state does not specify any privacy rights laws, it makes it legal for your employer to spy on you without your consent and usually without your knowledge. As a result, your employer may fire or discipline you for violating a company policy based on these covert activities. Only Connecticut and Delaware legally require employers to notify their workers in advance that company technology could be used to trace their movements

Most states only require that employers refrain from using surveillance tools on employees while they're changing their clothes or in the bathroom.

Many people rely on the Fourth Amendment to protect a person against unreasonable searches by the government. However, there are no Fourth Amendment protections from other citizens. The right to privacy does not extend to employees against their bosses. While police can't do it without probable cause, your employer can.

If an employee is advised that communications may be monitored, it may be implied that he or she consented to even highly intrusive monitoring by the employer. This is not a guarantee that simply notifying the worker will make the monitoring legal. However, most employers who have an IT policy signed during new hire onboarding or annual policy reviews do include a notification clause about monitoring of all company equipment. So make certain that you read everything you sign and keep a copy.

Employees should be aware that technology has given employers a powerful ability to collect information from employees in several different ways. Some example of data collection are through:

- background checks on credit and criminal records;
- resumes, cover letters and job applications;
- video surveillance of work premises and off-duty conduct;
- Global Positioning Systems for couriers, delivery and transport workers;
- telephone monitoring;
- keystroke logging;

- monitoring internet activities;
- "smart" ID cards that track attendance, access to the workplace and drug and dental plans;
- biometrics (fingerprint, handprint, voice and eye scanning to verify employee identity);
- drug and alcohol tests.

Whether any particular method of collection is permissible may depend on whether:

a) the employee is aware of the monitoring;
b) consent was obtained;
c) the level of intrusiveness of the collection;
d) the appropriate balance between employer and employee interests was fair; and
e) the facts of the situation warranted such collection.

Recently, Federal and state court decisions suggest that the U.S. may be moving towards a greater level of privacy protection for employees. A number of states have enacted statutes that prohibit employers from disclosing certain personal information about employees gathered during the employment relationship. Minnesota, for example, forbids public employers from disclosing information contained in an employee's personnel file. Georgia makes it unlawful for employers to obtain certain criminal history information about an employee or prospective employee without that person's consent. Alaska makes it unlawful for employers to require employees or job applicants take a polygraph examination. However, no state prohibits an employer from requiring an employee or job applicant to undergo a psychological evaluation for the purpose of assessing the test-taker's propensity for truthfulness or deceit.

Check your state's labor website for specifics. Here is an overview of the most common privacy concerns.

Credit Checks

When hiring for positions that require high levels of trust relating to financial matters, employers conduct credit checks to determine the appropriateness of an applicant. The most common reason employers cite for requiring employment credit checks is a concern that employees who are behind on their bills will be more likely to embezzle funds or engage in other criminal activity. Yet, there is little evidence to support this fear.

As of 2010, a spokesman for TransUnion, one of the largest companies selling credit reports to employers, admitted that there is no evidence of a link between credit problems and employees' propensity to commit financial crimes on the job. Eric Rosenberg, Director of State Government Relations for TransUnion, told Oregon legislators, "At this point we don't have any research to show any statistical correlation between what's in somebody's credit report and their job performance or their likelihood to commit fraud." Richard Tonowski, the Chief

Psychologist for the Equal Employment Opportunity Commission agreed with Mr. Rosenberg. In 2010, he testified that there is, "very little evidence that credit history is indicative of who can do the job better" and it is "hard to establish a predictive relationship between credit and crime."

The use of employment credit checks is creates a catch-22 for the unemployed. Workers who have fallen behind on their bills because they are unemployed are finding it harder to get the job that would make it possible for them to pay off their bills. Employment credit checks also subject job applicants to unwarranted intrusions on their privacy and, in the case of communities of color, can have an illegal discriminatory impact.

In 2010, Illinois and Oregon enacted legislation that limits the use of credit reports in employment scenarios. Similar laws are in place in Hawaii and Washington and are being considered in Connecticut, Illinois, Maryland, Michigan, Missouri, New Jersey, New York, Ohio, Oklahoma, South Carolina, Vermont and Wisconsin.

The Illinois law, the Employee Credit Privacy Act, became effective in 2011. The Act makes it illegal for employers to discriminate against job applicants on the basis of their credit histories and outlaws inquiries about applicants' and employees' credit histories. The law permits employers to conduct background investigations that do not include a credit history or report. In addition, the Act allows employers to obtain and consider credit reports in connection with jobs that involve (i) bonding or security (ii) custody of, or unsupervised access to, $2,500 or more in cash or marketable assets; (iii) signatory power over businesses assets of $100 or more per transaction; (iv) management and control of the business; or (v) access to personal, financial or confidential information, trade secrets, or state or national security information. The law includes the right to sue for injunctive relief and obtain attorneys' fees.

A similar Oregon law came into effect in 2010. With certain exceptions, the law prohibits Oregon employers from using credit history in making hiring decisions or any decision affecting current employees. The law exempts federally-insured banks and credit unions, businesses required by law to consider employee credit history, and police and other public employers when hiring for law enforcement or airport security positions. In addition, the law permits employers to conduct credit checks for "substantially job-related reasons" provided the reasons are disclosed to the employee in writing. The Oregon law gives individuals the right to file an administrative complaint or a private lawsuit and recovery of attorneys' fees.

While there is no federal prohibition against the use of credit reports for employment purposes, it appears that federal regulators may be seeking to curtail the practice. Specifically, in 2010, the Equal Employment Opportunity Commission ("EEOC") sued an employer in connection with use of credit reports in the hiring process. The EEOC alleged that the company used the reports in a way that discriminated against African-American job applicants. Emphasizing the broader reasons for the suit, the EEOC determined that employers are denying jobs to applicants with damaged credit histories in cases where creditworthiness does not appear to be directly relevant to the job. In the suit, the EEOC alleged this practice had a significant disparate impact on African-American applicants.

Background Security Check

Background reports can range from a verification of an applicant's Social Security number to a detailed account of the potential employee's history and acquaintances. It is now common practice that employers are now searching popular social networking Web sites such as Facebook, Twitter and MySpace for the profiles of applicants. An October 2007 survey from Vault.com found that 44% of employers use social networking sites to obtain information about job applicants while 39% have searched such sites for information about current employees.

Here are some of the pieces of information that might be included in a background check. Note that many of these sources are public records created by government agencies.

- Driving records
- Vehicle registration
- Credit records
- Criminal records
- Social Security no.
- Education records
- Court records
- Workers' compensation
- Bankruptcy
- Character references
- Neighbor interviews
- Medical records
- Property ownership
- Military records
- State licensing records
- Drug test records
- Past employers
- Personal references
- Incarceration records
- Sex offender lists

Information to be included in a background check will almost certainly depend to some extent on the employer and the job involved. For many jobs, a state or federal law requires the employer to conduct a background check. Jobs that involve work with children, the elderly or people with disabilities are examples of jobs that will almost certainly require a criminal background check.

The federal Fair Credit Reporting Act (FCRA) sets national standards for employment screening. However, the law only applies to background checks performed by an outside company, called a "consumer reporting agency". The law does not apply in situations where the employer conducts background checks in-house.

Under the FCRA, a background check report is called a consumer report. This is the same name given to your credit report, and the same limits on disclosure apply. The FCRA says the following *cannot* be reported:

- Bankruptcies after 10 years.
- Civil suits, civil judgments, and records of arrest, from date of entry, after seven years.
- Paid tax liens after seven years.
- Accounts placed for collection after seven years.
- Any other negative information (except criminal convictions) after seven years.

However, the above reporting restrictions imposed by the FCRA do *not* apply to jobs with an annual salary of $75,000 or more a year.

Other topics of a background security check include:

Arrest information. Although arrest record information is public record, in some states, employers cannot seek from any source the arrest record of a potential employee. However, if the arrest resulted in a conviction or if the applicant is out of jail but pending trial, that information can be used.

In California, an exception exists for the health care industry where any employer who has an interest in hiring a person with access to patients can ask about sex related arrests. And, when an employee may have access to medications, an employer can ask about drug related arrests.

In Florida, an exception exists when the person is (a) a candidate for employment with a criminal justice agency; (b) a defendant in a criminal prosecution; (c) petitioning to have his or her record expunged or sealed; (d) a candidate for admission to the Florida bar; (e) seeking to be employed or licensed by the state Department of Education, a district school board, or any local governmental entity that licenses child care facilities; or (f) seeking to be employed by, licensed by, or contracted with the state Department of Children and Family Services or Department of Juvenile Justice, or to be employed or used by a contractor or licensee in a position involving direct contact with children, the developmentally disabled, the aged, or the elderly.

Criminal history. In some states, conviction records are limited to when they can be used for hiring purposes especially when a conviction has been sealed or expunged.

In California, criminal histories compiled by police are not public record. Only certain employers such as public utilities, law enforcement, security guard firms, and child care facilities have access to this information. With the advent of computerized court records and arrest information, however, there are private companies that compile virtual "rap sheets." Also, in California, an employer may not inquire about a marijuana conviction that is more than two years old.

In Louisiana, individuals may not be disqualified from engaging in any profession requiring a state license solely because of a criminal record unless convicted of a felony directly relating to the position sought. Any decision by a Louisiana agency barring an applicant from engaging in such a profession that is based partially on a criminal record must be in writing and must explicitly state the reasons for the decision.

Employers need to use caution in checking criminal records. Information offered to the public by web-based information brokers is not always accurate or up to date. This violates both federal and some state laws when reported as such.

State employment laws may limit the questions an employer includes on a job application. For example, in California an application may ask job related questions about convictions except those that have been sealed, or expunged, or statutorily eradicated, but applications cannot ask general questions regarding an arrest.

Workers' compensation. In most states, when an employee's claim goes through the state system or the Workers' Compensation Appeals Board (WCAB), the case becomes public record. An employer may only use this information if an injury might interfere with one's ability to perform required duties. Under the federal Americans with Disabilities Act, employers cannot use medical information or the fact an applicant filed a workers' compensation claim to discriminate against applicants.

In California, employers may access workers' compensation records after making an offer of employment. To gain access, employers confirm with the WCAB that the records are being accessed for legitimate purposes. Although the agency may not reveal medical information and the employer may not rescind an offer due to a workers' compensation claim, employers sometimes discover that applicants have not revealed previous employers where they had filed claims. In such situations, employers often terminate the new hire because it appears they falsified the application.

Personnel Files, Résumés and Employment References

Under the federal Fair Credit Reporting Act ("FCRA"), the employer is required to get your permission before obtaining the following records.

Education records. Under both federal and some state laws, transcripts, recommendations, discipline records, and financial information are confidential. A school should not release student records without the authorization of the adult-age student or parent. However, a school may release "directory information," which can include name, address, dates of attendance, degrees earned, and activities, unless the student has given written notice otherwise.

Military service records. Under the federal Privacy Act, service records are confidential and can only be released under limited circumstances. Inquiries not authorized by the subject of the records must be made under the Freedom of Information Act. Even without the applicant's consent, the military may release name, rank, salary, duty assignments, awards, and duty status.

Past employers. Often a potential employer will contact an applicant's past employers. A former boss can say anything truthful about your performance. However, most employers have a policy to only confirm dates of employment, final salary, and other limited information. Some states prohibit employers from intentionally interfering with former employees' attempts to find jobs by giving out false or misleading references.

Personnel files. Under laws of many states, employees have a right to review their own personnel files and make copies of documents they have signed.

Medical Information

The federal Health Insurance Portability and Accountability Act (HIPAA) sets a national standard for privacy of health information. But HIPAA only applies to medical records maintained by health care providers, health plans, and health clearinghouses - and only if the facility maintains and transmits records in electronic form. A great deal of health-related information exists outside of health care facilities and the files of health plans, and therefore beyond the reach of HIPAA. The extent of privacy protection given to your medical information often depends on where the records are located and the purpose for which the information was compiled.

Employers usually obtain medical information about their employees by asking employees to authorize disclosure of medical records. This can occur in several ways not covered by HIPAA. Unfortunately, the laws in only a few states require employers to establish procedures to keep employee medical records confidential.

According to the federal Americans with Disabilities Act in workplaces with more than 15 employees:

- Employers may not ask job applicants about medical information or require a physical examination prior to offering employment. After employment is offered, an employer can only ask for a medical examination if it is required of all employees holding similar jobs.

- If you are turned down for work based on the results of a medical examination, the employer must prove that it is physically impossible for you to do the work required.

Several states limit the right of healthcare providers to release medical information to a patient's employer. For example, a Maryland statute generally requires the patient's consent before healthcare providers can disclose medical information to employers. Similar statutory restrictions in Maryland prohibit insurance carriers from disclosing medical information to an insured's employer without the insured's consent.

In California and many states, medical records are confidential. There are only a few instances when a medical record can be released without your knowledge or authorization. The FCRA also requires your specific permission for the release of medical records. If employers require physical examinations after they make a job offer, they will have access to the results. The Americans with Disabilities Act allows a potential employer to inquire only about your ability to perform specific job functions.

Videotape/Audiotape Surveillance

In order for an employer to legally videotape/audiotape you it must have some legitimate business purpose - but this is not hard to fulfill. In 2001, more than 15% of midsize and large companies videotaped employees to evaluate their job performance, and almost 38% filmed employees for security purposes.

Federal law seems to allow for the videotaping of any individual, even without his or her knowledge or consent, as long as it is not done to commit a crime. Some states, however, have placed further restrictions on videotaping, and may require that everyone involved in the conversation be aware of, and consent to, the taping. Further, some states, like Connecticut, have implemented stricter laws for employers, fining them for overuse of video cameras

The appropriate use of video cameras will also depend on the locations of the video cameras. Cameras focused on exits and entrances may be easier to justify in instances where security can be established as an issue in the workplace.

Videotaping employees in an area that they expect to be private, and where it is typical to be undressing, such as a locker room, violates the law. Courts have recently held that it is an unreasonable invasion of privacy to monitor employees undressing, and such monitoring violates both state and federal law..

Can My Employer Videotape Me When I Am Off-Duty?

A number of laws prohibit employers from intruding into their employees' lives outside of work. Some state constitutions specifically include a right to privacy, which prevents private employers from looking into their employees' off-duty activity. Some states have laws prohibiting employers from taking any job-related action against a worker based on that worker's lawful conduct off the job.

Even in those states that don't provide private workers with a constitutional or statutory right to privacy, it is generally illegal for an employer to intrude unreasonably into the "seclusion" of an employee. This means that physical areas in which you have a reasonable expectation of privacy are off-limits to employers, unless there is a very good reason to intrude. And an employer is never allowed to physically enter your home without consent (even when searching for allegedly stolen property belonging to the employer).

However in some cases (e.g. investigating insurance fraud) off-duty video surveillance conducted by a private investigator on behalf of the employer may be justified.

Employers are allowed to spy on their employees not only when they are suspicious that the employee is taking fraudulent leave under the FMLA, but also in any situation where the information gained by surveillance may be used as evidence to support the employer's honest belief the employee is taking fraudulent leave.

For example, in *Vail v. Raybestos*, Diana Vail was on FMLA leave due to chronic migraines and was suspected by her employer, Raybestos, of lying. Raybestos hired an off duty police officer to monitor Vail's activities while on FMLA leave. The officer observed Vail mowing lawns for her husband's landscaping company. The court upheld the employer's right to spy on an employee who is suspected of abusing FMLA granted leave. The court held that the employer's surveillance tactics were legal because they were used to supply the employer with an honest suspicion that the employee was using her leave in order to work another job. This ruling has a dramatic impact on employees willing to take FMLA leave from legitimate and legal reasons.

According to the *Vail* decision, employers are allowed to spy on their employees not only when they are suspicious that the employee is taking fraudulent leave, but also in any situation where the information gained by surveillance may be used as evidence to support a reasonable concern.

Overall, video surveillance of employees may or may not be legal depending on its necessity, effectiveness, and the extent of its impact on employee privacy interests.

Global Positioning System (GPS)

California and Texas have statutes addressing GPS tracking devices. In those states, placing a GPS device on a vehicle is unlawful without the owner's consent. Of course, these statutes have no impact on installing GPS devices in employer-owned vehicles. Still, because there is little statutory law addressing the use of GPS monitoring in the workplace, recent court rulings on privacy expectations continue to define the boundaries for tracking employee activity with GPS devices.

To date, few courts have addressed the privacy implications of GPS monitoring in the workplace. Those that have generally permit the practice. A Missouri federal court held in 2005 that use of a GPS device on a company vehicle did not constitute an invasion of privacy.

In 2009, a supervisor of carpenters employed by the New York City school system was fired because he repeatedly left work early while on the clock. How did his employers know? Because the cell phone that they had supplied him had a GPS antenna in it, and they had been using it to track his location for five months. His dismissal held up in court, because New York does not legally require employers to notify their workers in advance that company technology could be used to trace their movements.

Monitoring of Telephone Calls, Email or Websites Visited

Criteria similar to those used for judging video surveillance have also been used to evaluate other forms of surveillance, such as telephone, email and internet monitoring, and keystroke logging.

Under federal law, employers are only allowed to monitor business telephone conversations. Once they realize that the call is personal, they must hang up. However, employers can monitor your personal phone conversations if you have given them your consent. Some state laws provide further safeguards on telephone conversations by requiring that not only the employee, but the person on the other end of the phone line consent to the call being monitored.

Recent court cases have held that the employer may monitor voice messages. The best thing to do is to discourage anyone you know from leaving inappropriate messages on your employer's voicemail system, to avoid embarrassment or possible discipline. And as for messages that you have deleted, voice mail systems often retain deleted messages by permanently "backing them up" in your employer's computer system. So they are never completely gone and are available for monitoring.

Courts are heavily dependent on property-based concepts of ownership of computers or computer systems when determining an employee's privacy interest in her e-mails. In a Texas case, McLaren v. Microsoft, the plaintiff (McLaren) argued that by allowing McLaren to have a personal password for his online personal folders, he and the employer recognized an expectation that the personal folders would be free from "intrusion and interference". In two earlier Texas cases, the court had recognized that where an employer provides a locker for an employee and the employee uses his own lock on that locker, the employee has manifested and, the employer has recognized, a reasonable expectation of privacy in the contents of the locker, despite the fact that the locker itself is owned by the employer. However, the court asserted that the plaintiff, "even by creating a personal password," did not manifest "a reasonable expectation of privacy in the contents of the e-mail messages such that the employer was precluded from reviewing the messages."

The court distinguished an employee's e-mail storage system protected with a personal password from an employee's locker with a personal lock. The court stated that while a locker was provided to an employee for the strict purpose of storing personal belongings, the plaintiff's computer, which gave him the ability to send and receive e-mail messages, was part of the plaintiff's workstation provided to him by the employer so that he could perform the functions of his job. Therefore, the court reasoned, "the e-mail messages contained on the company computer were not the plaintiff's personal property, but were merely an inherent part of the office environment." Therefore, the court found that the plaintiff had no reasonable expectation of privacy in his e-mails.

However, it is not always the case that the computer used to send e-mails must be owned by the employer and/or have been given to the employee for work purposes. For instance, in Smyth vs. Pillsbury, the court had found that the employee had no reasonable expectation of privacy in his e-mail messages even though the e-mails were sent from his home computer. Ignoring the fact that the e-mails had originated on the plaintiff's home computer, the court emphasized that the e-mails had been sent over the defendant's e-mail communication system, maintained by the defendant in order to promote internal corporate communications between its employees.

Finally, most jurisdictions analyze an intrusion on privacy claim in an employment context with an evaluation of whether or not the intrusion would be highly offensive to a reasonable person, which most courts read as requiring a balancing test between the employer's interest in intruding and the employee's privacy interest. Using a balancing test on the McLaren case, the court stated that even if it had found that McLaren had a reasonable expectation of privacy in his e-mails, the privacy interest would be outweighed by Microsoft's "interest in preventing inappropriate and unprofessional comments, or even illegal activity, over its e-mail system."

As a result, the opinion only states that in "December 1996, Microsoft suspended McLaren's employment pending an investigation into accusations of sexual harassment and `inventory questions.`". His request for access to his e-mail in order to disprove the allegations was denied; on December 11, 1996, he was fired. Despite this suppression as to the contents of the e-mails in question and the facts alleged in the accusations, the court concluded that "a reasonable person would not consider Microsoft's interception of these communications to be a highly offensive invasion," because at the time of the interception, McLaren was on suspension pending an investigation and had notified Microsoft that some of the e-mails were relevant to the investigation

The court in Smyth vs. Pillsbury also weighed in an email privacy case noting that even if it were willing to recognize a privacy interest in e-mail communications, such an interest could not rise to the level where a "reasonable person would consider the defendant's interception of these communications to be a substantial and highly offensive invasion of his privacy." The defendant in Smyth had alleged that the e-mails "concerned sales management and contained threats to `kill the backstabbing bastards' and referred to the planned holiday party as the `Jim Jones Kool-Aid affair'. The court declared that once the plaintiff communicated the alleged unprofessional comments to a second person (his supervisor) over an e-mail system which was apparently utilized by the entire company, any reasonable expectation of privacy was lost.. The company's interest in preventing inappropriate and unprofessional comments or even illegal activity over its e-mail system outweighs any privacy interest the employee might have in those comments.

Thus, in both McLaren and Smyth, the courts first determined if the employee had a reasonable expectation of privacy in his email and concluded that they did not. Despite having already made that determination, the courts still chose to consider the interests of the employer "in preventing inappropriate and unprofessional comments, or even illegal activity, over its e-mail system," concluding that the employers' interests were stronger, on balance, than the employees' would-be privacy interests.

Employees who use company computers do not have a reasonable expectation of privacy regarding what they do on those computers. Employers have the right to track the websites visited by their employees on company computers, to block employees from visiting specific sites and to limit the amount of time an employee may spend on a specific website. This includes any time spent or activities conducted on the employer's premises during breaks and lunch hours.

In 2010, the New Jersey Supreme Court ruled for a former employee on the employee's claim that the state's common privacy law protected some of the employee's emails from review by her employer. The New Jersey Supreme Court considered whether the former employee – Ms. Stengart – had a reasonable expectation of privacy in certain emails she exchanged with her attorney. The email exchange took place over Stengart's personal, web-based email account. Stengart, however, used her company-issued computer for the communications. Images of the emails were saved by the employer's monitoring system, which retained every web page visited on the computer. In the course of subsequent litigation against Stengart, Loving Care – the former employer – retrieved Stengart's communications with her attorney from the laptop and sought to use the emails in the litigation. Stengart argued that the employer could neither review the emails nor use them in the litigation because she had a reasonable expectation of privacy in the communications. The New Jersey Supreme Court agreed.

The Court found the company's electronic communications policy to be ambiguous and interpreted the ambiguity against the employer. The policy stated that the company could review any matters on the company's media systems and services at any time, and that all emails and communications were not to be considered personal or private to employees. The Court found the policy's disclosure of employee monitoring insufficient because it did not inform employees that the company stored and could retrieve copies of employees' private web-based emails. The Court also concluded that the policy failed to state expressly that the company would monitor the content of email communications made from employees' personal email accounts when they were viewed on company-issued computers. The Court held that Stengart had a subjective expectation of privacy in communications she sent using her personal web-based email account, and that the company's ambiguous boilerplate electronic communications policy did not invalidate Stengart's expectation of privacy in the emails.

The Court acknowledged that employers may adopt and enforce lawful policies relating to computer use to protect the assets and productivity of a business. The Court held, however, that an employer may not read the contents of an employee's attorney-client communications sent or received using personal web-based email. The Court held that a policy that allows the employer to review such communications is unenforceable.

Although the decision dealt with attorney-client communications, it also has implications for any personal emails (such as communications regarding health or financial issues) employees send over private web-based email accounts. For example, the court noted that employers that record and review screen shots on workplace computers will need to provide employees with a detailed, specific notice of such monitoring to the extent the screen shots also record emails employees send or receive via private web-based accounts. The Court also cautioned that a policy that permits "occasional personal use" of workplace email systems may create an expectation of privacy by employees with respect to personal emails they send or receive via company email.

Fingerprint Scans and Other Biometrics

Biometrics is emerging as a new tool for employers to manage attendance and security in the workplace. Biometrics raise privacy concerns because they verify a person's identity using a person's unique physical characteristics such as their fingerprint, handprint, eye scan, or voice pattern.

Although federal law doesn't prohibit workplaces from implementing biometric time and attendance systems, some states have taken legal action in order to protect employees' privacy rights. Texas, Illinois and Washington have passed legislation restricting biometric data storage and mandating user consent prior to collecting it.

New York State Labor Law expressly prohibits the fingerprinting of job applicants and employees except in very limited circumstances. "Except as otherwise provided by law," the statute provides, "no person, as a condition of securing employment or of continuing employment shall be required to be fingerprinted (with exceptions such as jobs in the NYSE and NY Social Services for identification purposes). The statute speaks only to the fingerprinting of employees, not to other forms of characteristic identification, such as retinal scans or voice recognition.

Since biometric technology is so new, there are very few laws that specifically address its use and application. There are many laws that govern confidential information, such as the Sarbanes-Oxley Act and the Health Insurance Portability and Accountability Act (HIPAA). However, these are very general laws which deal with overall confidentiality in a given sector. As the use of biometrics increases, we should expect to see more specific laws.

Lie Detector Tests

A polygraph (lie detector) is an instrument that measures and records several physiological responses such as blood pressure, pulse, respiration, breathing rhythms, body temperature and skin conductivity while the subject is asked and answers a series of questions, on the theory that false answers will produce distinctive measurements.

The Employee Polygraph Protection Act ("EPPA") prohibits most private employers from using lie detector tests either for pre-employment screening or during the course of employment.

Employees have the right to refuse to take lie detectors tests requested by their employers. Even for an employer to ask or require that they take a lie detector test is a violation of their rights. These rules apply to applicants for employment as well.

No one can disclose to an employer that an employee has taken a lie detector test, and no one can disclose to an employer the results of a lie detector test taken by an employee.

Federal, state and local government employees are not protected by the law. Also, the law does not apply to tests given by the federal government to certain private individuals engaged in national security-related activities. The Act permits polygraph tests to be administered in the private sector, subject to restrictions, to certain prospective employees of security service firms (armored car, alarm, and guard), and of pharmaceutical manufacturers, distributors and dispensers. The Act also permits polygraph testing, subject to restrictions, of certain employees of private firms who are reasonably suspected of involvement in a workplace incident (theft, embezzlement, etc.) that resulted in economic loss to the employer.

Where polygraph tests are permitted, they are subject to numerous strict standards concerning the conduct and length of the test. Examinees have a number of specific rights, including the right to a written notice before testing, the right to refuse or discontinue a test, and the right not to have test results disclosed to unauthorized persons.

The ACLU has long favored protective legislation against indiscriminate "lie detector" testing in the American workplace, not only because it is unreliable, but also because it is an extreme invasion of privacy. For example, in order to establish "normal" physiological reactions of the person being tested, "lie detector" examiners ask questions that purposely embarrass, frighten and humiliate workers. An ACLU lawsuit in 1987 revealed that state employees in North Carolina were routinely asked to answer such questions as "When was the last time you unintentionally exposed yourself after drinking?" and "Who was the last child that got you sexy?" "Lie detectors" have been used by unscrupulous employers to harass union organizers and whistleblowers, and to coerce employees into "confessing" infractions they did not commit and falsely implicating fellow employees.

For example, the Texas Supreme Court invalidated a state agency's mandatory polygraph testing policy. The court found that the test was "highly offensive" to the average employee because of the extremely personal nature of the questions asked. The court also concluded that the test was not accurate enough to provide a reliable way of identifying misbehaving, inefficient, or unproductive employees.

Although polygraph tests are perhaps the most well known for lie detection, there are others. For instance, psychological stress evaluators (PSE's) claim to detect and record fluctuations in your voice produced by stress, which allegedly indicate if you are lying. These are just as unreliable as polygraph tests, and just as illegal.

Search and Seizure

Are you safe from your employer's intrusions into areas normally subject to your exclusive control (i.e. locker, desk drawer, etc.)? The answer may be a little murky.

A private workplace search may violate the employee's constitutional right of privacy. Employees may have a reasonable expectation of privacy in the workplace, such as in the contents of their desks. Because of the written policies of some employers stating that the employees do not have privacy interest in the contents of their desks, an employer may be allowed to randomly search company property used by an employee.

Without a clearly established policy or voluntary consent of the employee, employers may not conduct general searches of the employee's property or the employee's body, even if the employer suspects the employee has violated a crime, stolen company property, or has cause to believe the employee possesses illegal drugs.

There are a few rules to consider:

- **The more invasive the search, the stronger reason an employer needs.** Employees have a greater expectation of privacy when it comes to purses and bags than they do for the things on top of their desks. As well, employees have a much greater expectation of privacy in their bodies and reasonably so. An employer that wants to search more private areas needs an extremely compelling justification -- and there will virtually never be sufficient reason for an employer to require a full body search.

- **Employers can be proactive to manage an employee's expectations of privacy.** If the employer has a policy to inform employees that their desks and lockers are subject to search,, the employee will have a harder time convincing a court that they had a reasonable expectation of privacy in those areas.

- **Random searches are less likely to be upheld.** When an employer conducts a random search, it is essentially admitting that it has no basis to suspect a particular employee. This reflects poorly on the employer's justification for privacy violation.

- **An employer cannot detain you against your will.** Some employers detain workers in connection with a search -- to keep the worker out of the area being searched or to exert a little pressure on the worker to consent to a search. This is illegal and grounds for a lawsuit. An employee can sue an employer who makes the employee to believe that he is not free to leave.

Personal Blogging

Do you have a personal blog or Facebook page? If so, be mindful what you write. Yes, there is freedom of speech. But it doesn't mean that your employer has to like it. Freedom of speech keeps you from going to jail or being persecuted by the government, not necessarily from being fired. There are some limits to an employer's ability to disciplining **employees** for what they say online.

There are some laws that provide some limits on an employer's right to fire you for what you post about. The same rules that prohibit employers from retaliating against employees for raising particular types of issues also protect employees who blog or post about those topics. And, state laws protecting what employees do on their own time may also come into play.

Here are some of the laws that may protect an employee who keeps a private blog:

Off-duty conduct. A number of states have passed laws that prohibit employers from disciplining employees for activities they pursue off-site, on their own time. Although some of these laws were originally intended to protect smokers from discrimination others protect any employee conduct, as long as it doesn't break the law. These laws could provide legal protection for an employee who keeps a personal blog or posts on a social networking site or website.

Political views. Some states protect employees from discrimination based on their political views or affiliations. In these states, disciplining an employee for posts that endorse a particular candidate or political cause could be illegal.

"Whistlebloggers." An employee who raises concerns about safety hazards or illegal activity at work may be protected as a whistleblower (or a "whistleblogger). Whistleblower protections recognize that the public good is served by employees who are willing to come forward with these types of complaints -- and that very few employees will do so if they can be fired for it.

Retaliation. Several employment laws protect employees from retaliation for claiming that their rights have been violated. If your post complains of workplace discrimination, harassment, violation of the Family and Medical Leave Act, wage and hour violations, or other legal transgressions, you may be protected from disciplinary action.

Unfair Labor Practices. The National Labor Relations Act and similar state laws protect employees' rights to communicate with each other about the conditions of employment, and to join together to bring concerns about such issues to their employer. If you are fired for blogging or posting about low wages, poor benefits, or long work hours, you may have a claim against your employer. The National Labor Relations Board has been very active lately in bringing unfair labor practices claims against employers who fire or discipline employees based on posts that are critical of working conditions.

However, if your posts don't fit into one of the categories above you'll have to be careful about what you post. Here are some tips to avoid disciplinary action.

Don't use the internet as a substitute for an official complaint process. If you are a whistleblogger, make sure that you have filed complaints with the governing body first.

Don't criticize, mock, or make harassing comments about coworkers. Even if the people you're writing about are in on the joke, you can bet that your employer isn't going to get it. For example: The Automobile Club of Southern California eventually fired 27 workers for postings on MySpace about -- among other things -- the weight and sexual orientation of coworkers.

Don't post racist, sexist, or bigoted comments or rants. Again, even if you intend your comments as a joke, these topics are never funny and they reflect poorly on you. And your employer may even find itself under public pressure to get rid of you.

Don't reveal company trade secrets or confidential information. Michael Hansom, a temp was fired by Microsoft after he posted photos of Macintosh computers arriving at Microsoft, with the tag line: "Even Microsoft wants G5s."

Try to solve your problems privately before you post them publicly. While there are some protection laws for whistlebloggers, you would have to go to court to defend your right which can be costly both financially and emotionally.

Blog anonymously or restrict viewers to your blog. The Electronic Freedom Foundation, which supports the rights of bloggers, has a few of suggestions for making sure your employer doesn't identify you as the author of your blog, including:

- blogging anonymously or under a pseudonym (do not to reveal any identifying details about yourself or your job/company)
- restricting who can view your blog (either by region or name), and
- excluding your blog from major search engines.

Don't get careless with the fervor of your rants because on the internet, nothing gets deleted permanently and it can come back to haunt you.

Common Employer Wrongs

Dismissals

Wrongful Dismissal

You hear the phrase "wrongful dismissal" (or "wrongful discharge" or "wrongful termination"), but what is it really? A wrongful dismissal simply means that an employer fails to provide reasonable notice of termination. Most people equate the term 'wrongful' to mean some form of misconduct. This is not the case. Wrongful dismissal damages are provided only to compensate for lack of notice and not for misconduct, however, courts may award additional damages in a wrongful dismissed action for 'bad faith' conduct in the manner of termination over and above damages for failure to provide adequate notice. Keep in mind, there are no federal laws stipulating mandatory termination notice and very few state laws either.

Many people assume that any termination/severance package received is reasonable and that their employer would never try to take advantage of them. This concept ignores the fact that the employer is running a business and it makes business sense to pay less rather than more. Using that basic principle, it is rare that the opening offer will be its best offer. (Negotiation is discussed in a later chapter.) In the United States, there is no single "wrongful termination" law.

The rules for whether an employee was improperly fired or terminated from their job vary by state. All states, except Montana, follow the rules of "At Will" Employment. Employment is "at the will" of either the employer or the employee, or "at will." "At will" means that an employer can fire an employee for *any reason* the employer sees fit, provided it is not for an improper reason (listed below). It does not make a difference whether the employee actually did anything wrong, or whether the employer misunderstood the facts of the situation. If the employee is "at-will," any reason, including no reason, is a proper basis for termination.

The following are some exceptions when firing an at-will employee that amounts to wrongful termination:

- **Discrimination** - The employer cannot terminate employment because the employee is a certain race, nationality, religion, sex, age, or in some states, sexual orientation.

- **Retaliation** - An employer cannot fire an employee because the employee filed a claim of discrimination or is participating in an investigation for discrimination. This "retaliation" is forbidden under civil rights law. Also retaliation is not allowed in the case of whistle blowing either.

- **Illegal Acts** - An employer is not permitted to fire an employee because the employee refuses to commit an act that is illegal.

- **Family or Medical Leave** - Federal law permits most employees to take a leave of absence for specific family or medical problems. An employer is not permitted to fire an employee who takes family or medical leave for a reason outlined in the Family and Medical Leave Act.

- **Not Following Own Termination Procedures** - Often, the employee handbook or company policy outlines a procedure that must be followed before an employee is terminated. If the employer fires an employee without following this procedure, the employee may have a claim for wrongful termination.

Unless the company policy or employee handbook states otherwise, employers are not typically required to give the employee any advance notice of job termination. Likewise, employees are not required to give their employers advance notice of leaving the company absent a contract or stated company policy.

It is therefore extremely important that an employee understand what minimum payments they are entitled to, if any. Check your employment contract or offer letter or employee handbook.

Payment of Last Check

The federal government does not mandate when an employer must issue a terminated employee's final paycheck. However, many states have very specific rules. For employees who are fired or laid off, most states require payment on the next regularly scheduled payday, but some require it much earlier. For example, California requires you to pay the employee immediately upon termination. When employees quit, many states require only that the last check be issued on the next scheduled payday. However, states like Oregon require immediate payment, provided the employee has given two days' notice.

Here is a list of state requirements:

Source: www.nolo.com

State	Final Paycheck Deadline
Alabama	No statute
Alaska	**If employee is fired:** within three working days. **If employee quits:** next regular payday at least three days after employee gives notice.

Arizona	**If employee is fired:** within three working days or next payday, whichever is sooner. **If employee quits:** next payday.
Arkansas	**If employee is fired:** within seven days from discharge.
California	**If employee is fired:** immediately. **If employee quits:** within 72 hours, or immediately if employee has given at least 72 hours' notice.
Colorado	**If employee is fired:** immediately. (Within six hours of start of next workday, if payroll unit is closed; 24 hours if unit is offsite.) Employer decides check delivery. **If employee quits:** next scheduled payday.
Connecticut	**If employee is fired:** next business day after discharge. **If employee quits:** next scheduled payday.
Delaware	**If employee is fired:** next scheduled payday. **If employee quits:** next scheduled payday.
District of Columbia	**If employee is fired:** next business day. **If employee quits:** next scheduled payday or within seven days, whichever is sooner.
Florida	No statute
Georgia	No statute
Hawaii	**If employee is fired:** immediately or next business day, if conditions prevent immediate payment. **If employee quits:** next scheduled payday or immediately, if employee gives one pay period's notice
Idaho	**If employee is fired:** next payday or within 10 days (excluding weekends & holidays), whichever is sooner. If employee makes a written request for earlier payment, within 48 hours of receiving request (excluding weekends & holidays). **If employee quits:** next payday or within 10 days (excluding weekends & holidays), whichever is sooner. If employee makes a written request for earlier payment, within 48 hours of receiving request (excluding weekends & holidays).
Illinois	**If employee is fired:** at time of separation if possible, but no later than next payday. **If employee quits:** at time of separation if possible, but no later than next payday.

Indiana	**If employee is fired:** next scheduled payday. **If employee quits:** next scheduled payday. If employee has not provided a forwarding address, employer may wait until 10 days after employee demands wages or until employee provides an address where the check may be mailed.
Iowa	**If employee is fired:** next scheduled payday. **If employee quits:** next scheduled payday.
Kansas	**If employee is fired:** next scheduled payday. **If employee quits:** next scheduled payday.
Kentucky	**If employee is fired:** next scheduled payday or within 14 days, whichever is later. **If employee quits:** next scheduled payday or within 14 days, whichever is later.
Louisiana	**If employee is fired:** next payday or within 15 days, whichever is earlier. **If employee quits:** next payday or within 15 days, whichever is earlier.
Maine	**If employee is fired:** next scheduled payday or within two weeks after demand, whichever is earlier. **If employee quits:** next scheduled payday or within two weeks after demand, whichever is earlier.
Maryland	**If employee is fired:** next scheduled payday. **If employee quits:** next scheduled payday.
Massachusetts	**If employee is fired:** day of discharge. **If employee quits:** next payday. If no scheduled payday, then following Saturday.
Michigan	**If employee is fired:** next payday. **If employee quits:** next payday.
Minnesota	**If employee is fired:** immediately. **If employee quits:** next payday. If payday is less than five days after last day of work, employer may pay on the following payday or 20 days after last day of work, whichever is earlier.
Mississippi	No statute
Missouri	**If employee is fired:** day of discharge.

Montana	**If employee is laid off or fired for cause:** immediately. Employer may have a written policy extending this time to the next payday or within 15 days, whichever is earlier. **If employee quits:** next payday or within 15 days, whichever is earlier.
Nebraska	**If employee is fired:** next scheduled payday or within two weeks, whichever is earlier. **If employee quits:** next payday or within two weeks, whichever is earlier.
Nevada	**If employee is fired:** immediately. **If employee quits:** next scheduled payday or within seven days, whichever is earlier.
New Hampshire	**If employee is fired:** within 72 hours. If employee is laid off, employer may wait until the next payday. **If employee quits:** next scheduled payday or within 72 hours, if employee gives one pay period's notice.
New Jersey	**If employee is fired:** next scheduled payday. **If employee quits:** next scheduled payday.
New Mexico	**If employee is fired:** within five days. **If employee quits:** next payday.
New York	**If employee is fired:** next scheduled payday. **If employee quits:** next scheduled payday.
North Carolina	**If employee is fired:** next scheduled payday. **If employee quits:** next scheduled payday.
North Dakota	**If employee is fired:** next payday or within 15 days, whichever is earlier. **If employee quits:** next payday.
Ohio	**If employee is fired or quits:** first of the month for wages earned in the first half of prior month; fifteenth of the month for wages earned in second half of prior month.
Oklahoma	**If employee is fired:** next scheduled payday. **If employee quits:** next scheduled payday.
Oregon	**If employee is fired:** end of first business day after termination (must be within five days if employee submits time records to determine wages due). **If employee quits:** immediately, if employee has given 48 hours' notice (excluding

	weekends & holidays). Without notice, within five days or the next payday, whichever occurs first. (must be within five days if employee submits time records to determine wages due).
Pennsylvania	**If employee is fired:** next scheduled payday. **If employee quits:** next scheduled payday.
Rhode Island	**If employee is fired:** next scheduled payday. **If employee quits:** next scheduled payday.
South Carolina	**If employee is fired:** within 48 hours or next scheduled payday, but not more than 30 days.
South Dakota	**If employee is fired:** next payday or when employee returns employer's property. **If employee quits:** next payday or when employee returns employer's property.
Tennessee	**If employee is fired:** next scheduled payday or within 21 days, whichever is later. **If employee quits:** next scheduled payday or within 21 days, whichever is later.
Texas	**If employee is fired:** within six days. **If employee quits:** next payday.
Utah	**If employee is fired:** within 24 hours. **If employee quits:** next scheduled payday.
Vermont	**If employee is fired:** within 72 hours. **If employee quits:** next scheduled payday or, if no scheduled payday exists, the next Friday.
Virginia	**If employee is fired:** next scheduled payday. **If employee quits:** next scheduled payday.
Washington	**If employee is fired:** end of next pay period. **If employee quits:** end of next pay period.
West Virginia	**If employee is fired:** within 72 hours. **If employee quits:** Immediately, if employee has given one pay period's notice; otherwise, next scheduled payday.

Wisconsin	**If employee is fired:** next payday or within one month, whichever is earlier. If termination is due to merger, relocation, or liquidation of business, within 24 hours. **If employee quits:** next payday.
Wyoming	**If employee is fired:** five working days. **If employee quits:** five working days.

Just Cause

"Just cause" is a legal term that means an employer is justified in terminating an employee without providing termination notice or termination pay. There is no clear-cut method of determining what will constitute just cause. Each case is unique and must be reviewed with attention to all of the facts of the situation.

When resolving whether there is just cause for dismissal without notice in your situation, courts will look at answering the following two questions: (1) was misconduct by the employee proven?; and (2) was the level of the misconduct justifiable to dismiss the employee without any notice if the employee's contract or employee manual state otherwise? If the answer to both questions is *yes*, then just cause dismissal was reasonable; however, if an answer to either question is *no*, then the employer was obligated to give reasonable termination notice or termination pay as outlined in the employee contract and/or the employee manual.

What is the measure of misconduct that justifies termination for just cause? There are a number of factors. Firstly, a court will look at whether the employee's misconduct caused an irreparable disruption in the employment relationship, by either violating an important condition of the employment contract, or destroying the employer's trust in the employee. If the misconduct resulted in any of these events, then there is just cause.

Secondly, a court will look at the seniority of the employee in the organization. The more senior an employee, the more serious the conduct.

Thirdly, a court will look to see whether the employer gave any warnings (written or verbal) prior to termination. Where there was no warning prior to the dismissal that the misconduct was connected to, except in the most serious of cases (e.g. stealing, violence, leaking corporate secrets, etc.), the employer will have a harder time proving just cause in court.

Lastly, courts will look at whether the employee's misconduct was tolerated prior to the dismissal. If misconduct occurred before and the employer tolerated this behavior through inaction (i.e. not providing the employee with a formal warning that the misconduct would not be tolerated) then the employer's actions will be under scrutiny if the employee was dismissed without notice.

It is difficult enough for an individual to be suddenly told that his/her employment has come to an end. One of the top three stresses for adults in our society is losing a job. It is doubly so when the employer informs the employee that s/he has been terminated for "cause". Labor unions typically negotiate for a contract provision stating that an employee cannot be fired absent just cause.

Not every act of misconduct should lead to termination. The conduct by the employee must be serious enough to end the employment relationship. The types of conduct which the law recognizes as justifying termination have included: incompetence, insubordination or disobedience, abusive language or behavior, violence, chronic absenteeism, persistent lateness, intoxication, dishonesty, theft, destruction of property and sexual harassment.

When there is a cause for termination, the employer has no obligation to provide the employee with notice or termination pay. It is therefore not unusual for an employer to allege cause, even though it will be difficult to prove in order to discourage an employee from bringing an action for wrongful dismissal. Some employers try to take advantage of a terminated employee's shock and vulnerability.

And keep in mind; if an employee is fired for just cause and there is documentation provided by the employer, then the employee may be ineligible for unemployment insurance benefits. As well, it will impact securing a new job when you are asked why you left your previous place of employment.

Dishonesty

Not every employee who faces termination will have a legitimate lawsuit for wrongful dismissal. A termination is "wrongful" when an employee is terminated without cause and is not provided with reasonable notice of his/her termination.

"Dishonesty" includes not only theft or fraud but any form of untrustworthy behavior. Just cause based on dishonesty may happen whether the conduct in question occurs before the start of employment (e.g. lying on your résumé), during the course of employment or in relation to matters unconnected with employment. In determining when just cause for dishonesty exists, the courts are primarily concerned with whether the conduct of the employee is such that s/he can no longer be trusted or depended upon by the employer.

One of the most significant changes recently is distinguishing between varying "degrees" of lying and dishonesty within the workplace. For example, if the employee has demonstrated a history of lying in the workplace, the employer may have grounds for "just cause" since the trust level is damaged every time the employee lies.

If the employee is proven to act dishonestly yet continues to deny any wrongdoing then the more they try to conceal the act, the more susceptible they are to termination with cause. The degree of dishonesty is reflected in how much harm the lie caused, how it impacted the business, and whether the employee was in a position of authority and trust at the time of an incident. For instance, terminating with cause a manager who, on one occasion takes home a package of copy paper, may not have the same weight as that of an employee who repeatedly steals valuable product from the workplace.

Here are a few examples:

1. A company was hiring for a senior tool engineer. The hiring was based upon a personal interview together with a written application filed by the applicant following the interview. In order to be interviewed for work as an engineer, it was mandatory that applicants possess a college degree. The wage given to employees was dependent upon the number of years of college education completed. The applicant was aware of the employer's policy in this matter. On both the interview and the written application, the applicant informed the employer that he had a college degree, and was hired accordingly. The applicant actually did not earn a college degree. He was discharged was for misconduct due to dishonesty.

2. An employee was an auto mechanic. The employer's rule provided that the use of employer's or customers' cars for personal business, such as going to lunch, was prohibited. The employee was aware of this rule.

    The employee received a warning and guidance over his taking a vehicle owned by the employer home over the weekend without authorization. A few days later, he was assigned maintenance work on a customer's vehicle. The employer had promised the customer that he could pick up the car at 12:30 p.m. The employee completed the repairs and left the premises driving the customer's car without authorization and without notifying anyone. The customer arrived as scheduled. After waiting for an hour to pick up his car, the customer left irate.

    The claimant returned in the customer's car at about 2 p.m. and admitted to his supervisor that he had gone to lunch in the customer's vehicle. The claimant was fired the following day.

3. The employer's policy was that each employee must punch in his/her own time card. The employee was aware of the policy. However, the employee was observed punching in another person's time card even though that individual was not present. The employee claimed that he did it because the other individual had requested him to do so. The other

employee had just returned from a suspension because of attendance problems and was warned that any future attendance problems would lead to his termination. The employee was discharged because he punched in another person's time card which demonstrated dishonesty.

Breach of Trust

A breach of trust occurs when someone in a position of confidence violates the trust invested by someone else. In an employment situation, it typically occurs where the employee demonstrates misconduct that promotes his/her interests instead of the employer's interests. Where the employee's misconduct was motivated by a conflict of interest, the natural trust placed in the employee will have been destroyed. However, attention needs to be paid to the specific facts to confirm if a breach of trust has occurred.

An example occurs when a manager or employee becomes privy to information that another employee is about to be terminated. If the manager does anything to tip off the about-to-be-fired employee, s/he can be terminated for breach of trust. Whether the firing was justifiable or not is irrelevant. Through process or confidence, the manager was informed but has no latitude to be involved even if s/he is trying to help the fired employee.

Insubordination

Insubordination is a form of misconduct where the employee refuses to acknowledge and accept the authority of the employer and refuses to comply with the employer's clear instructions, policies and procedures without reasonable justification. Usually, the courts will not allow an employer to fire an employee for a single incident of insubordination, unless it was of some major significance.

A claim of insubordination must show the following:

1. That the employee was given a clearly expressed direct order (*preferably in writing*).

2. That the employee understood the order given (*acknowledged in the receipt of order*).

3. That the order was reasonable and work-related.

4. That the order did not place the employee in danger of his or her safety.

5. That the order did not violate public policy.

6. That the employee was informed of the consequences of not obeying the direct order. The employee <u>must</u> be told that failure to obey the order will result in discipline up to and including termination.

Insubordination may be active or passive.

Active insubordination occurs when an employee specifically refuses a directive or states the intention to not follow a directive. This refusal is usually verbal. Active insubordination can be confrontational. It may involve threats or even assault.

Passive insubordination occurs when the employee intentionally does not carry out the supervisor's directive, but there is no direct refusal. Passive insubordination is much harder to prove.

An employee disliked his job. He was very vocal about his contempt to coworkers. He mocked the policies which he felt were silly and often stated that he would be out of there as soon as he found another job.

The boss kept a record of his violations on file, so that when they fired him for insubordination, they would have evidence to back it up. After being caught by the boss for surfing the web for dating sites at his desk after being told not to (which he didn't even try to hide when anyone came into his cubicle), he was finally terminated for insubordination.

Absenteeism/Lateness

Absenteeism is defined as occasional absences from work which an employee may attempt to justify by through communication (phone call, email, text, discussion) indicating that s/he will not be reporting to work or that s/he is not feeling well. Lateness refers to reporting for work after one's schedule of hours has begun.

Many employers have in place attendance policies which set out the procedure that an employee must follow when not coming in to work or reporting late. This will often require that the employee report his/her non-attendance before the start of the shift, and provide doctor's notes when absences are illness-related and extend beyond a certain number of days. Non-compliance with an employer's attendance policy may result in discipline and if the conduct continues, be reason for the employer as cause for dismissal.

Even in establishments where there is no formal attendance policy, repeated lateness without a legitimate reason may be regarded as a serious breach of the employee's responsibility to the employer. Where the employee cannot justify his/her persistent lateness, warnings have been issued by the supervisor and the conduct persists, the employer will be able to terminate legally.

An employer will **not** be able to establish cause for dismissal where an employee is unable to attend work due to illness. In such circumstances, an employer will need to determine whether the employee is indeed sick. To do so, an employer has the right to request that an employee provide a doctor's note where the employee has been absent on a significant number of days.

An employer would, in most cases, be required to formally warn an employee before proceeding with outright dismissal under the ground of absenteeism. The employer could not justify firing an employee who was late on only one occasion. However, chronic lateness and absenteeism may justify dismissal if the employee had been given sufficient warnings and still failed to correct this behavior without valid reasons.

However, if an employee arrives at work late for his/her shift, an employer can demand that the employee remain on duty later than the normal end time to make up for time lost due to lateness. For example, if an employee showed up at 8:10am when his/her normal start time is 8:00am, then the employer is within his/her right to require the employee to stay until 5:10pm (if the normal day's end is 5:00pm). Additionally, in the same scenario, if the employee is paid an hourly wage, the employer can ask the tardy employee to leave and return at 8:30am to start work. This condition is allowed if the hours worked is based on a minimum of 30 minute intervals.

Misrepresentation at Time of Hiring

Misrepresentation at time of hiring occurs when an employee who was hired on the basis of a skill, experience or educational achievement that s/he indicated s/he possesses, but in reality does not. The employee in such a case may be dismissed with just cause for misrepresenting the skill. For example, a person who represented that he can swim and was hired as a lifeguard may be dismissed for just cause after the employer discovers the employee's lack of ability to swim. Or if an employee also claimed that she had an MBA during the interview phase and was later discovered that this was false after being hired may be fired for just cause.

Incompetence/Poor Performance

An employee is obliged to display a reasonable level of competence in relation to the job that they are hired for. Upon hiring, an employee may also indicate her/his awareness of the duties and responsibilities of the position s/he is applying for, and her/his qualifications and/or the experience s/he possess to do the job. Under these circumstances, where it is clear that the individual demonstrates that s/he is not up to the task or has misrepresented her/his qualifications and her/his ability, the employer may have cause for termination.

Employers are obligated to advise employees if there are performance-related concerns and provide a private opportunity to address them. What would constitute an adequate warning to an employee before an employer can use continued poor performance as cause for termination? Courts have repeatedly indicated that mere expressions of disappointment with an employee's work are not sufficient. The employee must be aware of the standard of performance expected of him/her and notified that s/he has failed to meet that standard. S/he must be given a reasonable amount of time to improve performance and be warned that failure to do so could result in termination. Courts have indicated that criticism of an employee's performance must be constructive and will only be deemed so where the employer has provided practical guidance on how to improve.

Intoxication

Can an employee who comes to work under the influence of drugs or alcohol be terminated for cause? Yes.

Since alcoholism is listed as a "disability" under the American Disabilities Act, can an intoxicated employee who is deemed an alcoholic be terminated for just cause? Mostly, yes.

The EEOC provides that employers are free to "discipline, discharge or deny employment to an alcoholic whose use of alcohol adversely affects job performance or conduct to the extent that s/he is not 'qualified.' " The EEOC elaborates with the following example:

If an individual who has alcoholism often is late to work, or is unable to perform the responsibilities of his/her job, an employer can take disciplinary action on the basis of the poor job performance and conduct. However, an employer may not discipline an alcoholic employee more severely than it does other employees for the same performance or conduct.

For example, if an alcoholic employee and a non-alcoholic employee are caught having a beer on the loading dock, the employer cannot fire the alcoholic employee while giving the other employee only a written warning. In Flynn v. Raytheon Co., the court dealt with this precise issue. It held that even though an employer can enforce its rules against intoxication on the job, it could not selectively enforce its rules in a way that treats alcoholics more harshly. In short, whatever policies the employer enacts must be uniformly applied.

The duty to provide reasonable accommodations to qualified individuals with disabilities is considered one of the most important statutory requirements of the ADA. Reasonable accommodation for an alcoholic would generally involve a modified work schedule so the employee could attend Alcoholics Anonymous meetings or a leave of absence so the employee could seek treatment. In Schmidt v. Safeway, Inc., for example, the court held that the employer must provide a leave of absence so the employee could obtain medical treatment for alcoholism. The ADA does not require an employer to provide an alcohol rehabilitation program or to offer rehabilitation in lieu of disciplining an employee for alcohol-related misconduct or performance problems.

The EEOC has held that "federal employers are no longer required to provide the reasonable accommodation of 'firm choice' under Section 501 of the Rehabilitation Act." "Firm choice" generally entails a warning to employees with alcohol-related employment problems that they will be disciplined if they do not receive alcohol treatment. The EEOC's rationale is that the Rehabilitation Act was amended in 1992 to apply ADA standards, and that the ADA does not require an employer to excuse misconduct for poor performance, even if it is related to alcoholism. In EEOC's "Enforcement Guidance on Reasonable Accommodation and Undue Hardship" statement, the EEOC reiterated that an employer "has no obligation to provide 'firm choice' or a 'last chance agreement' as a reasonable accommodation."

Moreover, an employer is generally not required to provide leave to an alcoholic employee if the treatment would appear to be futile. For example, in *Schmidt v. Safeway, Inc.*, the court said an employer would not be required "to provide repeated leaves of absence (or perhaps even a single leave of absence) for an alcoholic employee with a poor prognosis for recovery." And in *Fuller v. Frank*, the court held that the employer was not required to give an alcoholic employee another leave of absence when alcohol treatment had repeatedly failed in the past.

Finally, an employer generally is not required to provide an accommodation to an employee who has not asked for an accommodation and who denies having a disability. In Larson v. Koch Refining Co., the court dealt with this precise issue and held that the employer had no obligation to provide accommodation to an employee with alcoholism when the employee did not ask for an accommodation, and in fact expressly denied having an alcohol problem.

Courts routinely hold that employees cannot blame misconduct on alcoholism. For example, in Renaud v. Wyoming Department of Family Services, the court noted that even if alcoholism is assumed to be a disability, the ADA distinguishes between alcoholism and alcoholism-related misconduct. The court determined that the employer could lawfully terminate the employee (a school superintendent) for coming to work drunk, even though he claimed the conduct resulted from his alcoholism.

Insolence

Insolence is a form of insubordination where the employee openly shows disrespect for another person in the workplace. It could be through verbal tirades, badmouthing to others or even openly publicly mocking others such as on Facebook.

It usually requires more than one instance of insolence before termination can occur. However, a few circumstances can allow for immediate termination:

- Was the insolence in front of a customer, possibly affecting a business relationship?
- Was profanity or discriminatory slurs involved?
- Were unfounded criminal accusations about another employee or manager repeated?
- Did the incident of insolence involve violence or destruction of property or threats of such?
- Was the insolence in front of other employees and done in a manner that would affect the business relationship between the other employees and the target of insolence?

If any of these are the case, then an employee may be fired immediately for just cause.

Constructive Dismissal

A constructive dismissal occurs when an employer makes a significant change to a basic term or condition of employment without the employee's actual or implied consent. It describes situations where the employer has not directly fired the employee but, by unilaterally changing the terms of employment, forces the employee to quit. Constructive dismissal is sometimes called "disguised dismissal" or "quitting with cause" because it often occurs in situations where the employee is offered the alternative of leaving or of submitting to a unilateral and substantial change to a fundamental term or condition of his/her employment. The confirmation of a constructive dismissal is based on an objective view of the employer's conduct and not solely on the employee's perception.

To demonstrate, an employee may be constructively dismissed if the employer makes changes to conditions that result in a significant reduction in salary or a significant change in such things as work location, hours of work, threats of demotion, withdrawal of specific benefits required to do the job or position. Constructive dismissal may also include situations where an employer makes the working environment intolerable through harassment or abuse of an employee or an employer gives an employee an ultimatum to "quit or be fired" and the employee resigns in response.

The employee would have to resign in response to the significant change within a reasonable period of time in order for the employer's actions to be considered as constructive dismissal. However, throughout the United States, constructive discharge has differing meanings depending on the jurisdiction. The California Supreme Court defines constructive discharge as follows:

"In order to establish a constructive discharge, an employee must plead and prove, by the usual preponderance of the evidence standard, that the employer either intentionally created or knowingly permitted working conditions that were so intolerable or aggravated at the time of the employee's resignation that a reasonable employer would realize that a reasonable person in the employee's position would be compelled to resign."

If you feel you are being forced to resign, you need to be proactive if you hope to lodge a complaint. No matter which state you reside, the majority of courts always need to verify if you took the opportunity to resolve the problem yourself. It is your responsibility to make best efforts to address the problem, and go through the HR process to notify them of the issue, so the company has a chance to resolve it.

Taking these steps will help support your claim.

1. Keep a diary (see later reference to "job journal") of all the events. Include all names of witnesses, times and steps you have taken to correct the situation.
2. Make sure you follow company policy on filing issues, grievances etc. if you are not sure what those are, as your manager, or the HR/OD group.
3. Write down the series of events and your journey through the process if you are to be fired, or if there is a discipline issue against you. You want to make sure they don't fire you because you are kicking up a storm (which normally they can't, but they may try)
4. In all complaints be very specific about the issue, and about what you feel an effective resolution would be.
6. Do not take anything home that is company property. That includes emails or documents.
7. If there is no resolution, then before you quit you should try to consult with a lawyer and show him/her your supporting documents. A properly worded letter just before you quit can be very effective. The lawyer would advise you on how the letter should be written, so you give them proper notice. Be honest with your lawyer and don't leave anything out especially if there are any misconduct or performance issues in the past.

If you are being pushed out, then the steps you take before you quit are crucial to protecting yourself.

Temporary Layoff

An employee is on temporary layoff when an employer cuts back or stops the employee's work without ending his/her employment (e.g. laying someone off at times when there is not enough work to do). An employer may put an employee on a temporary layoff without confirming a date on which the employee will be recalled to work.

To provide some protection to the employee, the federal government has implemented the WARN (Workers Adjustment and Retraining Notification) Act. It requires most employers with 100 or more employees to provide employees at least 60 days notice of any plant closing and mass layoff.

The purpose of the WARN Act is to give workers and their families some transition time to prepare for the prospective loss of employment, to seek a new job, and, if necessary, to seek training in a new skill or retraining in an existing skill that will allow the workers to obtain replacement work.

Generally, WARN covers employers with 100 or more employees, not including:
- employees who have worked less than six (6) months in the last 12 months, and
- employees who work an average of less than 20 hours a week.

Employers must provide the WARN notice to all employees, including managers and supervisors.

An employer must provide the required notice when its closes a plant or effectuates a mass layoff. The number of affected workers is the total number laid off during a 30-day period.

A plant closing includes:
- the closing of a facility for more than six (6) months,
- the shutdown of an operating unit for more than six (6) months, or
- when 50 or more employees are laid off during any 30-day period at a single location.

A mass layoff occurs when a layoff, lasting at least six months, affects either:
- 500 or more workers. or
- at least 33% of the workforce when the layoff affects between 50 and 499 workers.

WARN allows workers time to make appropriate arrangements for a new job or retraining. It is within the discretion of the employer to give the worker paid time off to look for another job.

Most states follow the federal guideline, however, seven states have more stringent notification requirements than those in the WARN Act. The table below outlines those 7 state's WARN requirements.

State	Requirements
California	Applies to employers with 75 or more full or part-time employees where 50 or more employees are to be laid off due to a plant closing, mass layoff, or relocation of the employer's business. Unlike the federal law, there is no requirement that the number of employees to be laid off constitute a certain percentage of the employer's workforce. Relocation is

	defined as a move to a different location more than 100 miles from the prior location.
Illinois	Applies to employers with 75 or more full-time employees when: - 25 or more full-time employees are laid off if they constitute one-third or more of the full-time employees at the site, or - 250 or more full-time employees are laid off
Maryland	Maryland's version of WARN, the Maryland Economic Stabilization Act, is voluntary and applies to employers in the industrial, commercial, and business industries with 50 or more employees. Otherwise, an employer must comply with the federal requirements.

New Jersey	Applies to employers who have been in business at least three years and have at least 100 employees. It applies in situations where a covered employer:
	- transfers or terminates its operations during any continuous period of 30 days which results in the termination of employment of 50 or more full-time employees, or
	- conducts a mass layoff that results in an employment loss during any 30 day period of:
	
	    o 500 or more full-time employees, or
	
	    o 50 or more full-time employees representing one third or more of the full-time employees at the establishment

Tennessee	Applies to employers with 50 or more employees, instead of the 100 required by the federal law. All other federal requirements apply.
Wisconsin	Applies to employers with 50 or more employees. It applies in situations where a covered employer:

Exemptions

An employer does not need to give notice if a plant closing is the closing of a temporary facility, or if the closing or mass layoff is the result of the completion of a particular project or undertaking. This exemption applies only if the workers were hired with the understanding that their employment was limited to the duration of the facility, project or undertaking. An employer cannot label an ongoing project "temporary" in order to evade its obligations under WARN.

An employer does not need to provide notice to strikers or to workers who are part of the bargaining unit(s) which are involved in the labor negotiations that led to a lockout when the strike or lockout is equivalent to a plant closing or mass layoff. Non-striking employees who experience an employment loss as a direct or indirect result of a strike and workers who are not part of the bargaining unit(s) which are involved in the labor negotiations that led to a lockout are still entitled to notice.

The exceptions to 60-day notice are:

(1) Faltering company. This exception, to be narrowly construed, covers situations where a company has sought new capital or business in order to stay open and where giving notice would ruin the opportunity to get the new capital or business, and applies only to plant closings;

(2) Unforeseeable business circumstances. This exception applies to closings and layoffs that are caused by business circumstances that were not reasonably foreseeable at the time notice would otherwise have been required. If an employer believes their situation is the result an economic crisis, it may apply the unforeseen business circumstance exception; however, there could be a burden on the employer to prove why it could not plan 90 days in advance.; and

(3) Natural disaster. This applies where a closing or layoff is the direct result of a natural disaster, such as a flood, earthquake, drought or storm.

If an employer provides less than 60 days advance notice of a closing or layoff and relies on one of these three exceptions, the employer bears the burden of proof that the conditions for the exception have been met. The employer also must give as much notice as is practicable. When the notices are given, they must include a brief statement of the reason for reducing the notice period in addition to the items required in notices.

Probation

In some states, the legal rights of an employee are different during the employee's initial term of probation so it is important to determine if you are under probation to fully understand what your rights are.

Probation is defined as a trial period (usually 3 or 6 months) during which the employer will review and evaluate the employee to determine if s/he is suitable for ongoing employment. Under no circumstances does this status give the employer the right to discriminate or harass you.

A probationary period cannot be implied or assumed into a contract of employment and automatically imposed on the employee. In order to establish an employee's probationary status, it must be done within the written offer of employment and agreed to <u>before</u> the employee starts to work. If the employee accepts a verbal offer of employment that does not specify a probationary period, then no probationary period applies. The burden is on the employer to prove an alleged probationary term.

It is generally understood that the standards of proof for cause for termination is lower for probationary employees than it is for "regular" employees who have completed their probation. However, this does not give an employer a license to treat the employee unfairly; for example, to fire the employee after 3 days of 3 month probation or for a department's production decline unrelated to the probationary employee. Any termination must be performance related as outlined in the employment contract or offer letter.

An employer may not unilaterally extend a probationary period without the consent of the employee.

An employer has the right to terminate a probationary employee without notice or severance where the employer can establish that it acted fairly and with reasonable diligence in determining whether or not the proposed employee was suitable in the job for which s/he was being tested. As long as the probationary employee is given a reasonable opportunity to demonstrate his/her ability to meet the standards the employer sets out at the time of hiring, including the ability of the person to work in harmony with others, his/her potential value to the employer in the future and other factors deemed by the employer to be essential to the acceptable performance of the position, then the employee has no legal complaint.

What is important to note is that the employment standards allow the employer to terminate an employee on probation with no notice or pay in lieu of notice (assuming notice or notice pay is provided by the company in the first place).

Discrimination

Title VII of the Civil Rights Act of 1964 prohibits employers from harassing or discriminating against applicants and employees on the basis of race, color, religion, sex, and national origin (including membership in a Native American tribe). People who fall into these characteristic types are often referred to legally as a "protected class" or "protected characteristic". It also prohibits employers from retaliating against an applicant or employee who asserts his or her rights under the law.

Title VII prohibits discrimination in hiring, firing, compensation, benefits, job assignments, promotions, and discipline. It also prohibits practices that seem impartial but have an unbalanced impact on a protected group of people. An employer must justify a valid reason for using it. For example, a strength requirement might be legal -- even though it excludes disproportionate numbers of women -- if an employer is using it to fill a job that requires heavy lifting. Such a requirement would not be valid for a desk job.

Title VII applies to employers that fit into the following categories:

- private employers with at least 15 employees
- state governments and their political subdivisions and agencies
- the federal government
- employment agencies
- labor organizations, and
- joint labor-management committees and other training programs.

The U.S. Equal Employment Opportunity Commission (EEOC) enforces Title VII.

This type of discrimination can take two forms: "disparate treatment" or "disparate impact".

Disparate treatment discrimination occurs when an employer intentionally discriminates against an individual because they possess one of the protected characteristic listed above. The employer's motive is central to a determination of fault.

Disparate impact discrimination on the other hand requires no motive to discriminate. Disparate impact discrimination occurs when an employer's policy or procedure unduly burdens employees from one of the protected classes of individuals. The employer may have been attempting to act in the best interest of its employees and with no intent to discriminate when enacting the policy, but may still be liable under Title VII if, when applied, the rule has discriminatory effects. An employer can overcome liability for race, national origin, sex, and religion discrimination by showing it had a business necessity for the discriminatory policy or practice.

You may have a "gut feeling" that you were discriminated against. But how can you tell if you have a valid case? There are numerous questions that you can ask yourself to help determine whether discrimination played a part in your termination.

Evidence of Discrimination

Direct Evidence. "Direct Evidence" is the best way to show that discrimination occurred. Direct evidence of discrimination includes statements by managers or supervisors that directly relate the adverse action against you to your protected class status. For example, if your employer tells you that you are being let go because you are near retirement age and the company wants to go with a younger image, you have direct evidence that your protected class status was the cause of your termination. This evidence can be in the form of verbal comments or statements written in emails, letters, instant messages (IMs), texts, memos, or notes.

Circumstantial Evidence. The likelihood of obtaining direct evidence of discrimination is extremely low. Supervisors and other company personnel are usually too sophisticated and too well-trained to openly express their biases and prejudices. In almost every case, an employee must rely on circumstantial evidence. An example could be a policy or practice when a hiring manager repeatedly posts managerial job openings only in male dominated departments. It is not as blatant unless you have evidence to the intention of the hiring manager.

A person claiming discrimination who does not have direct evidence must produce enough circumstantial evidence of discrimination to allow a jury to find that the employer acted with prejudice. The law recognizes that persons can be discriminated against even if they were not replaced by someone outside of the protected class, for example during a mass layoff.

Questions to ask yourself:

- Are you a member of one or more of these protected classes? For example, if you are claiming age discrimination, are you over 40? If you are claiming disability discrimination, are you disabled?
- Were you qualified for your position? For example, if your job required you to be a licensed technician, were you licensed?
- Did your employer take unfavorable action against you? For instance, were you demoted or fired?
- Were you replaced by a person who is not in your protected class (or, in the case of age discrimination, someone substantially younger than you)?
- Were you treated differently than a similarly situated person who is not in your protected class?
- Did managers or supervisors regularly make rude or derogatory comments directed at your protected class status or at all members of your class and related to work? For example, "Women don't belong on a construction site" or "Older employees are set in their ways and make terrible managers".
- Are the circumstances of your treatment so unusual, outrageous, unjust, or severe as to suggest discrimination?
- Does your employer have a history of showing bias toward persons in your protected class?
- Are there noticeably few employees of your protected class at your workplace?
- Have you noticed that other employees of your protected class seem to be singled out for negative treatment or are put in dead-end jobs?

- Have you heard other employees in your protected class complain about discrimination, particularly by the supervisor or manager who took the adverse action against you?
- Are there statistics that show favoritism towards or bias against any group?
- Did your employer violate company policy in the way s/he treated you?
- Did your employer retain less qualified, non-protected employees in the same job?

Once you establish an action or pattern of discrimination, consider the reason that your company gave for terminating you. In court, an employer has the opportunity to offer a legitimate, non-discriminatory reason for its conduct. This is not very difficult for an employer to do. All that the law requires is that the employer states a legitimate reason. It does not have to prove that it is the true reason. A company can almost always come up with some reason for the action that it took. Once the employer articulates this reason, your proof of discrimination is gone and you will have to offer additional evidence, as discussed below.

If the employer cannot offer a valid reason for your termination, you have proven a case of discrimination. However, don't count on this happening. You may think, "my employer can never come up with a good reason for firing me!" You need to remember that your employer doesn't need a "good" reason, just any reason besides your protected status. The vast majority of employers can do this and do this regularly.

Assuming that your employer can offer any explanation at all for terminating your employment, you must next consider whether you can prove that the reason is just a cover-up for discrimination. There are several ways to do this.

Can you show that the stated reason is:

- Factually untrue?
- Insufficient to have actually motivated your discharge?
- So riddled with errors that your employer could not have legitimately relied upon it?
- Is false because you have direct or circumstantial evidence that demonstrates that your protected status is more likely to have motivated your employer than the stated reason?
- Inconsistent with a pattern of warnings, terminations or disciplinary action of others?

If you can demonstrate any of the above, you may be able to prove that the employer's stated reason is just a smoke screen for discrimination. The law requires you to show not only that the stated reason is false, but that the unlawful factor was the real reason, or that the employer's stated reason and your protected status both played a role in your termination.

Racial Discrimination

Let's look at a simple hypothetical example to illustrate discrimination based racial bias. Darryl is of minority race and has been at ABC Company for two years. Darryl feels discriminated against because of his race in relation to opportunities for promotion and job assignments. Generally, it seems like minorities are not being promoted as frequently as non-minorities in the company. Darryl wants to complain about how the races are being treated differently, but he wants to be discreet about it.

So Darryl goes to his supervisor and talks about how hard it is for people to move up at ABC, but doesn't use the word "race". He discusses how he knows he does a good job, and some co-workers don't perform as well, yet those co-workers get promoted and get better assignments. (Darryl is referring to the white co-workers, but he doesn't openly say that.) The supervisor speculates that the plant manager has it in for Darryl and they talk about some minor incidents that have happened and he agrees that those incidents might have caused the plant manager to dislike him. (Darryl knows that the plant manager also might have reason to dislike the white co-workers who still get promotions and good assignments, but he doesn't mention that.)

At no point does Darryl clarify that his complaint is based on how the races are treated differently. Darryl avoids saying "race discrimination". In addition, Darryl is also a bit scared of being too aggressive in raising the race issue as he fears losing his job.

Within six months, Darryl has been fired. The company does not like complainers. The company fears that Darryl is setting them up for a discrimination lawsuit. How did they justify his termination?

After the discussions, the supervisor began closely scrutinizing Darryl's work, watching his time, writing him up whenever justifiable (even though in the past most little things were overlooked). Eventually, Darryl is placed on formal discipline for poor performance or rule violations or attendance (minor infractions mostly). After another short time, Darryl is terminated for violating the terms of his discipline by committing additional poor performance or rule violations.

Darryl contacted a lawyer because he feels he has been wrongfully terminated because he got disciplined for infractions that others don't get disciplined for. The lawyer asks him about incidents that happened at work that might have caused the employer to want to be rid of Darryl. He recalls that he made the verbal complaint to the supervisor six months ago. He describes the circumstances.

Darryl might have two potential cases, one for discrimination and one for retaliation. Both cases have their challenges and problems.

Darryl's lawyer feels that Darryl committed several errors in how he made his complaint, errors that weaken his potential retaliation case. If a court concludes that Darryl's complaint was not a "discrimination" complaint, then his retaliation claim may get dismissed. If only Darryl had been less modest with his accusations. For example:

- Darryl did **not** say he felt discriminated against because of his race. It would have been to his advantage to state the legal category that might apply to his complaint that he was making, rather than be evasive because the employer will argue that he did not in fact make a race discrimination complaint and therefore did not gain protection against retaliation.

- Darryl did **not** state any facts in his complaint which directly tend to show that discrimination might be occurring. He could have talked about whites getting treated better, but he did not. It's not necessarily enough even if he had mentioned "race". Courts like to see examples of race-related mistreatment in order to objectively understand that a complaint is made in good faith. A good solid complaint will mention "race" and will use race-related examples.

- Darryl said damaging things during the complaint process about how he agreed that the plant manager might have it in for him due to some incidents in the past. This makes it look like Darryl did not believe he was being discriminated against due to race, but rather because of ongoing problems stemming from old events including long-simmering personality conflicts. So Darryl undermined both his potential retaliation claim and his potential race discrimination claim.

- Darryl did not complain to Human Resources or to some designated high-level manager. It's best to get the problem into the hands of Human Resources or people with more power to fix it than front-line supervisors, especially if front-line supervisors are the source of the problem.

There are big problems in Darryl's case now. Those problems could cause the case to get tossed out of court on the technicality that he didn't say enough of the right issues and he said too much of the wrong issues in his complaint. So what could have been a thriving retaliation case is now a more questionable case that may or may not be worthwhile depending on many other facts and circumstances.

In addition to the errors above, Darryl missed an opportunity. He did not complain in writing. It's best to make a written complaint using relevant facts. Darryl missed an opportunity. Verbal complaints allow the employer to dispute what he claims he said in his complaint, but he is still allowed to testify to his own recollection, however, a written complaint would end any speculation about what Darryl said.

Unfortunately, the problems Darryl faces in this example are not unique to racial discrimination. All such cases involve complaints and so any case could have the same problems as Darryl faces unless followed through properly.

Gender Discrimination

Gender discrimination occurs when actions or policies limit advancement due to gender, pregnancy, child bearing capacity, sterilization, fertility or related medical conditions. Examples include interview questions that focus on whether you are married or pregnant or plan to have a family. Some company policies such as classifying a job as "male" or "female"; paying different wages based on gender; or having separate paths for promotions or occupations based on gender.

Sexual Harassment

Sexual harassment, seen as a form of gender discrimination, is defined as being a recipient of unwelcome conduct of a sexual nature that negatively affects the work environment or leads to job-related consequences for the recipient of the harassment. It could amount to just cause for dismissal on the basis that it is conduct that is destructive to the employment relationship. A factor which significantly influences a court in deciding whether sexual harassment amounts to just cause for dismissal is whether the employer has a clear policy or procedure on sexual harassment which is enforced in the workplace on a daily basis. Was the employee told and understand that sexual harassment was completely unacceptable within the workplace.

Sexual harassment may occur when:

- Someone says or does things to you of a sexual nature which you do not welcome. This includes behavior that a person should know you do not expect, want or welcome including sexual comments, jokes, pictures and/or physical contact such as brushing up against you.

- A person having authority or power over you (manager, supervisor, etc.) makes sexual suggestions or demands that you do not want or welcome.

- A person having authority or power denies you something important, such as a promotion or review, punishes you or threatens to do something to you for refusing a request of a sexual or non-platonic nature.

A particularly tough battle occurs when you complain about sexual harassment and end up quitting your job. In such a situation, the company's conclusion might be that you did not properly go through the complaint process about sexual harassment before quitting and therefore you can't sue over the employer's failure to stop the harassment. For example: a woman who quit due to ongoing sexual harassment did not properly complete the complaint process. She quit her job too soon and therefore she loses her case in court.

Here is an example:

Paula, a full-time employee, complained that her immediate supervisor sexually harassed her by using a pornographic statuette as the basis for making offensive comments about her. The supervisor in reference to this statue said in front of other employees and Paula that: "Women are only good for two things: secretarial work and house work." On other occasions and in front of other employees, the supervisor would make numerous comments of a sexual nature about Paula's sex life. Furthermore, she argued that the supervisor's permission and encouragement to male employees to post posters of naked women in the workplace also constituted sexual harassment. The result is that the statuette and the posters in combination with the comments constituted sexual harassment.

In order to win a claim for sexual harassment, your evidence needs to show a pattern of behavior and that you have not been participating in it yourself. Therefore, if your work environment regularly shares raunchy jokes and you have willingly contributed to the discussions, then you would have a very difficult case as your participation can be seen as consent.

Age Discrimination

Age discrimination affects workers at both ends of the age spectrum. However, it is very difficult to prove in a court.

Age discrimination most commonly impacts people over the age of 50 as they are generally at the higher end of the wage scale, closer to taking their pension and require higher health benefits. What they don't realize is that studies have shown that a 50+ employee is less expensive to hire and train, has lower absences and turnover rates, is more flexible with their schedules, costs less in damage or theft liabilities, and is more efficient and more productive than younger workers are.

One example in which age discrimination:

Richard, a 69-year-old salesman, was the best in the organization and there were no complaints at any time about his performance. He was terminated on the basis of "a lack of potential in the area serviced by him", however, the first time this issue was ever raised was in the letter of termination. His position was not declared redundant but rather was filled by a younger person. Richard was awarded damages for lost wages and for hurt feelings and self-respect.

Age discrimination can happen to young employees as well. Most often, employers tend to discriminate against young people during the hiring process as they may fear the stereotype that young people are not reliable, party too hard, won't want to work long hours and won't be dedicated to being with an employer for a long period. Some other examples of age discrimination based on youth occurs when someone makes a "joking" statement directed at the young employee like "is this bring your kid to work day?".

While some younger employees say they've had their age held against them, older workers still bear the brunt of discrimination.

Duty to Accommodate/Disabilities

Employers have a duty to make reasonable accommodate disabled employees up to the point of "undue hardship." Undue hardship consists of several factors: financial cost, health & safety requirements and outside sources of funding. (Some states have more factors.)

Accommodating a worker means providing assistance or making changes in the job or workplace that will enable the worker to do the job. For example, an employer might lower the height of a desktop to accommodate a worker in a wheelchair; provide TDD telephone equipment for a worker whose hearing is impaired; or provide a quiet, distraction-free workspace for a worker with attention deficit disorder.

There are various disabilities that are protected from discrimination: mental, physical (mobility, blindness, deaf, etc.), disease (AIDS, Cancer, etc.), obesity, depression, color blindness, speech impediment, fear of flying, panic attacks and addiction.

Alcohol and drug pose special problems under the ADA. Employees who use (or have used) alcohol or drugs may have a disability under the law. However, an employer can require these employees to meet the same work standards -- including not drinking or using drugs on the job -- as employees who do not have a disability. Here are some guidelines to follow when dealing with these complicated issues:

- **Alcoholism.** Alcoholism is a disability covered by the ADA. This means that an employer cannot fire or discipline a worker simply for being an alcoholic. However, an employer can fire or discipline an alcoholic worker for failing to meet work-related performance and behavior standards imposed on all employees -- even if the worker fails to meet these standards because of alcohol abuse.

- **Illegal drug use.** The ADA does not protect employees who currently use or are addicted to illegal drugs. These workers do not have a disability within the meaning of the law and therefore don't have the right to be free from discrimination or to receive a reasonable accommodation. However, the ADA does cover workers who are no longer using drugs and have successfully completed (or are currently participating in) a supervised drug rehabilitation program.

- **Use of legal drugs.** If an employee is taking prescription medication or over-the-counter drugs to treat a disability, you may have to accommodate that employee's use of drugs and the side effects that the drugs have on the employee. However, you do not have to accommodate legal drug use if you cannot find a reasonable accommodation.

An employer is not required to make any accommodations if s/he is not aware of the need. Don't assume that they know about your disability or how to accommodate it.

Examples:

Source: www.csun.edu

Disability	Possible Access	Possible Solutions
Blind & vision Impaired (include not only those who are totally blind, but also those with limited vision)	• Path of travel • Displays of information • Controls with written directions • Elevators operating buttons • Completion of written forms	• "Talking" computers, calculators • Labeling in Braille • Respond to questions orally • Air radio announcements • Avoid clutter in passageways • Use writing, drawing, optical aids (e.g. magnifiers)
Deaf & Hearing Impaired (including not only those persons who are totally deaf, but also those with limited hearing)	Information obtained through: 1. Telephones 2. Warning devices(e.g., fire alarms, public address systems) 3. Equipment operating noises	• Use of amplification devices • Installations of TDD • Publication of written announcements • Allow mail-in-procedures to be used • Policy accommodating lip readers • Use visual cues for signage
Psychological Disabilities	Difficulty understanding: 1. Signs 2. Controls 3. Operating instructions	• Willingness of someone to assist and/or answer questions and provide directions

	4. Directions	
Difficulty with Upper Body Movement (including not only those persons who have limited use of arms, shoulder; persons who use wheelchairs or crutches; people of short stature; those who cannot perform certain hand movements, or have difficulty controlling movement)	Difficulty operating (or locating or reaching) certain hardware: 1. Hand controls on doors 2. Toilet room fixtures 3. Water fountains 4. Telephones 5. Vending machines 6. Light fixtures	• Relocating a program or service to accessible area • Use of adaptive equipment or modification of present hardware

Mobility Impairments (including those persons having difficulties, stamina limitations, as well as those who use wheelchairs and crutches	• No grasp bars. handrails, other supports
	 • No designated parking spaces for disabled people
	 • Distance from parking, public transportation stops
	 • Route of travel
	  1. Curbs, walks, unleveled surfaces
	  2. Carpeting, Textured title supports
	 • Entrances and doors
	 • Restrooms, phones, water fountains
	 • Location of controls, general hardware
		• Replace existing hardware, equipment
		 • Make necessary structural changes to eliminate barriers;
		 1. Install ramps
		 2. Widen doorways

National Origin/Ethnicity

Discrimination towards people of any ethnicity should never be tolerated. While most people are familiar with more blatant forms of racial discrimination such as not promoting people who are visible minorities, there are also more subtle forms. Employers cannot ask where you were born; however, they are allowed to ask if you are authorized to work in U.S. While the latter question can be asked for perfectly legitimate reasons, it can also be used to find out your citizenship.

Another form of discrimination occurs if an employer implements speaking English only rules in the workplace. There are times when it may be a business necessity (i.e. dealing with customers); however, an employer cannot enforce such a rule when you are on a meal or coffee break.

Example:
Bassam, who was born in Syria, applies for a position as a security guard with ABC Co., which provides security services at government office buildings. ABC requires Bassam to undergo a background investigation before he is hired. What are the legal implications?

ABC may require Bassam to undergo the same pre-employment security checks that apply to other applicants for the same position. As with its other employment practices, ABC may not perform background investigations or other screening procedures in a discriminatory manner.

Religion

Some religions have practices and rituals that need to be attended to during the work shift. Employers need to accommodate these activities as long as it does not impose any undue burden on the business activities such as altering work schedules or relaxing dress codes. However, there are times when it may be necessary for safety reasons to side with the employer (i.e., in construction jobs that require the use of a hard hat).

Religious discrimination complaints most commonly arise when employees lose their jobs after they refuse — for religious reasons — to work on certain days. This scenario represents the highest number of religious discrimination cases. However, it is important to recognize that the court will look at the effect of a particular rule, rather than its intent. If a rule has a discriminatory effect, the employer must take reasonable steps to accommodate, unless accommodation would create undue hardship. The responsibility of showing undue hardship falls to the employer. But it is the employee's responsibility to make the employer aware of his/her religious needs so that the employer has ample opportunity to accommodate.

For example, if an employee cannot work on Sunday due to his/ her sincerely held religious beliefs and requests Sunday off as his or her Sabbath, an employer has an affirmative obligation to accommodate the employee's sincerely held religious beliefs as long as it does not cause an undue hardship on the business. If the employer can get a person who is willing to work in the employee's place on Sunday, and the business can operate, the employer must accommodate the employee's sincerely held religious beliefs. For example, an employer found a reasonable accommodation for an employee's religious observance of Jewish holy days by excusing his attendance for a conference and allowing him to send his deputy director.

In another example, three of the 10 Muslim employees in ABC's 30-person accounting department approach their supervisor and ask that they be allowed to use a conference room in an adjacent building for prayer. Until making the request, those employees prayed at their work stations.

ABC would need to work with the employees to find an appropriate accommodation that meets their religious needs without causing an undue hardship for ABC. Whether a reasonable accommodation would impose undue hardship and therefore not be required depends on the particulars of the business and the requested accommodation. When the room is needed for business purposes, ABC can deny its use for personal religious purposes. However, allowing the employees to use the conference room for prayers likely would not impose an undue hardship on ABC in many other circumstances. Similarly, prayer often can be performed during breaks, so that providing sufficient time during work hours for prayer would not result in an undue hardship. If going to another building for prayer takes longer than the allotted break periods, the employees still can be accommodated if the nature of the accounting department's work makes flexible scheduling feasible. ABC can require employees to make up any work time missed for religious observance. In evaluating undue hardship, ABC should consider only whether it can accommodate the three employees who made the request. If ABC can accommodate three employees, it should do so. Because individual religious practices vary among members of the same religion, ABC should not deny the requested accommodation based on speculation that the other Muslim employees may seek the same accommodation. If other employees subsequently request the same accommodation and granting it to all of the requesters would cause undue hardship, ABC can make an appropriate adjustment at that time. For example, if accommodating five employees would not cause an undue hardship but accommodating six would impose such hardship, the sixth request could be denied. Like employees of other religions, Muslim employees may need accommodations such as time off for religious holidays or exceptions to dress and grooming codes.

Workplace Bullying or Mobbing

Bullying is usually seen as acts or verbal comments that could 'mentally' hurt or isolate a person in the workplace. Sometimes, bullying can involve negative physical contact as well. Bullying usually involves repeated incidents or a pattern of behavior that is intended to intimidate, offend, degrade or humiliate a particular person or group of people. It has also been described as the assertion of power through aggression.

Mobbing is an extreme form of workplace bullying that devastates the lives of its target. It refers to a social interaction, through which one individual is attacked by a group of individuals on almost a daily basis and for periods of many months, forcing the person into an almost helpless position. Some of the worst cases of mobbing go on for long periods of time and can actually continue for many years causing severe, sometimes irreparable psychological, emotional and physical health damage. In the worst cases this abuse has lead to suicide and even incidents of workplace violence. Not infrequently, mobbing can spell the end of the target's career, marriage, health, and livelihood. From a study of circumstances surrounding suicides in Sweden, it was estimated that about twelve percent of people who take their own lives have recently been mobbed at work. As many as one in six people in the American workplace are directly impacted by workplace mobbing/bullying.

While the US has discrimination laws, they protect only a specifically defined group of categories - race, gender, disability, religion, age, national origin, sexual orientation, and others. But even those groups are subjected to harassment without recourse if the workplace harassment or trauma is not obviously directed toward their protected characteristics. Therefore, workplace bullying is legal in the US.

Currently 13 states have workplace anti-bullying legislation pending. Many global corporations who maintain head offices in the US have anti-bullying policies where required, but usually instill no such policies in the US. Ironically, in addition to the emotional toll, studies indicate costs to US businesses due to bullying are estimated to be over $300 billion per year -- considerably more per capita than countries that have workplace anti-bullying laws.

Examples include:

- Spreading malicious rumors, gossip, or innuendo that is not true.
- Excluding or isolating someone socially.
- Intimidating a person.
- Undermining or deliberately impeding a person's work.
- Physically abusing or threatening abuse.
- Removing areas of responsibilities without cause.
- Constantly changing work guidelines.
- Establishing impossible deadlines that will set up the individual to fail.
- Withholding necessary information or purposefully giving the wrong information.
- Making jokes that are 'obviously offensive' by spoken word or e-mail.
- Intruding on a person's privacy by pestering, spying or stalking.

- Assigning unreasonable duties or workloads which are unfavorable to one person (in a way that creates unnecessary pressure).

- Underworked - creating a feeling of uselessness.

- Yelling or using profanity.

- Criticizing a person persistently or constantly.

- Belittling a person's opinions.

- Unwarranted (or undeserved) punishment.

- Blocking applications for training, leave or promotion.

- Tampering with a person's personal belongings or work equipment.

There is a "fine line" between strong management and bullying. Comments that are objective and are intended to provide constructive feedback are not usually considered bullying, but rather are intended to assist the employee with their work.

People who are the targets of bullying may experience a range of effects. These reactions include:

- Shock.

- Anger.

- Feelings of frustration and/or helplessness.

- Increased sense of vulnerability.

- Loss of confidence.

- Physical symptoms such as inability to sleep or loss of appetite.

- Psychosomatic symptoms such as stomach pains or headaches.

- Panic or anxiety, especially about going to work.

- Family tension and stress.

- Inability to concentrate.

- Low morale and productivity.

If you feel that you are being bullied, discriminated against, victimized or subjected to any form of harassment:

- Firmly tell the person that his/her behavior is not acceptable and request that they stop. You may ask a supervisor to be with you when you approach the person.
- Keep a factual journal or diary of daily events. Record:
    - ✓ The date, time and what happened in as much detail as possible
    - ✓ The names of witnesses.

✓ The outcome of the event.

Remember, it is not just the character of the incidents, but the number, frequency, and especially the pattern that can reveal the bullying or harassment.

- Keep copies of any letters, memos, e-mails, faxes, etc., received from the person.
- Report the harassment to the person listed in your workplace policy, your supervisor, or an HR manager. If your concerns are minimized, report to the next level of management.
- Do not retaliate! You may end up looking like the instigator. This may cause confusion and inconsistencies for the people responsible for evaluating and responding to your situation.

How to Tell You are Being Terminated

Most people are completely blindsided when they are terminated. But termination is not a process that happens overnight. It takes some time to get the paperwork ready and coordinate the parties that need to know (i.e. HR, IT, Security, etc.). Here are some typical signs that you may be marked for termination other than the obvious like losing a major account or screwing up a major project.

Has Your Area of Control Been Reduced? Any reorganization in which you no longer have the full level of control as before is a sign that you're getting moved out. If your manager tells you he's reassigning some of your responsibilities to another employee to lighten your heavy load, don't fall for it. It's just a diplomatic way for your manager to say he no longer believes you can do the job.

Have You Been Left Out of Key Meetings and Decisions? If you are respected and accomplished, you're asked for your opinion. So when you're suddenly no longer asked to weigh in on key issues, especially that affect your area or that you have been engaged in before, it can signify that your coworkers don't see you as strategic, your subordinates have lost confidence in you or you've become an barrier to getting things done and they'd sooner move ahead without you.

Are You Being Treated Like a Telemarketer Calling During the Dinner Hour When You Try to Get Buy-In? Not being able to get approval for your plans, individual projects or budget can indicate that your peers or management no longer support you. It shows you're not in tune with your colleagues or your company's needs. Or that your secret successor has been chosen. You can't be effective or successful without buy-in.

Do You Have to Constantly Fight to Get Anything Done? If colleagues are always arguing with you in meetings and they either don't listen to or rebuff your ideas, it indicates that your objectives are not the company's objectives or that you are being set up to fail.

Do You Find That Your Top Priorities No Longer Match Up With Your Manager's?
This is a clear indication that you and your manager are drifting apart and, unless you get back in alignment with him/her, s/he may decide to let you go. Similarly, if you find your lines of communication with your boss are vanishing—or worse, s/he assigns you to report to someone else—it means you no longer matter in his/her strategy. If you were, s/he'd devote a portion of his/her valuable time to you.

Does Your Supervisor Minimize Your Accomplishments? If you're doing back flips and your peers are saying they didn't notice or refuse to recognize, that's pretty bleak. It shows a lack of respect and that your colleagues don't see what you're doing as worthwhile or they sense that you will not be in the fold too long.

Does Your Boss Ask You to Work On "Special Projects"? Special projects are a euphemism for busy work. When you're assigned to special projects only, it means the boss has lost so much confidence in your ability to lead that s/he's trying to get you off the high-profile projects you had been working on until s/he can find a replacement for you. For example, if you are asked to work on a special project that involved investigating opportunities for a new product line in Eastern Europe but the company has no plans for expansion into Eastern Europe any time soon, and you weren't given a staff or a travel budget. This is a sure sign that you are in line to be thanked for coming out and let go.

Did You See a Confidential Search Ad That Describes Your Job to a Tee? You see (or worse a friend notices) a job posted on an online website that describes your job exactly in a company that sounds suspiciously like yours.

Are People Avoiding You At All Costs? Eye-contact is difficult to make with someone if you know his or her head is on the chopping block. Small talk is just as tough. It's best just to avoid that person altogether. So if people are no longer doing that fun "stop 'n' chat" in the hall or the coffee room empties or suddenly quiets down to an awkward silence when you enter, then guess what?…you may just be a marked man or woman for termination.

Are You Being Given Impossible Jobs With No Chance Of Success? This one is underhanded; which is why it's so popular. You are being set up for failure. The company needs a legitimate reason to give you the boot, especially if you've done everything right and are the key to your team. Enter the impossible project. If you've been given a thankless task, at least be thankful for the obvious tip-off that you're about to get the boot.

Are Your Responsibilities Redefined So That You Have Less Responsibility Than the Boss' Kid? Being "streamlined" of your responsibilities is a sure-fire sign that there's something unpleasant on the way. After all, you don't fire someone who's got a ton of important work to do, with loads of people underneath him/her. So, be mindful if you are given a new job title with less work, less budget, less people (or no people) and yet you have a hard time finding anything of any real value to do all day. Not long after this, you may be out.

Has Your Office, Cubicle or Working Space Recently Been Downsized? When employees are in the firing line, it's a lot easier to move them around and downsize their environment without worrying about their morale. If you are reading this in your new 6ft by 6ft cubicle with no lights on a 5 year old PC with a 200MB hard drive and dot matrix printer to match, you're not exactly a valued employee any more.

Do People Whisper More or Does the Conversation Change as You Approach? If you're marked for termination, you'll be the last one to know about it. And being the mature responsible people that they are, your co-workers will be quite happy to whisper about your impending doom in a corner of break room while sipping their coffees. Until you show up, when suddenly the conversation will change abruptly to something really original...like the weather.

Have You Recently Been Asked to Take Some Time Off? As we know, companies in North America are not prone to encouraging vacation time (compared to Europe, where they get tons of time off). If you are encouraged to take vacation but it is not to use up your annual allotment before end of the fiscal year before you lose it or for a genuine reward for a huge project you've just finished, then you are in trouble. When the boss tells you to take a break, they're more than likely telling you that they'd rather not have you in the office.

Are You Noticing Paper Trails Between Yourself and Your Superiors? Suddenly, you now notice everything is happening via emails instead of casual conversations. There's a reason for that. HR requires written/printed evidence of everything if there's to be a firing. A paper trail is necessary to determine that your manager did everything by the book, and to record every single one of your screw-ups. So, if you've gone from getting a few emails per week, to a daily deluge of paper and a full inbox, these are warning signs that you're being watched very closely.

Have You Recently Been Promoted to a Position of Less Responsibility? If the company promotes you into a newly created role, with less responsibility and no direct reports, then you may be faced with position elimination. It's hard to fire someone. It's easy to eliminate a position. You can get rid of anyone, even protected classes (older folks, pregnant women etc) if you simply eliminate a position. If you were formerly "Manager of Client Services" and are now "Director In Charge Of Special Project Development" (and there have never been any special projects), you may as well collect your personal effects from your cubicle now.

What To Do If You Are Targeted For Termination.

Here are some things to do that are essential to survive this process whether termination occurs or not.

Document, Document, Document!

Be sure to collect (hard and soft copies) of all documents (emails, memos, status reports, etc.) that confirms that you have done your work and have completed it on time. Ensure that you are not collecting documents that you are not authorized to have in your possession as this will backfire in any future claim. It shows an employee in a light of acting in bad faith and with dishonorable intentions and is therefore highly cautioned against. The reason for gathering hard copies is in case you are terminated and your network access is immediately removed as in the vast majority of cases. As well, network activity is monitored so you don't want them to see that you are emailing confidential company information to an external source even if it is yourself.

Create a Job Journal

Keep a log or journal of all pertinent events such as dates, times, locations and participants of activities that you have completed successfully. Don't bother tracking other people's issues as it will look that you have spent your time targeting other people. When you need to defend yourself, pointing the finger at others is not an effective or respectable strategy.

Create a Narrative of Events.

Include items such as:

- When you started work.
- How you performed early on.
- When your employment took a turn for the worse.
- To what do you attribute that turn.
- Basis as to why you attribute it to that cause.
- Significant events to date following that turn.
- Relevant comments made and by whom to whom.

Remember to make notes on a same-day basis at home. Do not make notes at work because that may either tip people off that you are preparing for legal action or co-workers may be disturbed thinking that you are writing about them.

Create a List of Witnesses

It is easier to make a list of potential witnesses while you are still employed. Make sure you list names, addresses and telephone numbers and any unsolicited relevant comments that they may have made.

Network

If you feel strongly that you are targeted for termination, then start looking for a new job now. Don't wait until you are fired as it is easier to find a job when you are still employed. This way, when interviewing for other job opportunities, you don't have to give a reason as to why you are no longer employed.

Do Your Job

Although you may be under a great deal of stress with the prospect of losing your job, keep doing it at the best performance level you can. Don't make it easy for your employer to fire you. This practice will not only make it difficult for an employer to terminate you, it will keep your good reputation, dignity and self respect intact by staying professional throughout this ordeal. Look at it as an exercise that is well worth the effort in the long run for your career growth especially when your work environment is in a state of flux. Learning to cope with stress in the workplace is one of the best career builders in today's economic environment.

Mend Fences

Make sure that your relationships with your co-workers are positive and they still see you as a team player. You don't want to give them reason to provide unfavorable information about you to your employer. Plus you will need good references in case you proceed with legal action. Always try to think about how your actions might affect things for you and others beyond the immediate moment.

Be Mindful of Upcoming Dates

Sometimes, companies will schedule terminations prior to an important date (i.e. the start of a new fiscal year, before a shareholder's meeting, prior to scheduled bonuses, etc.). Be aware of these types of dates and be prepared for them. As well, over the past decade, many corporations have an unwritten policy about which days of the week to let people go. The most popular days are Tuesdays and Wednesdays so if your supervisor schedules a last minute meeting on those days with little description of the topic and you can't find him/her all day to inquire, be prepared. Few companies fire people on Fridays anymore as studies have proven that anger and retaliation (i.e. going "postal") occurs most often when people are terminated on Fridays.

Avoid Traps

Managers are looking for a key excuse to terminate so don't make it easy for them. Therefore, don't be late, don't violate company rules, don't take long lunches, don't make mistakes on the job, don't make personal phone calls, don't have long chats with co-workers, etc. Focus on your work, be professional and don't give in to the pressure of their scrutiny.

Maintain Your Focus

Don't disengage because of the stress or the feeling that you have no options. Make sure that you are fully effective in your job and perform like nothing is wrong. Don't withdraw from discussions. Don't act like you are about to be fired because instead of getting people's support, you will end up with your co-workers distancing themselves from you so that they are associated with a "marked" man/woman.

Do Not Confront Your Boss

One of the worst things you can do is ask your boss if s/he is going to fire you. You are just reminding him/her that s/he can. It will put your supervisor in a defensive position. It will also show him/her that you are already mentally prepared to go which is advantageous to him.

Do Not Be Self Destructive

Do not file complaints or stress-related claims that have no written concrete evidence as it will make you look foolish. You don't want to look desperate or dramatic. If you feel that you want to proceed with this, you may want to consult a lawyer first.

Do Not Go On Vacation

Don't demand to have a vacation suddenly to avoid the situation at work. More terminations are planned while employees are on vacation because it gives management and HR opportunities to hold all the meetings they want about you. As well, it gives them the opportunity to sift through your desk and computer files to find an excuse to terminate you. Obviously, if you had booked a legitimate vacation prior to this situation, don't cancel it.

Do Not Just Quit

Some people feel so much stress that they quit. While tempting, don't do it until you get an objective opinion such as consulting a lawyer. You could be sacrificing income and benefits and any severance owed to you. You could also screw up a good case. Commonly, many people are paranoid and totally misread signals and never realize that they were not targeted for termination after all.

Do Not Make Illegal Media Recordings

It is illegal to make secret media recordings with your boss. If you wish to record a conversation, you must notify him/her prior to turning on the recorder. If you record them without prior consent, you will jeopardize your case (the tape is not admissible anyway), you will provide them grounds for dismissal, or you will permanently damage your reputation and/or relationships in the office.

Do Not Access Information Without Authority

When people feel that they are targeted for termination, they feel that it is within their right to find out what the plans are. In that regard, they sometimes access other people's files, go through papers on their boss's desk, go through drawers not belonging to them or try to access computer files that they are not authorized to read. These acts are all grounds for dismissal and will torpedo your case.

Collecting Your Evidence

Regardless of how righteous you are in your case, the evidence that you produce will be paramount to your success. Here are some key tips on collecting this evidence.

Building Your Case

To build a winning case, the onus is on you to gather as much truthful and relevant evidence, written and oral, as you can. After all, if you go to court, the burden of proof will be on your shoulders as you will have to prove that the employer willing engaged in misconduct in regard to your termination. Even if you don't end up in court, you need to support a case that a judge or arbitrator could find credible in order for your employer to consider settling the claim in your favor.

Organizing Your Documents

Collect and put in chronological order all of the documents that you can find concerning your employment every pay stub, every email, every review. Try, within your company's rules, to get copies of:

- Performance evaluations.
- Disciplinary warnings or reprimands.
- Letters of thanks or praise (from managers, customers, or co-workers).
- Internal memos.
- Company bulletins.
- Attendance record.
- Any document stating the reason for your dismissal.
- Handbooks, manuals, or other documents describing work rules, policies, and procedures.
- Pension benefits and retirement plan information.
- Documents related to your unemployment compensation claim.
- Copies of work assignments including special projects.
- Job description.
- Awards, accolades and/or accomplishments.
- Volunteer and/or charity participation through the company.
- Organizational charts, diagrams, floor plans, etc.

Do not take documents or access information to which you have no right and are not entitled. If you are a union member, ask your union to assist in acquiring documents that are otherwise difficult to obtain, but to which you are legally entitled.

Identifying Your Witnesses

If you think co-workers or others observed your unfair treatment, make a list of their names, home addresses, email addresses and home telephone numbers, along with a summary of what you expect them to say - good or bad. The "bad" or unfriendly witnesses are especially important to know about so that your lawyer can evaluate the damage they might do to your case. You don't want any surprises.

Ask friendly witnesses to give you a written statement of anything they saw or heard in person regarding your situation as soon as you decide to take action against your employer. Memories fade over time. Make sure the witnesses state only the facts of which they are personally aware and give specific examples of what they have seen themselves or what they were told directly. General statements such as, "Everyone knew that the manager was out to get her," are not helpful to your case. Get statements that specify the "who", "what", "when", and "where" of the biased behavior such as your manager's berating you or interfering with your ability to perform. If possible, have the written statement signed in front of a Notary Public.

Keep in mind that you shouldn't count on witnesses in your company that won't put their observations in writing. Many employees will be fearful of reprisals from the employer if they side with you. So don't assume that just because everyone tells you that they agree with you that they will testify on your behalf.

The most useful witness statements are fact-focused and objective. They should be detailed enough so that whoever reads them - the court, an attorney, or a mediator - will see the "big picture".

If you know of employees who were mistreated in the same way you were, ask them for statements about the way they were treated. If your supervisor, for example, made insulting and demeaning remarks to you and other workers, get statements from the other co-workers that quote or paraphrase the remarks, give the dates on which they were made, and name any others who were present.

Common Mistakes Employers Make

You might assume that even the biggest employers should be well-versed on how to deal with employee issues. But that is not the case. Most companies, regardless of the size, have been found to be sloppy in the way that they manage the rights of their employees. Be aware of these mistakes and ensure that you are not negatively impacted by them.

1. You warned them about the harassment but they didn't do anything about it.

   It is your employer's legal and moral obligation to take effective, direct and corrective action designed to put an immediate stop to the harassment as soon as it is reported. When they do not follow through, they open themselves to a wrongful dismissal lawsuit.

2. After you reported the harassment, they would not let the issue rest.

   Some companies overreact to charges of harassment. In that regard, they may call you into countless meetings to tell your story repeatedly. You end up getting frustrated, angry, intimidated and/or humiliated which makes your employer cynical and try to dissect your story. At this point, you will usually want to be left alone after filing the complaint. Often these post-complaint sessions become as harassing as the initial cause for the complaint.

3. They would not tell you what you did wrong.

   In reaction to increasing privacy concerns, some employers try to protect the identity of complainants against an employee. In doing so, they tend to not provide you with enough information to understand what you did wrong. Therefore, you cannot fix the performance problems effectively as the issues are not clarified.

4. They wouldn't follow up on the information you gave them.

   Sometimes, if an employer needs an investigation to lead to a particular outcome for their own sake, they tend to neglect to follow up on leads that do not result in their favor. This act shows disinterest in truly resolving the issue and disrespect to the complainants. This also has the potential to expose their vulnerability to a lawsuit if this development ever became publicly known.

5. Your supervisor constantly criticized you.

   When an employment relationship begins to deteriorate, the weaknesses in your performance become the target. This is reinforced through constant criticism and negativity either publicly and privately towards you. The employer is sending a strong subliminal message that you are no longer welcome. It is clear that the employer is invested in driving you to quit by trying to deflate and discourage your confidence about future prospects at the company.

6. Your supervisor was never consistent or clear about what was expected of you.

Whenever it becomes apparent that your supervisor refuses to give you objectives or targets, it shows that they are not investing in your future at the company. It implies that s/he has a different agenda.

7. They were setting you up to fail.

   Employees know when something is going on. You are given vague instructions, if any, and you are quickly condemned for doing it incorrectly. The level of support for you vs. your co-workers is blatantly lower. Your supervisor's response to your mistakes is very different compared to the ones towards your co-workers. Your supervisor sets unattainable performance goals. A jury will look at whether the goals set for you were realistic and achievable and whether any changes were justified.

8. They terminate you without hearing your version of events.

   Sometimes, employees are terminated prior to being able to provide their side of the story. If they refuse to hear you out, then that only reinforces the suspicion that the employer was only interested in using the complaint as an excuse for termination rather than assessing the situation objectively.

9. They terminated you without following their own procedures.

   One of the biggest concerns for an employee whether they are being treated fairly in regard to discipline. If your employer fails to follow its typical personnel practices in dealing with you, it may establish that you were targeted by the use of differential treatment. That failure of consistent treatment among all employs may serve favorably for your case.

10. They fired you just after you received a positive performance review.

    When this occurs, it undermines your employer's allegation that you are a poor performer. Performance reviews are to be taken seriously by employers. A jury would hold them to whatever was documented during those reviews. That is why it is key that you do not sign any review that you do not agree with, ever.

Bonus Mistake: HR was not involved during your time as an employee.

Sometimes the first time you meet your HR representative is when you are being terminated. (Sometimes not even then.) Employers should have their HR department engaged with the employees from the hiring interviews, to any disciplinary meetings, to regular employee policy updates, to the termination meeting to ensure that everything is being handled legally and professionally. If employees are unaware of changes in employee policies and procedures, how can they truly be held accountable to them? If managers are not trained properly to conduct themselves in a legal and professional manner and according to company policy, then it opens the door for discrimination and harassment lawsuits.

Disciplinary Action

Most terminations are preceded with some sort of disciplinary action whether in the form of verbal warnings or written ones. Receiving a warning or a reprimand is one of the most difficult and stressful experiences on the job. That is why many people unknowingly sabotage themselves when responding under such duress. If you know how to handle the disciplinary action (whether justified or not), you may avoid layoff terminations. You can survive employee discipline if you respond positively and constructively. Always be prepared and professional in any response you may give.

Even if you feel that the discipline is unwarranted, do not argue, raise your voice or be belligerent with your supervisor about the fairness or wisdom of the warning. If the matter becomes a struggle, your boss will interpret your actions as argumentative and that you are unwilling to be a team player. By behaving in an professional manner, you may be surprised how easily you can diffuse the potentially volatile situation. That may seem hard to do when you are feeling under such great stress but tune your perspective to focus on a "bigger picture" that includes a confident understanding of your rights.

After the discussion, think about the content of the discussion without being defensive or blinded by ego. For example, if you are being disciplined for lateness, don't think that because Jimmy does it, it is okay for you. Regardless of how any other employee conducts him/herself, you should always make the best effort to follow the established rules. You don't want to make it easy for management to select you in times of layoffs or cost cutting.

If your actions that are being disciplined are not your fault, for example, if a health problem is the reason for your tardiness, then it is still your responsibility to supply your employer with sufficient information to show it is a health issue and not a behavioral issue. Depending on the severity of your situation, you may require to provide a note from your doctor to verify your condition.

If a verbal warning is more subjective (i.e. bad attitude), it may be harder to manage. You may need to show your supervisor respect regardless of your actual feeling towards him/her. Keep disrespectful opinions to yourself when speaking to your supervisor or coworkers. Make sure you apply this to both verbal and nonverbal communication. Nothing shows disrespect more than a scowl, a heavy sigh, and crossed arms, rolling eyes or stares. Body language is the hardest thing to be aware of but one of the most noticeable forms of communication and belligerence.

Be very careful who you trust at the workplace. Many people feel comfortable to bad-mouth their boss or teammate to their "work" friends. Be mindful of what you are saying and to whom. Sometimes another co-worker overhears this conversation and will report it to someone else. Other times your friend may accidentally discuss what you said in another conversation. If your negative comments spread, there will be no way to resolve that issue if you are disciplined about it. Even if you aren't formally disciplined, you will create negative relationships that you may depend on. Like the old adage, you can't unring a bell.

If you have been unable to resolve the verbal warning(s), your supervisory may move it to the next disciplinary level by issuing you a written warning. Be sure to keep calm and professional. If you become enraged and challenge your supervisor for escalating the issue, you will easily convince your supervisor that you cannot work with him/her. Take time to reflect before you act.

If you need clarification, then ask for it. In many cases, a representative from Human Resources will be present. If you need further information (e.g. when the offense occurred, what specifically you have allegedly done, etc.), this is the perfect opportunity to ask questions as long as you are calm and thoughtful. If you have concrete information that can be beneficial to your defense, you can ask permission to say something in your defense. If the warning is based on misinformation, then you need to say so at this opportunity. Otherwise, silence can be interpreted as consent and a later response can be seen as suspicious by your supervisor.

Don't be pressured to sign any disciplinary documents that you don't agree with. You are not obligated to sign such documents unless you are in agreement. Once you sign, you will have great difficulty retracting that signature at a later date without diminishing your credibility.

PIPs

Performance Improvement Plans are often referred to as a "PIP". Usually, the plan outlines that your performance must improve within a certain period of time, otherwise, you will be terminated.

The goals and time frame must be realistic and objective. If you feel that the PIP is too subjective, then it is possible that you may negotiate clearer standards. If there are particular obstacles that prevent you from meeting certain PIP goals, you should outline them so that they are taken into account and not held against you. However, do not needlessly nitpick on the issues especially if it is reasonably clear. You will just reinforce the already prevailing negative perception of you.

Once the action on the PIP begins, you will probably meet with your supervisor on a regular basis to discuss your progress. Let your supervisor drive this process. Do not badger him to have a meeting if he misses one unless your PIP states that you have the responsibility to take the lead. Allow the issues between you and your supervisor to take lower priority if he chooses. Do not remind him that you are a problem employee by continually asking him "how am I doing?". And do not ask him if he is going to fire you. While it may be tempting because you are nervous of the next step, you will only be remind him that he can fire you. Resist the urge to put yourself in the line of fire. Remain calm and poised.

Suspensions and Involuntary Leaves

Most employers will terminate an employee for repeated negative behavior. However, some employers will address the issue with a suspension as a final warning. When you return, you must strictly comply with the required standards otherwise you are guaranteed to be terminated. What if you return and your behavior is exemplary? How long does the suspension remain an issue on your record? There are no laws as to a statute of limitation on the suspension.

An involuntary leave is more severe. It is usually applied when an employee is charged with serious misconduct. If an employee is charged with sexual harassment, suspected of theft or embezzlement or abusive conduct of peers are usually sent home with pay while the investigation proceeds. At any time, the leave can be converted to an unpaid leave if the employee is not cooperative with the investigation, abandons employment or is deemed to be guilty.

If this is your situation, remember that you are still an employee of the company. If you wish to keep your job, then you must be mindful to follow whatever directions your employer has given you even if it is a call-in requirement during certain times of the day or participate in the investigation. If you do not do so, then it can be interpreted as job abandonment and will merit termination. If you have a good wrongful termination case brewing, you do not want to torpedo it by engaging in conduct that justifies termination.

Handling a Termination Meeting

If you are summoned to a termination meeting, you must attend it otherwise you will immediately be terminated for insubordination. Usually, there will be more than one person attending this meeting (usually someone from HR) along with your supervisor. This additional person acts as a witness that all procedures where properly handled. Therefore, be mindful of your behavior. Do not lose control or curse out your manager. **Be professional at all times**.

Keep It Together!

You have a right to ask the reason if one is not provided. Keep your head clear because you will need to recall the reason given (if any). If the reason stated can later be proven as false, then this will help your case as it may infer that the real reason was an unlawful one. Sometimes if you wait long enough for the firing manager to drone on, s/he may give inconsistent reasons which will also help your case. Try traditional Japanese negotiation tactics by using silence. The Japanese believe that silence is golden and the mouth is the root of all trouble. You should use silence and let their mouth fill in the gaps. You may find it very useful as an information gathering tool as well as a protection tactic.

If you realize in the meeting that the reason is overtly false, you have the right to point that out in a professional and respectful manner. For example, if they provide a reason that you were over budget when telling you why you are being fired, you can simply say that "I have a copy of my reconciliation that shows I was not over budget. May I provide you with that document?". If this case were to escalate to the courtroom or arbitration, your act of offering the employer proof of your innocence would show a jury that you gave the employer an opportunity to correct the error. If the supervisor refuses to do so, a jury may see you as a victim to an uncaring and overtly arrogant employer.

Do Not Admit Or Agree to Any Wrongdoing!

If an employer offers you the option of resigning instead of being terminated, don't commit to an answer in this meeting. Request a day or two to think it over and decide what is best for you. Remember to keep your communications short, impersonal and professional.

The employer may provide you with an agreement to accept a severance package. Do not sign it there. If an employer is coercing you to sign it there, do not surrender. You have the legal right to request some time (a week minimum) to return a signed severance agreement. This will give you the opportunity to consult a lawyer and determine if the package offered is fair. If you require more than a week, feel free to contact the HR department near the week's end for an extension. Most will oblige for a few days extension as they do not want to be seen as making you sign a document under duress.

At this meeting, the employer may provide you with a check for your remaining pay, earned vacation pay and severance. You may take this check but do not cash it until you have decided that you don't want to pursue legal action. Cashing the check is a sign of consent and will impact you negatively if you plan to go forward with legal action. Consult a lawyer or check with Service Canada as to what minimums you are entitled to in order to ensure that you are being treated equitably. As well, you may be able to negotiate for more money or benefits (i.e. extension of health benefits, career placement service, training, etc.)

Security Escort

Don't be offended if you are escorted to your desk after the meeting to clean it out as well as escorted to the exit. This is legal and the company is trying to ensure that little disruption to the work environment occurs. Employees will be impacted enough by seeing you walk out with your belongings. The company will not want further morale reductions as a result from your play-by-play to your co-workers. It is in your best interest to say as little as possible.

Do Not File an Internal Grievance Immediately

Many employers offer employees the opportunity to file internal grievances. It is not recommended to file one immediately as it may hinder your legal action. When you tell your story, you want to do it as few times as possible. The more you tell it, the more it varies. This will create holes in your story that the employer's lawyer will walk right through. Plus, there is no guarantee that the employer's representative will be as diligent in recording your details. You want to ensure that your side of events is consistent with all people you discuss it with. As this person will be a witness for the employer if your case goes to trial so it may compromise your position if your story varies from person to person. If you are not consistent, the court will side with the employer's version of events.

Do Not Write to Upper Management

Some people feel that if upper management knew what was going on that they would rectify the issue. So they write a letter to the President of the company to explain the situation. Usually these letters are rambling, embellished or angry in tone. Letters like this will only hinder your situation and reinforce the contention that you deserved to be terminated.

Should I Sign a Release?

What's important to note is that employers are under no legal obligation to offer a severance (or termination) package. However, at termination, the employer may offer the employee one as a result of company policy. The severance package outlines the payments, benefits or other offers such as a letter of reference the employer is prepared to provide upon termination. Severance packages are often made conditional upon the signing of a release by the employee. The release is a contract which spells out the payments and any other elements to be provided by the employer in exchange for a release by the employee of any further legal claims he may have against the employer with respect to his employment and/or termination of employment. Put simply, if an employee signs the release, s/he is accepting the employer's offer in full and final satisfaction of any claims s/he may have and will therefore not be able to pursue any further legal action against the employer.

The release typically contains the type of jargon familiar to lawyers but not to most employees confronted with the document. Given what is a stake, employees are always advised to refrain from signing a release until they have obtained legal advice. The value of the offer is dependent upon a whole host of factors such the damages for wrongful dismissal the employee can obtain as well as the other remedies s/he can pursue. Few employees have the legal expertise to make a proper assessment of the offer contained in a release on his/her own. Pressure to sign on the spot should immediately raise suspicions that the employer is seeking to have the employee agree to an unfair deal and should be resisted if you can. You have the right to simply say "no, I will exercise and reserve my right to legal counsel before signing any document of a legally binding nature".

However, the law does not require your employer to offer you a severance package and the law does not require you to sign it. Your employer cannot force you to sign a severance package. However, an employer can legally refuse to pay you any severance funds if you refuse to sign a release of claims. If presented with a release and you are unsure about it, politely request some time to deal with the shock of termination. It is never a good policy to sign anything under duress.

Post – Termination Emotions

One of the biggest stresses after being terminated is to react emotionally. It is hard not to take things personally but, in all honesty, it is really just a business transaction. Don't fall into the trap of building your self-worth around your job because it is not healthy nor is it accurate. Be mindful of and try to avoid these emotional pitfalls:

1. **Seeing Yourself as a Failure in Life**. You are not a failure in any way. Even if you were fired for just cause, it means that this job or company was not a good fit for you. Many people blame themselves by saying:

   a. I should have seen this coming.
   b. I've let my family down.
   c. If I played my cards right, I would still have my job.
   d. Being fired doesn't happen to people like me.
   e. I should have worked harder.
   f. I should have kissed my boss's butt.

   While these feelings are normal and understandable, they are fruitless and a waste of your energy. A bad attitude, especially when it comes to your self-image, is the last thing that you need right now. Pick a set period of time to mourn and beat yourself up (say about a day or two tops) if you must and then put it behind you forever and move forward. You will be unable to negotiate an equitable severance package or land a new job with this attitude. And you will stress your friends and family further.

   Remember, almost everyone has been fired including: Mark Cuban, J.K. Rowling, Michael Bloomberg, Oprah Winfrey, Walt Disney, Thomas Edison, Jerry Seinfeld, and the list goes on. And everyone will tell you that it was the best thing that ever happened to them. Getting hired doesn't teach you anything. Getting fired does.

2. **Focusing on Revenge.** Many people feel hurt and maligned when they are fired. In order to regain their self respect, they feel the urge to exact revenge to "teach them a lesson". This is the wrong approach and is guaranteed to jeopardize any chance of a successful negotiation. It can only backfire on you by damaging your reputation, derailing your career, and, in some cases, bring criminal charges against you. It will also justify why you were

selected for termination. There is nothing truer than the old adage that "the best revenge is living well". Focus on the positive emotions and actions and you will be a lot happier.

3. **Being Engulfed By Behavior That Prevents You From Moving Forward.**

   a) **Isolation**: After termination, many people tend to isolate themselves from others. Start to network right away either through job search groups or outplacement services or taking a training course. Isolation is most likely to cause you to sink into depression and despair which will cause you to make irrational decisions, if any. It is this fear that many companies enact a policy not to fire employees on a Friday. The terminated employee tends to isolate themselves over the weekend which has led to the ex-employee returning to the office on Monday in a violent rage or committing suicide.

   b) **Denial**: Don't be in denial about your current state whether it be financial, emotional, or occupational. You are better off to know where you stand right away so that you can make educated decisions. Talk to someone you trust to get another perspective of your situation – good and bad. You will be surprised how well you will benefit from it.

   c) **Paralysis**: The shock of being terminated can put some people in a mental and emotional state of paralysis preventing them from moving forward. Establish an action plan and task list (e.g. update resume by the 12th, post resume to job sites on the 13th, call headhunters during the week of the 20th, etc.) Establish daily, weekly and monthly objectives. If you are not that organized or not a self-starter, ask friends for help. Make sure your goals are small and keep a record of the ones you have accomplished.

   Don't feel overwhelmed by what you need to do but be sure to feel fulfilled by what you have done.

4. **Don't Focus On Your Fears, Focus On Your Future.** Picture yourself successful, happy and in your ideal job. By visualizing your potential, you will work towards achieving it. If you continue to focus on your fears ("I can't do that", "I won't have any money", "I'll never get another job", etc.), you increase the chances of it coming true. It is like driving a car – wherever you look is where your car will veer. Don't see yourself as a victim but as a victor.

5. **Don't Be A Whiner.** The fact is that millions of people have worse problems than you do. Sure you lost your job but countless people suffer terminal diseases, threats of physical violence, and lack of food or shelter to name but a few. Would you want to trade places with them? I would think not. They have dire problems, you do not. Put everything in perspective and be grateful that you aren't worse off.

Tips For Managing Your Emotions

Here are some things that you should do in order to keep your negative emotions from blinding you from moving forward.

1) Involve your life partner in your severance decisions. They are your best support system and can give you an objective perspective on the situation. Keep communicating with them. Be sure to understand what they are feeling as well as they are apt to share some of your emotions with you. Don't assume that they can be the tower of strength for you at all times.

2) Get plenty of exercise and plenty of sleep. Whether it is walking or going to the gym, exercise is proven to relieve stress and make you feel good about yourself. Sufficient sleep will provide the rest you need to be clear headed and make effective decisions.

3) Do not increase your diet for sweets, caffeine or tobacco. Not only are these items not healthy for you, they are known to create agitation and stress even though at the time of consumption it feels like the opposite.

4) Do not spend too much time with your former co-workers. It can be depressing hearing about how life goes on without you at the company plus it may make them feel uncomfortable, at least at the beginning. Plus it may put them in an awkward spot if their employer knows about it since the employer may assume that you are trying to get confidential information from them.

5) Do not sit at home all day. Try to get a regular activity that will take you out of your house like meeting friends for lunch or seeing headhunters or going to the library to research careers. If you sit at home watching television all day, you will erode your self-worth and derail your focus. Even if there are days that you choose to stay home, don't spend the entire day in your pajamas. Put your clothes on first thing in the morning and complete your normal grooming process as you would if you were on a regular schedule.

6) Find a friend that you can lean on to be a sounding board. But remember; don't dwell on the same thing every time you chat with him/her. If you are not making progress in your discussions, you will lose that trusted supporter.

7) Join a networking or support group. There are lots of them in this economic climate. Search online for local Meetup groups to network with people searching for new employment opportunities. There are also online groups on LinkedIn.com. They may even lead you to a connection to a new job.

Severance Pay

If possible, review your employee contract/offer letter/ employee handbook first and then seek legal advice on the offer before you sign. If the offer is reasonable, it will likely be there after you have obtained advice. The more pressure that is put on you by the employer to sign, the greater is the likelihood that the offer is unreasonable. It is understood that seeing a lawyer is as much fun as going to see a dentist. However, in both cases they are necessary "evils".

(If you are an "at-will" employee and/or there is no stipulation in your contract/handbook to severance or notice, then you may be out of luck unless you can prove discrimination.)

Many people assume that any severance package received is reasonable, and that their employer would never try to take advantage of them. Such theories ignore the fact that the employer is running a business and it makes business sense to pay less rather than more.

Review the package to ensure that it includes:

1. Severance Pay as outlined in the employer's policy and/or a signed employment contract.

2. Back Pay – you may be owed back pay if, for some reason, you are owed wages from past work, overtime, bonuses or commissions. Generally, a two-year statute of limitations applies to the recovery of back pay. In the case of willful violations, a three-year statute of limitations applies.

3. Vacation/Holiday Pay – if your employer's policy is to provide you with earned vacation pay that you have not used, then you should receive such in your severance package. For example, if your employer's policy is to pay all employees for two weeks of vacation per calendar year and you are fired in early July without using any vacation for that year, then you should be entitled to one week's salary.

4. Benefits – depending on your company's policy, you may be eligible for retention of your health, dental and life insurance benefits for the term of your severance pay. Therefore, if your severance package provides three weeks salary then you may expect your benefits to be extended three weeks beyond your termination date. Other benefits that may be included are employee discounts, continuation of training programs and acquisition of company property such as company car, computer or smartphone.

Keep in mind that when you sign a severance package, you are signing away your right to litigate if you realize that you may have been treated unfairly later on. If you receive severance, it should not affect your eligibility for unemployment benefits.

Given the serious consequences which may result, individuals who are presented with a severance package and are asked to sign a release, are strongly advised to obtain independent legal advice before signing such an agreement. Only by doing so, you will be able to evaluate the employer's offer in relation to your rights and determine the best course of action including whether you might be better off bringing a civil action against the employer for wrongful dismissal. Besides, once you sign, you can't retract it unless you can prove without a doubt that you signed under duress or if the amount signed for was less than your rights afforded by your state's employment standards legislation. If you are not sure, seeking an employment lawyer's advice before you sign rather than after you sign is always in your best interest. And ensure that the lawyer you consult with is an experienced labor lawyer, not your cousin the real estate lawyer. It can make all the difference between a good settlement and the best settlement.

What Happens if the Business files for Bankruptcy?

If your employer has filed for bankruptcy, it means that the business can no longer pay its debts to its creditors, and the company has asked the court to help it either plan a repayment schedule ("Chapter 11" bankruptcy) or sell off all its property and use the money to pay off the creditors ("Chapter 7" bankruptcy). If the company owes you wages, you will be considered a creditor of the bankrupt company.

Creditors are prioritized in the order in which they will be paid off. Creditors who are owed wages, salaries, or commissions are given a high priority for repayment. Each individual employee of a bankrupt business is given a priority of up to $10,000 of the wages they earned up to 180 days before the company filed for bankruptcy. If you are owed more, then the rest goes into the pile for unsecured non-high priority creditors. However, secured creditors (banks, commercial lenders, etc.) are first in line, and therefore ahead of employees for repayment. Because secured creditors are generally owed the most money (usually for property and equipment loans), there often is not much money left over to give to the employees, who are in line after them. Sometimes, employees along with other creditors that are in line behind secured creditors will only receive a penny for every dollar they are actually owed.

In order to protect your rights as a creditor of your bankrupt employer, you should find out the county where the company filed the bankruptcy petition and call the clerk of the United States Bankruptcy Court for that county. (Look in the U.S. Government listings online.) Ask the clerk how to submit a "Proof of Claim" form, which is the form that the court will use to determine how much money to give you. Be sure to ask about the deadline by which you have to file your claim for wages. When completing the Proof of Claim form, you should include any supporting documentation, such as copies of contracts or timesheets.

As a creditor of the employer, you can participate in the bankruptcy court proceedings. Once you file the Proof of Claim form, the company's bankruptcy trustee should provide you with information and updates concerning the on-going bankruptcy proceedings.

If you filed a wage claim with the Labor Commissioner or already won a judgment, the bankruptcy law automatically freezes all legal actions against the employer as soon as they file for bankruptcy. If you have an unpaid wage award, or feel you are owed wages but have not yet begun wage claim proceedings, you should submit it as a claim to the bankruptcy court on a Proof of Claim form, not to the Labor Commissioner.

The "Consolidated Omnibus Budget Reconciliation Act" (COBRA) allow employees to continue their health insurance when they lose their job. However, in the case of bankruptcy, the type of bankruptcy determines whether an employee will be entitled to continued coverage. An employee may be able to exercise their COBRA rights in the case of a Chapter 11 bankruptcy, since the company will stay in business and may continue to provide a group plan for the employees it retains. In a Chapter 7 liquidation, where the entire company dissolves all group plans made available to employees, there will be no opportunity for workers to exercise their COBRA rights. The Health Insurance Portability and Accountability Act (HIPAA) will guarantee, under certain circumstances, that you could then convert the group plan into individual coverage. You will need to contact your insurance provider to clarify what you are entitled to and the process to obtain it.

What Happens if a Business is Sold?

Generally, an employee should not lose any rights or money because the business was sold.

If the employee had a contract with the seller, then the contract should still apply with the buyer. However, if you are an at-will employee (i.e. either you or the employer may end the working relationship at any time with no prior notice for any reason or no reason at all), you will likely have the same at-will relationship with the buyer. If the employee keeps his/her job, the employee is usually entitled (but not guaranteed) to maintain his/her seniority with respect to all the benefits and rights that were enjoyed before the business was sold.

Resignation

If you resign, are you entitled to severance pay or other entitlements or have you forfeited those as well as eligibility to Unemployment Insurance? In certain cases, especially when you are feel you have no choice, you may be entitled to payment and be eligible for Employment Insurance. The following are some common situations.

"I Quit!!"

What if I quit as a result of the workplace stress? If I yell "I quit" and walk out, is it binding?

Consider the following situation. Jimmy worked for a small company for last 8 yrs. Last year he was given a promotion to Supervisor. Since the promotion, Jimmy was overwhelmed because he felt undermined, bullied, and belittled by other staff members. After speaking to his manager regarding his concerns, Jimmy was disappointed at the cold response. He was told to deal with it.

A few months later, nothing had changed and Jimmy's stress was building due to the lack of co-operation from other employees and management. One day, Jimmy and one of his co-workers got into a verbal confrontation when the co-worker refused to take on the work Jimmy had assigned him. Jimmy expressed his frustration to his manager and discussed his concern on the constant stress and conflict.

During a follow-up meeting between Jimmy, his manager and the co-worker involved, Jimmy was told again that everyone needs to make an effort with get along. Suddenly, the co-worker ranted with abusive language at Jimmy for no reason. With no support from the manager forthcoming, Jimmy walked out of the meeting.

Jimmy felt threatened and intimidated as well as depressed and stressed. In an emotional state, Jimmy hastily sent his manager a text message asking him to release me from his contract thinking that he could claim benefits until he could find another job.

The following day Jimmy re-evaluated the situation in a calmer state of mind and called his manager and told him that he was going to see a doctor as this is out of character for him. The manager agreed.

After an examination, the doctor provided Jimmy with a sick note for one week due to work stress. Upon Jimmy returning home, there was a letter from his employer.
The letter confirmed the text message Jimmy sent to his manager and that they had accepted his resignation. Jimmy didn't respond to the letter. The next day, he received another letter saying that he was required to call in sick or forward sick notes to them as they had terminated his employment, and if this was not what he had intended and he wish to remain employed by them, then could he contact them to discuss the situation as soon as possible.

Is Jimmy's resignation via text binding? Since the second letter to him by his company states that they would like to discuss it further, it clearly wasn't seen as binding if Jimmy did not want it to be so. Jimmy has a good case to keep his job since he immediately pursued medical attention. However, if Jimmy does not respond to the letters in a timely manner, it will be considered binding.

Check your employment contract or handbook. Make sure you understand what their view and requirements of the protocol around resignation. Most will require a resignation to be in writing so if you yell "I quit!" in the heat of stress, it would not necessarily be binding. Some employers will allow a short grace period for employees who quit in a heat of passion but may not necessarily state it.

An indication from the employee that she is not satisfied with her employment and is looking for other work, or is thinking of quitting does not necessarily constitute a resignation. Similarly, a situation where an employee resigns, but soon thereafter withdraws the resignation will not likely constitute a resignation. This may be so even if an employer subsequently accepts the resignation.

This bigger issue here is if you do quit, whether you mean to or not, will you be eligible for benefits?

In order to receive unemployment you have to be unemployed through no fault of your own. If you quit your job you are voluntarily unemployed, and thus it is your own fault that you are unemployed, and therefore you are ineligible to receive unemployment benefits. However, there are some situations in which you may be found eligible for benefits. These situations are rare, and the resulting decision can seem somewhat arbitrary - and often only decided by going through the appeal process.

What are the situations where you may be able to get benefits if you quit your job?

1. If you quit your job because of a hostile working environment.

2. If you quit your job because your job reduces your hours and/or your pay significantly.

3. If you quit your job because of medical conditions or disability.

Every state is different, and each situation will be handled on a case-by-case basis. If you apply for unemployment after you just quit your job, you will almost certainly have your application denied.

After your claim is denied, you will have to file an unemployment appeal. If you have to file an appeal, this means that you employer is challenging your right to collect unemployment because you quit your job. After all, it may have legal implications on them too. You will have to have a special unemployment appeal hearing. Making an unemployment eligibility appeal can be a long, complicated process. It could take months for your appeal to be processed, and it could take months to get an actual eligibility hearing.

When you have quit your job and then apply for unemployment it is recommended that you apply for unemployment in person at your local unemployment office so that you can explain your situation fully to the unemployment counselor. When you file online or by phone it will be much more difficult -- the online system doesn't have a place for you to explain why you quit your job.

You will not be able to get unemployment if you quit your job:

1. If you quit your job because you don't like your job anymore.

2. If you quit your job because you don't like your boss.

3. If you quit your job because your work hours aren't convenient.

4. If you quit your job because you didn't get that raise you were expecting.

5. If you quit your job because you decide you want more money.

6. If you quit your job because you no longer wanted to do the commute.

If you are unhappy at your job, or need to make more money, or don't like your boss - don't quit your job just look for a new job. Make sure that you have found a new job before you quit your current job. It is much easier to find a job, when you already have a job. Also, it has been reported that many employers are not even considering job candidates that are currently unemployed.

Also, keep in mind how you plan to explain your departure from this employer during interviews with potential new employers. An abrupt resignation and its reasons will most likely reflect unfavorably on you for future opportunities.

Given the very serious consequences which can happen to an individual who resigns his or her employment, both in respect of entitlement to notice and unemployment benefits, those contemplating resignation are strongly urged to seek legal counsel before pursuing such action.

Constructive Discharge

As discussed earlier in this book, employees should also remember that resignations arising from pressure to accept different terms or leave the company could simply be a camouflaged termination. So when is quitting a constructive discharge/dismissal?

- If you were fired even if you had already quit.

- If your employer does something that makes it virtually impossible for you to continue on the job.

- If your employer changed some working conditions that led to your quitting (i.e. can't be something that bothered you since the start of your employment). This change must be recent enough that a cause and effect relationship or direct correlation can be established between the change(s) and quitting.

- A change in working conditions is so demeaning or upsetting or unfair. Note: If you are thin-skinned or the change(s) is done for business reasons in which most employees have accepted the change(s) without complaint, then you won't have a strong case.

Courts generally assess the intolerability of working conditions by considering whether a reasonable person in the employee's position would have felt pressured to resign. For example, an Illinois court ruled that an employee was constructively discharged because she had been forced to endure hostile environment sexual harassment. After the employee complained about harassment by her employer, a judge, her supervisor suggested that she either resign or transfer to another judge who clearly implied he would make her life miserable. In addition, when she was involuntarily transferred back to work to her harasser, he was cold and uncommunicative and indicated that he would continue to express his sexual interest in her.

In another case, a supervisor with the FDIC was stripped of his job title and supervisory responsibilities, reassigned to a less prestigious position of case manager, and told that he could either accept the reassignment, retire, or be involuntarily separated. The Court of Appeals held that a long-term supervisory employee would reasonably find these actions intolerable.

However, not all cases are successful for the employee. In another case, a claim for constructive discharge was denied by the court of a university professor who was put on paid administrative leave and given a temporary, though unsatisfying, reassignment, pending investigation of sexual harassment allegations against him. He then resigned rather than wait for the outcome of the university's due process hearing procedures. The Court held that however distasteful his temporary assignment was, his working conditions had not become so intolerable that a reasonable employee in his position would have felt compelled to resign.

It is important to note that most courts consider the employee's feelings or beliefs to be irrelevant. Many courts have stated that an employee's claims of depression and feelings of isolation, attributed to working conditions, are not enough evidence that a reasonable person would have viewed such working conditions as intolerable.

Employees with written contracts of employment are typically more successful in proving constructive discharge when their employers unilaterally change the nature of their jobs. For example, the Tennessee Supreme Court ruled that an employer breached an employment contract and constructively discharged its marketing director when it removed his job title and all of his work responsibilities specified in the contract. Similarly, the Nebraska Supreme Court found that an employee was constructively discharged when the employer unilaterally imposed additional duties that were not within the scope of the employee's contract.

In contrast, the Illinois Appellate Court ruled that a supermarket customer service manager who was demoted to cashier did not establish that she was constructively discharged. The employee did not have an explicit contract but the company did have an employee manual. However, these conditions were not in violation of the terms of an employment contract in such that the company's employee manual did not constitute a legal contract and that the employee was in fact an at-will employee.

If you feel that you are being constructively discharged, it is strongly recommended that you seek professional legal advice prior to resigning.

Termination Law

A number of expressions are commonly used to describe situations when employment is terminated. These include "let go," "discharged," "dismissed," "fired", "ousted", "cut" and "permanently laid off."

Recent studies have confirmed that the loss of a job is the fourth single most devastating event to an individual's emotional well being - just after death of a child, parent and divorce. The symptoms of depression which affect many who unexpectedly lose their employment - sleeplessness, anxiety, lack of appetite, indecision and irritability - closely resemble a person in mourning.

For many, the initial shock and humiliation quickly develops into a sense of abuse and outrage. The desire to strike back at your former employer, who so callously and foolishly destroyed your family's economic security, is to be expected and overwhelming.

Once the fog clears, many terminated employees question whether their former employer followed the law and did not infringe on the employee's rights. Here are some common areas that people question and how the law interprets them.

Job Role Discontinuance/Elimination

An employer should be allowed to make good faith re-organizations to grow with its business demands. What an employer is not allowed to do, however, is to pretend that the reason was job discontinuance or lack of work when really it was terminating a problem employee. If the employee can show that the real reason was the intent to cut him from the work force because he was a nuisance, then the complaint may be allowed.

For example, if an employee has a job function of "project manager" and the company decides to do away with this and create a position of "senior project manager", then there will be an examination of the real life job functions of the two positions to see if there is a real difference.

Several situations may indicate that a lack of work or job discontinuance is not dominant reason for a layoff including:

1. Where, shortly after an employee's termination, a replacement worker is hired to fill the employee's position and the duties performed by the replacement worker are substantially the same as those performed by the employee.

2. Where a decision to dismiss an employee comes right after a decision to re-organize the workplace, thus indicating that the reorganization was specially engineered so as to justify the employee's dismissal.

3. Where the employer first tells the employee that they have been dismissed for cause, and then later alleges it was because of a layoff.

4. Where the employee is replaced temporarily while he or she takes a leave of absence (or is otherwise re-assigned), and the employer later refuses to reinstate the employee claiming that there are no vacant positions.

5. Where the employee's old position becomes vacant and open for application within a reasonable time following the layoff but the employee is not offered the position.

In order to make a finding that the layoff resulted from a discontinuance of a function, the duties performed by the employee must no longer be performed in the workplace where he or she was employed. Where a set of activities is merely handed over in its entirety to another person, or the duty is simply given a new and different title so as to fit another job description, the discontinuance of a function test will not be met.

Where these responsibilities are subsequently contracted-out to individuals who engage in exactly the same work, on the same premises, with the same equipment, and pursuant to the same instructions, the Department of Labor deems this activity acceptable.

Common areas of termination law issues are:

Conflict of Interest

Conflict of interest is one of the most rapidly developing and complicated areas of just cause for dismissal. Seeking employment with another company or considering starting one's own business in competition with their employer will not amount to just cause for termination in most cases.

Whether an employer has just cause to terminate an employee in circumstances of a potential conflict of interest will depend upon the nature of the employment relationship, the details of the potential conflict and the circumstances surrounding the actions of the employee. Courts have increasingly recognized the very far reaching duties of management and senior level employees to avoid engaging in any conduct which could possibly amount to or be perceived as a potential conflict of interest.

A common example of conflict of interest occurs when an employee holds two jobs in the same industry. Then the employee's loyalty comes into question especially in the case where clients, new business leads or new products are confidential. Ideally, the employee manual should define conflict of interest usually under code of conduct.

Conduct Outside of Work

One of the most controversial grounds of just cause for termination involves the actions or activities of an employee outside of normal working hours. A court may conclude that such conduct could amount to just cause for termination if it occurs in the course of an event or activity that is somehow work related, is serious in nature and tends to reveal a less than honest or trustworthy character of the individual. For example, a judge held that a serious assault of a fellow employee with whom the individual was involved in a romantic relationship, outside of business hours, amounted to just cause for termination.

Unless there is some link or connection that is established between the misconduct in question and the individual's employment or employment relationship, conduct outside of working hours will not normally constitute just cause for termination.

Cause Discovered After Firing

It is a common misconception that an employer is not permitted to rely upon misconduct unknown to it at the time of termination as just cause for termination of the employment relationship. This is known in law as "after acquired cause" or "ex post facto justification for dismissal".

A common example of cause discovered after firing involves falsification of expense reports or theft of an employer's property. Such misconduct, if proven, could constitute just cause for dismissal, even though the employer was not aware of it at the time of termination.

Misstating Education, Qualifications, and Experience

Most court decisions involving misstatements or misleading information provided by employees at the hiring stage relate to the job candidate's education, qualifications and experience. An employee may be terminated for just cause as a result of misrepresentations made to the employer during pre-employment interviews and discussions.

The courts, in recent years, have emphasized the relationship of trust between an employer and an employee which begins at the point that the employee submits his or her resume to the employer, indirectly vouching for the accuracy of the information submitted to the employer. In many instances, it is difficult to draw the line between the typical "sales pitch" made by an employee in the course of job interviews verses misrepresentations (e.g. lying about working for IBM or earning an MBA, etc.) which may subsequently support a termination for just cause without notice and without compensation.

Not Providing Essential Information

In most cases, a person's failure to provide information to an employer during the hiring process will not amount to lying or falsifying information. This is due to the fact that courts historically have taken the position that an individual is not legally required to bring information to the attention of the employer where that information has not been requested.

In the case of senior management and executive employees, it is possible that a court may conclude that they have a duty to advise the employer of information which may affect their decision to hire the individual such as conflict of interest.

Damages for Injury to Reputation

The only recognized legal basis on which to award any damages for injury to reputation would be for loss of an opportunity to enhance one's reputation, which are limited to people such as actors and artists, where a very real benefit of their employment includes the opportunity to enhance their reputation and popularity within their profession.

In only the rarest situations will a wrongfully terminated employee have a valid claim for damages for defamation. Generally speaking, a written or verbal statement is defamatory if it harms the reputation of a person so as to lower him/her in the opinion of the community.

Spying on Employees Without Cause

In most large corporations, employees will be subject to various types of surveillance. Unlike surveillance conducted by law enforcement agencies, most forms of workplace surveillance do not require a search warrant or violate privacy laws. Since your choice of employment is voluntary, the law does not consider electronic monitoring in the workplace to infringe on constitutional guarantees of privacy. As a result, almost all communications and behavior on the job may be monitored through various surveillance systems with the flimsiest justification of cause.

Using surveillance cameras to monitor an employee at home, such as to determine if the employee is really sick or injured, is more risky for the employer. A court may allow an employer to monitor an employee at home if it is for a work-related reason. Stalking or recording an employee at home without good cause can lead to criminal charges for voyeurism. According to the National Institute of Standards and Technology, an employer can hire a detective to take pictures of an employee at home if it is for a valid reason such as a workman's compensation claim.

A reasonable expectation of privacy may apply to some work areas. State law may prohibit an employer from using surveillance cameras in private areas, such as bathrooms, changing rooms or employee break areas. The state of Connecticut, for example, prohibits employers from using monitoring systems in work locations designed to promote the employee's health or comfort. Federal law does not establish any of these restrictions.

What right do employers have to spy on their employees? Monitoring and surveillance are powerful tools against workplace theft. However, employers must have a reasonable apprehension of abuse by employees to justify their use. Employers have the right to install cameras in the workplace; however, that right is limited by the obligation to exercise it in good faith and fairness.

Reinstatement

There is no right to reinstatement. This is because both state and federal statutes do not provide for such a remedy in cases of termination.

Legal Action

Legal Advice

Are you wondering if you should speak to a lawyer? If you feel that your rights have been violated then you may want to go that route. Here are some tips that will assist you on your next step.

Hiring an Attorney

Should I hire my tax lawyer or the lawyer who handled my real estate transaction? No. You need a specialized employment and labor lawyer, especially one that has extensive experience working with employees. Some labor lawyers specialize on the employer's side of the disputes. If possible, you should lean towards a lawyer that focuses on the issues of the employee. And make sure that they do not have a conflict with the company that you are planning to sue. For example, if you work(ed) for XYZ Company and the lawyer works for XYZ on various labor issues, then there is a conflict of interest. In this case, a reputable lawyer will not take your case. Ask the lawyer *before* you present your case to him/her if there is a conflict.

How Do I Know if I Need an Attorney?

Firstly, just because you were fired or laid off does not mean you have a case. Assess your circumstances realistically and check what proof (documents, journal entries, witnesses) you have at your avail. What are you trying to get out of it? If you are doing this for pride, then this may not be justification for the stress and expense of this process.

Most lawyers will charge for an initial consultation so make sure that this investment is worth it. Plus, if you proceed, you will probably have to provide an initial retainer fee (average $1,500 – 3,000). And the fees can easily go above the retainer fee if the case goes to court.

Review one of the templates provided in this book to see if you can start the ball rolling. Remember, make sure that you are using the correct template or editing it appropriately otherwise, you may end up in a more difficult position with a simple typo or erroneous choice of words.

Legal representation is not a necessity unless you are destined to go to court. You may be better off not engaging an attorney in some cases especially at the beginning as a show of good faith. The following may be factors that can help you determine whether you should go directly to an experienced labor attorney.

1. **Understand What You Want.**

   If you have been terminated, you should think about what you are looking for out of these negotiations. Are you looking for retraining costs or a career coaching service to be added to your severance package? Are you looking for more money or extended benefits? Are you looking for revenge? If it is the latter, you should stop where you are and start the thinking process over once your emotions have subsided.

If you are still employed, what outcomes are you seeking that will rebuild the relationship with your employer? Are these reasonable for both you and your employer?

You can't effectively proceed on the following points until you complete this task. You want to ensure that whatever you do come up with, that it is business focused (not emotional or personal) and feasible for the employer. Now is not the time to "prove a point" or "show them". It is about finding a reasonable and workable solution so that everyone can move forward with dignity and respect.

2. Open Discussions With Your Employer.

Don't doubt the effectiveness of direct discussions about your termination/severance with your employer. An employer will most likely take a less defensive approach if you start talking to them directly versus immediately sending them a letter from a lawyer. Once you engage a lawyer, the employer will need to engage their lawyer which will cost them money. Plus it may become combative once lawyers are involved which leave less room for negotiation.

3. Your Knowledge of Employment Law In Your State.

If you are not knowledgeable in employment law (and unless you are a lawyer or have been through this before, you won't be), feel free to hire a lawyer to evaluate your case. S/he does not need to take anymore action than that. Don't just ask the lawyer if you have a good case; ask him/her if your employer has a good case against you. Make sure you reveal all the facts regardless of your indiscretions on the job. You will need an honest evaluation of what position you are actually in. Not being upfront about everything (even your misconduct) only ends up harming your case and costing you financially and emotionally.

4. Your Comfort Level With Negotiations.

If you are someone who is very uncomfortable with negotiations and how to make them work, then you may want to consider having an attorney by your side. S/he would be very experienced with these meetings and may bring a better resolution sooner.

5. Cost.

Lawyers, even for an initial consultation, are not cheap. Be sure that the outcome you are looking for is worth the cost. If you are looking for an attorney because you want revenge or a few extra dollars, then you may want to start negotiations yourself to begin with. You may want to hire a lawyer just to oversee or consult with you while you handle the direct employer communications.

How Do I Find The Right Lawyer?

If you know someone who has successfully sued his/her employer, then ask them for the attorney's name and phone number.

If you have another lawyer (real estate or will, etc.), then ask them for a referral to a labor lawyer. If s/he offers to take the case himself, be wary. You need someone who focuses on labor law. Ask them if they have handled similar cases and the outcome if those cases. If they have not handled several similar cases successfully, then they are not the lawyer you need. Tell them that you appreciate the offer but you simply need someone who specializes in employment and labor law. If possible, get a few names from your lawyer and ask him what order he recommends that you call them in.

You can also contact your local Bar association by searching for State Bar Association online.

Contact your state Legal Aid or Employment Insurance office to inquire about their recommendations.

Another recommendation for finding an appropriate lawyer is to go online to www.findlaw.com. You can search labor lawyers by jurisdiction and link to their website or profile.

When Should I See An Attorney?

Sooner rather than later! The time to see a lawyer is when you start to see your relationship with your employer deteriorating (if you are still employed). It doesn't mean that you will automatically sue. But you will have more opportunity to diffuse the situation through legal advice even if it means reconciling with your employer.

If you have just been terminated or served with a termination notice, then check out the termination pay regulations for your state. If it does not fall into these guidelines and you have tried to rectify the situation with your company to no avail, then contact a lawyer as soon as possible. Most states have strict time limitations in which you can contest a termination package.

What Happens on The Initial Consultation?

Just like interviewing for a job or someone to perform renovations to your home or hiring a babysitter, it is essential that you are finding the best person for your case. As well, you need to understand if this case is worth pursuing. The cost, the stress, the time, among many other variables are all factors in whether you should pursue legal action or just move on.

Different lawyers have different fees for the initial consultation. Some will charge a special initial consultation fee in order to evaluate your case. Some will provide a free consultation fee. Regardless of the fee, make sure that you are consulting with an experienced, successful labor lawyer who will be honest with you about the probabilities of your case.

Just as important, you should bring all documentation that you have with you that relates to your case/situation in anyway. Don't waste your initial consultation because you are ill prepared. The more info you can provide your lawyer, the easier it will be for your lawyer to assess your situation and less expensive for you.

What does the office look like? Is it professionally run and organized? Or is it disorganized and messy?

Is the lawyer confident in his/her field? Does s/he ask the right questions? Does s/he explain clearly? Does s/he outline options, benefits and consequences clearly? Does s/he discuss whether your case is worthwhile or is s/he promising big money?

Questions to Ask During This Session:

1. What are the fees?

2. Who will handle the case? If a partner will handle it, you should meet that partner. Or, if a junior lawyer is handling it, are you paying a senior lawyer's fees and how experienced is this junior? It may sound great to have a junior who charges a lower rate to take on all or part of your case, but keep in mind that some juniors require more time to do the same work as a senior. And at an hourly rate, this has the potential to cost more than a senior.

3. How often will contact be and through what method(s)?

4. Will you be able to discuss with them any actions prior to them proceeding?

5. Will you get copies of all letters and documents?

6. How realistic are my expectations?

7. What is the expected timeline(s) for my issue to conclude?

8. What further information/documentation is required from me for this to succeed?

9. What would be the next step?

Checklist of Info for Your Initial Meeting with Your Lawyer

It is advisable that you have all this typed out to hand to your lawyer to save time during your first meeting. (Time is money!) By providing all your information upfront, the lawyer will have a clearer picture of your current situation.

Your Personal Information:

Name:

_____

Address:

_____

_____

_____

Telephone

Home: _____

Cell: _____

Work: _____

Email:

_____

Date of Birth:

_____

Social Security Number:

_____

Current Employer Information:

Employer: _____

Employer's Address: _____
_____
_____

Employer's Telephone ____ _____

Number of Employees: _____

Date Hired: _____

Compensation:

Salary/Wage:_____

Bonus:_____

Awards:_____

Annual Vacation in weeks:_____

Title(s):

(Include every role you have had at this company) _____
_____

Level (Circle your current level):

Executive   Manager   Supervisor   Full-time Employee

Part-Time Employee   Contractor   Intern/Apprentice

Other: _____

Current Responsibilities: _____
_____
_____
_____

Supervisor: _____

HR Manager: _____

REASON FOR YOUR VISIT:

Terminated

Date of termination:_____

Date of notification:_____

Offered severance agreement

Deadline to sign:_____

Denied a promotion

Date I learned I would not be promoted:_____

Reasons given: _____

Harassment victim

Racial

Sexual

Other

Denied benefits

Date denial of benefits took place:_____

**Denied commission or bonus
or vacation pay**

Date denied:_____

Reasons given:_____

**Employer violated terms of
his own policies/handbook
or employment contract**

Violation: _____

Date violation occurred:_____

**Discrimination victim due to
my:**

Race   Gender   Age   Disability

Religion   Sexual Orientation   National origin/ancestry

Marital Status   Pregnancy   OSHA Claim   Illness/Injury

Other: _____

**Victim of retaliation because
I complained about/reported
employers illegal conduct**

Date of complaint/report:_____

Date of retaliation:_____

TERMS & CONDITIONS OF EMPLOYMENT

Union Member: Yes/No   Union Name:

Received employment letter when hired stating terms of employment. Yes/No (attach copy)

Company violated terms of this agreement as follows:

_____

_____

Received employee handbook when I was hired (copy attached) Yes/No

Company violated terms of this handbook as follows:

_____

_____

Company has specific policies that it goes by in making employment decisions but employees do not get a copy. I believe company violated terms of this handbook as follows:

_____

_____

Received periodic performance evaluations (copies attached). Yes/No

BASIS OF CLAIMS:

Treated unfairly. Yes/No   Description:

_____

_____

The following is my employer's explanation to me as to why I was treated as such:

_____

_____

The following is what I think is the REAL reason for this treatment:

_____

_____

I believe I was discriminated against. Evidence of this treatment:

_____

_____

I brought this discrimination to the attention of my employer:

      I reported discrimination of these dates: _____

      I reported discrimination to the following personnel: _____

      The following action was taken as a result of my complaint:

_____

_____

When I was terminated, I signed a resignation letter/waiver/release (copy attached)

Here are the circumstances in which I signed the document:

_____

_____

INJURIES OR DAMAGES

I suffered the following physical and/or emotional damage as a result of my employer's actions:

_____

_____

I sought medical and/or psychiatric attention as a result:

Doctor's name and address: _____

Telephone: _____

Diagnosis: _____

I have lost wages as a result of my employer's actions

Amount of wages lost to date: _____

I have suffered other financial losses as a direct result of my employer's actions.

Amount: $_____

Description of loss: _____

I have not received all of the direct payments I have earned and that are due to me from my employer.

Salary due:

Bonuses due:

Vacation pay:

Commissions:

Other (specify)

PREVIOUS LAWSUITS

I have filed complaints or sued an employer before (present or past employer)

Date of complaint/lawsuit_____

Reason for complaint/lawsuit_____

Result: _____

While you don't have to include everything listed above, you should try to include everything you can that does relate to your case or situation.

Costs

So, how much can it cost to go the lawyer route? Well, it depends on several factors:

Lawyers Fees

Hourly rates on average is $300 per hour. Contingency fees, where a lawyer doesn't charge you an hourly fee but takes their fee as a percentage of your winnings, are on average 33.3% plus expenses (court costs, photocopying, travel, long-distance calls, etc.). You will most likely be paying the hourly rate. Ideally, you should ensure that your lawyer is willing to reassess the situation after each communication with your employer. This way you can limit your costs depending on whether you want to continue to pursue the case any further.

Settlement

How willing are you or your company willing to settle? If not, then the case can drag on for a long time and increase costs.

How Effective Is The Counsel For The Employer?

If they are not particularly competent, they may be more willing to settle sooner which is advantageous to you.

Court

If you decide to have your case heard in court, there are filing fees, deposition costs, attorney's travel fees, etc.

Costs, of wrongful dismissal cases can escalate quickly, especially if you end up in court. Make sure it is worth it and that your lawyer is interested in providing the best arrangement for you, not him/her. The following is an example of a case that outlines the issue of cost and their risks when pursuing a case in court.

When an employer wins a case, they usually ask for the plaintiff (i.e. losing employee) to reimburse them for legal costs (not uncommon in any court case for the loser to pay the winner's legal fees). In this example, the judge notes that the employer's lawyers billed the employer close to $250,000 to defend the lawsuit. If the judge feels that the case brought by the employee was frivolous, the judge may grant the employer's request for total reimbursement. So not only did the employee not win his claim for damages, he is also responsible for paying both the employer's legal fees as well as his own. This result was far more costly to the employee than a private negotiation could have produced. If the employee cannot pay the employer's legal fees and needs to declare bankruptcy, the cost of not settling this case through negotiation is now considerable to both parties.

In the same example, after a review of the employer's request for reimbursement, the judge rules that some of the costs on the lawyer's bill were excessive, including 75 hours of legal research by three articling students at $70 per hour. The judge believes that the legal issues were basic and an experienced employment law firm should not have needed that much research done. In the end, the judge orders the plaintiff (the losing employee) to pay $37,000 (instead of $250,000) towards the employer's legal bill. Again, that would be on top of the money he had already paid his own lawyer. The employer has to pay the difference between the legal bill (around $250,000) and the $37,000 the employee was ordered to pay. So the lawsuit cost both the employer and employee a sizeable financial expense.

If the judge had decided that the employer was responsible for all the employer's legal expenses ($250,000) and the employee was suing for $230,000, then the lawsuit cost both parties far more than negotiating a settlement in private.

Litigating a wrongful dismissal case can be a costly, risky, and an economically unsound thing to do for both the employer and the employee. The only difference is that a large corporation can absorb the cost.

It is strongly recommended that you ensure that you have attempted all avenues to settle your complaint out of court before incurring the potentially high costs of the court system. You may end up settling for less money that you originally hoped, but your legal expenses may end up being less which may even out the financial outcome. However, be sure that you are not settling for less than what you are entitled to in the Employment Standards Act of your state or territory.

The Court Process

The court process is divided into two distinct categories: cases involving potential claims of $25,000 or less and those claims above $25,000. In regards to the former, there are different "simplified rules" that may expedite the process. For cases which exceed $25,000, the rules are more complicated and thus tend to draw out the process over a longer period of time. For example, a case in Toronto courts will take roughly 12 to 18 months to get to trial for larger claims. In addition to the time to get to trial, each party has a right to appeal which could easily take another 18 months. Therefore, it could take years to resolve your lawsuit if you are seeking a large settlement so be prepared.

Pre-Trial Discovery

Each case requires the opposing parties to produce all relevant documents. Then each party has the right to question the other party under oath to understand what the evidence will be to defend the position. Unlike the United States, where any person in the world may be deposed before trial, in Canada, one representative of the company is produced for pre-trial discovery.

After discoveries have been completed, the case is set for trial and assigned a court date for hearing.

Mediation

Typically mediation occurs at the early stages of a lawsuit when costs are much lower and the case will have lesser obstacles to settlement. The parties appoint an experienced lawyer or a retired judge to hear what is in dispute. The clients are encouraged to speak about why they feel they are right and also what other motivations have brought about the conflict. The mediator has no power to order anything. His/her influence is strictly persuasive. When entered into voluntarily, it has proven to be very successful.

One essential aspect has been that both parties have a desire to settle. In addition particularly in cases of wrongful dismissal, the company representative should be empowered to make decisions. Quite often the company may send someone as a figure head with no real decision making power or only up to a specific dollar figure.

In cases of mandatory mediation, both parties are dragged to the meeting as opposed to wanting to be there to settle. It is likely that it will not be as successful as the voluntary variety, but nonetheless will no doubt settle cases that would have required a trial otherwise.

Arbitration

This is an alternative to the court process. Sometimes the parties complete pre-trial discoveries and instead of going to trial, agree to use an arbitrator. The result is an agreement which is binding with no right of appeal. The advantages that drive the arbitration decision are usually the ability to litigate in privacy, the right to know who the decision maker will be, and a certainty of the date. The disadvantages are the costs involved. One party no doubt will lament the loss of appeal rights.

Negotiating a Package

Upon termination, employers usually anticipate that most employees will accept whatever package is given (provided it is within legal guidelines) to them. They tend to hope that the vulnerable state of the terminated employee will get them to agree to the first offer immediately. However, depending on the situation, there may be room for negotiation even if you do not have a legal case.

Step 1: Understand Your Losses

Call a local recruiter and tell them who you are, what you do, how much you make and how long it would take for your to get a similar job. They should tell you that it would take x months. Take that information to your employer and let them know that you cannot afford to be without income and benefits that long. Ask if the company is willing to help out.

You aren't threatening a lawsuit; you're appealing to the employer's fairness to assist you. Even if you do have a legal case, it is not a bad idea to use this as an initial tactic in order to get a better severance package in lieu of litigation.

You should also track what your benefit costs are (i.e. health, dental, life insurance) and what it will take to continue them while you are unemployed. Don't forget to include professional membership fees, training expenses, occupational certification costs, health memberships and business discounts that you were afforded as an employee. You may be able to recoup some of these losses during negotiation.

Take note of any other compensation that was due to you including bonuses, commissions, overtime pay, unused vacation and stock options. You want to ensure that you still receive what you earned or what you had been promised prior to termination. In addition, if you have been provided equipment or services such as a computer for your home, smartphone, home internet service, etc. document these items and source the costs if you were to pay for them yourself. Many companies allow some terminated employees to keep some of these items as part of their package.

You have a decent chance to open negotiation with your employer. If they are unwilling to cover you until you find another job, then feel free to counter propose. Just don't propose too low otherwise you will limit your lawyer's ability to negotiate if you go the litigation route. Further, don't propose an amount that is ridiculously high otherwise no one will take you seriously. A good rule of thumb here is, if your proposal denotes what is fair and reasonable, then your chances at succeeding with your negotiations will improve when you're at this stage.

Step 2: Evaluate the Contents of Your Package

In some cases, you can negotiate other aspects of the package aside from the financial aspect. Don't forget that severance can include extension of health benefits, extension of employee discounts, training allowance, career transition service, résumé service, outplacement services, computer equipment, company car purchase, etc. Be certain to use any of these items in your negotiation. For example, if your employer is offering a résumé service as part of your package and you already have a current effective résumé, then you may request to trade that benefit for an equitable training allowance.

Other items that may be negotiable: a letter of recommendation or ability to resign instead of termination to protect your employment record.

If you receive stock options, ensure that you understand how long they are valid for. While it is standard that you have the right to exercise the stock options until the end of your notice period, some employers insist that they become invalid at the date of termination. If the latter is the case, track the stock during your notice period. If there is a positive difference, then you may be entitled to that difference if the employer insisted that they expire on the date of termination.

If you were enrolled in a program that allowed you to purchase shares in the employer's company at a reduced rate through your payroll, find out what happens to those shares upon termination. Most companies will force you to sell them at the market rate shortly after your date of termination. If this is the case, be prepared for any possible capital gains taxes and include this added expense if you choose to renegotiate your package.

You may also be able to negotiate the pay out of your severance package if you were a long time employee of the company. If you have been with the company a long time and your severance payment equals 2 months' salary or more, many companies will pay you out as an employee on a regular pay period. Some people prefer to have a lump sum payment. Some things to consider in this case:

1. Make sure that the benefits extension lasts the full term of the original severance (e.g. if you are getting a lump sum payment for 3 months salary, your health insurance should still last 3 months past your termination).

2. It is possible that the lump sum option will be slightly less than the full term or you may be required to return some of the money if you find a job in less time than expected. Severance is meant to bridge some of the time until you secure another job.

3. Be mindful of your tax situation if your choose lump sum. If you choose a lump sum payment, you may increase your tax bracket for that year if you get another job quickly. The employer will only retain taxes at the level you were employed at and are not obligated to calculate your new rate.

For example, if you received a lump sum payment of three months' salary in July and you get a new job at your previous salary in August, you are increasing your annual salary by 2 months. If you are in a higher tax bracket, and you are being taxed for all your annual income at the lower tax bracket, you will get a nasty surprise in April from the IRS.

Another example would be if you are entitled to a termination package due to an employee of 20 years, then you may be entitled to as much as 20 weeks' severance pay. If you receive this lump sum in November or December, you just added 5 months of salary in a year that you already worked most of the year. Unless you are already at the highest tax bracket, your tax rate (and taxed owed in April) will skyrocket. If you had the option of spreading this payment out for 5 months, then you have a better chance of keeping more in your bank account as the payments will spread out over the next calendar year. Therefore, sometimes a long term payroll may be more beneficial for taxes if it extends into the next calendar year or put a portion of your lump sum into an IRA.

4. If you choose a lump sum payment, it will not shorten the time period in which you are eligible for unemployment insurance. If you get 3 months' salary in a lump sum payment, the government will still see 3 months' severance on your Record of Employment.

5. There may be a provision in your agreement that stipulates that if you get a job before the severance payments are completed, you will need to return a certain portion of the severance ("Clawback"). If you agree to it, it is legal.

Step 3: Understand What is Negotiable

The key to negotiation is to understand what motivates your employer to negotiate and what motivates you to stop negotiating.

Usually there are three common motivators that may open negotiations:

1. **Fear of negative publicity** – Some companies rely on having a positive image in the public. Therefore, if your company has a history of terminating a particular protected group (i.e. women, disabled, visible minority, etc.), you may be able to leverage this information.

2. **Fear of losing a lawsuit** – When terminations are conducted under "fishy" conditions, companies are more willing to open the door to negotiations to avoid a lawsuit. For example, if you had a record of positive performance evaluations and suddenly you are

terminated and replaced with a friend of your supervisor, then there may be something suspicious about your termination. As well, if proper procedure was not followed, then you have facts that should motivate your employer.

3. **Deadlines** – Sometimes terminations occur on a certain schedule (i.e. before a shareholder's meeting, prior to new fiscal year, etc.) to appease upper management. If this is the case, then you can motivate your employer by alluding that you don't think you can sign your current package by that time period.

Many times, you have motivators that will force you to accept an offer. Employers will try to reveal what these drivers are and exploit them. Be careful not to show your weaknesses.

1. **Fear of losing income** – Many people take the company's first severance offer out of their perceived desperation for the money. Sometimes two months' salary looks great in a lump sum when you have a stack of bills to pay and no knowledge of the current job market. However, if you have worked for the company for 8 years, this is unlikely to be a sufficient settlement. Take the necessary time to think about the offer and its complete implications and consult with a professional before settling.

2. **Fear of being seen negatively** – Too many people are worried about being seen as "greedy" or "not nice" if they demand more compensation. Firstly, you are fighting for what you deserve. Secondly, if you accept the first offer just to be likable, you will not be respected. Respect should be more important to you than being liked. After all, if "liking" meant anything to your employer, you would not be terminated to begin with. Thirdly, who cares what you perceive people think about you?

3. **Fear of retribution** – Don't be afraid that because you want to re-negotiate that the company will blackball you in the industry. This practice is illegal and they can be sued for large sums of money if they are proven to do so.

4. **Fear of the offer being rescinded** – Don't be afraid that the employer will rescind its offer if you don't accept it immediately. Especially if the offer isn't that great to begin with or only gives you a little above the required amount by law. Many employers will be eager to resolve this situation and if they take back the offer, this will only prolong it.

5. **Lack of knowledge of your legal rights** – Many employers assume that employees have limited knowledge of what is legal and equitable. Don't let them know this is your situation if this is the case. Tell them that you reserve your rights to consult with a lawyer and would need some time before you sign anything.

6. **Employer's hands are tied** – If you are part of a mass layoff, many employees think (or are told) that if they give you more, then they have to do that for everyone. This is malarkey and a common tactic used for severance negotiations by employers. All severance agreements are held to a confidentiality agreement that you will sign, therefore,

other employees will not be privy to your settlement. Remember, other employees are probably settling for a bigger severance package too. Besides, even if it were true that the employer would have to match your settlement to other terminated employees, then that is not your problem.

Therefore, it is essential that you are well prepared before opening negotiations. Be prepared to give up points where you see fit if it moves negotiations further. Don't think that you will get everything you want – it is a negotiation, not a robbery.

Bear in mind that this is a mutual game of pushing buttons so don't fall for some of the tactics from your employer such as threats, anger and condescending attitudes. The employers' negotiator is most likely very experienced at this process and thinks s/he knows how to rattle your cage. The goal for the both of you is to get a resolution that both of you can live with, so stay on track and don't allow yourself to get distracted or deterred from your goals.

Step Four: Remember What You Are Negotiating For.

1. Family: People tend to negotiate better when they negotiate on behalf of their family instead of just themselves. Some people keep a picture of their family in their jacket pocket and touch it unobtrusively during discussions as a reminder and incentive.

2. Stress, wrongful treatment, needs, and fairness: These four things can be very persuasive in negotiations. Be prepared to discuss your claims, your basis for them, and your willingness to address the company's point of view as well.

3. Goals: Remind yourself of your true goals which you have determined beforehand. Don't be distracted by extraneous matters such as your emotions, your company's financial issues, or your counterpart's sympathy. These are all techniques to throw you off your game and break your focus.

Step Five: Prepare for Alternatives

Prepare a second list of settlement requests in case your initial request is turned down. If there is a stalemate, one of you will need to break it and it may be in your best interest to do so to progress the discussion. Your negotiation goals and substitute goals should be very clear in your mind and you should be prepared to express them clearly and confidently.

Understand all the options available. For example:

- Intellectual property – will you be able to retain samples to use in your portfolio?

- Positive reference.

- Departure statement or public announcement – will you be able to review or contribute to ensure a positive spin?

- Will outplacement or education assistance be provided?

- Technology - Can you retain computer equipment, cell phone, etc.?

- Car - Can you retain the company car until the lease expires?

- New business – if you decide to open a new business, will the employer agree to be a client?

- Non-competition clause – will the employer be willing to forgo or limit a non-competition clause if it exists?

- Solicitation of customers – Companies do not want you pilfering their customers. If this becomes a negotiation point, then get specifications – current customers only? Include employees? Does it include working for a company that would be doing the solicitation?

- Reimbursement for legal expenses.

- Message and mail forwarding

- Payments upon death – it is hard to think about this point but you should consider it if your severance payments are over a long period of time, you may want to establish a continuance of payments in case of your death.

- Bankruptcy protection – in case of the company's bankruptcy prior to completing the payout of severance, the outstanding sum shall become an obligation of the shareholders.

- Mergers/acquisitions – in the case of a merger, acquisition, reorganization or sell-off of assets, the company is obligated to continue your outstanding payments.

- Bonus – Present Year – if you are terminated without cause, you should still be entitled to the anticipated bonus for the year of termination.

- Royalties, copyrights, or patent rights. – If you have participated in written works or inventions while employed, then you may be entitled to proceeds or royalties the employer may later collect. Make sure that this is outlined in the severance package.

- Credit for creative works – if you contributed creatively to your employer's projects, ensure that the appropriate creative credits are maintained. If royalties are due to you, ensure that they continue to come to you.

- Deferral – To avoid moving into a higher tax bracket, you may request for part or all severance payment to be deferred to January 2nd of the next calendar year.

- First Rehire Right – if you are part of a mass layoff or downsizing, you may request a "right of first rehire" when circumstances improve.

- Payback Inapplicable – Many severance agreements contain a stipulation that if you are rehired by the employer or another company before the severance period ends, you need to report it and reimburse severance moneys owed. Although common, you should be wary of such a clause.

- Voicemail and email continuation – In order to transition to unemployment, request continuation through reemployment or for a period of three to six months.

Step Six: Be Positive

Keep a positive attitude and don't take negotiations personally. This is just business. Your goal is to get what you need. Don't see results in terms of winners and losers. Experienced negotiators will try to intimidate, overpower, or even scare you. They may try to make you feel guilty or greedy. Always display a positive, friendly and happy demeanor regardless of your feelings churning inside you. Sarcasm, scowling and eye rolling will get you nowhere and will indicate to your counterpart that their technique is working.

Step Seven: Get It In Writing

As you come to an agreement, write the details down. Don't depend on your memory and definitely don't depend on the memory of your employer. At the conclusion of each meeting, review with your counterpart to the items agreed to for their confirmation. Once you have an agreement, ask them if they want a photocopy.

When the final agreement is documented, review your notes to ensure it is thorough and correct. Do not leave anything open to interpretation or assumption. If something is not completely clear or is omitted, then do not sign the document. Make your counterpart aware and ask for revisions to ensure that you are both on the same page.

Preparing For Severance Negotiation

Here is a checklist of items that you should gather prior to starting negotiations.

1. Gather any documentation that outlines your job responsibilities from when you were hired until now. Include as much of the following as possible:

    a) Employment contracts or letter of offer and any written modifications since then.

    b) Any performance evaluations that may describe your job duties and written modifications since then.

    c) Any HR-type job descriptions that outline your duties, responsibilities and terms. This could be any recent job postings within your company that have the same title as yours. For example, if there is more than one Accounts Payable Clerk in the company, the most recent job posting may be very similar to your job description.

    d) Any evidence of common knowledge that you and your employer have always worked under. (i.e. your title, your wage, your job grade, your pension program and/or benefits, your vacation entitlement, etc.)

    e) Any paperwork that outlines a termination agreement (or known for executives as a "golden parachute clause") or any reprimands that you received that you did not agree with.

2. Collect all other papers that may suggest or outline your terms of employment.

    a) Offer letter or onboarding material (documents given to you when you are first hired).

    b) New Hire memo that went out to co-workers when you started.

    c) "Welcome Aboard" letter.

    d) Original posting for the position.

    e) Pay stubs.

    f) Personnel policy manuals or policy statements.

3. Organize a list of records and amounts reflecting your current compensation including all employment related benefits that you are entitled to receive.

    a) Salary.

b) Bonus/Cost of living allowances.

c) Pension or 401k contribution.

d) Stock options.

e) Vacation entitlement.

f) On-call or overtime pay.

g) Discounted house/car insurance, travel accommodations or other perks.

h) Salary grade.

i) Any inclusion in company succession planning or promotional expectations.

j) Business partnership discounts (home use software, discounted tickets, etc.).

k) Parking allowance or reserved spot.

l) Free public transit passes.

m) Health and/or life insurance.

n) Disability insurance.

o) Educational allowance or assistance.

p) Car or mileage allowance.

q) Company computer or cell phone or service to run them.

r) Discounted public transit passes.

s) Employee discounts (e.g. purchasing or lowered bank fees).

t) Club memberships.

u) Matching gift programs.

v) Other contribution programs.

w) Travel allowances.

4. Prepare any evidence of satisfactory employment performance.

a) Performance evaluations and annual reviews.

b) Awards and/or honours.

c) Promotions.

d) New titles.

e) New responsibilities.

f) Raises.

g) Emails/cards from supervisor or co-workers thanking you or crediting your efforts.

h) Bonuses.

i) Company newsletter articles.

j) Succession planning or promotional plans discussed between you and your manager.

5. Determine any benefit of any type that is scheduled to accrue in the upcoming months or years.

   a) Stock options.

   b) IRA or Pension adjustments.

   c) Deferred compensation on deferred benefit programs.

   d) Bridging program to retirement or retirement program eligibility.

   e) Special programs (e.g. free lifetime health coverage for those with 25 years employment).

   f) Bonus or gift for defined number of years of employment.

   g) Performance bonus or cost of living allowance.

   h) Deferred commissions or earned bonuses based on performance or company performance.

6. Design a timetable of all matters pertaining to stock options.

   a) Number of shares optioned.

   b) Dates offered.

   c) Granted or to be granted.

   d) All exercise dates and methods.

   e) All strike prices.

   f) Current market prices.

7. Verify your insurance coverage and upcoming needs.

   a) Coverage for your or family members medical condition, disability, physical ailment or impairment.

b) Upcoming treatment, surgery, procedure, tests or rehabilitation for you or your family.

c) Upcoming follow up care or expenses related to above conditions.

d) Special accommodations, dispensations or arrangements.

e) Upcoming maternal/paternal leave or parental care leave.

8. Devise a schedule of available liquid assets (cash or short-term investments).

a) List bank accounts, short term investment accounts, stocks, GICs, etc.

b) Lines of credits or loans available.

c) List financial obligations – child care expenses, education expenses, parent-care expenses, debts coming due, etc.

9. Prepare a written account of misconduct by your employer relative to your complaint.

a) Discrimination/harassment/mistreatment claims.

b) How they took place.

c) Witnesses.

d) Other victims.

e) Complaints made by you or others.

f) Was senior management made aware.

g) Documentation involved (emails, memos, instant messages, etc.).

h) Any journal that you may have to track these events.

10. Specific requests for your severance package that relates to your particular field.

a) Upgrading technical skills for IT people.

b) Registered Representatives in Securities field termination designation with their governing body.

c) Executive MBA enrollment.

d) Memberships in professional associations.

e) Training to maintain your certifications.

11. Request a copy of your personnel file from HR.

12. Company's policies in negotiating severance packages.

   a) Ask around on the policy especially among former employees. If any of them were successful in re-negotiating, then they probably won't talk about it as they are usually bound to a confidentiality agreement. If they were not successful, they will blab and blab.

13. Strategic developments at the company that would make them concerned about litigation.

   a) Mergers.

   b) Acquisitions.

   c) Public offering or refinancing.

   d) Employee Stock Option Plans.

   e) Bankruptcy.

   f) CEO retirement.

   g) Partnerships with ethical programs or partners.

   h) New business planning.

   i) Negative image or process of re-building image.

14. Skeletons in your closet should be shared with your attorney.

   a) Dating a subordinate.

   b) Overextending an expense account.

   c) Borrowed funds without authority.

   d) Use company resources for personal use.

   e) Complaints filed against you.

   f) Unsatisfactory performance reviews or PIPs (Performance Improvement Plans).

   g) Warnings or reprimands that you have received.

15. Outline a realistic career plan to understand your future needs.

   a) Career plan over the next 5-10 years.

b) Job progression plan.

c) Salary and compensation plan needed to sustain your lifestyle needs.

d) Training needed.

e) Resources needed to find your next job.

f) Update your résumé and cover letter.

g) Costs associated to find a new job – wardrobe, travel, printing, etc.

h) Look into a career counselor for assistance.

i) Networking plan.

j) Professional associations you need to join.

Tips For Lawyer-Assisted Negotiations

If you choose to use a lawyer, you should ensure that you understand the most effective way to utilize him/her during negotiations. Ensure that both you and your lawyer are in sync prior to meeting with your employer.

1. **Be Firm About Your Goals Before You Meet Your Lawyer.**

   You should be able to recite your negotiation goals without notes. You must also be knowledgeable what your minimal acceptable terms are. Your lawyer should be well aware of these as well and be able to advise you how realistic they are. Remember, if your employer was not willing to negotiate with you, they would not participate in a negotiation session.

2. **Be Clear About Your Strategy.**

   Are you asking for $5,000 more but are willing to take $3,500? Is one aspect of your package a "deal breaker" but another part not of much value to you? You should prepare separate lists of items that you want but you are willing to sacrifice. Keep this list alongside the one that has your non-negotiable items.

3. **Your Lawyer Needs To Set The Agenda Before Negotiations Commence.**

   The agenda should be outlined and distributed to the employer's team. Agenda items typically include:

   - The purpose of the meeting.
   - The anticipated outcome.
   - The current state due to initial offer proposed.
   - The specific topics to be discussed.

- The parties who will actively participate in negotiation.
- The understanding that neither plaintiff nor defendant will be deposed by attorneys.
- Determining who will take notes or recording and distribute results.
- Determining if any discussion is to be "off the record".
- Determining time allotment or restrictions on the meeting.
- Determining who of the parties are authorized to enter into an agreement.

4. At The Meeting, Sit Back and Let Your Lawyer Run The Show.

As the client, you have the authority to approve the strategy, goals and direction your lawyer will take. But during the negotiation meetings, you must take a backseat to your lawyer. Never overtly disagree with your lawyer or give any indication of dissention through your body language during these sessions. Any questions or concerns you have with your attorney should be done only in private. If you need to consult with your lawyer, you can ask for a private discussion alone with your lawyer.

5. Inform Your Lawyer of Any Issue That You Don't Want Raised or Concerned Will Be Mentioned During The Session Beforehand.

The more sensitive the topic, the more important it is that your lawyer is aware of it. Your attorney is on your side so don't be afraid to tell him/her about it beforehand. If you don't, then you run the risk of your opponent raising it which will blindside your lawyer and your case.

6. Avoid Nervous, Anxious or Self-Doubting Emotions.

Pretend you are playing poker. Do not express your anger, betrayal, frustration or any other negative emotion. Remember, this is only business.

7. Don't Hasten The Negotiation or Settlement Process.

If you are anxious, you are more likely to make concessions and compromises. Once you reveal them, then it is almost impossible to withdraw them from the negotiation process. Your attitude should be one of good faith and willingness to compromise. Just don't openly initiate the compromise yourself. Ask the other side to suggest the compromise.

8. Don't Be Aggressive or Menacing.

Don't try to play games by threatening to sue or go to the media. Don't try to intimidate your negotiation partners by yelling or being abusive. This will hinder the process. These stunts never act in your favor.

9. **Never Be Pressured Into Any Decision or Concession Unless Your Gut Is Comfortable With It.**

10. **Never Agree To Anything Unless Your Lawyer Agrees With The Decision.**

How Much Should I Ask For?

Your initial offer from your employer may not be what you expected. Sometimes you don't really know what to expect so how can you determine whether to agree to an offer. Here are some guidelines that you may find helpful. Remember, however that a severance package is just that – a package. When deciding how good or bad an offer is, you need to consider all the elements included. Some items may be more important to you than others (e.g. continuance of full health benefits if you are a single parent or educational assistance if you wish to get your MBA).

Salary Compensation

Firstly, be well versed on what the minimums are in your jurisdiction or company policy so that you are not asking for less than you deserve by law. This is the first place people review to evaluate a package. Where employment has been ongoing for a prolonged period of time, a simple multiplier can provide a gauge as to what to expect.

For example:

Level	Current Norm
Senior Management	One month per year of service
Middle Management	2-3 weeks per year of service
Support staff	1-2 weeks per year of service

A common clause recently is employers requiring "mitigation of severance", a claw-back of salary payments if and when the terminated employee secures new employment. However, its popularity is decreasing as it is increasingly viewed as discouraging reemployment efforts and is difficult to administer.

Bonuses

The norm is to provide an employee with a portion earned of their bonus, incentive bonus or profit sharing on a pro rata basis (the amount they had accrued until termination). In some cases, companies will establish a policy that an employee must be employed by the company on the date of the bonus distribution in order to receive their bonus. If your bonus makes up a large portion of your compensation, this may be a key negotiating point for you.

Pension and Retirement

For older workers, pension rights are significant. Many people have stayed with their employer for decades in order to ensure pension security in their retirement. To lose all of that especially when the employee is close to retirement can be devastating. This is because it is statistically proven to be harder for an older worker to gain employment.

Those who fear either long-term difficulty or complete inability to secure employment can request to accelerate commencement of their pension payout. Increasingly common, is a measure called "bridging to retirement" by which an employee's period of salary continuance during severance is not paid out on a full-time basis but is instead stretched out through smaller payments to reach a minimum retirement age or period of service. For example, if an employee is entitled to 6 months of full salary continuance as part of a settlement, the bridge to retirement could be payment of 1/3 of the salary over eighteen months. In this example, employment is "bridged" to the necessary attainment of service or age.

Outplacement Assistance

Basic outplacement services consist of career assessment and counseling, telephone answering, resume preparation as well as seminars on such topics as job search and stress management.

Three months' outplacement assistance is now common when it comes to the duration of this benefit. While rarely seen a decade ago, it has become almost a standard in severance packages.

For those that don't need outplacement services (i.e. if you are a career counselor), you can request a cash payment in lieu of this benefit. Depending on your level, the standard compensation is between $3,000 to $9,000.

Departure Statement

Some employees, especially those in a managerial or executive level, are concerned about how their termination will be announced to other employees or the media (for high ranking public-facing employees). Most employers are willing to work with the employee toward the preparation of a mutually agreeable departure statement (i.e. reason for leaving the company) because it poses a win-win resolution that doesn't cost a dime. It gives both parties to save face and protect their reputations.

Stock Option Extensions

More companies are offering stock options to all level of employees these days. Some stock options have restrictions including loss upon employment termination.

Because stock options are often seen as valuable to the employee and low in cost to the employer, more and more companies are viewing requests for stock option extensions in a positive light. This allows the stock option holder to have at least the duration of the termination notice period to exercise his/her stock options.

Appendix A: Termination Laws by State

There are numerous federal and state laws protecting employees from losing their jobs due to discrimination or retaliation for what is known as "whistle blowing" reports. In addition there are mechanisms for filing claims if wrongful termination can be proven.

Most local laws covering employment vary by state; however, the most common federal employment legislation is the Federal Labor Standards Act of 1938, which addresses minimum wage, overtime, and working hours. The Federal Civil Rights Act of 1964 also addresses civil rights, age discrimination, disabilities, nationality, and race. State laws may expand on those protections and provide specific remedies for those terminated unfairly.

Most states are "at will" states, meaning that an employee can quit at any time and for any reason, and the employer can fire an employee at any time for any reason, other those prohibited by other legislation.

These listings are a guideline of the current laws at time of printing. Please make sure that you check your state's labor website for any updates or specifics.

Alabama

Alabama has a few laws expanding on federal employment laws, but in general, Alabama adheres to federal laws in most areas, with the following exceptions:

Benefit	State Law	Additional Benefits
Right to Work	Yes	
State Military Leave	Yes	30 days minimum; USERRA rules apply
Jury Duty	Yes	Paid leave; employer penalty for penalizing employee: actual & punitive damages
Voting	Yes	Unpaid time off with notice
State Family & Medical Leave	No	
Arrest & Conviction Records	No	
Discrimination	Yes	20 or more employees; Age (40 and older)
Whistleblower	Yes	Child labor laws
Plant Closings	Yes	Legal, credit, & financial information and/or assistance

Alabama Discrimination Laws

Alabama also follows federal anti-discrimination laws in employment as in other aspects of public policy, with the one addition of prohibition against age discrimination for workers over 40. In Alabama, if an employee suspects their employer is guilty of age discrimination, there are agencies to handle such claims, but the employee has additional rights:

- There is no administrative preemption prohibiting an employee from filing a private lawsuit

- Employees are permitted to recover attorneys fees from the defendant if they win their case

- There is a statute of limitations of 300 days for age discrimination cases

Alaska

Alaska is an "at will" state, meaning employment can be terminated by employees or employers for any reason that is not specifically outlawed by federal or state laws. The Equal Employment Opportunity Commission (EEOC) oversees employment rights and has processes by which employees can file claims or pursue lawsuits for wrongful termination.

Alaska's Specific Labor Laws

Alaska has initiated a number of state laws expanding the protections against discrimination in employee hiring and firing. Some of the laws specific to the state of Alaska include the following:

Benefit	State Law	Additional Benefits
Right to Work	No	
State Military Leave	Yes	Unlimited unpaid leave and guaranteed reinstatement
Jury Duty	Yes	Unpaid leave; employee may not be threatened, coerced, or penalized; employer may be liable for lost wages, damages, and/or reinstatement
Voting	Yes	Time off not always required, but when it is, it is paid time off
State Family & Medical Leave	No	
Arrest & Conviction Records	No	

Discrimination	Yes	1 or more employees; Age (40 and older), national origin, disability, AIDS/HIV, gender, marital status, pregnancy/childbirth, race, religion, mental illness
Whistleblower	Yes	Health & safety, and nurses specifically protected; claim must be filed within 30 days of violation for reinstatement, back pay, etc.
Plant Closings	Yes	Employment & training programs

Alaska Job Discrimination Laws

Alaska has included a number of specific regulations concerning discrimination which federal laws do not address. In addition to federal laws outlawing discrimination based on race, color, religion, sex, or national origin, Alaska includes a number of family, marital, sexual, mental, and disability issues. If an employee suspects wrongful termination based on discrimination, there are agencies to handle such claims, but the employee has additional rights.

An employee is not prohibited from filing a private lawsuit to include the employee's ability to recover attorney's fees from the defendant at the discretion of the court.

Arkansas

Arkansas has included several civil rights statutes in their labor laws which further protect employees in both public and private occupations beyond the basics of race, color, religion, sex, or national origin. There are, however, additional guidelines for discrimination cases in the state:

- Public employees are prohibited from filing private lawsuits; however, private employees are not

- Public employees are prohibited from recovering attorney's fees from a defendant; however, private employees are not

- Arkansas Statute of limitations is 2 years for a lawsuit concerning wrongful termination

Arizona

Arizona is an "at will" work state. Arizona laws address a number of civil rights issues not covered under federal civil rights laws. For abuses, employees should contact their state or local office of the Equal Employment Opportunity Commission (EEOC) to begin the claims process. Arizona does allow individual lawsuits, however, if state claims are ineffective.

Arizona's Specific Labor Laws

The Arizona state laws concerning employee rights are more extensive than federal laws in a number of areas, including the following:

Benefit	State Law	Additional Benefits
Right to Work	Yes	
State Military Leave	Yes	Unlimited unpaid leave and guaranteed reinstatement for National Guard maneuvers; employers may not threaten employees to dissuade enlistment
Jury Duty	Yes	Unpaid leave; employee may not lose sick or vacation time
Voting	Yes	Paid time off if required and requested 1 day in advance
State Family & Medical Leave	No	
Arrest & Conviction Records	Yes	Occupational license may be denied when misdemeanor or felony conviction is in related occupation
Discrimination	Yes	15 or more employees; Age (40 and older), national origin, disability, AIDS/HIV, gender, race, religion, genetic testing information
Whistleblower	Yes	Both public & private employees; for health & safety issues, public employees for public policy issues
Plant Closings	No	

Arizona Discrimination Laws

While Arizona does not have the most extensive civil rights laws in the nation, they do have a number of additional statutes protecting workers from job discrimination. If there are abuses beyond the basic protections under federal law, which include race, color, religion, sex, or national origin, Arizona's specific statutes allow the following actions for wrongful termination claims:

- An employee is not prohibited from filing a private lawsuit

- Employees are permitted to recover attorney's fees from the defendant
- Arizona Statute of limitations is 2 years for a lawsuit, or 180 days to file a claim through the Civil Rights Division

California

California has some of the most widespread civil rights laws in the nation, adding a number of categories to those provided in the Federal Labor Standards Act of 1938 and the Civil Rights Act of 1964. In addition, California is an "at will" state, which allows employees and employers to terminate the working relationship for any reason that is not otherwise prohibited in federal and state labor laws. However, if an employee does have a claim for wrongful termination, as long as they file claim within the state's statute of limitations with the state or local office of the Equal Employment Opportunity Commission (EEOC), they may be able to be reinstated, recover compensation, or damages.

California's Specific Labor Laws

There is a long list of special state laws in California protecting employees from wrongful termination, in addition to federal employment laws. Those state laws include the following:

Benefit	State Law	Additional Benefits
Right to Work	No	
State Military Leave	Yes	Unlimited unpaid leave and reinstatement without loss of benefits or termination without cause for 1 year; 52 weeks of unpaid disability leave due to military service; no discrimination due to military service
Jury Duty	Yes	Vacation, sick time, or comp time used for unpaid leave; employees making court appearances as victims of crime, sexual assault, or domestic violence cannot be penalized
Voting	Yes	2 hours paid time off if necessary, & if requested 2 days in advance
State Family & Medical Leave	Yes	5 or more employees, pregnancy leave; 25 or more, domestic violence, sexual assault, school activity leave; 50 or more, domestic partner leave; if employees contribute to state temporary disability ins. Fund, employees must be allowed to

		participate in state paid family leave benefits program; 55% of regular earnings for up to 4 months pregnancy leave, 12 weeks domestic partner care, 6 weeks for SDI contributors with ill family member or new child; 40 hours/yr. school activities; reasonable time for victims of domestic violence or sexual assault, their families, or domestic partners.
Arrest & Conviction Records	Yes	No questions about arrests without convictions; no questions about diversion programs; may ask about pending trials & convictions even without sentencing
Discrimination	Yes	5 or more employees; age discrimination (40 & older); national origin, disability, AIDS/HIV; gender, marital status; pregnancy & child birth, race, religion, sexual orientation; genetic testing information; medical conditions; political activities or associations
Whistleblower	Yes	Both public & private employees
Plant Closings	No	

California Discrimination Laws

California discrimination laws have wide leeway for employees to pursue remedies, beyond those that may be pursued by government labor agencies. The basic areas of federal civil rights protection include race, color, religion, sex, or national origin. Employees filing for remedies from those and specific state abuses have the following options:

- Employees are permitted to file private lawsuits

- Employees are permitted to recover attorney's fees from a defendant

- California statute of limitations is 3 years for civil actions, and 1 year for government/agency claims

Colorado

In addition to federal civil rights and labor laws, Colorado has a number of state laws protecting employees from wrongful termination. Those laws limit the "at will" standing of Colorado, which allows both workers and employers from terminating a work relationship for any reason, except those specifically stated in federal and state laws. The primary federal laws include the Federal Labor Standards Act of 1938 and the Civil Rights Act of 1964. Workers who suspect wrongful termination may contact their local office of the Equal Employment Opportunity Commission (EEOC), for remedies or, if state agencies fail to provide satisfaction, may contact an employee rights attorney to pursue private legal remedies or a lawsuit.

Colorado's Specific Labor Laws

Colorado provides some additional statutes protecting employees from wrongful termination in the workplace. Among the most prominent local statutes are the following:

Benefit	State Law	Additional Benefits
Right to Work	No	
State Military Leave	Yes	15 days unpaid leave for National Guard or reserve training, plus reinstatement and benefits; for National Guard active duty, unlimited unpaid leave and full reinstatement and benefits
Jury Duty	Yes	Paid leave for all employees, up to $50/day for first 3 days; no employer demands to interfere with effective performance of jury duty
Voting	Yes	Up to 3 hours paid time off, if necessary, at start or end of work shift, & if requested in advance
State Family & Medical Leave	Yes	Same leave allowed for adoption as for childbirth; 50 or more employees, 3 days domestic violence leave for employees with 1 year or more of service
Arrest & Conviction Records	Yes	No questions about arrests without convictions; may respond concerning sealed arrests or convictions as if they never occurred
Discrimination	Yes	1 or more employees; age discrimination (40-70); national origin, disability (physical, mental, learning), AIDS/HIV; gender, pregnancy & child birth, race,

		religion, genetic testing information; lawful conduct out of work; mental illness
Whistleblower	Yes	For public employees, no retribution permitted as long as revelation known to be accurate; for private employees, must provide information to supervisor before reporting to outside officials
Plant Closings	Yes	When occurs due to technological changes, state provides retraining

Colorado Discrimination Laws

In general, Colorado state agencies take priority in pursuing employers for wrongful termination under federal laws, which prohibit discrimination based on race, color, religion, sex, or national origin. In addition, abuse of state statutes must first be pursued by local EEOC offices. At that point, employees may pursue private options with an employee rights attorney:

- Enforcement, administration, and investigation by the state takes precedence over private suits

- Employees are permitted to file private lawsuits only after pursuing a claim through the appropriate government agency

- Employees are permitted to recover attorney's fees from a defendant

- Statutes of limitations are variable

Connecticut

Connecticut has gone above and beyond federal employee protection laws, as found in statutes such as the Federal Labor Standards Act of 1938 and the Civil Rights Act of 1964. As an "at will" state, employees may quit a job for any reason, and employers may terminate an employee for any reason except those specifically outlined in those federal laws and any additional state laws. That means employees who believe they have a case for wrongful termination have many federal and state laws that provide protections that might enable them to file a claim with the EEOC or a lawsuit in civil court.

Connecticut's Specific Labor Laws

Connecticut provides a number of very specific state statutes that expand the employee protections provided in federal laws. Some of those specific states laws include:

Benefit	State Law	Additional Benefits
Right to Work	No	
State Military Leave	Yes	USERRA applies except in relation to life insurance; leave for meetings or training allowed during working hours without discrimination or loss of benefits
Jury Duty	Yes	Paid leave for all full-time employees for 5 days, state pays up to $50/day thereafter
Voting	No	
State Family & Medical Leave	Yes	For businesses with 75 employees-childbirth, adoption, serious health issue; 3 employees-maternity and disability; for all employees with 1 year and 1,000 hours of service in last 12 months; Family Medical leave includes 16 weeks in a 24-month period for childbirth, adoption, serious health condition for employee, serious health condition for family member, bone marrow transplant or becoming an organ donor; "reasonable" maternity disability; up to 2 weeks sick leave
Arrest & Conviction Records	Yes	Cannot ask about criminal records that have been erased; must inform applicants that they may respond as if such convictions never happened and how to have records erased; if other convictions used to reject employment, reasons and evidence must be provided in writing
Discrimination	Yes	3 or more employees; age discrimination (40 & older); national origin, disability (physical, mental, learning), AIDS/HIV; gender, marital status; pregnancy & child birth, race, religion, sexual orientation, genetic testing information; mental retardation
Whistleblower	Yes	For both public and private employees, no retribution permitted as long as revelation known to be accurate

Plant Closings	Yes	For permanent closure or out of state relocation except for bankruptcy; applies to plants employing 100 or more at any time in previous 12 months; employer continues health coverage for 120 days or until employee is eligible for other coverage

Connecticut Discrimination Laws

Connecticut provides a wide range of discrimination laws protecting citizens in all walks of life from wrongful termination or discrimination in hiring and firing in the workplace. Those state laws require that claims filed in state agencies take precedence over private suits, although individuals are allowed to pursue private suits if agency claims fail:

- Enforcement, administration, and investigation by the state takes precedence over private suits

- Employees are permitted to file private lawsuits only after pursuing a claim through the appropriate government agency

- Employees are permitted to recover attorney's fees from a defendant

- Statutes of limitations are 180 days in all instances except for violation of discrimination based on arrest and conviction, which is 30 days.

Delaware

The state of Delaware employs federal regulations in most areas of employment legislation; however, there are some additional protections provided for in state statutes. The Federal Labor Standards Act of 1938 is the state standard for wages and hours; although the Civil Rights Act of 1964 is only the starting point for discrimination protection. Delaware is an "at will" state, which means that employees may quit a job for any reason, and employers may terminate an employee for any reason except those specifically outlined in federal and state laws. Employees who believe they have been wrongfully terminated should file a claim with the local EEOC first, and then seek the additional option of employing an employee rights attorney to help them file a lawsuit in civil court.

Delaware's Specific Labor Laws

The state laws in Delaware's statutes which supplement the federal employment guidelines include the following:

Benefit	State Law	Additional Benefits
Right to Work	No	
State Military Leave	No	
Jury Duty	Yes	Unpaid leave
Voting	No	
State Family & Medical Leave	No	
Arrest & Conviction Records	Yes	Employees do not have to reveal expunged arrests or convictions
Discrimination	Yes	4 or more employees; age discrimination (40 & older); national origin, disability (physical, mental), AIDS/HIV; gender, marital status; pregnancy & child birth, race, religion, genetic testing information
Whistleblower	Yes	For public employees
Plant Closings	No	

Delaware Discrimination Laws

Delaware statutes include a number of additional provisions protecting employees from wrongful termination or discrimination in the workplace. And while claims for abuses must first be processed through state agencies, individuals are allowed to pursue private suits in the event that agency claims produce no results:

- Enforcement, administration, and investigation by the state takes precedence over private suits

- Employees are permitted to file private lawsuits only after pursuing a claim through the appropriate government agency

- Employees are permitted to recover attorney's fees from a defendant

- Statutes of limitations are 90 to 180 days, depending on the violation.

District of Columbia

The District of Columbia has some of the most comprehensive civil rights protection laws in the country, with numerous local laws supplementing the Federal Labor Standards Act of 1938 and the Civil Rights Act of 1964. And while there is a local EEOC office which employees can contact for help, claims, or advice, employees may also file private civil suits with the help of an attorney. The District of Columbia is also an "at will" municipality, allowing both employees and employers to have the right to terminate employment for any reason except those specifically outlined in federal and local laws.

District of Columbia' Specific Labor Laws

In addition to federal laws, there are an extensive number of supplemental anti-discrimination laws relating to the workplace, which include the following:

Benefit	State Law	Additional Benefits
Right to Work	No	
State Military Leave	No	
Jury Duty	Yes	Paid leave for full time employees, regular pay for first 5 days
Voting	No	
State Family & Medical Leave	Yes	For employers with 20 or more employees; employees who have worked a year or at least 1,000 hours or more in previous 12 months; 16 weeks leave in any 12-month period for childbirth, adoption, maternity, or serious health condition of employee or family member; leave for school events up to 24 hours/year; family members must be related by blood, custody, or marriage, share the residence, a committed relationship, or a permanent parent-child responsibility/relationship
Arrest & Conviction Records	Yes	Employee not required to reveal any record that has been expunged
Discrimination	Yes	1 or more employees; age (18 and older); national origin; disability (physical or mental), HIV/AIDS; gender; marital status (including domestic partnerships); pregnancy, child birth, & parenthood; race; religion; sexual orientation; genetic testing; enrollment in vocational or higher education; family duties; source of income; place of residence or business; personal appearance; political affiliation; smoking; anything other than individual merit
Whistleblower	Yes	Public employees
Plant Closings	Yes	For new contractors assuming service contracts with 25 or more nonprofessional

		employees (food, health, janitorial); within 10 days new contractor must hire all former employees with at least 8 months service for 90 days, after which a written performance review is the basis for retaining only satisfactory employees; replaced contractors awarded similar contracts within 30 days must hire 50% or more of former employees

District of Columbia Discrimination Laws

District of Columbia has a wide range of supplemental local laws protecting employees from wrongful termination. Those laws are in addition to the federal laws protecting the basic rights of race, color, religion, sex or national origin. If discrimination occurs, employees may file a claim with local agencies or through a private employee rights attorney, according to these guidelines:

- The state does not preempt the right of employees to privately pursue discrimination claims for wrongful termination.

- Employees are permitted to recover attorney's fees from a defendant.

- Statute of limitations is 1 year.

Florida

Wrongful termination laws can be found within federal employment statutes such as the Federal Labor Standards Act of 1938 and the Civil Rights Act of 1964. However, Florida has additional rights provided through state laws that cover many areas of employee protection. Florida is also an "at will" state, which means that both employees and employers may terminate employment for any reason except those specifically outlined in federal and state laws. Employees may file claims for wrongful termination with the local office of the EEOC, and if that fails to bring relief, pursue a lawsuit in civil court.

Florida's Specific Labor Laws

Florida state laws which supplement the federal employment guidelines include the following:

Benefit	State Law	Additional Benefits
Right to Work	Yes	

State Military Leave	Yes	No penalties when called into active duty; employees terminated while on active duty who do not have COBRA are entitled to 18 months of benefits when active service or job ends
Jury Duty	Yes	Unpaid leave; dismissal threats illegal
Voting	No	
State Family & Medical Leave	No	
Arrest & Conviction Records	Yes	No employee may be disqualified for employment unless prior conviction is a felony/misdemeanor directly related to the disputed position.
Discrimination	Yes	15 or more employees; age; national origin, disability (handicap), AIDS/HIV; gender, marital status; race; religion; sickle cell trait
Whistleblower	Yes	For both public and private employees of companies with 10 employees or more; employee must submit reports in writing and give employer appropriate time to correct
Plant Closings	Yes	For job loss due to industry changes; counseling, training, and placement services through Workforce Florida for those in telecommunications and defense industries; priority in state employment agencies for those formerly in the saltwater fishing industry

Florida Discrimination Laws

Florida puts great emphasis on protecting the civil and employment rights of employees in the state. Federal laws protect the basic rights of race, color, **religion**, **sex** or national origin. State agencies are responsible to pursue claims for wrongful termination initially under these guidelines:

- Enforcement, administration, and investigation by the state takes precedence over private suits
- Employees are permitted to file private lawsuits only after pursuing a claim through the appropriate government agency
- Employees are permitted to recover attorney's fees from a defendant
- Statutes of limitations are 365 days.

Georgia

Georgia has few laws that supplement or extend the employment protections under federal laws such as the Federal Labor Standards Act of 1938 and the Civil Rights Act of 1964. And in fact, state agencies are given the authority to pursue all wrongful termination cases. Georgia is an "at will" state, as well, which means that both employees and employers have the right to terminate employment for any reason except those specifically outlined in federal and state laws.

Georgia's Specific Labor Laws

Those state laws which permit Georgia employees to supplement the federal employment guidelines include the following:

Benefit	State Law	Additional Benefits
Right to Work	Yes	
State Military Leave	Yes	Unlimited unpaid leave; up to 6 months leave in any 4-year period for education or training; guaranteed reinstatement with full benefits if employer circumstances remains unchanged; 90 days after discharge to apply for reinstatement
Jury Duty	Yes	No penalties for responding to a subpoena or court appearance after reasonable notice
Voting	Yes	Unpaid time off if necessary; reasonable notice required
State Family & Medical Leave	No	
Arrest & Conviction Records	Yes	Employer must provide fingerprints or employee consent to obtain; if used to disqualify, must report all reasons in writing to employee; probation is not considered conviction and employment decisions cannot be based upon probation time served
Discrimination	Yes	15 or more employees for disability; 10 or more employees for gender; disability (physical or mental), gender (for wage discrimination only)
Whistleblower	Yes	Public employees
Plant Closings	No	

*These laws change often, so consult state statutes for the most up-to-date information.

Georgia Discrimination Laws

Federal laws protect the basic rights of race, color, religion, sex or national origin for Georgia employees, and state statutes have additional protections in a few areas. If those rights are abused, employees may file a claim with a state office of the EEOC to pursue remedies according to the following standards:

- Enforcement, administration, and investigation of wrongful termination cases is permitted by state agencies only

- Employees are not permitted to file private lawsuits

- Employees are permitted to recover attorney's fees from a defendant at the discretion of the court

- Statutes of limitations are 180 days.

Hawaii

Hawaii is one of the states that has a high degree of commitment to employee rights in all walks and situations of life, and they show that commitment through their numerous and comprehensive state laws supplementing the Federal Labor Standards Act of 1938 and the Civil Rights Act of 1964. However, those rights can only be remedied by claims through state EEOC agencies. In addition, Hawaii is an "at will" state, which means that both employees and employers have the right to terminate employment for any reason except those specifically outlined in federal and state laws.

Hawaii's Specific Labor Laws

There are numerous state laws supplementing federal employment protection legislation, which include the following:

Benefit	State Law	Additional Benefits
Right to Work	No	
State Military Leave	Yes	Unlimited unpaid leave and comparable benefits; if disabled and cannot perform former duties, employee entitled to comparable position; termination without cause prohibited for 1 year
Jury Duty	Yes	Unpaid leave
Voting	Yes	2 consecutive hours of paid time off if

		necessary; proof of voting required; if no proof, hours may be deducted from pay
State Family & Medical Leave	Yes	Leave for childbirth, adoption, & serious health conditions for employers with at least 100 employees, & employees with 6 months service, granted 4 weeks leave per calendar year; leave for pregnancy and domestic violence for all employers, all employees are eligible, a "reasonable period" of leave is due; leave for domestic violence for employers with over 50 employees, must allow up to 30 days unpaid leave per year for employee or child; employers with 49 or fewer employees, 5 days leave; may also include 10 days accrued leave or sick leave; eligible family members include reciprocal beneficiary, parents-in-law, grandparents, grandparents-in-law, stepparents;
Arrest & Conviction Records	Yes	No discrimination based on arrest records; conviction inquiries allowed only after conditional offer of position, and only on convictions within 10 years; expunged records treated as if they never occurred
Discrimination	Yes	1 or more employees; age; national origin; disability (physical or mental), HIV/ AIDS; gender; marital status; pregnancy & child birth; race; religion; sexual orientation; genetic testing; arrest & court records unless directly related to job
Whistleblower	Yes	Public and private employees have possible remedies within a 2-year statute of limitations
Plant Closings	Yes	For companies with 50 or more employees at any time in past 12 months; for companies closing or partially closing and/or moving out of state; 4 weeks dislocated worker allowance to supplement unemployment compensation to equal former wage; employer must provide 60 days written notice; job assistance and training

Hawaii Discrimination Laws

While federal laws protect the basic rights of race, color, religion, sex or national origin for employees in Hawaii, state statutes contain a large number of additional protections. If those rights are abused, employees may file a claim with a state office of the EEOC to pursue remedies according to the following standards:

- Enforcement, administration, and investigation by the state is the only claim method for wrongful termination.

- Employees are not permitted to file private lawsuits.

- Employees are permitted to recover attorney's fees from a defendant.

- Statute of limitations is 90 days.

Idaho

Any employee who believes they have been the victim of wrongful termination has several options by which they can pursue remedies under both federal laws such as the Federal Labor Standards Act of 1938 and the Civil Rights Act of 1964, plus additional state laws to supplement and expand those protections. In most states, claims are filed through EEOC state offices, however, in Idaho; they can be filed through the Idaho Commission on Human Rights. Because Idaho is an "at will" state, both employees and employers have the right to terminate employment for any reason except those specifically outlined in federal and state laws, but those laws allow claims through state agencies as well as through civil lawsuits with the help of an employee rights lawyer.

Idaho's Specific Labor Laws

In addition to federal laws, there are a number of supplemental state laws, which include the following:

Benefit	State Law	Additional Benefits
Right to Work	Yes	
State Military Leave	Yes	1 year unpaid leave for state national guard plus reinstatement & benefits; if disabled and cannot perform former duties, employee entitled to comparable position; must apply for reinstatement within 30 days; termination without cause prohibited for 1 year; U.S. National Guard & reserves have 15 days training leave per year

		without affecting vacation, sick leave, and other benefits; 90 days notice required for training dates
Jury Duty	Yes	Unpaid leave
Voting	No	
State Family & Medical Leave	No	
Arrest & Conviction Records	No	
Discrimination	Yes	5 or more employees; age (40 and older); national origin; disability (physical or mental), gender; pregnancy & child birth; race; religion; genetic testing
Whistleblower	Yes	Public employees; 180-day statute of limitations
Plant Closings	No	

Idaho Discrimination Laws

Federal laws protect the basic rights of race, color, religion, sex or national origin for employees in Idaho, but there are state statutes that provide additional protections. If those rights are abused, employees may file a claim with state agencies or in civil court, with the help of an employee rights attorney according to the following guidelines:

- Employees are permitted to file private lawsuits for wrongful termination.

- Employees are not permitted to recover attorney's fees from a defendant.

- Statute of limitations is 1 year

Illinois

Illinois has made a strong legal commitment to employee rights through a number of supplemental state laws that expand on the protections found in federal laws such as the Federal Labor Standards Act of 1938 and the Civil Rights Act of 1964. Employees have the right to file claims through EEOC state offices as well as through the Illinois Department of Human Rights. Illinois is another "at will" state, allowing both employees and employers to have the right to terminate employment for any reason except those specifically outlined in federal and state laws.

Illinois' Specific Labor Laws

In addition to federal laws, there are a number of supplemental state laws, which include the following:

Benefit	State Law	Additional Benefits
Right to Work	No	
State Military Leave	Yes	Unlimited leave for state national guard plus reinstatement & benefits, with comparable increases; if disabled and cannot perform former duties, employee entitled to comparable position; must give reasonable notice of deployment if possible; request for reinstatement 1 day after 30-day deployment or less, 14 days after 30 day deployment, 90 days after 180 day deployment or longer; termination without cause prohibited for 1 year; U.S. uniformed service people must request reinstatement within 90 days
Jury Duty	Yes	Unpaid leave; night shift employee allowed time off without penalty; notice to employer within 10 days of summons
Voting	Yes	Paid time off; time scheduled at employer's discretion; 1 day notice by employee required
State Family & Medical Leave	Yes	For employers with 50 or more employees; those who have worked at least half time for 6 months or more; school events, 4 hours/day or 8 hours/year for employees with no paid leave; domestic violence or sexual assault for employee or family/household member, 12 weeks unpaid leave
Arrest & Conviction Records	Yes	Unlawful to ask about arrest or conviction that has been expunged or to use arrest or criminal record to influence employment
Discrimination	Yes	15 or more employees (1 or more employees/disability); age (40 and older); national origin; disability (physical or mental), HIV/AIDS; gender; marital status; pregnancy & child birth; race; religion; sexual orientation; genetic testing;

		citizen status; military status; arrest record
Whistleblower	Yes	Public employees
Plant Closings	Yes	For mass layoff, relocation, or employment loss; for employers with 75 or more employees or those whose employees work an aggregate 4,000 hours/week excluding overtime; 60 days notice required;

Illinois Discrimination Laws

Illinois has a wide range of supplemental state laws protecting employees from wrongful termination. Those laws are in addition to the federal laws protecting the basic rights of race, color, religion, sex or national origin. If those rights are abused, employees may file a claim with state agencies, which follow these guidelines:

- Enforcement, administration, and investigation by the state is the primary claim method for wrongful termination.

- Employees are permitted to file a wrongful termination private lawsuit for temporary relief only.

- Employees are permitted to recover attorney's fees from a defendant.

- Statute of limitations is 180 days

Indiana

Wrongful termination is a crime under federal laws, but many states have individual laws supplementing the protections offered by the Labor Standards Act of 1938 and the Civil Rights Act of 1964. Indiana is one of those states, although they have far fewer of those specific restrictions than many other states. Employees who have been discriminated against in this way may contact the local EEOC office to file claims or ask questions; however, they also have the right to file a private lawsuit with the help of an employee rights lawyer independently. Indiana is also an "at will" state, providing employees and employers with the right to terminate employment for any reason except those specifically outlined in federal and local laws.

Indiana's Specific Labor Laws

In addition to federal laws, Indiana has some supplemental anti-discrimination and workplace protection laws, including the following:

Benefit	State Law	Additional Benefits
Right to Work	No	
State Military Leave	Yes	U.S. military reserves allowed up to 15 days unpaid leave (although employers may award regular pay at their discretion) upon employee evidence of dates and completion; does not affect vacation, sick leave, bonuses, or seniority. Reinstatement is guaranteed.
Jury Duty	Yes	Unpaid leave
Voting	No	
State Family & Medical Leave	No	
Arrest & Conviction Records	No	
Discrimination	Yes	6 or more employees; age (40 to 70); national origin; disability (physical or mental-15 or more employees), gender; race; religion
Whistleblower	Yes	Both public and private employees; violation first reported to employer or appropriate agency; if reparations not made in reasonable time, employee may report in writing to any agency, organization, or person.
Plant Closings	No	

Indiana Discrimination Laws

Indiana's supplemental discrimination laws provide protection in addition to the federal laws which protect the basic rights of race, color, religion, sex or national origin. If discrimination occurs, employees may file a claim with local agencies or through a private employee rights attorney, according to these guidelines:

- The state does not preempt the right of employees to privately pursue discrimination claims for wrongful termination.

- Employees are not permitted to recover attorney's fees from a defendant.

- There is no statute of limitations specified in Indiana law.

Iowa

Iowa generally supports and aligns its wrongful termination statutes with federal laws such as the Labor Standards Act of 1938 as well as the Civil Rights Act of 1964. However, there are some supplemental protections allowed under Iowa state laws. In addition, Iowa's wrongful termination violations are generally addressed in the local Iowa Civil Rights Commission rather than an EEOC office. And while Iowa is also an "at will" employment state, meaning that employers and employees have the right to terminate employment for all reasons other than those specifically spelled out in federal and local laws, wrongful termination or discrimination in the workplace is always a crime for which employees can file claims.

Iowa's Specific Labor Laws

Iowa's supplemental workplace protection and anti-discrimination laws, include the following:

Benefit	State Law	Additional Benefits
Right to Work	Yes	
State Military Leave	Yes	U.S. national guard, reserves, or civil air patrol leave does not affect vacation, sick leave, bonuses, or other benefits; guaranteed reinstatement to same or similar position upon proof of satisfactory completion of service and ability to perform former job.
Jury Duty	Yes	Unpaid leave
Voting	Yes	Paid leave, up to 3 hours combined with nonpaid time, if necessary; hours selected at employer's discretion; leaves must be requested in advance in writing
State Family & Medical Leave	Yes	Employers with 4 or more employees; all employees eligible; up to 8 weeks leave for pregnancy, childbirth, or legal abortion.
Arrest & Conviction Records	No	
Discrimination	Yes	4 or more employees; age (18 or older); national origin; disability (physical or mental), HIV/AIDS; gender; pregnancy/childbirth; race; religion; genetic testing
Whistleblower	Yes	Public employees eligible for civil action for remedies if employer is not a supervisor or department head in executive branch of state government; for

		permanent employees, remedies are classified.
Plant Closings	No	

Iowa Discrimination Laws

Federal laws provide basic protections against discrimination based on race, color, religion, sex or national origin. However, Iowa state laws provide additional protection which employees may pursue through the Iowa Civil Rights Commission according to the following guidelines:

- The state does not allow employees to privately pursue discrimination claims for wrongful termination; they must be pursued through EEOC agencies or the state's Civil Rights Commission.

- Employees are not permitted to recover attorney's fees from a defendant.

- There is no statute of limitations specified in Iowa law

Kansas

Kansas has legislated a number of specific supplemental statutes in addition to the federal protections already in place regarding wrongful termination. The federal laws, Labor Standards Act of 1938 as well as the Civil Rights Act of 1964, cover basic protections, which state statutes include some more local and detailed legislation. All states, including Kansas, are now "at will" employment states, which means that employees and employers both have the right to terminate employment for any reason other than those specifically spelled out in federal and local laws. Kansas has state agencies which will assist employees who believe they have been terminated unlawfully.

Kansas's Specific Labor Laws

Supplemental discrimination and wrongful termination laws in the state of Kansas include the following:

Benefit	State Law	Additional Benefits
Right to Work	Yes	
State Military Leave	Yes	Unlimited leave for state military forces called to active duty, as well as guaranteed reinstatement and full benefits unless disabled, then entitled to comparable position, seniority, and benefits; employee has 72 hours to report after completion of service or recovery from injury/illness; 5

		to 10 days leave/year for training
Jury Duty	Yes	Unpaid leave for permanent employees; job, seniority, or benefits are guaranteed
Voting	Yes	Paid leave for up to 2 hours combined with nonworking hours, if necessary; employer decides leave hours, but not during break periods
State Family & Medical Leave	No	
Arrest & Conviction Records	Yes	Employer cannot require employees to inspect or challenge a record in order to review it themselves; employer may require applicant to sign release so they can review record to screen employee; Certain businesses can require access to criminal records
Discrimination	Yes	4 or more employees; age (18 or older); national origin; disability (physical or mental), HIV/AIDS; gender; race; religion; genetic testing; military status
Whistleblower	Yes	Public, permanent, & classified employees can appeal to state civil service board, courts, or administrative hearings within 30-day statute of limitations; unclassified employee can file civil suit within 90 days; remedies include reinstatement, back wages, reasonable attorney's fees, & witness fees.
Plant Closings	Yes	Certain employers (public utilities, transportation, manufacture/ transportation/ preparation of food products/clothing; fuel mining/ production) need state Secretary of Labor approval to limit or discontinue business operations.

Kansas Discrimination Laws

While Kansas does not generally allow victims of discrimination to file private lawsuits against their employers, the state EEOC office and office of Human Rights Commission are tasked with pursuing claims on behalf of those employees suffering discrimination because of race, color, religion, sex, or national origin contrary to federal laws, and supplemental state laws, as well, according to these procedures:

- State agencies are primarily responsible for enforcement, administration, and investigation of wrongful termination claims due to discrimination.

- The state does not allow employees to privately pursue discrimination claims.

- Employees are not permitted to recover attorney's fees from a defendant.

- The statute of limitations for discrimination claims is 300 days.

Kentucky

Federal laws such as the Labor Standards Act of 1938 and the Civil Rights Act of 1964, protect employees from most forms of discrimination and wrongful termination. However, many states have additional statutes to provide further protection for workers in their state. Kentucky is one of those states with additional statutes in addition to it being an "at will" employment state in which employees and employers both have the right to terminate employment for any reason except those specified in federal and state laws. State agencies are the employee's primary recourse for remedy and reinstatement, when applicable, under Kentucky law.

Kentucky's Specific Labor Laws

Kentucky has several additional laws covering specific areas of workplace protections:

Benefit	State Law	Additional Benefits
Right to Work	No	
State Military Leave	Yes	Unlimited unpaid leave for Kentucky National Guard members for active duty or training; reinstatement, benefits, and seniority guaranteed
Jury Duty	Yes	Unpaid leave
Voting	Yes	Unpaid time off, up to 4 hours, at the employer's discretion; 1 day notice from employee required; no proof of voting is required, but if employer learns employee did not vote, disciplinary action may be taken
State Family & Medical Leave	Yes	For all employers and all employees; up to 6 weeks adoption leave for a child under 7 years of age
Arrest & Conviction Records	No	
Discrimination	Yes	8 or more employees; age (40 or older);

		national origin; disability (physical or mental), HIV/AIDS; gender; race; religion; smoking; occupational pneumoconiosis (with no respiratory impairment) due to coal dust exposure
Whistleblower	Yes	Protections for both public and private employees who report safety & health violations; protections for public employees who report any abuses in the workplace, who may file civil action within 90 days
Plant Closings	No	

Kentucky Discrimination Laws

Federal laws protect employees from discrimination in the workplace based on race, color, religion, sex, or national origin, and state laws provide additional protections for Kentucky workers. If employers are not complying with those laws, employees may file claims with state EEOC offices and the Kentucky Human Rights Commission for relief and/or damages according to these state guidelines:

State agencies are primarily responsible for enforcement, administration, and investigation of wrongful termination claims due to discrimination.

The state does allow employees to privately pursue discrimination claims after agency options are exhausted.

Employees are allowed to recover attorney's fees from a defendant.

The statute of limitations for discrimination claims is 180 days.

Louisiana

There are no excuses for discrimination in the workplace, especially when an employee is wrongfully terminated as a result. Federal laws protect employees across the country, primarily through the Federal Labor Standards Act of 1938 and the Civil Rights Act of 1964. There are additional laws in each state supplementing those federal laws, and Louisiana is no exception. As an "at will" employment state, employees and employers have the right to terminate employment for any reason apart from those specifically listed in state and federal laws. Louisiana has EEOC and human rights agencies to assist employees; however, employees have the right to file their own civil lawsuit without going through those state agencies.

Louisiana's Specific Labor Laws

While Louisiana doesn't have the most stringent supplemental laws addressing wrongful termination, they do have a number of very specific statutes covering most areas of the workplace:

Benefit	State Law	Additional Benefits
Right to Work	Yes	
State Military Leave	Yes	State military forces entitled to the same rights as found in USERRA; guaranteed same benefits as employees on other types of leave; required to report back to work within 72 hours of release from duty or recovery from disability; guaranteed reinstatement; cannot be terminated without cause for 1 year; U.S. National Guard members guaranteed 15 days paid leave/year for training.
Jury Duty	Yes	Regular employee, 1 paid day; cannot lose other leave or benefits as a result; no retribution; must give reasonable notice;
Voting	No	
State Family & Medical Leave	Yes	Pregnancy/maternity leave in businesses with more than 25 employees; bone marrow donation provisions for those with 20 or more employees; school activities leave for all employees; bone marrow leave only for employees with 20+ hours/week; leave periods should be reasonable time periods, not longer than 4 months for pregnancy/maternity leave; up to 40 hours' paid leave/year for bone marrow donation; school activities, 16 hours/year
Arrest & Conviction Records	Yes	Employers cannot use prior convictions as the only bases for disqualification for employment or professional/occupational licenses unless field directly related to felony conviction; exceptions: medical, engineering/architecture, or funeral/embalming licenses, among others.
Discrimination	Yes	20 or more employees; age (40 or older); national origin; disability (physical or mental), gender; race; religion; genetic

		testing; sickle cell trait
Whistleblower	Yes	Primarily apply to labor/insurance and environmental laws, rules, and regulations (including lead hazard); for public employees reporting governmental abuses, may apply to government ethics agencies for remedies; for public and private employees reporting environmental abuses, eligible for triple damages, court costs, attorney's fees, plus other civil and criminal remedies
Plant Closings	Yes	Applies to job loss due to environmental protection agency laws; those out of work due to relocation or technology changes resulting from EPA laws entitled to assistance from Displaced Worker Retraining Program through Department of Workforce Development

Louisiana Discrimination Laws

Workplace discrimination is against both state and federal laws. The federal laws cover discrimination based on race, color, religion, sex, or national origin. With Louisiana's supplemental employment protection laws, citizens of the state have many options for procuring their rights in the workplace, including state EEOC and human rights agencies, as well as private lawsuits, according to these guidelines:

- State agencies do not preempt private lawsuits for wrongful termination due to discrimination abuses

- The state allows employees to privately pursue discrimination claims

- Employees are allowed to recover attorney's fees from a defendant

- The statute of limitations for discrimination claims is not specified

Maine

Maine provides a wide range of labor protection laws for employees in addition to federal laws such as the Federal Labor Standards Act of 1938 and the Civil Rights Act of 1964. As an "at will" employment state, employers and employees have the right to terminate an employment relationship for any reason other than those specifically protected in federal and state labor laws. Since those laws are comprehensive in this state, there are many opportunities for employees to have their rights protected and restored with the help of state agencies and employee rights attorneys.

Maine's Specific Labor Laws

Maine's supplemental labor laws are detailed and specific. Those laws cover a range of workplace issues, including:

Benefit	State Law	Additional Benefits
Right to Work	No	
State Military Leave	Yes	No discrimination for membership in state military force
Jury Duty	Yes	Unpaid leave; may not be penalized for jury duty with loss of health insurance coverage
Voting	No	
State Family & Medical Leave	Yes	All employees eligible for domestic violence leave; employers with at least 15 employees at one workplace eligible for family medical leave; eligible employees are those with 1 year of service or more; leave for childbirth, serious health conditions, or family member with such illnesses include 10 weeks in any 2-year period; "reasonable and necessary" leave available for victims dealing with aftereffects of domestic violence, sexual assault, stalking, or family members involved in such cases
Arrest & Conviction Records	Yes	Convictions can only influence employment decisions when directly related to position, when they include dishonesty or false statements, when they result in more than a year's imprisonment, or when they involve sexual misconduct.
Discrimination	Yes	1 or more employees; age; national origin; disability (physical or mental), gender; pregnancy/childbirth; race; religion; sexual orientation; genetic testing; gender identity or expression; former worker's compensation claims; past whistleblowing
Whistleblower	Yes	Applies to both public and private employees; must report to supervisor first

		and allow a reasonable chance to correct violation unless it is obvious the employer will not do so.
Plant Closings	Yes	For employers with 100 or more employees at any one time during previous 12 months who discontinue or relocate business more than 100 miles; must give 1 week severance for each 1 year of employment for those with company for 3 years or more, which is due within 1 pay period; notification in writing required 60 days or more in advance to employee and to Bureau of Labor Standards and officials in plant location

Maine Discrimination Laws

Discrimination can often be at the center of wrongful termination cases. In Maine, those who believe they have either been discriminated against according to federal workplace discrimination protections from race, color, religion, sex, or national origin, or state supplemental discrimination laws, Maine's statutes require that employees file a claim with a local human rights agency first, before pursuing a private lawsuit. Other guidelines include the following:

- State agencies preempt private lawsuits in discrimination cases.

- The state does allow employees to pursue private discrimination claims once state agency options have been exhausted.

- Employees are allowed to recover attorney's fees from a defendant under certain conditions.

- The statute of limitations for discrimination claims is 6 months.

Maryland

Wrongful termination is a form of labor discrimination that is protected by federal laws such as the Labor Standards Act of 1938 and the Civil Rights Act of 1964. In addition, many states including Maryland have a number of supplemental laws protecting citizens in the workplace. Since Maryland is an "at will" employment state, employees and employers may terminate employment for any reason except those protected by state and federal laws; therefore, the state guarantees the appropriate protections in state statutes.

Maryland's Specific Labor Laws

State supplemental labor laws in Maryland include the following:

Benefit	State Law	Additional Benefits
Right to Work	No	
State Military Leave	Yes	USERRA laws provide equal benefits to state national guard and Maryland defense force called into military service
Jury Duty	Yes	Unpaid leave without relinquishing vacation, sick, or annual leave
Voting	Yes	Paid leave, if necessary; 2 consecutive hours of paid leave + non work hours required when polls are open; proof of voting, or attempting to vote, required
State Family & Medical Leave	Yes	Applies to employers who allow childbirth leave; all employees eligible; same leave allowed for adoption as for childbirth
Arrest & Conviction Records	Yes	No inquiries concerning expunged records; refusal to disclose conviction information cannot be sole reason for employment decisions; convictions may not be sole reason for refusing or revoking professional or occupational licenses, must consider conviction's relationship to the position, when it occurred, and applicant's behavior before and after conviction
Discrimination	Yes	15 or more employees; age; national origin; disability (physical or mental), gender; marital status; pregnancy/childbirth; race; religion; sexual orientation; genetic testing
Whistleblower	Yes	Public employees; remedies include submitting complaint to officials within 6 months of violation; if violation is proved, remedies include removing any related information from employee personnel record, reinstatement, lost wages, benefits, court costs, and attorney's fees
Plant Closings	Yes	For employers with 50 or more employees and in business for 1 year or more; applies to business with 25% or more employee layoffs or 15, whichever is more, in 3

		months; 90-day notification required whenever possible; employers encouraged to follow Department of Labor guidelines for severance, benefits, and notifications; exceptions for bankruptcy, seasonal fluctuations, labor disputes, temporary businesses, or construction jobs.

Maryland Discrimination Laws

Discrimination laws in Maryland are based on federal standards, which include protections from discrimination based on race, color, religion, sex, or national origin. However, state supplemental discrimination laws provide additional protections for certain situations or classes of workers under the following standards:

- Private lawsuits for discrimination claims are preempted by state agencies.

- Employees may only pursue personal lawsuits after state agencies have processed discrimination claims.

- Employees may recover attorney's fees from a defendant at the agency's or court's discretion

- The statute of limitations for discrimination claims is 6 months.

Massachusetts

Massachusetts not only enforces federal anti-discrimination and wrongful termination labor laws, such as the Federal Labor Standards Act of 1938 and the Civil Rights Act of 1964, they have a wide range of state statutes supplementing those protections. As an "at will" employment state, both employers and employees have the right to terminate that work relationship at any time for any reason except those stated in state and federal laws. Those protections are powerful, and can be pursued by claims through state EEOC offices and civil rights agencies. However, if those claims are dropped or ineffective, employees and their employee rights lawyers may file private lawsuits.

Massachusetts's Specific Labor Laws

There are a number of state statutes in Massachusetts which supplement federal laws protecting employees from wrongful termination and discrimination:

Benefit	State Law	Additional Benefits

Right to Work	No	
State Military Leave	Yes	U.S. reserves or state forces may take up to 17 days leave/year for training without affecting vacation, sick time, bonuses, or seniority; reinstatement is guaranteed; notice to employer of start and end date of service is required
Jury Duty	Yes	All full-time, part-time, and temporary employees working for 3 months prior to call; paid leave for first 3 days, after which state pays $50/day; if incurs "extreme hardship" on employer, state pays those wages
Voting	Yes	Unpaid time off for first 2 hours polls are open (for manufacturing, mechanical, or retail industries); leave must be requested in advance
State Family & Medical Leave	Yes	Maternity & adoption leave for employers with 6 or more employees; applies to full-time female employees past probationary, or initial 3 month period; school activities leave for employers with 50 or more employees; FMLA eligible employees also eligible for state family leave protection; childbirth/maternity family leave, or for adoption of child under 18 (23 if disabled), entitled to 8 weeks leave; leave of 24 hours/year for school activities or to accompany minor child or relative 60 or older to medical/dental appointments
Arrest & Conviction Records	Yes	If job applications ask about arrests or convictions, must include standard statement (from statute) enabling applicant to answer "no record" for sealed records; prohibited from asking about arrests that did not lead to convictions; prohibited from asking about 1st offenses for drunkenness, simple assault, speeding, minor traffic violations, or disturbing the peace; prohibited from asking about misdemeanor convictions more than 4 years old
Discrimination	Yes	6 or more employees; age (40 or older); national origin; disability (physical or

		mental), HIV/AIDS; gender; marital status; race; religion; sexual orientation; genetic testing; military service; arrests
Whistleblower	Yes	Public employees; employee required to report violations to supervisor to allow them to correct unless supervisor knows of problem and emergency arises, employee fears physical harm from making report, or report includes evidence of criminal activity; civil action permitted within 2 years of incident
Plant Closings	Yes	For sale or transfer of ownership of business with 50 or more employees; must include permanent separation of at least 90% of employees within 6 months; employers must be receiving state assistance; employers must provide 90 days of group health insurance coverage at same terms as prior to closing; upon sale, new employer must provide severance equal to 2 weeks compensation for every year of service over 3 years to employees terminated within 1 year of sale; 90 day notice of closing required; employers with 12 or more employees must notify Director of Labor and Workforce Development concerning change of location; new owners of business with 60 or more employees must provide written employee rights within 30 days; reemployment assistance available through state agency; employees with more than 1 year service entitled to up to 13 weeks reemployment assistance benefits

Massachusetts Discrimination Laws

Massachusetts has a significant legal interest in protecting employees from wrongful termination or discrimination. In addition to federal laws protecting employees from discrimination based on race, color, religion, sex, or national origin, state laws provide additional avenues for employees to pursue compensation or remedies for unlawful employer actions according to the following provisions:

- Private lawsuits for discrimination claims are preempted by state agencies

- Employees may not pursue personal lawsuits after state agencies have processed discrimination claims
- Employees may recover attorney's fees from a defendant
- The statute of limitations for discrimination claims is 300 days; 3 years for civil actions

Michigan

Michigan has a number of protections in place for their employees in addition to federal laws, which include the Federal Labor Standards Act of 1938 and the Civil Rights Act of 1964, although Michigan aligns with federal statutes in general. As an "at will" employment state, workers and employers may both terminate the work relationship for any reason, as long as it does not fall under state or federal laws. Those laws can be pursued by claims through the state EEOC or human rights offices, or by private lawsuits by the employee and their employee rights attorney.

Michigan's Specific Labor Laws

The state statutes with supplement federal labor laws include the following:

Benefit	State Law	Additional Benefits
Right to Work	No	
State Military Leave	Yes	State or U.S. servicemen may take unpaid leave, as may employees enlisting or applying for enlistment; reinstatement is generally guaranteed; application for reinstatement must be within 15 days of service termination
Jury Duty	Yes	Unpaid leave; no additional hours required beyond normal working hours to make up time off
Voting	No	
State Family & Medical Leave	No	
Arrest & Conviction Records	Yes	Prohibited from asking about arrests or misdemeanor charges that did not result in conviction; employees may refuse to disclose information that is protected under state/federal civil rights laws
Discrimination	Yes	1 or more employees; age; national origin;

		disability (physical or mental), HIV/AIDS; gender; marital status; pregnancy/childbirth; race; religion; genetic testing; height or weight; arrest record
Whistleblower	Yes	For both public and private employees; may file civil suit within 90 days to recover damages, attorney's fees, court costs, lost wages, benefits, reinstatement, injunction, and seniority
Plant Closings	Yes	For permanent closure of businesses with 25 or more employees; encouraged to give notice to employees, their representatives, and the community as soon as possible; Department of Labor may help study the option of employees forming their own business.

Michigan Discrimination Laws

Michigan has enacted discrimination laws to supplement federal discrimination laws providing protection based on race, color, religion, sex, or national origin. The following provisions reveal the state guidelines for filing discrimination claims or lawsuits within the state of Michigan:

- Private lawsuits for discrimination claims are not preempted by state agencies.

- Employees are permitted to pursue private lawsuits whether or not they have pursued claims through state agencies.

- Employees with winning claims or suits are permitted to recover attorney's fees from a defendant

- The statute of limitations for Michigan discrimination claims is 3 years

Minnesota

Minnesota has a strong commitment to protecting its citizens from wrongful termination and discrimination in the workplace with a significant number of state laws supplementing the federal legislation found in the Federal Labor Standards Act of 1938 and the Civil Rights Act of 1964. In addition, while this "at will" state allows employers and employees to terminate an employment relationship for any reason that is not protected in state and federal laws, employees who believe they have a claim for wrongful termination or discrimination may pursue that claim through state agencies or private lawsuits with their employee rights attorney.

Minnesota's Specific Labor Laws

The long list of state supplemental labor laws including the following specifications:

Benefit	State Law	Additional Benefits
Right to Work	No	
State Military Leave	Yes	For all U.S. and local military servicemen; no threats to employee jobs for enlisting or serving
Jury Duty	Yes	Unpaid leave
Voting	Yes	Paid time off during election day morning
State Family & Medical Leave	Yes	Childbirth/maternity/adoption leave for employers with 21 employees or more at one site, and employees who have worked at least half-time for 1 year, 6 weeks of leave; bone marrow donation for employers with at least 20 employees, employees with at least 20 hours per week, up to 40 hours paid leave per year; school leave for all employers, employees with at least 1 year service, 16 hours leave in a 12-month period, including other activities related to child care, preschool, or special education; parents may also use sick leave to care for sick/injured child
Arrest & Conviction Records	Yes	No one can be disqualified due to criminal record unless crime directly relates to occupation or license (and then significant evidence of rehabilitation may supersede this opportunity to disqualify); state encourages rehabilitation for all, and considers employment essential part of rehabilitation
Discrimination	Yes	1 or more employees; age (18 to 70); national origin; disability (physical or mental), HIV/AIDS; gender; marital status; pregnancy/childbirth; race; religion; genetic testing; gender identity; membership on local commission; perceived sexual orientation; receiving public assistance
Whistleblower	Yes	For both public and private employees; no

		penalties for reporting or refusing to participate in illegal actions or those against policy; civil lawsuits allowed for damages, attorney's fees, & injunctive relief
Plant Closings	Yes	For permanent closure of a single business site or substantial layoff of 50 or more employees for 30 or more days; employers encouraged to give at least 60 days notice to the Department of Trade and Economic Development; when WARN applies, employers must give notice to state commissioner; department provides rapid response assistance and on-site emergency assistance, information about employment resources, & assistance in establishing employment committees

Minnesota Discrimination Laws

Federal discrimination laws protect employees from discrimination due to race, color, religion, sex, or national origin. Minnesota state laws also add to those protections, and both sets of laws can be pursued under the following specifications:

- Discrimination claims may be pursued through either state agencies (with no preemption) or private lawsuits

- Employees have the right to recover attorney's fees in a winning claim or lawsuit

- Discrimination claims must be filed within the Minnesota statute of limitations, which is 1 year.

Mississippi

Mississippi relies heavily on federal laws governing wrongful termination and discrimination in the workplace, although they have enacted some state statutes supplementing the Federal Labor Standards Act of 1938 and the Civil Rights Act of 1964. As an "at will" state, they allow great freedom for both employers and employees to terminate a work relationship for any reason except those specifically protected under federal and state laws. However, when an employee believes they have reason to file a complaint for either of these abuses, state EEOC offices, human rights agencies, and civil courts all provide options for remedies and, if appropriate, compensation.

Mississippi's Specific Labor Laws

The state laws enacted to supplement federal anti-discrimination in the workplace and wrongful termination are few, but detailed, as can be seen in the list below:

Benefit	State Law	Additional Benefits
Right to Work	Yes	
State Military Leave	Yes	Unpaid leave for all U.S. and local military active duty or training; guaranteed reinstatement if still qualified for former job or employer must provide similar one; proof of service required
Jury Duty	Yes	Unpaid leave; employer cannot take sick leave, vacation time, or other leave time to compensate; reasonable notice is required; employers with 5 employees or less may have court postpone jury duty for 1 employee if another is already serving
Voting	No	
State Family & Medical Leave	No	
Arrest & Conviction Records	No	
Discrimination	Yes	Military service (all employers); only other protected categories apply only to employers who receive public funding
Whistleblower	Yes	For public employees; no penalties for reporting or testifying to investigators; civil lawsuits allowed to recover lost wages and reinstatement
Plant Closings	No	

Mississippi Discrimination Laws

Federal laws are very comprehensive in protecting Mississippi citizens from discrimination based on race, color, religion, sex, or national origin, and state statutes supplement those laws as needed by workers according to these standards:

- There is a preemption for all claims by state service employees to be pursued through state agencies only

- Mississippi does not allow discrimination claims for state service employees to be pursued through private lawsuits

- State service employees do not have the right to recover attorney's fees in a winning claim

- There is no statute of limitations specified for claims by state service employees for discrimination or wrongful termination

Missouri

Every state depends on federal wrongful termination and discrimination laws to protect their citizens in the workplace, primarily based on the Federal Labor Standards Act of 1938 and the Civil Rights Act of 1964. However, most states have additional supplemental statutes to further insure the civil rights of its workers. "At will" states like Missouri allow both employees and employers to terminate employment for any reason other than those outlined in state and federal laws, so state EEOC and human rights agencies play a big part in helping employees understand their rights and pursue them if they are abused.

Missouri's Specific Labor Laws

Missouri has enacted a limited number of supplemental labor laws covering such areas of anti-discrimination and wrongful termination as those listed in the chart below:

Benefit	State Law	Additional Benefits
Right to Work	No	
State Military Leave	Yes	Employer prohibited from interfering with any employee's state or U.S. military service, enlistment, leave, or return to the job
Jury Duty	Yes	Unpaid leave; employer cannot penalize employee in any way; employer cannot take sick leave, vacation time, or other leave time to compensate
Voting	Yes	Paid leave, if necessary, to allow employee 3 consecutive hours off when polls are open; pay contingent upon actual vote by employee (but no proof of voting required); at least 1 day employee notice required
State Family & Medical Leave	No	
Arrest & Conviction Records	No	
Discrimination	Yes	6 or more employees; age (40 to 70); national origin; disability (physical or mental); AIDS/HIV; gender; pregnancy/childbirth; race; religion;

		genetic testing
Whistleblower	Yes	For public employees; no penalties for reporting; can appeal through state personnel advisory board within 30-day statute of limitations for modification or reversal of employer's disciplinary actions and other lawful relief
Plant Closings	Yes	Plant takeovers must be reported to state securities commission concerning future plans to sell, liquidate, or in any way change corporate or employment structure

Missouri Discrimination Laws

Specific federal statutes protecting Missouri citizens from discrimination because of race, color, religion, sex, or national origin, as well as state statutes supplementing those laws, can be pursued according to these standards under Missouri discrimination laws:

- Private discrimination lawsuits are preempted by actions through state agencies.

- Employees are not limited to EEOC or human rights claims, but may pursue personal lawsuits for discrimination remedies.

- Employees may recover attorney's fees from a defendant as part of a successful discrimination settlement.

- The statute of limitations for Missouri discrimination claims is 180 days.

Montana

Montana relies heavily on federal wrongful termination and discrimination laws, such as the Federal Labor Standards Act of 1938 and the Civil Rights Act of 1964, to protect employees within their state. However, they have enacted some state statutes to supplement those laws and further protect workers. While Montana is an "at will" state, they have enacted the Wrongful Discharge from Employment Act to further specify employer and employee rights to terminate the working relationship. All employees in the state who believe they have been wrongfully terminated from a position have the right to file claims with the local human rights offices or in the courts with the help of employee rights attorneys.

Montana's Specific Labor Laws

The state statutes Montana employs to supplement federal laws include the following:

Benefit	State Law	Additional Benefits
Right to Work	No	
State Military Leave	Yes	State militia members called up for emergency/disaster service receive unpaid leave for duration of emergency; employer prohibited from discriminating because of militia service, enlistment, leave, or return to the job; leave may not be deducted from vacation, sick, or other employee leave unless employee volunteers to do so
Jury Duty	No	
Voting	No	
State Family & Medical Leave	Yes	All employers covered; all employees eligible; leave is "reasonable leave of absence" for pregnancy, maternity, & childbirth
Arrest & Conviction Records	No	
Discrimination	Yes	For 1 or more employees; age; national origin; disability (physical or mental); gender; marital status; pregnancy/childbirth; race; religion
Whistleblower	Yes	For both public and private employees; retaliation or termination for reporting prohibited
Plant Closings	No	

Montana Discrimination Laws

Federal laws provide a high level of protection for Montana workers against discrimination due to race, color, religion, sex, or national origin; and state laws provide additional protections. However, if employers violate those laws, employees may file claims or lawsuits in accordance with the following standards:

- Private discrimination lawsuits are preempted by actions through state agencies.

- Employees are not limited to human rights claims, but may pursue personal lawsuits for discrimination remedies.

- Employees may recover attorney's fees from a defendant as part of a successful discrimination settlement.

- The statute of limitations for Montana discrimination claims is 180 to 300 days.

Nebraska

There are a number of statutes provided for in federal laws protecting all U.S. workers from wrongful termination. However, most states have additional laws governing these claims and expanding their protections. Nebraska is no different; with state statutes limiting the "at will" nature of Nebraska employment by which both employers and employees have the right to terminate the employment relationship for any reason other than those covered in state and federal laws. The primary federal laws governing wrongful termination are the Federal Labor Standards Act of 1938 and the Civil Rights Act of 1964. Both federal and state laws also provide means for employees whose rights have been violated to file claims through state agencies and, if those claims are ineffective, in civil courts with an experienced employee rights attorney.

Nebraska's Specific Labor Laws

Nebraska state statutes which supplement federal laws include the following:

Benefit	State Law	Additional Benefits
Right to Work	Yes	
State Military Leave	Yes	Active state national guard members have the same reinstatement and leave rights as USERRA
Jury Duty	Yes	Paid leave at normal rate (minus court compensation); no make-up hours allowed (day or night shift); reasonable notice required;
Voting	Yes	Paid time off if necessary to equal 2 consecutive hours during polling hours, at employer's discretion; notification required
State Family & Medical Leave	Yes	Adoption leave for all employers who grant childbirth leave; all employees eligible; leave guaranteed for those adopting child under 9 or special needs child under 19; does not apply to foster parent or stepparent adoption
Arrest & Conviction Records	Yes	No access to arrest records after 1 year if no charges pending or completed
Discrimination	Yes	For 15 or more employees; age (40 to 70 for employers with 25 or more employees); national origin; disability (physical or

		mental); gender; marital status; pregnancy/childbirth; race; religion; genetic testing (all employers)
Whistleblower	Yes	For employers receiving public funding and that employ 15 or more employees; applies to public employees
Plant Closings	No	

Nebraska Discrimination Laws

In addition to wrongful termination laws, federal discrimination laws protect employees from inequities in the workplace based on race, color, religion, sex, or national origin. State laws also protect employees and provide guidelines for filing claims for remedies:

- State agency claims preempt private suits by employees

- Employees may file personal lawsuits once agency claims for discrimination violations have been exhausted

- Employees are eligible to recover attorney's fees in winning actions

- Nebraska discrimination claims must be filed within 300 days of violation

Nevada

Nevada adheres to federal wrongful termination and employment discrimination laws under the Federal Labor Standards Act of 1938 and the Civil Rights Act of 1964. However, they have some stringent penalties and statutes in state legislation that supplement those laws. While it is an "at will" employment state, and employees and employers can both terminate employment for any reason not specifically protected in federal and state laws, employees whose rights have been violated under those laws have legal options to file claims and/or lawsuits.

Nevada's Specific Labor Laws

Supplemental laws protecting employees in the state of Nevada are enumerated in the chart below:

Benefit	State Law	Additional Benefits
Right to Work	Yes	
State Military Leave	Yes	Discrimination based on Nevada National Guard service prohibited

Jury Duty	Yes	Unpaid leave; discrimination for jury duty prohibited; minimum 1 day's notice required
Voting	Yes	Paid time off if required, based on work hours and distance from polls: 1 hour off for those who work 2 miles or less from polls, 2 hours off for those 2 to 10 miles from polls, 3 hours off for those more than 10 miles from polls; time off not required if employee has sufficient non-work time during polling hours; at least 1 day notification required
State Family & Medical Leave	Yes	All employers covered; parent, guardian, or child custodian eligible; family leave same as sick or medical leave policies; leave must apply to pregnancy, miscarriage, and childbirth
Arrest & Conviction Records	Yes	Records available only if they contain convictions or pending charges (including parole or probation); gaming board may access records for convictions related to gaming
Discrimination	Yes	For 15 or more employees; age (40 or older); national origin; disability (physical or mental); gender; pregnancy/childbirth; race; religion; sexual orientation; genetic testing; lawful use of any product while not on work time; use of service animal
Whistleblower	Yes	Applies to employees of physicians; public and private employees who report health and safety violations; public employees who report violations of regulations/laws, authority, abuses, and waste
Plant Closings	No	

Nevada Discrimination Laws

Discrimination can be the basis for wrongful termination as well. Nevada has guidelines by which violations of federal laws prohibiting discrimination for race, color, religion, sex, or national origin can be remedied:

- Private lawsuits are preempted by claims made through state agencies

- Once agency claims dropped or exhausted, employee may file private lawsuit

- Employees do have the right to recover attorney's fees
- The statute of limitations for Nevada discrimination claims is 180 days from violation

New Hampshire

New Hampshire adheres to federal discrimination and wrongful termination laws without supplementation in the majority of cases. However, there are some additional statutes that New Hampshire employers must comply with to avoid penalties. As an "at will" employment state, the only reasons for which employers and employees cannot terminate employment relationships are spelled out in state and federal laws such as the Federal Labor Standards Act of 1938 and the Civil Rights Act of 1964. These discrimination and wrongful termination statutes provide measures for employees to pursue remedies for violations.

New Hampshire's Specific Labor Laws

New Hampshire employees are protected by federal discrimination and wrongful termination laws and state supplemental statutes, which include the following:

Benefit	State Law	Additional Benefits
Right to Work	No	
State Military Leave	Yes	State national guard and militia on active duty have the same leave and reinstatement rights as USERRA; discrimination based on military service prohibited
Jury Duty	Yes	Unpaid leave
Voting	No	
State Family & Medical Leave	Yes	Employers with minimum 6 employees covered; all employees eligible; family leave for temporary disability due to childbirth or related condition
Arrest & Conviction Records	Yes	Employer may only ask about arrests or convictions that have not been legally annulled; cannot require applicants to have no arrest record; cannot base hiring decisions on arrest records unless a "business necessity"; cannot ask about arrest records to discourage applicants of a particular race or national origin

Discrimination	Yes	For 6 or more employees; age; national origin; disability (physical or mental); gender; marital status; pregnancy/childbirth; race; religion; sexual orientation; genetic testing
Whistleblower	Yes	Employee must present report to employer or supervisor in order to allow them to correct abuses (except when it is reasonable to assume employer will not correct); employers may not interfere with rights of public employee to discuss work topics that are not confidential;
Plant Closings	Yes	Any business making a takeover offer must notify secretary of state and target company of future plans to liquidate or change any management or employment systems

New Hampshire Discrimination Laws

There are a number of state discrimination laws in addition to the basic federal protections from discrimination based on race, color, religion, sex, or national origin. New Hampshire mandates the following guidelines to employees seeking remedies for violations of discrimination laws:

- State agencies preempt private lawsuits for discrimination claims

- There is no provision in New Hampshire law for private lawsuits

- It is at the state agency or court's discretion whether an employee has the right to recover attorney's fees

- The New Hampshire statute of limitations is 180 days from date of discrimination violation

New Jersey

New Jersey has enacted a number of state statutes supplementing federal wrongful termination and discrimination laws, the most common of which are the Civil Rights Act of 1964 and the Federal Labor Standards Act of 1938. New Jersey workers have the right, in this "at will" employment state, to quit a job for any reason, and an employer has the right to terminate an employee for any reason except those which are specifically protected in federal and state laws. If an employer illegally terminates an employee, federal and state laws provide guidelines for filing claims and/or lawsuits to obtain the remedies that are available.

New Jersey's Specific Labor Laws

There are a number of detailed state laws in New Jersey relating to discrimination and wrongful termination, which can be found in the following table:

Benefit	State Law	Additional Benefits
Right to Work	No	
State Military Leave	Yes	Unpaid leave for U.S. or state military service; guaranteed reinstatement unless employer's circumstances change and make it impossible; must apply for reinstatement within 90 days; termination without cause in less than 1 year prohibited; up to 3 months training leave allowed every 4 yeara; employee must apply for reinstatement within 10 days
Jury Duty	Yes	Unpaid leave
Voting	No	
State Family & Medical Leave	Yes	Employers with minimum 50 employees covered; eligible employees have 1 year service & at least 1,000 hours in previous 12 months; 12 weeks family leave (24 weeks reduced leave) in 24 months for pregnancy/maternity, childbirth, adoption, or family care for serious condition; family members include domestic partners, parents-in-law (child includes legal wards; parents include those with visitation rights)
Arrest & Conviction Records	Yes	Employers may obtain information on convictions and pending arrests or charges to aid in determining applicant's qualifications; must provide sufficient time for applicant to challenge, complete, or correct record; cannot presume guilt for pending actions
Discrimination	Yes	For 1 or more employees; age (18 to 70); national origin; disability (past or present, physical or mental); HIV/AIDS; gender; marital status (including domestic partners); pregnancy/childbirth; race; religion; sexual orientation; genetic testing; predisposing genetic characteristics; military service or status; smoker;

		accompanied by service animal; gender identity
Whistleblower	Yes	Employee must present report to employer or supervisor in order to allow them to correct abuses, except in emergency or when employee faces physical threat or when it is reasonable to assume employer will not correct)
Plant Closings	Yes	Possible plant closing; Department of Labor and other government agencies may assist (and commissioner of commerce may fund) employees in employee ownership plans, especially in economically challenged community

New Jersey Discrimination Laws

Federal discrimination laws provide the basic protections based on race, color, religion, sex, or national origin. In addition, New Jersey has added legislation supplementing those laws and providing guidelines for pursing remedies for violations:

- Private lawsuits are not preempted by state agency discrimination claims.

- Employees in New Jersey are permitted to file private lawsuits for discrimination abuses.

- New Jersey employment discrimination victims have the right to recover attorney's fees in successful lawsuits and claims.

- There is a 180-day statute of limitations for agency claims and a 2-year statute of limitations for private lawsuits in employment discrimination cases.

New Mexico

Federal laws protect employees from discrimination and wrongful termination in the workplace on a number of bases. The most common statutes governing these issues are the Civil Rights Act of 1964 and the Federal Labor Standards Act of 1938. However, most states have passed additional legislation addressing these areas, limiting the "at law" employment status of most states, including New Mexico, which permit employers and employees to terminate employment for any reason except those specifically covered in those state and federal laws. They also include provisions for employees to find remedies, either through EEOC claims or private lawsuits, for employer violations.

New Mexico's Specific Labor Laws

New Mexico has enacted the following state laws supplementing federal regulations concerning wrongful termination and discrimination in the workplace:

Benefit	State Law	Additional Benefits
Right to Work	No	
State Military Leave	Yes	Unpaid leave for U.S. armed forces, state national guard, or militia; guaranteed reinstatement in same or similar position; must apply for reinstatement within 90 days; termination without cause in less than 1 year prohibited;
Jury Duty	Yes	Unpaid leave; cannot be made to use vacation, sick, or annual leave to make up time lost
Voting	Yes	Paid time off, if required; if employee has 2 hours before or 3 hours after work while polls open, time off not required
State Family & Medical Leave	No	
Arrest & Conviction Records	Yes	In order for potential employee to obtain a permit, license, or authority to work in a regulated business or profession, felony and misdemeanor convictions may be considered for moral character, but may not be an automatic bar to employment
Discrimination	Yes	For 4 or more employees; age (40+, applies to employers with 20+ employees); national origin; disability (physical or mental); gender; marital status (applies to employers with 50+ employees); pregnancy/ childbirth; race; religion; sexual orientation (applies to employers with 15+ employees); genetic testing; gender identity (for employers with 15+ employees); serious medical condition
Whistleblower	Yes	For both private and public employees; discrimination or discharge because of complaint, testimony, exercising a right, or beginning an action based on OSHA standards prohibited
Plant Closings	No	

New Mexico Discrimination Laws

The basic protections for race, color, religion, sex, or national origin provided by federal laws and supplemented and/or expanded on in state laws can be legally pursued in New Mexico according to the following guidelines:

- Private lawsuits for discrimination are not preempted by state agency claims.

- Private lawsuits are allowed for New Mexico employees suffering discrimination abuses.

- Employees who win New Mexico employment discrimination claims or lawsuits have the right to recover attorney's fees.

- The statute of limitations for filing a New Mexico discrimination claim is 180 days for claims; for private lawsuits it is 30 days.

New York

New York has made a strong commitment to employee rights through supplemental state statutes in addition to federal discrimination and wrongful termination laws. The most common federal laws are found in the Civil Rights Act of 1964 and the Federal Labor Standards Act of 1938. While New York is an "at law" employment state, in which employees and employers may terminate employment for any reason, state and federal laws limit those reasons. They also provide avenues by which employees can file claims and civil actions to recover lost positions or receive compensation for employer violations.

New York's Specific Labor Laws

The many New York supplemental discrimination and wrongful termination laws can be found in the chart below:

Benefit	State Law	Additional Benefits
Right to Work	No	
State Military Leave	Yes	Unpaid leave for U.S. uniformed services and state military forces for active duty, training, or reserve drills; guaranteed reinstatement in same or similar position unless employer changes make it impossible or unreasonable; must apply for reinstatement after completion of service, which is 90 days for active duty, 10 days for training or drills, or 60 days for initial training

Jury Duty	Yes	Unpaid leave for all employers; employers with more than 10 employees must pay $40 for first 3 days; employer notification required
Voting	Yes	Up to 2 hours paid time off if required; not required if employee has 4 consecutive nonwork hours before or after shift while polls are open; time off combined with nonwork hours at employers discretion; at least 2 days, but not more than 10 days, notice required
State Family & Medical Leave	Yes	Employers allowing childbirth leave must also allow adoption leave for employees adopting preschool age child or younger, or disabled child of 18 or younger; bone marrow donation leave for employers with 20 or more employees at one site, those working at least 20 hours per week eligible for up to 24 hours leave
Arrest & Conviction Records	Yes	Employer cannot ask about arrests or charges not resulting in convictions unless pending; employers with 10 or more employees cannot deny employment based on convictions unless directly related to job or offense threatens property or safety; if applicants denied employment request it, employer must provide written explanation within 30 days
Discrimination	Yes	For 4 or more employees; age (18 and older); national origin; disability (physical or mental); HIV/AIDS; gender; marital status; pregnancy/ childbirth; race; religion; sexual orientation; genetic testing; lawful use of any product during nonwork hours; military status; observation of Sabbath; political activities; accompanied by service dog
Whistleblower	Yes	For both private and public employees; discrimination or discharge because of complaint, testimony, refusing an unlawful action prohibited; employee must first report violation to supervisor and allow reasonable time to correct
Plant Closings	Yes	Applies to plant closings that results in job

		losses to at least 25 full-time employees in 30 days or substantial layoffs that result in job losses for at least 33% of full-time and 50 part-time employees, or 500 full-time employees in 30 days, or a business takeover; company taking over another must register statement with New York City attorney general's office and target company disclosing plans for closures or major changes in employment policies; city agencies provide emergency readjustment services, information about retraining, unemployment insurance, technical assistance, and assistance in creating an employee-owned enterprise

New York Discrimination Laws

Federal laws provide New York workers with basic protections from discrimination for race, color, religion, sex, or national origin. State laws provide additional protections, as well as the following legal parameters for filing claims or lawsuits:

- State agency claims cannot preempt private lawsuits for discrimination

- Employee victims may file private lawsuits without being required to file prior state claims

- Employees are not permitted to recover attorney's fees in discrimination claims or suits

- The statute of limitations for discrimination claims or lawsuits varies, depending on the specific offense

North Carolina

Wrongful termination and discrimination in the workplace is outlawed in every state in the union. However, in addition to federal regulations such as the Federal Labor Standards Act of 1938 and the Civil Rights Act of 1964, all states have supplemental laws that expand those protections and in some cases, increase the penalties for employers. North Carolina is an "at will" employment state, which allows employers and employees to terminate employment at any time and for any reason except those prohibited in federal and state statutes. Those statutes also provide methods for victims to file claims for reinstatement and compensation when their rights have been violated.

North Carolina's Specific Labor Laws

The specific state labor statutes enacted by the North Carolina legislature include the following:

Benefit	State Law	Additional Benefits
Right to Work	Yes	
State Military Leave	Yes	Unpaid leave for North Carolina National Guard members on active duty; guaranteed reinstatement in same or similar position unless employer changes make it unreasonable; must apply for reinstatement 5 after completion of service; termination or discrimination based on military service is prohibited
Jury Duty	Yes	Unpaid leave; demotion for serving jury duty is prohibited
Voting	No	
State Family & Medical Leave	Yes	All employers covered; all employees eligible; up to 4 hours family leave for school activities per year
Arrest & Conviction Records	No	
Discrimination	Yes	For 15 or more employees; for age; national origin; disability (physical or mental); HIV/AIDS; gender; race; religion; genetic testing; lawful use of any product during nonwork hours; military service; sickle cell trait
Whistleblower	Yes	For public and private employees, discrimination or discharge because of complaint, testimony, refusing an unlawful action, or filing OSHA complaint prohibited
Plant Closings	No	

North Carolina Discrimination Laws

Based on federal laws barring discrimination based on race, color, religion, sex, or national origin and the state supplemental statutes listed above, the following parameters guide employees in filing for relief under North Carolina law:

- Victims of discrimination the workplace or wrongful termination may not file private lawsuits, but must file claims through state EEOC or human rights agencies

- Employees are not eligible to recover attorney's fees in discrimination claims or suits

- There are no state statutes of limitations on discrimination or wrongful termination claims

North Dakota

American legislators have become much more aware of discrimination throughout society and especially in the workplace. As a result, most states have added supplemental statutes providing protections in addition to federal laws found in the Federal Labor Standards Act of 1938 and the Civil Rights Act of 1964. While North Dakota is an "at will" employment state, and both employees and employers have the right to terminate employment for any reason that is not prohibited in federal and state laws, they have added a number of laws to protect employees in their state from discrimination. When such violations occur, those laws also provide avenues for victims to seek legal remedies.

North Dakota's Specific Labor Laws

The supplemental state labor laws enacted in North Dakota for wrongful termination and discrimination include those on the following chart:

Benefit	State Law	Additional Benefits
Right to Work	Yes	
State Military Leave	No	
Jury Duty	Yes	Unpaid leave; demotion for serving jury duty is prohibited
Voting	Yes	Unpaid time off is encouraged when regular work hours conflict with polling hours
State Family & Medical Leave	No	
Arrest & Conviction Records	Yes	Employers may obtain records of criminal charges and convictions for adults from the last 3 years for those instances that have not been purged or sealed
Discrimination	Yes	For 1 or more employees; for age (40 or older); national origin; disability (physical or mental); gender; marital status; race; religion; lawful conduct during nonwork hours; receiving public assistance
Whistleblower	Yes	For public employees; employee must have objective, factual basis for refusing work order; employee must inform employer of reasons for refusal
Plant Closings	No	

North Dakota Discrimination Laws

North Dakota has established specific guidelines which apply to filing claims for discrimination in the workplace:

- There is no statute requiring employees to file discrimination claims through state agencies before pursing private lawsuits

- Employees are eligible to file private lawsuits for discrimination in the workplace

- Employees may recover attorney's fees when they win discrimination claims or suits

- Employees have 300 days to file claims for discrimination or wrongful termination in North Dakota

Ohio

There is no place for discrimination or wrongful termination in America's workplaces, and Ohio legislators agree, since there are not only federal laws, such as the Federal Labor Standards Act of 1938 and the Civil Rights Act of 1964, but numerous state statutes as well. That means that while Ohio is an "at will" employment state, employees and employers are allowed to terminate employment for any reason at any time except for reasons prohibited in federal and state statutes. Those statutes also provide means by which employees can find relief from employers who violate those laws and subject employees to discrimination or wrongful termination.

Ohio's Specific Labor Laws

Ohio laws designate a number of supplemental labor laws in addition to federal regulations:

Benefit	State Law	Additional Benefits
Right to Work	No	
State Military Leave	Yes	Employees called into active duty during times of war or emergency in the Ohio militia, Ohio national guard, public health service corps, or other uniformed service, have equal leave and reinstatement rights as provided under USERRA
Jury Duty	Yes	Unpaid leave; employee may not be required to use personal leave; reasonable notice to employer is required; employers with 25 or fewer employees may postpone jury duty for one employee when another is already serving

Voting	Yes	Paid time off; reasonable time necessary for voting
State Family & Medical Leave	No	
Arrest & Conviction Records	Yes	Employers may not ask about sealed convictions or sealed bail forfeitures unless they have direct and substantial impact on the job; employee may respond to such questions as though sealed arrests never occurred
Discrimination	Yes	For 4 or more employees; for age (40 or older); national origin; disability (physical, mental, or learning); gender; pregnancy/childbirth; race; religion
Whistleblower	Yes	For both public and private employees; employee must notify supervisor and file a written report to them, allowing them 24 hours to correct or make good faith effort to correct violation
Plant Closings	Yes	For businesses with 25 employees or more planning permanent shutdown; or relocation of business at least 100 miles away; Department of Development provides advice and feasibility study for employee ownership

Ohio Discrimination Laws

The parameters under which employees may file claims or lawsuits for violations of Ohio's discrimination and wrongful termination laws include the following:

Private lawsuits are permissible in Ohio for those suffering discrimination in the workplace

It is up to the discretion of the court whether employees with winning claims or lawsuits may recover attorney's fees

Discrimination claims or lawsuits in the state of Ohio must file within 1 year of the violation

Oklahoma

Oklahoma legislators have enacted a number of supplemental statutes enhancing and strengthening federal wrongful termination and discrimination laws, which are most commonly found in the Federal Labor Standards Act of 1938 and the Civil Rights Act of 1964. These laws place limits on the "at will" nature of Oklahoma's labor laws, permitting employers and employees to terminate employment "at will" except where those reasons are prohibited by federal and state regulations. Those laws also provide avenues by which employees victimized by wrongful termination and discrimination in the workplace can pursue remedies and compensation.

Oklahoma's Specific Labor Laws

The laws enacted by Oklahoma legislators cover a wide range of protections from wrongful termination and discrimination in the following areas:

Benefit	State Law	Additional Benefits
Right to Work	Yes	
State Military Leave	Yes	Employees called into active duty with the Oklahoma National Guard have equal leave and reinstatement rights as provided under USERRA; leave allowed for state training, drills, or ceremony as well
Jury Duty	Yes	Unpaid leave; employee may not be required to use personal leave; reasonable notice to employer is required; employers with 25 or fewer employees may postpone jury duty for one employee when another is already serving
Voting	Yes	Paid time off, if required; not required if employee has minimum of 3 hours off after polls open or before polls close; employer has discretion in scheduling 2 paid hours off in most cases, more if distance from polling place requires it; request must be made at least one day in advance; employee required to show proof of voting
State Family & Medical Leave	No	
Arrest & Conviction Records	Yes	Employers may not ask about any criminal record that has been expunged; employee may respond to such questions as though no criminal action ever occurred; employment may not be denied for failure to disclose sealed criminal information
Discrimination	Yes	For 15 or more employees; for age (40 or older); national origin; disability (physical or mental); gender; race; religion; genetic

		testing; military service; smoking
Whistleblower	Yes	For public employees, employer cannot terminate or discriminate against employee for reporting or testifying about OSHA and other violations, must allow opportunity for employer to correct; for public employees of state agencies, employer cannot terminate or discriminate for adverse reports in any area
Plant Closings	Yes	For companies planning a business takeover; company must file statement with state securities commission disclosing plans to close, relocate, or substantially change employment policies

Oklahoma Discrimination Laws

Oklahoma discrimination laws also contain guidelines under which employees can file claims for discrimination or wrongful termination:

- Oklahoma law requires employees to file such claims through state agencies before filing private civil actions

- Employees are not permitted to file private civil suits unless state agencies exhaust their ability to pursue the case or drop it entirely

- Employees do have the right to recover attorney's fees in winning claims or lawsuits

- Oklahoma discrimination claims must be filed within 180 days of the violation

Oregon

Wrongful termination and discrimination in the workplace are against the law, including both federal and state laws, such as the Federal Labor Standards Act of 1938 and the Civil Rights Act of 1964. State statutes supplement those laws, limiting the rights of employers and employees to terminate employment for any reason under "at will" statutes in the state. There are numerous options for employees to file claims and lawsuits to compensate them or provide relief from such violations.

Oregon's Specific Labor Laws

The Oregon legislature has provided supplemental labor protections for employees in the state through the following statutes:

Benefit	State Law	Additional Benefits
Right to Work	No	
State Military Leave	Yes	Employees called into active duty with state organized militia have unpaid leave; entitled to benefits and reinstatement rights upon return; employee must return to work within 7 days of release
Jury Duty	Yes	Unpaid leave (or policy adopted by employer); employee may not be penalized or discriminated against for serving
Voting	No	
State Family & Medical Leave	Yes	12 weeks yearly leave for childbirth and adoption, with an additional 12 weeks yearly for employees or family members with serious health conditions, required from employers with 25 or more employees, eligible employees must have worked 25 or more hours per week for 180 days or more; up to 40 hours or amount of accrued paid leave for bone marrow donation, required from all employers, eligible employees must work 20 or more hours per week
Arrest & Conviction Records	Yes	Employers may only request records after notifying employee/applicant and the state police; qualified records released 14 days later; may not discriminate on basis of expunged juvenile record unless there is a "bona fide occupational qualification"; may only request information about arrests less than 1 year old that are not dismissed or acquitted; employee/ applicant must be informed of procedures to challenge records
Discrimination	Yes	For 1 or more employees; for age (18 or older); national origin; disability (physical or mental; applies to employers with 6 or more employees); gender; marital status; pregnancy/ childbirth; race; religion; genetic testing
Whistleblower	Yes	For both public and private employees;

		employer cannot terminate or discriminate against employee for reporting violations
Plant Closings	Yes	Applies to employers with 100 or more full-time employees; for plant closings resulting in job losses for 50 or more full-time employees in any 30-day period; for mass layoffs resulting in job losses of 33% of workforce and 50 full-time employees, or 500 full-time employees during any 30-day period; must notify the Department of Community Colleges & Workforce Development; state provides assistance and professional/technical training, unemployment compensation, and benefits

Oregon Discrimination Laws

The guidelines for filing claims and lawsuits under Oregon state statutes include the following:

- Oregon does not require claims through state agencies to take precedence over private lawsuits.

- Employees have the right to file private lawsuits for discrimination and wrongful termination.

- Employees in Oregon have the legal right to recover attorney's fees in successful claims or civil suits.

- Employees have 1 year to file claims or lawsuits for violations of discrimination laws in Oregon

Pennsylvania

Pennsylvania has a number of complex state statutes that add to federal discrimination laws protecting employees from wrongful termination. The primary examples of federal laws are the Federal Labor Standards Act of 1938 and the Civil Rights Act of 1964. As an "at will" state, Pennsylvania allows employees and employers to terminate employment relationships for any reason; however, that freedom is somewhat limited by the protections for employees found in discrimination and wrongful termination laws. When those laws are violated, they provide legal opportunities for employees to file claims and civil actions for remedies.

Pennsylvania's Specific Labor Laws

The Pennsylvania wrongful termination and discrimination laws that supplement federal regulations are found in the following chart:

Benefit	State Law	Additional Benefits
Right to Work	No	
State Military Leave	Yes	Employees drafted, who enlist, or who are called into active duty with state or U.S. forces are entitled to unpaid leave; guaranteed reinstatement, benefits, and seniority upon return; termination or discrimination prohibited; employee entitled to 30 days' health insurance continuation benefits at no cost
Jury Duty	Yes	Unpaid leave (for retail or service employers with 15 or more employees & manufacturers with 40 or more employees); employee may not be penalized or discriminated against for serving; employees not eligible for unpaid leave may be excused; employees called as witnesses or victims, or family members of victims or witnesses also entitled to unpaid leave
Voting	No	
State Family & Medical Leave	No	
Arrest & Conviction Records	Yes	Employers may only consider felony and misdemeanor convictions if they directly influence employee's ability to do the job; employee must be informed in writing if disqualification is due to criminal record
Discrimination	Yes	For 4 or more employees; for age (40 to 70); national origin; disability (physical or mental); gender; pregnancy/ childbirth; race; religion; familial status; GED rather than high school diploma; use of guide or service animal
Whistleblower	Yes	For both public and private employees; employer cannot terminate or discriminate against employee for

		reporting violations; apply to motor carrier safety standards, laws, or regulations when employee refuses to operate commercial vehicle that does not comply with safety laws
Plant Closings	Yes	Applies to current or planned plant closings and business takeovers; potential new owner must notify state securities commission, target company, and collective bargaining agent in writing 20 days in advance about plans for closing down, making major changes in employment policies, or changing collective bargaining agreements

Pennsylvania Discrimination Laws

There are a number of state standards to guide employees in filing claims and lawsuits against employers who violate discrimination laws:

- Pennsylvania law allows state agency claims to preempt private lawsuits.

- While state agency claims have priority, when those claims are exhausted or dropped, employees may file private lawsuits

- Employees may have the right to recover attorney's fees for successful lawsuits or claims at the discretion of the courts.

- Employees are required to file claims or civil suits for discrimination or wrongful termination within 180 days through state agencies, and within 2 years for private actions.

Rhode Island

Bias or discrimination in the workplace can lead to wrongful termination, which is illegal under federal laws, like the Federal Labor Standards Act of 1938 and the Civil Rights Act of 1964, and often under supplemental state laws across the country as well. Rhode Island is one such state, which establishes limits on its "at will" status for employment. As a result, employees and employers have the right to terminate an employment relationship for any reason except those prohibited in state and federal laws. Those laws also provide employees with legal avenues to pursue remedies and compensation for employer violations.

Rhode Island's Specific Labor Laws

Rhode Island's supplemental laws protecting workers from wrongful termination and discrimination can be found in the following chart:

Benefit	State Law	Additional Benefits
Right to Work	No	
State Military Leave	Yes	Employees called into active duty with state military or national guard have the same leave and reinstatement guarantees provided for in the USERRA; employees allowed unpaid leave for training with guaranteed reinstatement, benefits, and seniority upon return unless changes in employer circumstances make that impossible or unreasonable; employee must request reinstatement within 40 days; termination or discrimination prohibited
Jury Duty	Yes	Unpaid leave; employee may not be penalized or discriminated against for serving
Voting	No	
State Family & Medical Leave	Yes	Employers with 50 or more employees covered; eligible employees have worked 30 or more hours per week for 12 consecutive months or more; 13 weeks leave in any two calendar years for childbirth, adoption of child up to 16 years of age; serious health condition of employee or family member; up to 10 hours leave for school activities; family member includes parents-in-law
Arrest & Conviction Records	Yes	Asking about previous arrest records on applications or employee interviews is prohibited; asking about convictions is permitted; employee is not required to reveal any convictions that have been expunged
Discrimination	Yes	For 4 or more employees; 1 or more employees – gender-based wage discrimination; for age (40 or older); national origin; disability (physical or mental); HIV/AIDS; gender; pregnancy/ childbirth; race; religion; sexual orientation; genetic testing; domestic abuse victim; gender identity or expression

Whistleblower	Yes	For both public and private employees; employer cannot terminate or discriminate against employee for reporting violations
Plant Closings	Yes	Applies to involuntary layoff and permanent reduction in workforce; employees entitled to at least 18 months' health coverage continuation at same rate as under group plan, paid for at employee's expense; length of coverage not to exceed length of employment

Rhode Island Discrimination Laws

In order to find relief from violations of those state laws, there are provisions for pursuing claims and civil suits in Rhode Island statutes:

- Rhode Island state agencies have priority in pursuing claims for discrimination in the workplace or wrongful termination

- If state agencies fail to pursue the claim successfully or choose to drop it, employee may file their own private civil suit.

- If employee claims or civil suits are successful, Rhode Island statutes allow them to recover attorney's fees.

- Discrimination or wrongful termination claims must be filed within the 1 year statute of limitations for such cases in Rhode Island.

South Carolina

American laws are attempting to eliminate bias and discrimination from our culture and workplace, as evidenced by federal laws such as the Federal Labor Standards Act of 1938 and the Civil Rights Act of 1964. States have additional statutes supplementing those laws to protect employees in the workplace from wrongful termination. While South Carolina is an "at will" employment state, and employees and employers both have the right to terminate employment relationships for any reason, that right is limited by protections from state and federal discrimination laws. Those laws also provide legal remedies to compensate employees and penalize employers for violations.

South Carolina's Specific Labor Laws

South Carolina state labor laws that supplement federal laws can be detailed and powerful, as is evident in the chart below:

Benefit	State Law	Additional Benefits
Right to Work	Yes	
State Military Leave	Yes	Employees on active duty with SC National Guard and State guard are entitled to unpaid leave; guaranteed reinstatement, benefits, & seniority upon return unless changes in employer circumstances make it impossible or unreasonable; employee must request reinstatement in writing within 5 days of release
Jury Duty	Yes	Unpaid leave; employee may not be penalized/terminated if subpoenaed
Voting	No	
State Family & Medical Leave	Yes	Employers with 20 or more employees covered; eligible employees work 20 hours or more per week; up to 40 hours paid leave per year is available for bone marrow donations
Arrest & Conviction Records	No	
Discrimination	Yes	For 15 or more employees; for age (40+); national origin; disability (physical or mental); gender; pregnancy/childbirth; race; religion
Whistleblower	Yes	For both public and private employees; employer cannot terminate or discriminate against employee for reporting violations; if employee reports result in savings of public funds, may result in rewards for employees
Plant Closings	Yes	Applies to employers who require notice from employees before resignation; employers must give same notice required from employees or at least 2 week's notice; notice must be in writing and posted in every room of the work building

South Carolina Discrimination Laws

There are specific parameters spelled out in South Carolina discrimination laws outlining the steps employees can take to pursue claims and civil actions for violations:

- South Carolina EEOC agencies and the state Human Affairs Commission have priority in pursuing complaints against employer violations of discrimination laws.

- In this state, employees do not have the option to file private claims or civil actions against an employer who violates discrimination laws.

- If state agency claims are successful, employees may have the right to recover attorney's fees.

- All claims for discrimination or wrongful termination must be pursued before the statute of limitations runs out, which is 180 days.

South Dakota

South Dakota generally aligns with federal wrongful termination and discrimination laws, like the Federal Labor Standards Act of 1938 and the Civil Rights Act of 1964. While they have enacted some supplemental statutes in the state, they are few in number and not as complex as those in some other states. And while South Dakota is also an "at will" employment state, federal laws limit the formerly unrestricted right of employees and employers to terminate the employment relationship for any reason. Federal and state laws also provide legal relief which the employee can pursue through state agencies or private civil suits.

South Dakota's Specific Labor Laws

The following chart contains the state labor laws enacted to supplement the federal wrongful termination and discrimination laws that apply throughout the country:

Benefit	State Law	Additional Benefits
Right to Work	Yes	
State Military Leave	Yes	Employees ordered to active duty with South Dakota National Guard are guaranteed the same leave and reinstatement benefits as those provided under USERRA
Jury Duty	Yes	Unpaid leave; employee may not be penalized or terminated if called to serve
Voting	Yes	Paid time off, if required; employee allowed 2 consecutive hours at employer's discretion; not required if employee has 2 consecutive nonwork hours while polls are open

State Family & Medical Leave	No	
Arrest & Conviction Records	Yes	Employer is not to ask about arrests or convictions unless they are significantly relevant to the job
Discrimination	Yes	For 1 or more employees; for national origin; disability (physical, mental, and learning); gender; race; religion; gender testing; pre-existing injury
Whistleblower	Yes	For both public and private employees; employer cannot terminate, discriminate, or retaliate against employee for reporting violations
Plant Closings	No	

South Dakota Discrimination Laws

There is great freedom in South Dakota for employees to file discrimination claims with state agencies first, and then through private civil actions.

- South Dakota mandates that the state office of the Division of Human rights take priority in pursing claims for discrimination or wrongful termination.

- If the state agency is unable to provide a satisfactory resolution to an employee's claim against an employer who violated discrimination laws, the employee and their employee rights lawyer may pursue a private civil action.

- In successful discrimination claims, either by state agencies or employee rights attorneys, the employee has the right to recover attorney's fees.

- Employees must ensure that the state agency or their employee rights attorney file discrimination claims within the 180-day statute of limitations.

Tennessee

Federal laws such as the Federal Labor Standards Act of 1938 and the Civil Rights Act of 1964 protect employees from wrongful termination and discrimination in the workplace. However, in addition to those laws, most states have statutes to supplement and expand those protections. And while Tennessee is an "at will" employment state that allows employers and employees to terminate the work relationship for any reason, that guarantee is limited by discrimination laws in order to protect employees. If violations do occur, these regulations provide remedies by way of claims filed through state agencies or private suits filed with employee rights lawyers.

Tennessee's Specific Labor Laws

There are a number of state-specific labor laws in Tennessee that supplement federal wrongful termination and discrimination laws, as seen in the chart below:

Benefit	State Law	Additional Benefits
Right to Work	Yes	
State Military Leave	Yes	Disqualification of applicants and termination of employees due to national guard membership or required leave for training or drills is prohibited
Jury Duty	Yes	Employers with 5 employees or more; not applicable to temporary employees with less than 6 months service; paid leave, regular wages minus jury fees; night shift workers not required to work during and the night before serving jury duty; employee must notify employer the day after receiving jury summons
Voting	Yes	Paid time off, if required; reasonable time off, up to 3 hours if necessary; not required if employee has 3 nonwork hours after polls open or before they close; employee must request leave before noon the day prior to elections
State Family & Medical Leave	Yes	Employers with at least 100 employees covered; eligible employees have worked 12 consecutive months; up to 4 months of unpaid leave for maternity/pregnancy and childbirth (which includes nursing); 3 month's notice required unless it is a medical emergency; employer must include these laws in employee handbook
Arrest & Conviction Records	No	
Discrimination	Yes	For 8 or more employees (1 or more employee for gender-based wage discrimination); for age (40 or older); national origin; disability (physical or mental); gender; race; religion
Whistleblower	Yes	For both public and private employees; employer cannot terminate, discriminate, or retaliate against employee for

		reporting violations
Plant Closings	Yes	Applies to company closings, modernization, relocation, or new management; those that lay off 50 or more employees either permanently or temporarily during a 3-month period; required for companies with 50 to 99 full-time, in-state employees; notification required for employees first, then the Commissioner of Labor and Workforce Development, with details of closing and employees being laid off; does not apply to construction sites or common seasonal fluctuations

Tennessee Discrimination Laws

Employees have great leeway in filing discrimination claims and civil actions in Tennessee, according to the parameters outlined in state statutes:

- Tennessee laws allow employees who are victims of workplace discrimination or wrongful termination to file a claim with state agencies or through their employee rights lawyer in civil court.

- If discrimination claims or suits are successful, Tennessee law allows employees to recover attorney's fees.

- Employees, state agencies, and employee rights lawyers must be sure to file claims or civil actions before the statute of limitations runs out, which is 180 days for agency claims, or 1 year for private actions.

Texas

Texas generally complies with federal wrongful termination and discrimination laws; however, it has enacted several state statutes to supplement regulations like the Federal Labor Standards Act of 1938 and the Civil Rights Act of 1964. Texas is an "at will" employment state, which means that what would normally provide both employees and employers complete freedom to terminate employment for any reason is now limited according to state and federal laws in order to protect the civil rights of employees. When employers violate those laws, there are processes in place to allow the employee to file claims or private suits for remedies.

Texas's Specific Labor Laws

The state laws in Texas that supplement federal discrimination and wrongful termination regulations are included in the table below:

Benefit	State Law	Additional Benefits
Right to Work	Yes	
State Military Leave	Yes	Employees called to active duty in state military forces entitled to unpaid leave; guaranteed reinstatement to same position, benefits, vacation, seniority, unless employer's circumstances have changed, making it impossible or unreasonable
Jury Duty	Yes	Unpaid leave for permanent employees; employees required to give notice of intent to return after jury service complete
Voting	Yes	Paid time off, if required; time off must be allowed, but no time period specified; not required if employee has 2 consecutive nonwork hours while polls are open
State Family & Medical Leave	No	
Arrest & Conviction Records	No	
Discrimination	Yes	For 15 or more employees; for age (40 or older); national origin; disability (physical or mental); gender; pregnancy/childbirth; race; religion; genetic testing
Whistleblower	Yes	For public employees; employer cannot terminate, discriminate, or retaliate against employee for reporting violations
Plant Closings	No	

Texas Discrimination Laws

The regulations governing how employees can file claims or suits for remedies from violations of discrimination laws allow for the following actions:

- Victims of discrimination are allowed to file claims with state agencies or private suits through employee rights attorneys in civil court.

- Texas laws do not allow employees to recover attorney's fees in discrimination claims or civil actions.

- The statute of limitations on discrimination claims filed through state agencies is 180 days, and for private actions, it is 2 years.

Utah

Utah is an "at will" employment state, which means that employees have the right to end employment relationships for any reason, as do employers. However, that freedom is limited by federal laws which supersede that right in order to provide protections for the civil rights of those very employees. In addition, most states have enacted supplemental labor statutes to expand and refine the most common federal civil rights laws, such as the Federal Labor Standards Act of 1938 and the Civil Rights Act of 1964. Within those laws are also legal measures by which employees can file claims or civil actions for remedies from employers who violate them.

Utah's Specific Labor Laws

Utah's supplemental labor laws provide specific protections for citizens in the workplace from the following violations:

Benefit	State Law	Additional Benefits
Right to Work	Yes	
State Military Leave	Yes	Employees called to active duty in U.S. armed forces reserves, active duty training, inactive duty training, or state active duty, eligible for up to 5 years of unpaid leave; guaranteed reinstatement to same position, benefits, vacation, or seniority; discrimination or disqualification of applicants who are members of the state or federal national guard is prohibited
Jury Duty	Yes	Unpaid leave; employees cannot be required to use annual, sick, or vacation leave; threats or coercion are prohibited
Voting	Yes	Paid time off, if required; 2 hours off at beginning or end of shift; not required if employee has at least 3 nonwork hours when polls open; must be requested before election day

State Family & Medical Leave	No	
Arrest & Conviction Records	Yes	Employers not permitted to ask about arrests; employers are permitted to ask about convictions, but are advised not to unless relevant to job
Discrimination	Yes	For 15 or more employees; for age (40 or older); national origin; disability (follows federal law); AIDS/HIV; gender; pregnancy/childbirth; race; religion; genetic testing
Whistleblower	Yes	For public employees; employer cannot terminate, discriminate, or retaliate against employee for reporting violations
Plant Closings	Yes	For defense industry layoffs; workers may apply to Office of Job Training for assistance in retraining or reeducation for job skills in demand

Utah Discrimination Laws

In order for Utah employees to take advantage of the state discrimination statutes, they must pursue relief within the following parameters:

- In Utah, state agencies preempt the opportunity for employees to file private claims for discrimination and wrongful termination.

- Once state agencies have had the opportunity to file claims or pursue remedies; an employee and their employee rights lawyer have the right to file private civil actions.

- Employees do not have the right to recover attorney's fees when winning discrimination claims or civil actions.

- Employees and their legal representatives must be sure to file all claims or civil actions within the 180-day statute of limitations for discrimination violations.

Vermont

Federal and state laws throughout this country prohibit wrongful termination and job discrimination, primarily through the Federal Labor Standards Act of 1938 and the Civil Rights Act of 1964. However, states like Vermont have enacted numerous supplemental statutes increasing those protections, even in "at will" employment states like Vermont that allow employers and employees to terminate employment relationships for any reason except those prohibited by law. When those laws are broken, victims are empowered to file claims and civil actions for relief and compensation for those abuses.

Vermont's Specific Labor Laws

Vermont has a number of state laws against discrimination and wrongful termination, as enumerated in the table below:

Benefit	State Law	Additional Benefits
Right to Work	No	
State Military Leave	Yes	Employees called to active duty in national guard or ready reserves entitled to unpaid leave; 30 day's notice required for U.S. training and as much notice as possible for state training; guaranteed reinstatement to same position, benefits, vacation, seniority; discrimination or disqualification of applicants who are members of the state or federal national guard is prohibited
Jury Duty	Yes	Unpaid leave without loss of any benefits or seniority that are available to other employees; same protections apply to those called as witnesses in court or before commissions, boards, or tribunals
Voting	No	
State Family & Medical Leave	Yes	For childbirth and adoption leave, employers with at least 10 employees covered; for employee or family member's serious illnesses, employers with at least 15 employees are covered; eligible employees must have worked 30 or more hours per week, on average, for at least a year; leave of 12 weeks per year for childbirth, adoption, serious illness, medical appointments, or medical emergencies; 4 hours total unpaid leave in 30-day period (but not more than 24 hours per year) for school activities; family members include parents-in-law
Arrest & Conviction Records	Yes	Employers involved in caring for children, the elderly, the disabled, or those running post-secondary schools with residential facilities may request

		information on criminal records of employees or applicants offered positions and who have signed and notarized releases; release form must inform applicant of their right to appeal any information in those records
Discrimination	Yes	For 1 or more employees; for age (18 or older); national origin; disability (physical or mental); gender; race; religion; sexual orientation; genetic testing; place of birth
Whistleblower	Yes	For both public and private employees, particularly those in health care industry; employer cannot terminate, discriminate, or retaliate against employee for reporting violations
Plant Closings	No	

Vermont Discrimination Laws

Discrimination laws also outline the parameters under which employees can seek relief and remedies for violations:

- Vermont state laws allow victims of discrimination to seek remedies through state agency claims or private civil suits.

- Employees are eligible to recover attorney's fees in successful discrimination claims or suits.

- There is a statute of limitations of 6 years from the date of the violation on Vermont discrimination claims.

Virginia

While there are numerous federal wrongful termination and discrimination laws protecting employees from civil rights abuses in the workplace, violations of those laws still occur, trampling employee rights. In fact, there are not only federal laws, such as the Federal Labor Standards Act of 1938 and the Civil Rights Act of 1964, most states have supplemental labor laws providing more protections for employees as well as legal measures enabling them to respond to employer violations. As an "at will" employment state, employees and employers generally have the right to terminate employment for any reason; however, that right is limited by the vital protections to employee civil rights provided by wrongful termination and discrimination laws.

Virginia's Specific Labor Laws

Virginia has enacted a wide range of supplemental labor laws to provide further protections for its citizens in the workplace:

Benefit	State Law	Additional Benefits
Right to Work	Yes	
State Military Leave	Yes	Employees called to active duty in the Virginia National Guard, Virginia State Defense Force, or naval militia, are eligible for unpaid leave; employers may not require employees to take vacation or other leave (except by choice); guaranteed reinstatement to same or comparable position, benefits, vacation, or seniority, unless employer's circumstance have changed and make that unreasonable; employee must request reinstatement in writing within 5 days of release; discrimination against members of the state military service is prohibited
Jury Duty	Yes	Unpaid leave; employees cannot be required to use annual, sick, or vacation leave; employees who have served 4 hours or more in 1 day cannot be made to start shift after 5 p.m. or before 3 a.m. the next morning; discrimination or termination for serving are prohibited; employees summoned or subpoenaed to appear in court have the same protections, except criminal defendants
Voting	No	
State Family & Medical Leave	No	
Arrest & Conviction Records	Yes	Employers not permitted to require applicants to reveal information about criminal charges that have been expunged; applicants not required to reveal information about such records
Discrimination	Yes	For all employees; for age; national origin; disability (physical or mental); gender; marital status; pregnancy/

		childbirth; race; religion; genetic testing; use of a service animal
Whistleblower	Yes	For private employees; particularly asbestos and lead workers, and contractors; employer cannot terminate, discriminate, or retaliate against employee for reporting violations;
Plant Closings	No	

Virginia Discrimination Laws

State laws provide guidelines which Virginia employees can use to file claims or civil suits if their rights are violated in the workplace:

- Employees have the option under Virginia state laws to pursue discrimination claims through EEOC or other state agencies, or through filing a civil suit, often with the help of an employee rights attorney.

- If an employee's claim or suit is successful, they have the right to recover attorney's fees from the defendant.

- State statute of limitations laws require that discrimination or wrongful termination claims or civil suits be filed within 180 days of the original violation.

Washington

Federal laws governing wrongful termination and discrimination in employment practices are primarily found in the Federal Labor Standards Act of 1938 and the Civil Rights Act of 1964. However, every state has enacted supplemental laws that apply to its citizens, expanding those protections and enabling relief for employees from violations by their employers. In Washington, which is an "at will" employment state, employees and employers have the right to end an employment relationship for any reason except those specified in federal and state laws, which protect those employees from abuses.

Washington's Specific Labor Laws

The labor laws specific to the state of Washington concerning wrongful termination and discrimination in the workplace include the following:

Benefit	State Law	Additional Benefits
Right to Work	No	
State Military Leave	Yes	Employees on active duty in the

		uniformed services are guaranteed reinstatement to same or comparable position, benefits, vacation, or seniority, unless employer's circumstance have changed and make that unreasonable, impossible, or a hardship; discrimination against members of the state military is prohibited
Jury Duty	Yes	Unpaid leave; discrimination or termination for serving are prohibited
Voting	Yes	Paid time off, if required; employer must schedule work time to allow enough time to vote, generally 2 hours (not including break periods); not required if employee has 2 nonwork hours when polls are open or is able to obtain an absentee ballot
State Family & Medical Leave	Yes	Accrued paid family leave available to all employees for family members with serious health conditions; for newborn, adopted, or foster children, employers with 50 or more employees must provide up to 12 weeks in any 12-month period for employees who have worked at least 1,250 hours in previous year; family members include parents-in-law, grandparents, and stepparents
Arrest & Conviction Records	Yes	Employer inquiries must determine if arrests/charges are pending, dismissed, or resulted in conviction relevant to job performance and occurred within 10 years; employees must be notified within 30 days that employer has obtained conviction record and be able to review it; employment decisions can only be based upon such information if relevant to job; expunged records treated as if they never occurred
Discrimination	Yes	For 8 or more employees (1 or more employees for gender-based wage discrimination); for age (40 or older); national origin; disability (physical, mental, or sensory); AIDS/HIV; gender; marital status; pregnancy/ childbirth;

		race; religion; sexual orientation; genetic testing; use of trained guide dog; hepatitis C infection; member of state militia; gender identity
Whistleblower	Yes	For public employees; employer cannot terminate, discriminate, or retaliate against employee for reporting violations
Plant Closings	Yes	Applies to employees who have been terminated and are unlikely to return to principal occupation; The Department of Employment Security provides special training and counseling for workers in aerospace, thermal electric generation, and forest products industries plus regular unemployment compensation

Washington Discrimination Laws

Washington statutes have spelled out specific guidelines for employees to be able to file claims and lawsuits for remedies when their rights have been violated:

- Washington statutes allow employees to file discrimination claims with state offices of the EEOC, the Washington Human Rights Commission, or through an employee rights attorney in civil court.

- Winning claims and lawsuits entitle employees to recover attorney's fees.

- The statute of limitations in Washington for discrimination claims and lawsuits is 6 months from the date of the violation.

West Virginia

There is no excuse for an employee suffering silently as a result of wrongful termination or job discrimination in today's society, since there are numerous federal and state laws protecting employees from such violations. The primary federal legislation is found in the Federal Labor Standards Act of 1938 and the Civil Rights Act of 1964. However, West Virginia has additional state laws that modify its "at will" status, limiting the right of every employee and employer to terminate an employment relationship for any reason. The exceptions are found in state and federal laws, which also provide legal measures for employees to reclaim lost income, damages, and other remedies for abuses.

West Virginia's Specific Labor Laws

West Virginia's state labor laws are not extensive, but they are powerful protections for its citizens in the workforce:

Benefit	State Law	Additional Benefits
Right to Work	No	
State Military Leave	Yes	Employees on active duty in the organized militia are guaranteed the same leave and reinstatement rights as those found USERRA
Jury Duty	Yes	Unpaid leave; discrimination or termination for serving are prohibited
Voting	Yes	Paid time off, if required, and if employee votes; employer must schedule work hours to allow enough time to vote, generally 3 hours; not required if employee has 3 nonwork hours when polls are open; employee must request leave in writing at least 3 days before election
State Family & Medical Leave	No	
Arrest & Conviction Records	Yes	Employer inquiries only permitted concerning convictions relevant to job; conviction cannot necessarily bar employment
Discrimination	Yes	For 12 or more employees; for age (40 or older); national origin; disability (physical or mental); AIDS/HIV; gender (equal pay provisions apply to employers with 1 or more employees); race; religion; smoking away from work
Whistleblower	Yes	For public employees; employer cannot terminate, discriminate, or retaliate against employee for reporting violations
Plant Closings	No	

West Virginia Discrimination Laws

State laws provide guidelines by which employees who have been victimized by employers and suffered wrongful termination or discrimination find resolution and remedies:

- The West Virginia Human Rights Commission provides information, support, and legal representation to employees who have faced discrimination on the job, as do employee rights lawyers who can help employees file civil actions.

- State law allows those employees whose discrimination claims or civil suits are victorious to claim attorney's fees from the defendant.

- State agencies must be sure to file all claims before the 1-year statute of limitations runs out, and employee rights lawyers must file civil actions before their 2-year deadline.

Wisconsin

Wisconsin has enacted a wide array of wrongful termination and discrimination statutes in the state to supplement the already strong federal laws governing those issues. As an "at will" state, without these laws employees and employers could terminate employment at any time for any reason, allowing employers to violate employee's rights at will. However, current laws provide powerful civil rights protections for employees, both in the workplace and by providing a way to seek compensation and restitution when their rights have been violated.

Wisconsin's Specific Labor Laws

The very detailed state laws in Wisconsin that address civil rights in the workplace include the following:

Benefit	State Law	Additional Benefits
Right to Work	No	
State Military Leave	Yes	Employees on active duty in the uniformed services, or civilians performing defense work during an emergency may take up to 4 years leave unless that period is extended by law; upon completion, they are entitled to reinstatement to the same position with the same benefits and seniority, or a similar one, unless employer's conditions have changed so as to make that unreasonable; employee must apply for reinstatement within 90 days of completion or 6 months of rehabilitation; must present proof of completion; may not be fired without cause for 1 year from reinstatement
Jury Duty	Yes	Unpaid leave; discrimination or

		termination for serving are prohibited
Voting	Yes	Unpaid time off, up to 3 consecutive hours, scheduled at employer's discretion; employee must request leave before election day
State Family & Medical Leave	Yes	6 weeks leave in a 12-month period for pregnancy/maternity, childbirth, or adoption, available to employees who have worked minimum of 1 year and 1,000 hours in previous 12 months; applies to employers with 50 or more employees, additional 2 weeks' leave per 12-month period for serious health condition or to care for family member with such condition
Arrest & Conviction Records	Yes	Discrimination based on prior arrest or conviction record prohibited; exceptions – pending arrest charges; may only ask about convictions that are substantially relevant to job, and for jobs that require bonding, or burglar alarm installers;
Discrimination	Yes	For 1 or more employees; for age (40 or older); national origin; disability (physical or mental); AIDS/HIV; gender; marital status; pregnancy/ maternity; race; religion; sexual orientation; genetic testing; arrest or conviction; lawful use of any product when not at work; military service or status
Whistleblower	Yes	For public employees; specifically those in the health care industry; employer cannot terminate, discriminate, or retaliate against employee for reporting violations
Plant Closings	Yes	Applies to business closings, permanent or temporary, that affect 25 or more employees; mass layoffs that affect 25% or 25 employees, whichever is greater, or at least 500 employees; employees who have worked at least 6 of last 12 months and put in 20 or more hours per week; and employers with 50 or more employees in the state; notification required at least 60 days in advance in

		writing to Dislocated Worker Committee in the Department of Workforce Development; affected employees, collective bargaining representatives; highest municipal officials in business locale

Wisconsin Discrimination Laws

In order to pursue remedies and relief in Wisconsin, employees must adhere to the following guidelines for filing discrimination claims and civil actions:

- Wisconsin state laws require that wrongful termination and discrimination claims be processed first through state EEOC offices or the Equal Rights Division before private civil claims can be filed by employees and their employee rights lawyers.

- However, if state agencies drop the claim or are unsuccessful at the mediation level, an employee and their employee rights attorney may continue the legal process through a private claim in civil court.

- Wisconsin laws do not allow employees to recover attorney's fees from defendants.

- State agencies and employee rights attorneys have 300 days to file claims and civil suits under Wisconsin statute of limitations deadlines.

Wyoming

Wyoming allows federal laws to have sole jurisdiction over most wrongful termination and employment discrimination issues in their state, although they have enacted a limited number of supplemental state laws. Even though Wyoming is an "at will" state, employers and employees do not have unlimited right to terminate an employment relationship. Rather, there are state and federal laws to limit that right due to their protection of employee's civil rights in the workplace. If an employee's rights are being ignored or abused, discrimination laws provide options for pursing remedies and relief.

Wyoming's Specific Labor Laws

The state laws that Wyoming has enacted to supplement federal employment and labor laws include the following:

Benefit	State Law	Additional Benefits
Right to Work	Yes	
State Military Leave	Yes	Employees on active duty in the uniformed services may take up to 5

		years leave; upon completion, they are entitled to reinstatement to the same position with the same benefits and seniority (as well as what they would have accrued if they had never left), or a similar one, unless employer's conditions have changed so as to make that unreasonable; may not be fired without cause for 1 year from reinstatement; discrimination or penalties are prohibited
Jury Duty	Yes	Unpaid leave; discrimination or termination for serving are prohibited
Voting	Yes	Paid time off, if required; 1 hour other than breaks; not required if employee has 3 consecutive nonwork hours when polls are open
State Family & Medical Leave	No	
Arrest & Conviction Records	No	
Discrimination	Yes	For 2 or more employees; for age (40 or older); national origin; disability; gender; race; religion; military service or status; smoking off duty
Whistleblower	Yes	For both public and private employees; employer cannot terminate, discriminate, or retaliate against employee for reporting violations
Plant Closings	Yes	Applies to plant closings or substantial layoffs; Department of Employment and other state agencies offer occupation transfer and retraining for displaced workers

Wyoming Discrimination Laws

In order to find relief from discrimination and wrongful termination in Wyoming, employees must file claims according to the following guidelines:

- State agencies such as the Department of Employment are the source for resolving discrimination claims in Wyoming.

- Private actions are not allowed in employment discrimination or wrongful termination cases in the state.

- Wyoming law does not allow employees to recover attorney's fees from defendants in civil suits.

- Those state agencies with authority to pursue discrimination claims in Wyoming must do so within 300 days of the original violation, under the Wyoming statute of limitations.

Appendix B: Complaint Process

U.S. Equal Employment Opportunity Commission (EEOC) is responsible for enforcing federal laws that make it illegal to discriminate against a job applicant or an employee because of the person's race, color, religion, sex (including pregnancy), national origin, age (40 or older), disability or genetic information. It is also illegal to discriminate against a person because the person complained about discrimination, filed a charge of discrimination, or participated in an employment discrimination investigation or lawsuit.

The EEOC has the authority to investigate charges of discrimination against employers who are covered by the law. Their role in an investigation is to fairly and accurately assess the allegations in the charge and then make a finding.

To complete an online assessment, use this link: https://egov.eeoc.gov/eas/

In general, you need to file a charge within 180 calendar days from the day the discrimination took place. The 180 calendar day filing deadline is extended to 300 calendar days if a state or local agency enforces a law that prohibits employment discrimination on the same basis. The rules are slightly different for age discrimination charges. For age discrimination, the filing deadline is only extended to 300 days if there is a **state** law prohibiting age discrimination in employment and a state agency or authority enforcing that law. The deadline is not extended if only a local law prohibits age discrimination.

Note: Federal employees and job applicants have a different complaint process, and generally must contact an agency EEO Counselor within 45 days. The time limit can be extended under certain circumstances.

Federal and job applicants' complaint process:
http://www.eeoc.gov/federal/fed_employees/complaint_overview.cfm

Contacting an EEOC Counselor: http://www.eeoc.gov/federal/fed_employees/counselor.cfm

If more than one discriminatory event took place, the deadline usually applies to each event. For example, let's say you were demoted and then fired a year later. You believe the employer based its decision to demote and fire you on your race, and you file a charge the day after your discharge. In this case, only your claim of discriminatory discharge is timely. In other words, you must have filed a charge challenging the demotion within 180/300 days from the day you were demoted. If you didn't, we would only investigate your discharge. There is one exception to this general rule and that is if you are alleging ongoing harassment.

In harassment cases, you must file your charge within 180 or 300 days of the last incident of harassment, although they will review all incidents of harassment when investigating your charge, even if the earlier incidents happened more than 180/300 days earlier.

Alabama:

If an employee believes they have a case for wrongful termination, their first step is to file a claim with their local EEOC office. An employee has 180 days from the date they learned of the violation to file their claim. The EEOC will then begin the process of procuring or suing for the employee's rights by:

- Investigation
- Mediation/Conciliation
- Filing a lawsuit

Legal Remedies for Wrongful Termination

If the EEOC does not file suit within 60 days of an individual's claim, the employee may file their own personal lawsuit against the employer. However, there are other options, beginning with retaining an employee rights attorney. They may be able to negotiate a settlement with the employer, which includes financial compensation, damages, back pay, reinstatement, and more. If that is impossible, and a lawsuit is inevitable, an employee rights attorney can pursue such a lawsuit on behalf of the employee.

EEOC Offices

Birmingham District Office

1130 22nd Street S, Suite 2000
Birmingham, AL 35205
205-212-2100 or 800-669-4000
FAX: 205-212-2105

Mobile Local Office

63 South Royal Street, Suite 504
Mobile, AL 36602
800-669-4000
FAX: 251-690-2581

For age discrimination issues, contact:

Alabama Department of Economic and Community Affairs
401 Adams Avenue
Montgomery, AL 36104
Phone: (334)242-5100; Fax: (334)242-5099;
e-mail: ADECA.webmaster.Info@adeca.alabama.gov

Alaska:

Every claim for wrongful termination must begin with the local EEOC office. Employees have 180 days from the date of the violation to file that claim, at which time the EEOC will evaluate the claim and, if appropriate, begin pursing it through the following steps:

- Investigation
- Mediation/Conciliation
- Filing a lawsuit

Legal Remedies for Wrongful Termination

The EEOC is faced with more and more claims for wrongful termination as more civil rights laws have been enacted, both at the federal and state levels. That means that it is easy to have the 60-day limit pass without remedies for a case filed with that agency. If that happens, the employee has the option to retain an employee rights lawyer. That lawyer may advise employees to drop their case, pursue negotiation for remedies, seek arbitration or conciliation, or file a lawsuit. Some of the remedies possible include reinstatement to the job, back pay, damages for stress or suffering on the part of the employee and/or punitive damages to stop the employer from similar abuse in the future, and in some cases injunctive relief, requiring the employer to write new policies company-wide in order to prevent future abuses.

In addition, Alaska has specific laws protecting whistleblower activity, imposing a fine of up to $10,000 for abuse.

Commission for Human Rights
Anchorage, AK
907-274-4692
800-478-4692
http://gov.state.ak.us/aschr

Arkansas:

www.eeoc.gov/littlerock/index.html

820 Louisiana Street
Suite 200
Little Rock, Arkansas 72201

1-800-669-4000

While no appointment is needed to file a charge in person, please contact the office if you are traveling a long distance or have limited time to verify that EEOC has jurisdiction and determine the best time to visit the office. In an effort to provide better customer service, EEOC staff may conduct either an interview in the EEOC office or a telephone interview. Although less time may be required, please allow at least 1 to 2 hours for an office visit. To avoid delay, please let the office know beforehand if you need special assistance, such as an interpreter, to file a charge.

Individuals who are interested in filing charges of discrimination are initially screened by an EEOC representative to determine whether your employment experiences are covered by the laws EEOC enforces. You may also use our online assessment (https://egov.eeoc.gov/eas/) and complete a questionnaire to be sent or taken to our office. *(Note: the online assessment will be unavailable each week for up to 30 minutes, Saturday evening or Sunday morning.)* The EEOC representative will ask questions about your allegations, about the evidence available to support the allegations, and about jurisdiction (whether the charge is timely, and the employer, charging party and subject matter are covered under the statutes enforced by EEOC).

The staff will advise you whether your employment concern is covered by EEOC. If it is not covered, you will be provided with information on where you might receive assistance. If covered by EEOC, you will be advised on the procedures for filing a charge of employment discrimination with EEOC.

When completing the questionnaire you should be prepared to provide the following information:

1. The name, address, and telephone number of the person filing the charge;
2. The name, address, and telephone number of the company, employment agency, or union that the charge is filed against, and the number of employees (or union members), if known;
3. A short description of the event(s) with supporting documentation (if any) which caused the person filing the charge to believe that his or her rights were violated;
4. The date(s) the event(s) took place;
5. The names, addresses, and telephone numbers of any witnesses;
6. Whether the individual has filed the same or similar charge with a state or local fair employment practice agency; and
7. The name, address, and telephone number of a person who always knows where to contact the person wishing to file a charge.

Arizona:

In general, employees who file claims for wrongful termination have several remedies they may pursue, including reinstatement, back pay, compensation for stress and suffering, punitive damages to discourage repetition of the abuse by the employer, and even policy changes in the company to prevent further similar abuses. In addition, Arizona provides specific remedies for certain abuses:

- **Jury duty** – misdemeanor conviction and fines of up to $500 and/or 30 days in jail
- **Child or spousal support garnishment** – contempt of court fines, liability for unpaid support, attorney's fees, damages, and employee reinstatement.
- **Whistleblower**– fines between $5,000 and $7,000 for each violation and attorney's fees

Civil Rights Division

Phoenix, AZ
602-542-5263
877-491-5742
www.azag.gov/civil_rights/index.html

EEOC

Phoenix District Office

3300 N. Central Avenue,
Suite 690
Phoenix, AZ 85012
602-640-5000 or 800-669-4000

California:

While EEOC claims may not always be justified or successful, there are some common remedies employees may pursue, or that may be further pursued in private lawsuits:

- Reinstatement
- Back pay
- Compensation for stress and suffering
- Punitive damages to prevent further abuses by the employer
- Mandated policy changes to protect other employees in that company

California provides for some specific remedies in the following areas:

- **Jury duty** – reinstatement with back pay and/or lost wages and benefits; if the judge determines the violation is willful, misdemeanor charges may be filed.

- **Child support garnishment** – contempt of court for willful refusal to garnish wages, possible liability for support amounts plus interest.
- **Whistleblower Protections**– misdemeanor charges with penalties of up to 1 year in jail and $1,000 fine for individual employers, up to $5,000 fines for corporate employers

Victims of wrongful termination must begin the claim process with the EEOC; however, if that does not provide the relief or compensation they believe they are due, they may contact an employee rights attorney to pursue further negotiations with their employer or a lawsuit.

Equal Employment Opportunity Commission Offices

Fresno Local Office

2300 Tulare Street
Suite 215
Fresno, CA 93721
559-487-5837 or 800-669-4000

Los Angeles District Office

255 E. Temple Street
4th Floor
Los Angeles, CA 90012
213-894-1000 or 800-669-4000

Oakland Local Office

1301 Clay Street
Suite 1170-N
Oakland, CA 94612
510-637-3230 or 800-669-4000

San Diego Area Office

401 B Street, Suite 510
San Diego, CA 92101
619-557-7235 or 800-669-4000

San Francisco District Office

350 Embarcadero, Suite 500
San Francisco, CA 94105
415-625-5600 or 800-669-4000

San Jose Local Office

96 N. Third Street
Suite 200
San Jose, CA 95112
408-291-7352 or 800-669-4000

Department of Fair Employment and Housing

Sacramento District Office

Sacramento, CA
916-445-5523 or 800-884-1684
www.dfeh.ca.gov

Colorado:

Employees who have been wrongfully terminated have the right to pursue a number of remedies under federal and state laws:

- Reinstatement
- Back pay
- Compensation for stress and suffering
- Punitive damages to prevent further abuses by the employer
- Mandated policy changes to protect other employees in that company

In Colorado, employers may face additional penalties when found guilty of wrongful termination under state laws:

- **Jury duty** – Class 2 misdemeanor convictions, with fines of $250 to $2,000, and/or between 3 and 12 months in jail; may also be liable to the employee for triple damages and attorney's fees.

- **Child support, medical support, and health insurance garnishment** – May be liable to terminated employee for up to 6 week's wages, reinstatement, court costs and attorney's fees.

- **Whistleblower**– Public employees may file a written complaint within 30 days for back pay, reinstatement, lost seniority, expunged records, and any other relief deemed appropriate. Private employees may file civil suits for damages, court costs, and other appropriate remedies.

The EEOC begins the process of filing claims and seeking remedies for wrongful termination; however, the employee may want to contact an employee rights attorney at any time to ensure that they are pursuing all the avenue of compensation and relief available in Colorado. If state remedies do not prove satisfactory, that attorney may then be prepared to pursue civil action much more quickly and efficiently.

Equal Employment Opportunity Commission Offices

Denver District Office

303 E. 17th Avenue, Suite 510
Denver, CO 80203
303-866-1300 or 800-669-4000

Civil Rights Division

Denver, CO
303-894-2997 or 800-262-4845
www.dora.state.co.us/Civil-Rights

Connecticut:

EEOC claims are thoroughly investigated for validity before the agency will consider filing suit. If the employee is deemed to have case, the EEOC will proceed to the next steps:

- Mediation/Conciliation
- When appropriate, filing a lawsuit

Only after agency measures are concluded, or after 180 days, will an employee be able to pursue private legal remedies.

Legal Remedies for Wrongful Termination

Legal remedies available for employees determined to be the victims of wrongful termination include:

- Reinstatement
- Back pay
- Compensation for stress and suffering
- Punitive damages to prevent further abuses by the employer
- Mandated policy changes to protect other employees in that company

In Connecticut, employers may face additional penalties when found guilty of wrongful termination under state laws:

Jury duty – criminal contempt of court, with fines of up to $500 and/or jail terms of up to 30 days; may also be liable for 10 weeks of back pay. If employer fails to comply, they may be liable for triple damages and attorney's fees.

Garnishment – employers are liable for all back wages from time of termination and until reinstatement. For child support or child health care garnishment, employer is liable for fines of up to $1,000.

Whistleblower – employee can bring suit within 90 days for violations after utilizing all agency remedies. Public employees may file claim within 30 days.

Connecticut requires employees to file claims through EEOC agencies exclusively first. If those processes fail to provide the compensation or damages the employee feels they are due, they can then file private suits with the help of an employee rights attorney.

Commission on Human Rights and Opportunities

Hartford, CT
860-541-3400 or 800-477-5737
www.state.ct.us/chro

Delaware:

For any employee that believes they have been the victim of wrongful termination, the first step in Delaware is to file a claim with the local office of the EEOC. They will follow standard procedures to validate and, if appropriate, pursue the claim:

- Mediation/Conciliation
- When appropriate, file a lawsuit

If either the agency deems the claim to be invalid, is unwilling or unable to pursue it further, or 180 days have passed without resolution, an employee is able to pursue private legal remedies.

Legal Remedies for Wrongful Termination

Employees may pursue their own legal means, with the help of an employee rights attorney, for any or all of the following remedies:

- Reinstatement
- Back pay

- Compensation for stress and suffering

- Punitive damages to prevent further abuses by the employer

- Mandated policy changes to protect other employees in that company

Delaware employers who are found guilty of wrongful termination under state laws may face the following penalties:

Jury duty – criminal contempt of court, with fines of up to $500 and/or jail terms of up to 6 months; may also be liable to employee for lost wages and attorney's fees, and possibly reinstatement.

Garnishment– fines of up to $1,000 and/or 90 days in jail for first offense. For additional offenses, penalties may include fines of up to $5,000 and/or 1 year in jail. If employment is denied because of garnishment, fines of up to $500 may be imposed for each offense. Corporate employers may also be subject to criminal charges.

Whistleblower– public employees can bring suit within 90 days for violations, which can produce injunctive relief for the violation and/or damages.

In modern times, discrimination in any walk of life is illegal and employers who break those laws face penalties, either from public agencies such as the EEOC, or in civil court at the hands of an employee and their employee rights lawyer.

Office of Labor Law Enforcement, Division of Industrial Affairs
Wilmington, DE
302-761-8200
www.delawareworks.com/industrialaffairs/welcome.shtml

District of Columbia:

Those who are victims of wrongful termination may file a claim with the District of Columbia EEOC as well as the Office of Human Rights, which, if they deem the case valid, will pursue the following procedures:

- Investigation

- Mediation/Conciliation

- File a lawsuit, when appropriate

Legal Remedies for Wrongful Termination

Employees may expect any or all of the following remedies from local agencies or private lawsuits:

- Reinstatement
- Reinstatement of benefits and seniority
- Back pay
- Compensation for stress and suffering
- Punitive damages to prevent further abuses by the employer
- Mandated policy changes to protect other employees in that company
- Possibly court costs and attorney's fees

District of Columbia employers who fail to abide by federal or state employment standards for hiring and firing may face the following penalties:

- **Jury duty** – criminal contempt of court with fines of up to $300 and/or 30 days in jail for first offense, up to $5,000 and/or 180 days in jail thereafter; also liable to employee for lost wages, reinstatement, and attorney's fees.

- **Garnishment** – for discrimination based on child support withholding (which includes taking longer than 90 days to comply with garnishment requests), penalties include fines of up to $10,000 paid to employee for use in satisfying child support payments.

- **Whistleblower** – may file civil suit within 1 year statute of limitations.

Employees are free to contact the EEOC office or the local Office of Human Rights in the District of Columbia, or they can consult an employee rights attorney to protect their rights in relation to wrongful termination claims. And while the statute of limitations is 1 year for most cases, it is wise to move quickly and give EEOC officials or a lawyer time to investigate these cases thoroughly to determine the proper course of action and receive the appropriate solution.

District of Columbia EEOC Offices

Washington Field Office

1801 L Street, NW, Suite 100
Washington, DC 20507
202-419-0700 or 800-669-4000

Office of Human Rights

Washington, DC
202-727-4559
http://ohr.dc.gov/ohr/site/default.asp

Florida:

The Equal Employment Opportunity Commission is the agency primarily responsible for enforcing federal and state claims for wrongful termination using these processes:

- Investigation
- Mediation/Conciliation
- When appropriate, file a lawsuit

If the agency deems the claim to be invalid, is unwilling or unable to pursue it further, or has discontinued its pursuit of the case for a sufficient period of time, an employee is able to pursue private legal remedies.

Legal Remedies for Wrongful Termination

Employees may expect any or all of the following remedies when pursuing a case for wrongful termination either through a state EEOC agency or with the help of their own employee rights attorney:

- Reinstatement
- Back pay
- Compensation for stress and suffering
- Punitive damages to prevent further abuses by the employer
- Mandated policy changes to protect other employees in that company

Florida employers who fail to abide by federal or state employment standards for hiring and firing may face the following penalties:

- **Jury duty** – criminal contempt of court; may also be liable to employee for lost wages, punitive damages, and attorney's fees.
- **Garnishment**– contempt of court for violation; fines of up to $250 for first offense, and $500 for additional offenses.
- **Whistleblower**– state agency employees can bring suit within 180 days of when state agency terminates investigation.

Local public employees must file a complaint within 60 days of violation or, if there is no agency action, 180 days to file a civil suit; if an agency complaint is terminated, they have 180 days to file a civil action, which can produce injunctive relief for the violation and/or damages. Private employees must pursue all contractual and administrative options; if they bring no relief, they have 180 days after the violation to file a civil action.

Discrimination is illegal, and employers who break the federal and Florida laws against discrimination in the workplace can face penalties, either through the EEOC claims process, or at the hands of an employee and their employee rights attorney pursuing their rights in civil court.

Florida EEOC Offices

Miami District Office

One Biscayne Tower
2 S. Biscayne Boulevard
Suite 2700
Miami, FL 33131
305-536-4491 or 800-669-4000

Tampa Area Office

501 E. Polk Street SW
Suite 1000
Tampa, FL 33602
813-228-2310 or 800-669-4000

Commission on Human Relations

Tallahassee, FL
850-488-7082
http://fchr.state.fl.us

Georgia:

The Equal Employment Opportunity Commission (EEOC) is primarily responsible for pursuing federal and state claims for wrongful termination using these processes:

- Investigation

- Mediation/Conciliation

- File a lawsuit, when appropriate

If the employee is not compensated or reinstated as a result of agency action, state law does not allow them to pursue private civil actions.

Legal Remedies for Wrongful Termination

Employees may expect any or all of the following remedies when pursuing a case for wrongful termination through a state EEOC agency:

- Reinstatement

- Back pay

- Compensation for stress and suffering

- Punitive damages to prevent further abuses by the employer

- Mandated policy changes to protect other employees in that company

Georgia employers who fail to abide by federal or state employment standards for hiring and firing may face the following penalties:

- **Jury duty** – employers may be liable for damages and attorney's fees.

- **Whistleblower**– public employees may be able to have prohibited employer action set aside

State EEOC agencies are primarily responsible for pursuing claims for wrongful termination. However, if an employee has a more complex case or is unsure of how to secure proper pursuit of their rights, they may need call on an employee rights attorney to advise them during the EEOC claim process.

Georgia EEOC Offices

Atlanta District Office

100 Alabama Street, SW
Suite 4R30
Atlanta, GA 30303
404-562-6800 or 800-669-4000

Savannah Local Office

410 Mall Boulevard
Suite G
Savannah, GA 31406
912-652-4234 or 800-669-4000

Atlanta District Office

U.S. Equal Employment Opportunity Commission

Atlanta, GA
404-562-6800 or 800-669-4000
www.eeoc.gov/atlanta/index.html

Hawaii:

Those who are victims of wrongful termination may file a claim with the Equal Employment Opportunity Commission (EEOC) which follows these procedures:

- Investigation

- Mediation/Conciliation

- File a lawsuit, when appropriate

If the employee is not compensated or reinstated as a result of agency action, state law does not allow them to pursue private civil actions.

Legal Remedies for Wrongful Termination

Employees may expect any or all of the following remedies from an EEOC claim for wrongful termination:

- Reinstatement

- Reinstatement of benefits and seniority

- Back pay

- Compensation for stress and suffering

- Punitive damages to prevent further abuses by the employer

- Mandated policy changes to protect other employees in that company

- Possibly court costs and attorney's fees

Hawaii employers who fail to abide by federal or state employment standards for hiring and firing may face the following penalties:

Jury duty – petty misdemeanor charges with penalties of fines up to $1,000 and/or jail terms of up to 30 days. Employer may also be required to reinstate the employee and pay 6 weeks back wages

Garnishment– criminal contempt of court.

Whistleblower– fines of between $500 and $5,000 for each violation

Plant closings – failure to provide required notice and severance results in employer liability for 3 months compensation to each employee

Federal and state laws provide a great deal of protection for employees in Hawaii, as well as recourse to seek remedies for wrongful termination. However, the only avenue to seek those remedies is through state agencies. If any employees feel that those agencies are not properly pursuing their case, they may want to consult an employee rights lawyer to help them receive the protections they deserve.

Hawaii EEOC Offices

Honolulu Local Office

300 Ala Moana Boulevard
Room 7-127, P.O. Box 50082
Honolulu, HI 96850
808-541-3120 or 800-669-4000

Hawaii Civil Rights Commission

Honolulu, HI
808-586-8636
www.hawaii.gov/labor/hcrc/

Idaho:

Those who are victims of wrongful termination may file a claim with the Idaho Commission on Human Rights, which, if they deem the case valid, will pursue the following procedures:

- Investigation
- Mediation/Conciliation
- File a lawsuit, when appropriate

If the employee is not compensated or chooses not to file a claim with a state agency first, they may pursue a private law suit for remediation.

Legal Remedies for Wrongful Termination

Employees may expect any or all of the following remedies from state agencies or personal civil lawsuits:

- Reinstatement

- Reinstatement of benefits and seniority

- Back pay

- Compensation for stress and suffering

- Punitive damages to prevent further abuses by the employer

- Mandated policy changes to protect other employees in that company

- Possibly court costs and attorney's fees

Idaho employers who fail to abide by federal or state employment standards for hiring and firing may face the following penalties:

Jury duty – criminal contempt of court, carrying a fine of up to $300 plus liability for three times the amount of lost wages to the employee.

Garnishment– fines of up to $300; reinstatement of employee; liability for two times the amount of employee's lost wages plus additional damages, court costs, and attorney's fees.

Whistleblower– civil fines of up to $500

Employees victimized by wrongful termination have great leeway in Idaho to file a claim in state agencies or to file a personal lawsuit in civil court with the assistance of an employee rights attorney.

Idaho Commission on Human Rights

Boise, ID

208-334-2873

http://humanrights.idaho.gov/

Illinois:

Those who are victims of wrongful termination may file a claim with the Illinois EEOC as well as their Department of Human Rights, which, if they deem the case valid, will pursue the following procedures:

- Investigation

- Mediation/Conciliation
- File a lawsuit, when appropriate
- Employees may file for temporary relief only in civil court.

Legal Remedies for Wrongful Termination

Employees may expect any or all of the following remedies from state agencies:

- Reinstatement
- Reinstatement of benefits and seniority
- Back pay
- Compensation for stress and suffering
- Punitive damages to prevent further abuses by the employer
- Mandated policy changes to protect other employees in that company
- Possibly court costs and attorney's fees

Illinois employers who fail to abide by federal or state employment standards for hiring and firing may face the following penalties:

Jury duty – civil and/or criminal contempt of court, and possible liability for lost wages and benefits.

Garnishment– retribution for one garnishment can result in a class A misdemeanor charge, which includes a fine of up to $2,500 and/or 1 year in jail. For child support withholding, employer may be liable for the amount of wages not garnished, fined up to $200, and ordered to reinstate employee.

Plant closings – employers who fail to give appropriate notice may be liable for up to 60 days of back pay and benefits for the same period; up to $500/day civil penalties unless back pay is paid within 3 weeks of announced layoffs; federal penalties accrue toward state penalties.

Employees are limited to agency claims for wrongful termination violations in the state of Illinois. However, since they have only 180 days to file those claims, it may be wise to consult an employee rights attorney to ensure their case is pursued effectively.

Illinois EEOC Offices

Chicago District Office

500 W. Madison Street
Suite 2800
Chicago, IL 60661
312-353-2713 or 800-669-4000

Department of Human Rights

Chicago, IL

312-814-6200

www.state.il.us/dhr

Indiana:

If an Indiana employee files a claim or lawsuit for wrongful termination, their representative will pursue the following procedures:

- Investigation
- Mediation/Conciliation
- File a lawsuit, when appropriate

Legal Remedies for Wrongful Termination

Employees may expect any or all of the following remedies from local agencies or private lawsuits:

- Reinstatement
- Reinstatement of benefits and seniority
- Back pay
- Compensation for stress and suffering
- Punitive damages to prevent further abuses by the employer
- Mandated policy changes to protect other employees in that company
- Court costs and attorney's fees

Indiana employers who fail to abide by federal or state employment standards for hiring and firing may face the following penalties:

Jury duty – class B misdemeanor with up to $1,000 in fines and/or 180 days in jail; liable to employee for lost wages, attorney's fees, and possibly reinstatement.

Whistleblower– Class A infraction

There are strict penalties for Indiana employers who discriminate against their employees contrary to state of federal guidelines. However, employees also have the right to pursue claims in the local EEOC office or private civil suits to receive compensation and even punitive damages for abuses. An employee rights attorney can help an employee determine what route to take to best have their rights protected and be compensated for wrongful actions by their employers.

Indianapolis District Office

101 W. Ohio Street, Suite 1900
Indianapolis, IN 46204
317-226-7212 or 800-669-4000

Civil Rights Commission

Indianapolis, IN
317-232-2600 or 800-628-2909
www.in.gov/icrc

Iowa:

The Iowa Civil Rights Commission pursues claims for wrongful termination through investigation, mediation and/or conciliation; however, if those methods don't work, they will file a lawsuit when appropriate.

Legal Remedies for Wrongful Termination

There are a number of remedies employees may expect through agency claims or civil lawsuits, when allowed:

- Reinstatement; and reinstatement of seniority and benefits
- Compensation for stress and suffering
- Back pay
- Mandated policy changes to protect other employees in that company
- Punitive damages to prevent further abuses by the employer
- Possibly court costs and attorney's fees

In addition, in Iowa the following specific penalties may be imposed upon employers who are found guilty of wrongful termination:

Jury duty – contempt of court, liable for lost wages for as much as 6 weeks, attorney's fees, and reinstatement

Garnishment– failure to withhold child support results in misdemeanor charge for 1st offense, serious misdemeanor for additional offenses, liable for costs, interest, and attorney's fees for collection of support; general garnishment, simple misdemeanor and contempt of court

Whistleblower– simple misdemeanor

The Iowa Civil Rights commission has primary jurisdiction over wrongful termination cases in the state. However, anyone who believes their rights have been abused in this area, especially in more complex cases, may want to consult with an employee rights attorney to ensure they are pursuing every means possible for remedies, reinstatement, or compensation.

Iowa Civil Rights Commission
Des Moines, IA
515-281-4121 or 800-457-4416
www.state.ia.us/government/crc

Kansas:

The Kansas office of the EEOC and the Kansas Human Rights Commission will assist employees who have been wrongfully terminated according to either federal or state laws, by investigating those claims, attempting to mediate a settlement, and filing a lawsuit on the claimant's behalf when appropriate.

Legal Remedies for Wrongful Termination

- Remedies vary depending on the discrimination or wrongful termination; however, some of the possible solutions include the following:
- Reinstatement; and reinstatement of seniority and benefits
- Back pay
- Compensation for stress and suffering
- Mandated policy changes to protect other employees in that company
- Possibly court costs and attorney's fees
- Punitive damages to prevent further abuses by the employer

Kansas imposes some specific additional penalties in the following areas:

Jury duty – may be liable for back wages and benefits, attorney's fees, damages, and reinstatement

Garnishment– for refusal to comply with child support withholding requests, fines of up to $500

Whistleblower– for permanent, classified officer, penalties include suspension without pay for 30 days; for willful/repeated violations, may require resignation or disqualification for state officer for up to 2 years

While employees are required to file wrongful employment claims through state agencies and offices, these can be difficult cases to pursue. Any employee filing such a claim may find additional help and guidance from an employee rights attorney who is skilled is these areas and may have additional avenues to help them follow.

Kansas City Area Office

4th & State Avenue, 9th Floor
Kansas City, KS 66101
913-551-5655 or 800-669-4000

Human Rights Commission

Topeka, KS
785-296-3206
www.khrc.net

Kentucky:

The local EEOC office and the Kentucky Human Rights Commission are the first options for claimants who have been discriminated against by their employers. After their investigation, if there is cause for action, they will seek mediation or conciliation; and if that is ineffective, they may file a lawsuit on the employee's behalf. If those efforts fail, the employee has the right to file a private lawsuit.

Legal Remedies for Wrongful Termination

There are a number of options that may be available for an employee who has been subjected to discrimination. Some of those options, whether pursued through state agency claims or individual lawsuits, may include reinstatement of the former position, benefits, and/or seniority; back wages; compensation for mental pain and suffering; court costs and attorney's fees; injunctive relief in the workplace to protect other employees; punitive damages.

Kentucky law also allows additional penalties in the following specific areas of abuse:

Jury duty – class B misdemeanor with fines of up to $250 and/or 89 days in jail; liable for back pay and attorney's fees; reinstatement with full benefits and seniority

Garnishment– for child support, fines of up to $500 and/or 1 year in county jail

Whistleblower– for all employers who willfully or repeatedly violate employee protections for reporting safety and health infractions, fines of $5,000 to $70,000 per violation; civil penalties of up to $10,000 per violation

Clearly, Kentucky has some stiff penalties for those who abuse employee rights in the workplace. State agencies have established processes to help employees pursue those rights in the governmental system. However, there are many claims passing through those agencies, and to ensure that all their options are explored, employees may want to consult with an employee rights lawyer for assistance.

Louisville Area Office

600 Dr. Martin Luther King Jr. Place, Suite 268
Louisville, KY 40202
502-582-6082 or 800-669-4000

Human Rights Commission

Louisville, KY
502-595-4024 or 800-292-5566
www.kchr.ky.gov

Louisiana:

Claims filed according to those guidelines can be assured that agencies will investigate and attempt to mediate a settlement. If those measures fail, the agency may also file a lawsuit on the employee's behalf. However, the employee may bypass the agency process and file their own lawsuit with the help of an employee rights lawyer.

Legal Remedies for Wrongful Termination

If the employee and the agency or lawyer representing them can prove a case for wrongful termination, there are a number of remedies they may obtain, including reinstatement of their job and benefits, back pay, compensation for their stress and difficulties, injunctive relief in the workplace, court costs and attorney's fees, and punitive damages.

Employers may also face additional penalties for violation of wrongful termination laws:

Jury duty – for wrongful termination, fines of between $100 and $1,000 for each employee and reinstatement with full benefits; for failure to grant paid leave when applicable, fines of $100 to $500, liable for full day's lost wages

Garnishment– for wrongful termination, reinstatement and lost wages (though no damages); for denial of employment, reasonable damages

Louisiana has taken great pains to provide additional protection for employees in their state. While state EEOC and human rights agencies may provide assistance, there are also civil options available to the employee, which they may pursue with the assistance of an employee rights attorney. There are many details involved in these laws that apply in a number of specific situations. Without the advice of a lawyer, it can be all too easy for the employee to be unaware of some of their rights and protections.

New Orleans Field Office
1555 Poydras Street, Suite 1900
New Orleans, LA 70112
800-669-4000 TTY: 800-669-6820
FAX: 504-589-6861

Commission on Human Rights
Baton Rouge, LA
225-342-6969
www.gov.state.la.us/HumanRights/humanrightshome.htm

Maine:

Those claims filed in public human rights agencies begin with a thorough investigation of the wrongful termination case. If the case is found to have merit, the agency will generally pursue mediation or conciliation. If that is unsuccessful, they may file a lawsuit on behalf of the employee. If those means are unsuccessful, or if the agency discontinues its case, the employee and their employee rights lawyer may then pursue their own lawsuit.

Legal Remedies for Wrongful Termination

The remedies state agencies and/or private lawsuits may obtain, under federal or state labor laws, may include:

- Reinstatement of former position and benefits
- Lost wages
- Compensation for stress and suffering
- Injunctive relief in the workplace

- Attorney's fees and court costs

- Punitive damages

In addition to those remedies, there are additional penalties for employers under supplemental laws for some violations:

Jury duty – class E crime, punishable by fines of up to $1,000 and/or 6 months in county jail; liable for up to 6 weeks back pay, attorney's fees, and benefits

Garnishment– for knowingly failing to withhold and/or remit child support payments, fines of up to $100; for terminating, disciplining, or failing to employ those with garnishments, fines of up to $5,000; liable for actual and punitive damages, attorney's fees, and court costs

Main laws provide a number of supplemental statutes in addition to federal laws protecting Maine employees. While violations must first be pursued through state agencies, it can be in the employee's best interests to consult an employee rights lawyer to ensure that every avenue of remedy and compensation is considered. If agency measures fail, that lawyer is then prepared to continue pursuing the claim in civil court and bring it to a quicker resolution.

Human Rights Commission

Augusta, ME
207-624-6050
www.maine.gov/mhrc

Maryland:

State EEOC or human rights agencies are primarily responsible for investigating claims and determining whether they are viable. If so, those agencies may pursue mediation or, if that fails, lawsuits on the employee's behalf. If the agency's claim is dropped or fails, the employee has the right to retain an employee rights attorney to file suit in civil court.

Legal Remedies for Wrongful Termination

Agency claims or civil lawsuits may be able to obtain some or all of the following remedies under federal and state labor laws:

- Reinstatement of former position and benefits

- Lost wages

- Compensation for stress and suffering

- Injunctive relief in the workplace

- Attorney's fees and court costs

- Punitive damages

State statutes also provide the following specific penalties for employers who abuse employee rights:

Jury duty – fines of up to $1,000

Garnishment– for general wage garnishments, discharging employees carries a fine of up to $10,000 and/or 1 year in prison; for child support withholding, liable for amount of wages failed to withhold or make support payments

Maryland has an extensive array of state statutes supplementing federal labor and discrimination laws. And while the first step in protecting employee rights is to file a claim with state EEOC and human rights agencies, employees may need the help of employee rights attorneys to oversee the claim and make sure every effort for remedy is pursued. In addition, if agency claims are unsuccessful, employees and their employee rights lawyers may file private lawsuits.

10 S. Howard Street
3rd Floor
Baltimore, MD 21201
410-962-3932 or 800-669-4000

Commission on Human Relations
Baltimore, MD
410-767-8600
www.mchr.state.md.us

Massachusetts:

Massachusetts state law requires that all claims for wrongful termination or workplace discrimination be filed first through state EEOC or human rights offices. Those offices will investigate such claims, and if viable, pursue mediation or conciliation or, if appropriate, a lawsuit on behalf of the employee. If those processes fail, Massachusetts law allows employees to pursue their own private lawsuit.

Legal Remedies for Wrongful Termination

Agencies and employee rights lawyers may seek any or all of the following remedies, depending on the violation and the specific federal or state penalties:

- Reinstatement of former benefits and position

- Back pay

- Compensation for stress and suffering

- Injunctive relief in the workplace

- Attorney's fees and court costs
- Punitive damages

Additional penalties enumerated in Massachusetts state law against employers include the following:

Garnishment– for child support, employer who terminates illegally liable for back pay and benefits, plus fines of up to $1,000; for failure to follow withholding order, liable for amount requested to be withheld or fine of up to $500, whichever is more

These legal options begin with claims through state EEOC and civil right agencies. The more complex the violation and claim, the more helpful it can be to have an employee rights attorney representing the employee. In such a case, if the agency resolutions are ineffective, the employee's attorney will be prepared to file a private suit more quickly and represent the employee more effectively.

Boston Area Office

John F. Kennedy Federal Building
475 Government Center
Boston, MA 02203
617-565-3200 or 800-669-4000

Commission Against Discrimination

Boston, MA
617-994-6000
www.state.ma.us/mcad

Michigan:

Claims for wrongful termination generally begin with an investigation to determination their validity. If they are found to have merit, agencies generally proceed to mediate a settlement or seek conciliation. If that is impossible, the agency may file a lawsuit on the employee's behalf, or the agency may drop the claim and allow the employee to pursue it in a private lawsuit.

Legal Remedies for Wrongful Termination

There are a number of possible remedies that may be obtained through EEOC claims or lawsuits. They may include the following, depending on the violation:

- Reinstatement of former benefits and position
- Back pay

- Compensation for stress and suffering

- Injunctive relief in the workplace

- Attorney's fees and court costs

- Punitive damages

Employers in Michigan who violate federal or state discrimination laws may also face additional penalties:

Jury duty – misdemeanor charge, with fines of up to $500 and/or 90 days in prison; or contempt of court charges, with fines of up to $7,500 and/or up to 93 days in jail

Garnishment– general garnishment, for illegal termination, reinstatement and lost wages and benefits; for child support withholding violations, misdemeanor conviction, with fines of up to $500, reinstatement; and back pay

Whistleblower– civil fines of up to $500

While Michigan has only a few supplemental labor laws addressing wrongful termination or discrimination in firing, state agencies and employee rights attorneys also pursue claims and suits addressing violations of federal laws. With all of the details that vary so widely by state, it is wise to retain an employee rights attorney to assure that employees are being thoroughly protected under discrimination and wrongful termination laws.

477 Michigan Avenue, Room 865
Detroit, MI 48226
313-226-4600 or 800-669-4000

Department of Civil Rights

Detroit, MI
313-456-3700
www.michigan.gov/mdcr

Minnesota:

When pursuing a claim or lawsuit for wrongful termination, agencies or attorneys will generally investigate the claim to determine its validity before attempting mediation or conciliation. If a valid claim is not settled in this way, a lawsuit is generally the next step, either through a state agency or private lawsuit.

Legal Remedies for Wrongful Termination

There are a number of remedies an employee may pursue with their employee rights attorney in Minnesota. Those remedies may vary depending on the violation and the degree of willfulness; however, they may include any or all of the following:

- Reinstatement of former benefits and position

- Compensation for stress and suffering

- Back pay

- Attorney's fees and court costs

- Punitive damages

- Injunctive relief in the workplace

Minnesota laws also have additional penalties for employers who violate certain labor laws:

Jury duty –criminal contempt with fines of up to $700 and/or 6 months in jail; liable for up to 6 months of back pay, attorney's fees, and reinstatement.

Garnishment– for general wage garnishment, reinstatement and employer liability for double back pay; for child support withholding, liable for support employer failed to withhold plus interest, attorney's fees, contempt of court, liable for double back pay, and fines of $500 or more.

Whistleblower– fines of $25 per day for each injured employee, up to $750 for each employee

With the considerable number of state statutes supplementing federal wrongful termination and discrimination laws, there are many avenues of relief for employee to pursue in response to workplace abuses. In addition, while state agencies can be extremely helpful, for more complex cases, it can be essential to have the advice of an employee rights attorney to ensure that all the employee's rights are protected and all their remedies are considered.

Minneapolis Area Office

330 S. Second Avenue, Suite 430
Minneapolis, MN 55401
612-335-4040 or 800-669-4000

Department of Human Rights

St. Paul, MN
651-296-5663
www.humanrights.state.mn.us

Mississippi:

Since private employees are not preempted in pursuing their employment rights under federal or Mississippi state laws, they have the option of obtaining help through EEOC or human rights agencies, or retaining an employee rights attorney to help them file a private suit. Many discrimination or wrongful termination cases can be complex, and may not justify a claim or lawsuit. A full investigation determines the validity of the case and, if it is found to be justified, will begin by attempting mediation or conciliation. If those processes fail, a lawsuit may be justified.

Legal Remedies for Wrongful Termination

Whether a claim or lawsuit is the end result, agencies and employee rights attorneys may seek a number of remedies, depending on the violation, state laws, and the seriousness of the abuse:

- Lost wages
- Reinstatement of benefits and position
- Attorney's fees and court costs
- Compensation for stress and suffering
- Punitive damages
- Injunctive relief in the workplace

Mississippi laws also require additional penalties for employer violations in some specific areas:

Jury duty –employers found guilty of interfering with the administration of justice can face fines of up to $500 and/or 1 month in county jail up to 2 years in the state penitentiary; contempt of court with fines of up to $1,000 and/or 6 months in prison

Whistleblower– each member of governing board, authority, or executive leadership may be fined up to $10,000 per violation

Employees have a number of options open to them if they believe their rights have been violated in the workplace. The state EEOC and human rights agencies provide assistance for workplace abuse, and an employee rights attorney can advise any employee about the most effective means to protect their rights and pursue remedies for abuses in the workplace.

Dr. A. H. McCoy Federal Building
100 West Capitol Street, Suite 207
Jackson, MS 39269
601-965-4537 or 800-669-4000

Department of Employment Security

Jackson, MS
601-321-6000
www.mdes.ms.gov

Montana:

Whether an employee chooses to pursue a claim through state agencies or a lawsuit through an employee rights attorney, it is important to thoroughly investigate the applicable state laws to ensure their case is valid. Conciliation or mediation can often solve the problem out of court; however, if those efforts fail, employees in Montana have the right to file a private lawsuit.

Legal Remedies for Wrongful Termination

Either through federal or state laws, there are many possible remedies for wrongful termination, especially when it is based on discrimination. Employees and their lawyers should be sure they pursue all of the options that are open to them under Montana law:

- Lost wages
- Punitive damages
- Reinstatement of benefits and position
- Compensation for stress and suffering
- Injunctive relief in the workplace
- Attorney's fees and court costs

Montana law also provides additional penalties for employers who violate wrongful termination protection laws:

Jury duty –employer may be liable for back pay, damages, attorney's fees, and reinstatement

Garnishment – for wrongful termination because of garnishment, employer liable for fines of $150 to $500, reinstatement, full restitution, lost wages

Whistleblower– employee may file internal appeals for wrongful termination; after 90 days or exhausting internal actions, may file claim or suit up to 1 year after termination for lost wages, fringe benefits (for up to 4 years from termination), and punitive damages

The Human Rights Bureau is the source of information and claim options for Montana workers whose rights have been violated. However, employees are not limited to agency claims. They may also choose to take more complicated cases to an employee rights attorney to ensure that all avenues of remedy are being pursued as thoroughly as possible.

Human Rights Bureau

Employment Relations Division
Department of Labor and Industry
Helena, MT
406-444-2884 or 800-542-0807
http://erd.dli.state.mt.us/HumanRight/HRhome.asp

Nebraska:

Employees whose rights have been abused by an employer and wrongfully terminated may file a claim through the Nebraska Equal Opportunity Commission. Only when they have investigated and validated that claim and pursued conciliation or mediation with the offending employer may the employee take their claim to court, first through the state agency, and only after that case is concluded or dropped, in a private civil action.

Legal Remedies for Wrongful Termination

The remedies a civil agency or employee rights attorney may pursue can vary, depending on the type of offense and the applicable state laws; however, they may include any of the following:

- Reinstatement of benefits and position

- Punitive damages

- Lost wages

- Compensation for stress and suffering

- Attorney's fees and court costs

- Injunctive relief in the workplace

Additional state penalties for employers who violate wrongful termination or discrimination laws can be harsh:

Jury duty – class IV misdemeanor with fines of $100 to $500

Garnishment –child support withholding, for failing to comply with withholding orders liable for amount owed plus interest, legal costs, attorney's fees; for violating employee's rights, liable for damages plus interest, legal costs, attorney's fees, fines of up to $500 for state administered support, and may be required to provide complete restitution, reinstatement, and lost wages

Whistleblower– public counsel and appeals board may grant lost wages, reasonable attorney's fees, and other appropriate relief; employee may also pursue action under Administrative Procedures Act for damages, reinstatement lost wages, attorney's fees, or other appropriate relief

The Nebraska Equal Opportunity Commission is experienced in filing wrongful termination or discrimination claims, and the employee should contact them quickly to ensure they meet the state statute of limitations. However, for complicated claims or those that the agency may not pursue to the end, it can be a tremendous help to consult an employee rights lawyer immediately and take advantage of their expertise each step of the claims process.

Lincoln, NE
402-471-2024 or 800-642-6112
www.neoc.ne.gov

Nevada:

In Nevada, employees must first pursue a claim for wrongful termination or discrimination in the workplace through state EEOC offices. After a thorough investigation and an attempt at mediation and conciliation, if the claim is still not satisfied, either the agency or the employee and their employee rights attorney may pursue a civil lawsuit.

Legal Remedies for Wrongful Termination

Claims, mediation negotiations, and civil lawsuits may pursue a number of remedies under federal and state labor laws:

- Reinstatement of benefits and position
- Lost wages
- Compensation for stress and suffering
- Punitive damages
- Attorney's fees and court costs
- Injunctive relief in the workplace

Nevada state laws provide additional penalties for employers guilty of violating wrongful termination laws which can be quite stiff:

Jury duty –termination or threatening to terminate is gross misdemeanor with fines of up to $2,000 and/or 1 year in prison; may be liable for back pay, damages equal to back pay, punitive damages up to $50,000, and reinstatement; dissuading or threatening to dissuade is a misdemeanor with fines of up to $1,000 and/or up to 6 months in jail.

Garnishment – for willfully refusing to withhold general garnishments or misrepresenting employee's income, liable for entire withholding amount and punitive damages up to $1,000 per pay period; wrongful termination for child support withholding, reinstatement and liability for payments not withheld plus fines of up to $1,000; upon employee victory in court, liability for minimum $2,500 plus legal costs and attorney's fees; willful non-compliance or misrepresenting employee's income, liable for entire support amount not paid and damages to obligee for punitive damages up to $1,000 per pay period

Whistleblower– public and private employees discriminated against may file complaint within 30 days of violation, only after notifying employer and division, employer may be liable for lost wages and benefits; public employees discriminated against may appeal to personnel department within 2 years of report, hearing officer may order employer to refrain from discrimination

In many cases, Nevada laws, legislators, and courts place stiff penalties on employers who discriminate against employees and terminate employment in violation of federal and state laws. In order to ensure that those penalties are imposed, employees should consult an experienced employee rights lawyer to advise them through the claims, mediation, and court processes to receive the legal remedies under U.S. and Nevada statutes.

Las Vegas Local Office
333 Las Vegas Blvd. South, Suite 8112
Las Vegas, NV 89101
800-669-4000

Equal Rights Commission
Reno, NV
775-688-1288
http://detr.state.nv.us/nerc/NERC_index.htm

New Hampshire:

A claim for wrongful termination violations must be pursued through state agencies, where they will investigate the claim for validity, attempt to negotiate mediation or conciliation, and take the claim to civil court if all else fails.

Legal Remedies for Wrongful Termination

There are many remedies the EEOC office may pursue through claims, negotiations, and lawsuits:

- Injunctive relief in the workplace
- Reinstatement of benefits and position
- Lost wages
- Punitive damages
- Attorney's fees and court costs
- Compensation for stress and suffering

Additional penalties that can be imposed upon employers who violate discrimination and wrongful termination laws as a result of EEOC claims or lawsuits include the following:

Jury duty –contempt of court, liable to employee for back pay, attorney's fees, and reinstatement.

Garnishment – for non-compliance with child support withholding order or disciplining employee for such order, misdemeanor with fines of up to $1,000 for failure to withhold payments and fines of up to $100 per pay period

Whistleblower– employee must seek conciliation in-house before seeking hearing with labor commissioner; remedies include reinstatement, lost wages, fringe benefits, seniority, and injunctive relief; continued violations may bring daily penalties

New Hampshire places a great emphasis on employer compliance with federal discrimination and wrongful termination laws. There are additional state penalties for violations, and state agencies are the sole avenue of remedies for employees whose rights have been violated. However, it is a complex process with many details that only experienced employee rights attorneys can easily navigate. It may speed the case of an employee to consult such an attorney to ensure they receive the protections and compensation they deserve.

Commission for Human Rights
Concord, NH
603-271-2767
www.nh.gov/hrc

New Mexico:

Not all claims or lawsuits for wrongful termination are justified. Therefore, public agencies and employee rights attorneys generally investigate those claims thoroughly for validity first, and then pursue some form or mediation or conciliation before taking action in civil court.

Legal Remedies for Wrongful Termination

Many remedies for wrongful termination and discrimination in the workplace are provided under state and federal laws. Those remedies vary, however, depending on the severity of the violation, the type of abuse, and state laws. Employees may seek one or more of the following:

- Reinstatement of benefits and position
- Lost wages
- Punitive damages
- Attorney's fees and court costs
- Compensation for stress and suffering

- Injunctive relief in the workplace

New Mexico has additional penalties for employers guilty of employee discrimination or wrongful termination in the following areas:

Jury duty – petty misdemeanor, with fines of up to $500 and/or 6 months in jail

Garnishment –willful refusal to pay child support garnishment liable to fines for total amount not withheld; for wrongful termination or other penalties, liable for damages, reinstatement, and possible contempt of court

Wrongful termination and employee discrimination are outlawed in every state. New Mexico is no different, enacting supplemental statutes to increase penalties and restraints on employers for abuse. New Mexico has mechanisms whereby victims may file EEOC claims or employ employee rights attorneys to file private lawsuits in the courts for a number of remedies, including reinstatement, compensation, and damages. Because of the complex nature of these laws and the workplace conditions that accompany violations, an experienced lawyer can provide essential counsel to ensure employees take advantage of all the options available to them.

Albuquerque Area Office
505 Marquette Street, NW, Suite 900
Albuquerque, NM 87102
505-248-5201 or 800-669-4000

Human Rights Division
Santa Fe, NM
505-827-6838 or 800-566-9471
www.dol.state.nm.us/dol_hrd.html

New Jersey:

An employee may either pursue legal remedies for unlawful termination or discrimination by filing a claim through a state agency or retaining an employee rights attorney to file a private lawsuit. Once the violation has been thoroughly investigated and deemed valid, legal representatives will generally attempt to settle the claim or suit by mediation or conciliation. If those methods fail, the case may go to court, either in the hands of agency lawyers or the employee's employee rights attorney.

Legal Remedies for Wrongful Termination

Once a claim reaches negotiation or litigation in court, the remedies the employee and their legal representative can pursue are many, although they vary according to the violation, the state laws, and the degree of abuse. Those remedies generally include one or more of the following:

- Lost wages

- Injunctive relief in the workplace

- Punitive damages

- Reinstatement of benefits and position

- Attorney's fees and court costs

- Compensation for stress and suffering

In addition to the remedies provided for the employee, there are penalties for the employer that violates these laws. Some states have additional penalties to those found in federal laws, and in New Jersey, they include the following:

Jury duty –disorderly person charge with fines of up to $1,000 and/or up to 6 months in jail; may be liable for economic damages, attorney's fees, and reinstatement

Garnishment – for general garnishment, results in unlawful termination, disorderly person charge, reinstatement and damages; for child support withholding, wrongful termination, liable for fines, civil damages, reinstatement, attorney's fees, twofold compensatory damages, legal costs, and back pay; for noncompliance with withholding order, liable for fine or amount not withheld, interest, attorney's fees; for noncompliance with medical support order, liable for children's medical expenses and all other withholding amounts not collected

Whistleblower– employee can file civil actions up to 1 year after violation to receive injunction, reinstatement, benefits, seniority, lost wages, legal and attorney's fees, punitive damages, and civil fines of up to $1,000 for first offense and up to $5,000 for repeat offenses

New Jersey employees have several options to pursue reinstatement and compensation for wrongful termination or discrimination in the workplace. State EEOC offices can answer most questions concerning these issues, but if there is a complicated case of employer violations, it may be wise to enlist the counsel of an employee rights lawyer to ensure the rights of the employee are being protected and all of their options for remedies are being explored.

Newark Area Office
1 Newark Center, 21st Floor
Newark, NJ 07102
973-645-6383 or 800-669-4000

Division on Civil Rights
Newark, NJ
973-648-2700
www.state.nj.us/lps/dcr

New York:

After determining the validity of a wrongful termination claim, state agencies generally attempt mediation or conciliation to settle these claims out of court. If those efforts fail, however, the agency may file a civil suit or drop their claim and allow the employee to contact an employee rights attorney to file a private lawsuit.

Legal Remedies for Wrongful Termination

Victims of wrongful termination have a number of remedies which they may pursue through claims or civil suits, including one or more of the following:

- Reinstatement of benefits and position
- Lost wages
- Punitive damages
- Attorney's fees and court costs
- Compensation for stress and suffering
- Injunctive relief in the workplace

State statutes include additional penalties for employers who violate wrongful termination and discrimination regulations in these areas:

Jury duty –contempt of court with fines of up to $1,000 and/or 30 days in county jail

Garnishment – for wrongful termination, liable for reinstatement, up to 6 weeks lost wages, fines of up to $500 for first offense and up to $1,000 for repeat offenses, and possibly contempt of court

Victims of discrimination and wrongful termination in New York have many protections and options for remedies under federal and state statutes. Because they can be very detailed and specific, employees may benefit from retaining a skilled employee rights attorney to guide them through the process of filing an EEOC or human rights claim or civil suit to ensure that they take advantage of all the legal opportunities provided in these important protections.

Buffalo Local Office
6 Fountain Plaza, Suite 350
Buffalo, NY 14202
716-551-4441 or 800-669-4000

Division of Human Rights
Bronx, NY
718-741-8400
www.dhr.state.ny.us

North Carolina:

State agencies do not always validate and pursue wrongful termination claims. To determine whether or not to file a claim, the agency investigates the case thoroughly and, if they find it viable, generally begin by attempting mediation or conciliation to avoid the time and cost of court cases. If those efforts are ineffective, however, they may file a lawsuit on behalf of the employee.

Legal Remedies for Wrongful Termination

The remedies a state EEOC or human rights agency can pursue, depending on the violation and the state statutes, include any or all of the following:

- Injunctive relief in the workplace
- Reinstatement of benefits and position
- Lost wages
- Compensation for stress and suffering
- Punitive damages
- Attorney's fees and court costs

In North Carolina, state statutes have additional penalties for discrimination or wrongful termination violations in the following areas:

Jury duty –liable for damages and reinstatement

Garnishment – for child support withholding that results in wrongful termination or discrimination, liable for fines of up to $100 for first offense, $500 for second offense, and $1,000 for third; for noncompliance with child support withholding order, liable for contempt of court

Whistleblower– public employers willfully violating wrongful termination or discrimination laws liable for three times legal costs and reasonable attorney's fees; for private employers willfully violating wrongful termination or discrimination laws, liable for triple damages

For victims of wrongful termination and discrimination in the workplace, the primary avenue of relief under North Carolina law is filing a claim through state EEOC offices and the Department of Labor. Because of the number of cases they generally have pending, it can be vital for employees to have their own employee rights attorney to represent them and ensure that all remedies are being aggressively pursued on their behalf.

Charlotte District Office

129 W. Trade Street, Suite 400
Charlotte, NC 28202
704-344-6682 or 800-669-4000

Greensboro Local Office

2303 W. Meadowview Road, Suite 201
Greensboro, NC 27407
336-547-4188 or 800-669-4000

Raleigh Area Office

1309 Annapolis Drive
Raleigh, NC 27608
919-856-4064 or 800-669-4000

Employment Discrimination Bureau

Department of Labor
Raleigh, NC
919-807-2796 or 800-NC-LABOR
www.nclabor.com/edb/edb.htm

North Dakota:

Employees may believe they have a claim for wrongful termination or discrimination in firing, but the basis for their claim may be invalid. That is why state agencies and employee rights attorneys must begin by investigating the claim and comparing the facts with federal and state laws. If the claim is deemed valid, lawyers and agencies will generally attempt mediation and conciliation before investing the time and expense that a court case requires.

Legal Remedies for Wrongful Termination

The remedies provided under federal and state statutes may vary, depending on state laws and the specific violation. But they generally include one or more of the following:

- Punitive damages

- Reinstatement of benefits and position

- Lost wages

- Compensation for stress and suffering

- Injunctive relief in the workplace

- Attorney's fees and court costs

North Dakota state laws also include some additional penalties for employers who violate discrimination and wrongful termination laws:

Jury duty – Class B misdemeanor, with fines of up to $1,000 and/or 30 days in jail; may also be liable for up to 6 weeks of lost wages, attorney's fees, and reinstatement

Garnishment – for wrongful termination, liable for double lost wages and reinstatement; for failure to comply with child support withholding orders, contempt of court, liable for missing payment, legal costs, interest, and attorney's fees; noncompliance for 7 days may result in late fees of $25 to $75 per business day; more than 14 days, liable for $200 or more in damages, legal costs, interest, and attorney's fees

Whistleblower– Class B misdemeanor

North Dakota provides not only federal and state laws prohibiting discrimination and wrongful termination, but legal means for pursuing relief, compensation, and restitution. However, because of the number of laws and the specific parameters of application, it may be wise to enlist the help of an experienced employee rights lawyer to make sure all of those statutes are thoroughly and correctly applied.

Human Rights Division

Department of Labor
Bismarck, ND
701-328-2660 or 800-582-8032
www.nd.gov/labor

Ohio:

Filing a claim for wrongful termination or discrimination in the workplace is a simple matter of contacting the local EEOC agency, Civil Rights Commission, or employee rights attorney; cooperating with their investigation; participating in mediation and conciliation negotiations; and, if necessary, filing a civil suit.

Legal Remedies for Wrongful Termination

State agencies and employee rights attorneys can pursue a number of remedies, as provided for in state and federal regulations. Depending on the state laws, the violation, and the seriousness of the violation, those remedies may include any of the following:

- Punitive damages
- Reinstatement of benefits and position
- Lost wages
- Compensation for stress and suffering
- Injunctive relief in the workplace

- Attorney's fees and court costs

There are additional penalties in Ohio law for employers who violate discrimination and wrongful termination laws in the following areas:

Jury duty – contempt of court, with fines of up to $250 and/or 30 days in jail for first offense, fines of up to $500 and/or 60 days in jail for second offense; fines of up to $1,000 and/or up to 90 days in jail for third offense.

Garnishment – for wrongful termination, fines of $50 to $200 and 10 to 30 days in jail

Employers cannot discriminate or wrongfully terminate an employee for any of the issues outlined in federal and state laws. Employees have the right to pursue state national guard reserve service, vote, fulfill jury duty, and more. If employers make that impossible, or discipline employees for exercising those rights, employees can pursue remedies such as claims and civil actions. Because of the number of statutes involved, it can be essential to be able to call on the expertise of an employee rights attorney to ensure the success of those claims or suits.

Cincinnati Area Office
550 Main Street
10th Floor
Cincinnati, OH 45202
513-684-2851 or 800-669-4000

Cleveland Field Office
1240 E. 9th Street, Suite 3001
Cleveland, OH 44199
Skylight Office Tower
216-522-2003 or 800-669-4000

Civil Rights Commission
Columbus, OH
614-466-5928 or 888-278-7101
www.crc.ohio.gov

Oklahoma:

Not all situations which employees believe are cases of wrongful termination or discrimination can be considered so under Oklahoma law. Therefore, state agencies must first investigate those claims for validity. Once that is established, agencies generally attempt mediation or conciliation to solve the dispute. If those efforts are ineffective, the agency may choose to file a civil suit for the employee or allow them to retain an employee rights attorney to file a private civil suit.

Legal Remedies for Wrongful Termination

Whether through agency claims or civil lawsuits, state and federal laws provide a number of remedies for wrongful termination violations:

- Reinstatement of benefits and position
- Punitive damages
- Lost wages
- Compensation for stress and suffering
- Attorney's fees and court costs
- Injunctive relief in the workplace

Additional penalties are included under Oklahoma law for employers who violate these specific aspects of discrimination and wrongful termination laws:

Jury duty – misdemeanor, with fines of up to $5,000, liable for past and future lost wages, damages for mental anguish, and costs of finding appropriate alternate employment

Garnishment – for noncompliance with child support withholding, liable for amount not withheld and fines of up to $200 for each payment not made.

Whistleblower –state officials may be suspended without pay, demoted, discharged, or put on probation for 6 months; for willful violations, court will forfeit their position and hold them ineligible for employment for 1 to 5 years

Employers have a duty to their company, their customers, but also their employees. No employee can have their rights ignored, abused, or sacrificed in order for an employer to have a healthy bottom line. Oklahoma provides the opportunity for employees victimized by their employers to file claims with EEOC agencies or the Human Rights Commission to find relief. And while they may not file private civil suits until those state options are exhausted or abandoned, they may still need to have the advice of an employee rights attorney to ensure that the agency is pursing every possible avenue of relief.

Oklahoma Area Office
215 Dean A. McGee Avenue, Suite 524
Oklahoma City
Oklahoma 73102
405-231-4911 or 800-669-4000

Human Rights Commission
Oklahoma City, OK
405-521-2360
www.hrc.state.ok.us

Oregon:

The procedure for filing those claims begins with contacting the Civil Rights Division of the Oregon Bureau of Labor and Industries, or retaining an employee rights lawyer to verify the claim. Legal representatives begin by attempting mediation or conciliation, in an attempt to avoid the time and costs of going to court. If that proves impossible, either the agency or an attorney must argue the wrongful termination case in civil court.

Legal Remedies for Wrongful Termination

Whether through mediation or civil action, the remedies an employee is entitled to seek vary by violation and severity of the abuse, but generally include one or more of the following:

- Reinstatement of benefits and position
- Punitive damages
- Lost wages
- Compensation for stress and suffering
- Attorney's fees and court costs
- Injunctive relief in the workplace

Oregon statutes include additional penalties for employers who violate the following discrimination laws:

Jury duty – reinstatement and back pay

Garnishment –noncompliance with child support withholding order, liable for all amounts not paid, fines of up to $250 for each willful failure to pay; for wrongful termination, discrimination, or retaliation, liable for reinstatement, lost wages, the greater of compensatory damages or $200, punitive damages, legal costs, and attorney's fees

No one should have to suffer the losses and humiliation of wrongful termination or discrimination in the workplace. However, if their employer violates the federal or state protections that are in place, they have the right to file a claim or lawsuit to recover damages, wages, and even reinstatement of their position. Employee rights lawyers are skilled at determining the validity of a case and pursing it aggressively to help employees regain the rights and benefits that are guaranteed under current laws.

Civil Rights Division, Bureau of Labor and Industries
Portland, OR
971-673-0761
www.oregon.gov/BOLI/CRD

Pennsylvania:

Employees who find themselves victimized by wrongful termination or discrimination in the workplace should contact the local EEOC office or the Human Relations Commission and file a claim. Once they investigate and determine if that claim is valid, they will attempt to mediate a settlement with the employer. If that is unsuccessful, they may file a civil suit for remedies, or they may drop the case and allow the employee and their employee relations lawyer to file a private lawsuit.

Legal Remedies for Wrongful Termination

Federal and state laws provide for a number of remedies that an employee may pursue through a claim or lawsuit, depending on the violation and the applicable statutes:

- Reinstatement of benefits and position

- Lost wages

- Punitive damages

- Attorney's fees and court costs

- Compensation for stress and suffering

- Injunctive relief in the workplace

In addition to the standard remedies in wrongful termination and discrimination laws, there are some additional penalties employers may face for certain violations:

Jury duty – liable for back pay, benefits, attorney's fees, and possible reinstatement

Garnishment – child support withholding, for violating employee rights, fines of up to $1,000 and damages; for noncompliance with support orders, contempt of court and possibly jail

Whistleblower – fines of up to $500; for intent to discourage disclosure of criminal activity, subject to suspension from public service for up to 6 months unless official holds an elected public office

No employer has the right to take advantage of an employee and deny their civil rights. That is why there are so many specific and detailed protections in federal and state laws against wrongful termination and discrimination today. Employees should consult an employee rights lawyer to discover if they have grounds to file a claim through stage agencies. If so, their attorney can help ensure the agency pursues their case aggressively, and if the case goes to civil court, that attorney may be prepared to help provide a winning strategy.

Philadelphia District Office

21 S. Fifth Street, Suite 400
Philadelphia, PA 19106
215-440-2600 or 800-669-4000

Pittsburgh Area Office

1001 Liberty Avenue. Suite 300
Pittsburgh, PA 15222
412-644-3444 or 800-669-4000

Human Relations Commission

Harrisburg, PA
717-787-4410
www.phrc.state.pa.us

Rhode Island:

In keeping with the Rhode Island guidelines for filing claims and lawsuits for wrongful termination and discrimination, victims should contact the state Commission for Human Rights office to file a claim. After their investigation into the evidence, if that claim is valid, agency representatives will pursue negotiations to settle the claim out of court. If that negotiation is unsuccessful, the agency may file a civil suit, or drop the case and allow the employee and their employee rights attorney to file a private suit.

Legal Remedies for Wrongful Termination

The remedies which state agencies and employee rights lawyers can pursue in claims and suits vary by violation and the relevant statutes, but they may include any or all of the following:

- Compensation for stress and suffering

- Reinstatement of benefits and position

- Lost wages

- Attorney's fees and court costs

- Injunctive relief in the workplace

- Punitive damages

Rhode Island laws includes additional penalties for employers who violate employment discrimination laws in some specific areas:

Jury duty – misdemeanor with fines of up to $1,000 and/or 1 year in prison

Garnishment –child support withholding: for discriminating or penalizing employee, liable for damages, interest, legal costs, attorney's fees, and possibly reinstatement and lost wages; fines of up to $100; for noncompliance with child support withholding order, liable for $100 fine

The penalties for discrimination and wrongful termination can be difficult and expensive. However, the opportunity for victimized employees to pursue legal remedies can be well worth the time and expense if it means reinstatement, compensation, and damages. Because these laws are so complex and detailed, even if Rhode Island state agencies have priority in pursuing those claims, an employee rights attorney can be of tremendous help in determining which laws apply and in preparing for civil action if it becomes necessary.

Commission for Human Rights
Providence, RI
401-222-2661
www.richr.state.ri.us/frames.html

South Carolina:

Victims of workplace discrimination and wrongful termination must file a claim with the local EEOC branch office or the Human Affairs Commission in South Carolina. Once they investigate the claim to determine its validity, they will attempt to mediate a settlement out of court. If that proves unsuccessful, they may pursue civil action.

Legal Remedies for Wrongful Termination

State agencies will pursue the appropriate remedies for the violations for which an employee files a claim. While there are a number of possibilities, they vary according to type of violation and severity of abuse:

- Lost wages
- Reinstatement of benefits and position
- Compensation for stress and suffering
- Attorney's fees and court costs
- Punitive damages

- Injunctive relief in the workplace

State laws in South Carolina also provide additional penalties for employers who are guilty of the following violations:

Jury duty – for wrongful termination, liable for 1 year's salary; for demotion, liable for 1 year's difference between previous and lower salary

Garnishment –child support withholding, for employee rights violations, fines of up to $500

Plant Closings –employers who do not give notice equal to that required of employees who resign, liable for damages to every employee for what they suffer as a result of the failure to give notice

While state agencies handle all claims and civil suits under South Carolina law, they have many cases to pursue. In addition, the laws against wrongful termination and discrimination are complicated and specific claims can get overlooked. For thorough representation and experienced handling of their case, it can be to the advantage of employees to retain their own employee rights lawyer to assist them through this difficult process and ensure their rights are protected.

Greenville Local Office
301 N. Main Street
Greenville, SC 29601
864-241-4400 or 800-669-4000

Human Affairs Commission
Columbia, SC
803-737-7800 or 800-521-0725
www.state.sc.us/schac

South Dakota:

While employees must first file their wrongful termination claims with the state Division of Human Rights, if the agency decides not to pursue that claim, the employee and their employee rights attorney then have the right to file a private civil suit.

Legal Remedies for Wrongful Termination

The remedies employees may pursue for relief from wrongful termination or discrimination in the workplace include one or more of the following:

- Reinstatement of benefits and position

- Lost wages

- Compensation for stress and suffering

- Punitive damages

- Attorney's fees and court costs

- Injunctive relief in the workplace

Additional South Dakota penalties for employers who are guilty of discrimination or wrongful termination are as follows:

Jury duty – Class 2 misdemeanor, fines of up to $500 and/or 30 days in county jail

Garnishment – child support withholding only; for violating employee rights or noncompliance with support orders, petty offense

While South Dakota does not have the extensive list of state labor laws that some other states do, it does not minimize the seriousness of those violations that do occur. Employees who must begin their quest for remedies may be required to pursue the process through the state Division of Human Rights, but they may still want to consult an employee rights attorney to ensure that they are moving in the right direction and, if necessary, that they have a skilled legal advisor to call upon if it becomes necessary to file a private civil suit.

Division of Human Rights
Pierre, SD
605-773-4493
www.state.sd.us/dol/boards/hr

Tennessee:

Tennessee statutes allow employees to file wrongful termination claims or lawsuits, with no priority for state agencies in their requirements. Generally, state representatives or employee rights attorneys will attempt mediation before arguing civil suits in state courts.

Legal Remedies for Wrongful Termination

The remedies for wrongful termination vary, depending on the violation and whether it was willful or not. Some of the remedies that may apply include

- Injunctive relief in the workplace

- Reinstatement of benefits and position

- Lost wages

- Punitive damages

- Compensation for stress and suffering

- Attorney's fees and court costs

Tennessee includes additional penalties for employers who violate statutes in the following areas:

Jury duty – Class A misdemeanor, with fines of up to $2,500 and/or up to 11 months, 29 days in jail, liable for back pay, benefits, and reinstatement

Garnishment – penalties relating to child support withholding, for employee discrimination or noncompliance with support orders, class C misdemeanor, with fines of up to $50 and/or up to 30 days in jail

In these difficult economic times, wrongful termination becomes an even more serious violation of an employee's civil rights. That is why it is so important for a victim to have skilled and experienced representation when filing a claim or private suit. Experienced employee rights attorneys can help their clients determine which, and often how many, discrimination laws have been violated and how to best pursue the remedies that Tennessee law provides.

Memphis District Office
1407 Union Avenue, Suite 621
Memphis, TN 38104
901-544-0115 or 800-669-4000

Human Rights Commission
Knoxville, TN
865-594-6500
www.tennessee.gov/humanrights

Texas:

While Texas EEOC offices and the Texas Human Rights Commission are responsible for filing agency claims for discrimination violations, employees and their employee rights lawyers are free to file private actions as well. The first option, however, is generally to pursue mediation. Yet if mediation is unsuccessful, often civil actions cannot be avoided.

Legal Remedies for Wrongful Termination in Texas

The resolutions and forms of compensation available to employees who are victims of discrimination in the workplace are many and varied. However, victims will generally be awarded one or more of the following:

- Compensation for stress and suffering

- Lost wages

- Reinstatement of benefits and position

- Punitive damages

- Attorney's fees and court costs

- Injunctive relief in the workplace

In addition to remedies for the victim, Texas law provides penalties for employers who violate the following specific statutes:

Jury duty – liable for 1 to 5 year's compensation, attorney's fees, and reinstatement

Garnishment – penalties relating to child support withholding, for noncompliance with child or spousal support orders, liable for amount that should have been withheld, attorney's fees, legal costs, plus $200 for each instance

Whistleblower –penalties for supervisors, maximum $15,000 fine

Victims of discrimination and wrongful termination in the workplace are allowed to seek help from EEOC and human rights agencies in Texas to learn the best means of having their rights restored and receiving compensation for their abuses. However, to receive personal attention from an expert in the field, it can be worthwhile to consult an employee rights attorney and file a private civil action for the remedies that are due.

Memphis District Office
1407 Union Avenue, Suite 621
Memphis, TN 38104
901-544-0115 or 800-669-4000

Human Rights Commission
Knoxville, TN
865-594-6500
www.Texas.gov/humanrights

Utah:

Within the guidelines laid down within state statutes, Utah employees must first pursue relief by filing claims through the state Anti-Discrimination and Labor Division of the Labor Commission. They generally pursue these claims through mediation first, and if that fails, then consider filing civil action in the courts. If they choose to drop the claim at any point, employees then have the right to pursue private civil actions.

Legal Remedies for Wrongful Termination

The primary remedies available to victims of discrimination and wrongful termination in the workplace include:

- Reinstatement of benefits and position
- Injunctive relief in the workplace
- Compensation for stress and suffering
- Punitive damages
- Lost wages
- Attorney's fees and court costs

In addition to remedies for victims of discrimination, employers face penalties for violating state discrimination laws in some specific areas of employee rights:

Jury duty – criminal contempt, with fines of up to $500 and/or up to 6 months in jail; liable to employee for up to 6 weeks' lost wages, attorney's fees, and reinstatement

Garnishment– penalties relating to child support withholding; for noncompliance with support orders, liable for amount of garnishment or $1,000, whichever is greater, plus interest, legal costs, and attorney's fees.

Whistleblower- civil fines of up to $500

The protections provided by federal and state discrimination and wrongful termination laws are powerful tools for protecting the civil rights of all citizens in the workforce. State anti-discrimination agencies are adept at filing claims when violations occur, but for the fullest protection, victims may need to consult an employee rights attorney to represent them and ensure that their rights are protected throughout the legal processes allowed under Utah regulations.

Labor Commission
Salt Lake City, UT
801-530-6801 or 800-222-1238

Vermont:

Vermont state agencies such as the Civil Rights Division of the Attorney General's Office can provide guidance and answers for those seeking remedies for civil rights violations. They can also help employees file claims for those remedies, which will generally be pursued, first, by mediation. If that fails, state agencies can then pursue civil actions. However, in Vermont, employees can also retain employee rights lawyers to help them file private civil lawsuits without the assistance of state agencies.

Legal Remedies for Wrongful Termination

Victims have the freedom to seek a number of remedies under Vermont laws, including one or more of the following:

- Injunctive relief in the workplace

- Compensation for stress and suffering

- Lost wages

- Reinstatement of benefits and position

- Attorney's fees and court costs

- Punitive damages

State and federal laws also provide penalties for employers who violate discrimination and wrongful termination laws. Vermont laws with additional penalties include:

Jury duty – fines of up to $200.

Garnishment– penalties under general wage garnishment, for noncompliance with garnishment orders, liable for amount of garnishment, interest, and attorney's fees; penalties under child support withholding, for noncompliance with support orders, fines of $100 to $1,000

While legal remedies for violations of discrimination and wrongful termination laws take time and effort, it is important to remember that it is not only important for the victim to find relief from such discrimination, employers must learn that such violations will not be allowed to continue. Employee rights lawyers can help achieve both those results through their experience and skill in this complex field, and ensure that the civil rights of the victim are preserved, as well.

Attorney General's Office, Civil Rights Division
Montpelier, VT
802-828-3657
www.atg.state.vt.us

Virginia:

Employees who have had their rights violated through wrongful termination or discrimination have the option to file a claim for remedies under Virginia statutes. There are state offices of the EEOC to help, as well as the state Council on Human Rights. Victims may also retain an employee rights attorney to help them file a civil suit to obtain the remedies provided in state laws.

Legal Remedies for Wrongful Termination

There are significant remedies available to victims of wrongful termination and discrimination in Virginia, including any or all of the following:

- Injunctive relief in the workplace
- Compensation for stress and suffering
- Reinstatement of benefits and position
- Punitive damages
- Lost wages
- Attorney's fees and court costs

Employers who violate discrimination and wrongful termination laws may have specific penalties imposed upon them according to Virginia laws, as well:

- Jury duty – Class 3 misdemeanor, with fines of up to $500.
- Garnishment– penalties relating to child support withholding, for termination or discrimination, fines of up to $1,000

The federal and state wrongful termination laws that exist today have many elements to protect employees and help them respond to violations by employers. However, it is important to have an advocate who understands those laws and is able to determine the proper elements to employ in claims and civil suits on behalf of victims. An employee rights lawyer can provide that representation and expertise in a challenging legal action, possibly making the difference between success and failure.

Norfolk Local Office

200 Granby Street, Suite 739
Norfolk, VA 23510
757-441-3470 or 800-669-4000

Richmond Local Office

830 E. Main Street, 6th Floor
Richmond, VA 23219
804-771-2200 or 800-669-4000

Council on Human Rights
Richmond, VA
804-225-2292
http://chr.vipnet.org

Washington:

There are state agencies to aid employees who face discrimination on the job or who have been wrongfully terminated due to discrimination. While those state agencies may file claims for employees, employees may also file private suits in civil court with the aid of an employee rights lawyer.

Legal Remedies for Wrongful Termination

The remedies provided in federal and state laws for wrongful termination and discrimination are many, although they do not all apply to every violation:

- Reinstatement of benefits and position
- Lost wages
- Injunctive relief in the workplace
- Punitive damages
- Compensation for stress and suffering
- Attorney's fees and court costs

Not only can employees seek remedies for their losses due to wrongful termination or discrimination, the state may impose penalties on employers for such violations:

- **Jury duty** – misdemeanor, with fines of up to $1,000 and/or 90 days in prison, liable for damages, attorney's fees, and reinstatement
- **Garnishment** – for civil rights violations, liable for double back pay, damages, legal costs, attorney's fees, possible reinstatement, civil fines of up to $2,500 per violation; for noncompliance with withholding orders (including child support, child health support, and spousal support), liable for full payment, plus costs, interest, and attorney's fees
- **Whistleblower** – fines of up to $3,000, and suspension or dismissal

The more information an employee has about federal and state labor laws and protections, the better claim they will have through state agencies, or the better civil suit they will have in the courts. State agencies can provide a great deal of information, but it may take the personal care of an employee rights attorney to prepare the kind of thorough case needed to repair all the damage from abuses by an uninformed or unscrupulous employer.

Seattle Field Office
909 1st Avenue, Suite 400
Seattle, WA 98104
206-220-6883 or 800-669-4000

Human Rights Commission
Seattle, WA
206-464-6500 or 800-233-3247
www.hum.wa.gov

West Virginia:

Employees may begin the legal process by filing a claim with state agencies or a civil suit through an employee rights lawyer. The first effort may be to attempt mediation or negotiation for a settlement out of court. However, if that fails, the case may need to go to civil court for adjudication.

Legal Remedies for Wrongful Termination

The specific remedies state agencies and employee rights attorneys may pursue through the legal process include one or more of these resolutions:

- Injunctive relief in the workplace
- Reinstatement of benefits and position
- Lost wages
- Compensation for stress and suffering
- Punitive damages
- Attorney's fees and court costs

Employee relief under West Virginia laws doesn't stop there; there are also penalties employers may suffer for specific violations under state statutes:

Jury duty – contempt of court, with fines of $100 to $500, liable for reinstatement, lost wages, and attorney's fees.

Garnishment– penalties in relation to child support withholding, wrongful termination or discrimination violations are misdemeanors, with fines of $500 to $1,000

Whistleblower– civil fines of up to $500, elected or appointed public officials who commit violations with intent to discourage disclosure, suspension for up to 6 months

With all of these options available to employees suffering from wrongful termination or discrimination on the job, it is only a question of finding the right legal representative, either in a state agency or in an employee rights law firm, who will take the time to thoroughly understand their case and pursue it until their rights are honored and compensation is won.

Human Rights Commission

Charleston, WV
304-558-2616 or 888-676-5546
www.wvf.state.wv.us/wvhrc

Wisconsin:

In accordance with state parameters for wrongful termination and discrimination claims, employees must work through state agencies to begin the claims process. If attempts at mediation and conciliation are unsuccessful, the agency may either pursue the case into civil court or allow the employee to retain an employee rights attorney to file that civil action.

Legal Remedies for Wrongful Termination

Claims and civil actions in Wisconsin are aimed at obtaining any or all of the following remedies:

- Lost wages
- Injunctive relief in the workplace
- Reinstatement of benefits and position
- Compensation for stress and suffering
- Punitive damages
- Attorney's fees and court costs

In addition to those remedies, there are penalties employers who have violated Wisconsin discrimination laws must face:

Jury duty – fines of up to $200, possible reinstatement and lost wages

Garnishment– penalties for child support withholding: for wrongful termination, fines of up to $500

Whistleblower– fines of $10 to $100 for every day of violation

Plant closings – Employers who do not provide required notification are liable for pay and value of benefits employees would have received if closing or layoff had not occurred, payable from the day notice was required to the day notice was actually given, the day business closed, or the day mass layoff occurred, whichever is earlier

While the legal process begins with claims filed through Wisconsin branch offices of the EEOC or the Wisconsin Equal Rights Division, these cases can involve so many details of employment law that it may be wise to have an employee rights attorney involved to insure that all avenues of relief, compensation, and damages are being pursued and that the case is receiving all the attention it deserves.

Milwaukee District Office

310 W. Wisconsin Avenue, Suite 800
Milwaukee, WI 53203
414-297-1111 or 800-669-4000

Equal Rights Division

Madison, WI
608-266-6860
www.dwd.state.wi.us/er

Wyoming:

Once an employee contacts a state agency in order to file a wrongful termination claim, that agency will generally attempt to negotiate a settlement or pursue mediation so as to settle the claim out of court. If those efforts fail, however, that agency will then be required to take the claim to civil court for an official decision.

Legal Remedies for Wrongful Termination

Any or all of the following remedies are available to employees in the state of Wyoming as a result of claims or civil suits for violations of discrimination or wrongful termination laws:

- Reinstatement of benefits and position
- Lost wages
- Injunctive relief in the workplace
- Compensation for stress and suffering
- Punitive damages
- Attorney's fees and court costs

The punitive element of discrimination laws in the state of Wyoming provides penalties for employers who commit the following violations:

Jury duty – liable to employee for damages up to $1,000, legal costs, attorney's fees, and possible reinstatement

Garnishment– penalties for child support withholding, for discrimination, fines of up to $200; for noncompliance with support orders, liable for amount that should have been withheld

Representatives of state agencies such as the Wyoming Department of Employment are generally highly skilled in the legal processes necessary to pursue a claim or civil suit for discrimination or wrongful termination. However, they are often overworked and understaffed, making it difficult for each case to receive the attention it deserves. It may be of benefit for an employee to retain their own employee rights lawyer to advise them through the claims process to ensure that nothing is overlooked and they receive the relief and compensation they are due.

Cheyenne, WY
307-777-7261
http://wydoe.state.wy.us

Appendix C: Sample Letters

Writing an effective complaint letter is a skill that everyone needs to perfect in today's litigious society. In order to protect your legal rights and start the document process, you should always lodge your complaints in writing and send them via registered mail. Even if a registered letter is not required to present your complaint, it is still often a sound idea to spend the few dollars to send the letter. And we recommend that you send a copy in sealed envelope to yourself so that you have an authentic date stamp to verify what was sent in case your employer tries to deny the contents of your complaint.

The key to an effective letter is to:

- Include relevant business information. Don't get emotional or go on unrelated tangents.

- Send copies of documentation if you feel it is important to back up the contents of your letter. Do not send originals!

- Put thought into your letter. You want to sound professional. Don't use inappropriate language or slang and do not make accusations or threats. You don't want to hinder any possible legal case you may have.

- Don't be dramatic. If you use statements like: "I feel that I have been compromised in every regard and cannot function any longer in this climate." You may be expressing your stress; however, the reader(s) of this line will assume that you have resigned.

- Do not be disrespectful or sarcastic. This will result in justifying cause for dismissal. You need to prove that you are a professional.

- Do not question the abilities or motives of the person you are filing the complaint against. For example, do not describe your manager as taking no action out of fear or weakness or surmising that your supervisor had it in for you. This mistake will highlight insolence on your part.

- Make sure there is a reasonable action statement assigned to the employer (i.e. send missed wages to you, contact you, etc.) and within a set period of time (e.g. 5 business days). Otherwise, it will be unlikely that the employer will respond and the ball will remain in your court.

- Keep it brief. Try to keep it to one page.

- Start with a rough draft and keep editing it until you are comfortable with the contents. Have a trusted friend or family member read it over to get the perspective of a recipient.

- When you are satisfied with the above tasks, write the final draft. Remember, to be careful on tone and content as it will be used as evidence in any legal case or complaint to the Labor Board.

- Send it via registered mail so that you have a record of their receipt. At the same time, send an exact copy to yourself via mail and don't open it on receipt. Just file it with the registered mail receipts.

The following are some sample letters that we have included that should assist you in your composition. While your exact situation or information may not be listed, one of them should inspire you in how to compose a professional letter while getting your points across.

If you are uncomfortable to send a letter on your own, please consult an experienced labor lawyer.

Sample Demand Letter For Unpaid Wages

[insert date]

[Insert Employer's Address]

Dear *[EMPLOYER'S NAME]*:

My job ended on *[insert the day of your firing, lay-off or resignation here]*. More than 15 days have passed since then and you still owe me money for my work outstanding equivalent to *[insert number of unpaid days/ hours]*. You owe me at least *[insert the amount you believe you are owed here]*. I ask for immediate payment of the amount due. If you do not pay this in full, you may become liable for payment of all costs and attorney's fees if I have to hire a lawyer and file a lawsuit to get what you owe me. You may also be liable for payment of additional money as a penalty, as well as legal interest.

If you believe you do not owe me the full amount I have stated, but only a part of it, the law requires you to pay me immediately the amount you agree you owe me. You should also tell me the reason why you are not paying the full amount.

Please send the amount due me to my current address by *[insert date within two weeks]*:

[insert your address here]

Sincerely,

[Insert your name]

Sample Letter To Retract Spontaneous Resignation

[Insert date]

[Insert Name of Supervisor]

[Insert Employer Company & Address]

Dear *[Insert Supervisor's Name]*:

I am sending this letter via registered mail in response to your letter received today.

For the record, I vehemently dispute the contents of your letter; in particular to the statement that "I quit *[insert in the exact wording from situation]*". My understanding from our discussion on Thursday, October 29th is that I was given some time (with pay) to recover from the stress of the events of the day's conflict. In that regard, I had planned to return to work *[Insert date you plan to return]* to resume my responsibilities.

As you are aware from my *[insert number of years with the company]* years of employment with your company, I am a dedicated and capable employee who would never abandon her position regardless of the mounting duress existing in the work environment. However, as a result of your letter with the inaccurate claim of my resignation, I feel that I have suffered great embarrassment and damage to my reputation.

[Insert Supervisor's Name], this issue needs resolution as soon as possible. I will expect to hear from you within five (5) business days from delivery of this letter to discuss this issue further.

Sincerely and without malice, ill-will, prejudice or vexation,

[Insert Your Name]

All Rights Reserved, Non-Assumpsit

Sample Wrongful Termination Complaint Letter

[insert date]

[Insert Employer's Address]

Dear *[Insert name]*:

I am writing regarding your recent decision to *[insert details about the job action you are complaining about; for example, "your recent decision to fire me from my job" or "your recent decision to write me up for absences" or "your recent decision to put me on probation"]* at *[insert your employer's name]*. I have obtained information about my legal rights and I believe that your termination of me from my job was in violation of my rights under the Family and Medical Leave Act *(verify any additional state labor act)*.

[Insert details regarding situation. An example follows.] As you know, I have been a loyal employee of *[insert your employer's name]* for the last two years. As your primary receptionist, I have received nothing but positive employment evaluations from you. Over the last six months, I have been forced to use my vacation and sick leave to attend to personal issues and injuries.

Most recently, I missed a week of work to heal from a bruised rib and other injuries. I called you the morning of April 4, 2005 before my shift to inform you of my need for leave and I faxed you a note from my doctor the same day indicating that I was unable to work for the week. Nonetheless, when I returned to work the following week, you informed me that I was fired and handed me my termination letter. This letter stated that you fired me for excess absences from work. I believe that your termination of me was in violation of my rights and I would like to be reinstated as soon as possible and to receive compensation for my lost wages.

The Family and Medical Leave covers employers like *[insert your employer's name]* that employee fifty or more employees. Eligible employees under the FMLA are employees who have worked for the employer for at least a year and at least 1250 hours in the last 12 months *(verify for your jurisdiction as each one is slightly different)*, which I have. An employee may take job-guaranteed leave under the for a "serious health condition" that makes her unable to perform her job. In April, I went to the emergency room and saw my doctor to receive treatment for my bruised rib and other injuries. I was prescribed pain killers and other prescription medication and was directed by my doctor not to work for a week. This qualifies as a "serious health condition" under the act. It is illegal for an employer to punish or retaliate against an employee for taking FMLA-qualifying leave. Because the leave that I took was FMLA-qualifying, your decision to terminate me for taking this leave is in violation of my rights under the FMLA.

This is a very private issue and it is very important to me that my situation be kept confidential. I understand that you may need to consult with a limited number of other managers about my specific situation, but I request that you let me know whom you speak with.

Additionally, I expect that, in compliance with the law, you will only discuss my request for time off with other managers who need to know about the situation, and that you will ensure that they too keep this information confidential.

As you might imagine, I would prefer to address this situation informally rather than by filing a claim with the [State/Federal] Labor Board or pursuing a claim in court. I would like to be returned to my job and receive back pay as soon as possible.

Please contact me by [*insert date in one week*] at [*insert phone number*]. If I do not hear from you I will take further action to enforce my rights to the full extent of the law.

Sincerely,

[*Insert name and address*]

Sample Sexual Harassment Complaint

[Insert date]

[Insert Employer's Address]

Dear Ms. Jones:

Since *[month, year]*, I has been employed by *[Insert company name]* as a *[Insert title or position]*. Within two weeks of my start at *[Insert company name]* (mid-June 2003), I was approached by *[insert name of harasser and title]*. *[Insert name of harasser]* asked me if we be able to have sex now. During the time that he asked this question, he put his hands on my rear end and patted it. Later that day, he asked me about _____, a prospective client and person I had recently met, who worked for _____. *[Insert name of harasser]* instructed me to sleep with Mr. _____ in order to acquire the new account for *[insert company name]*. I protested and said that I would do no such thing.

Immediately after being spoken to by *[Insert name of harasser]*, I went to my own supervisor, _____, and explained what had happened. To her knowledge and as the following facts indicate, no action was taken.

In [month, year], *[Insert name of harasser]* again confronted me and asked if I was interested in him. I told him no and walked away.

At the Christmas party, 2009, *[Insert name of harasser]* approached me and asked me if I wanted to go up to his suite and "do it," saying that they should take advantage of the room and make use of it. *[Insert name of harasser]* went so far as to reach into his coat pocket and produce the key to confirm the room number he had mentioned me. I declined the offer and again told him to refrain from dealing with her in this way.

After the Christmas party and on or before [date], I and *[Insert name of harasser]* had a telephone conversation where I informed him, again, unequivocally, that she did not want to have anything romantically or sexually to do with him. *[Insert name of harasser]* responded that he had more to lose than she did. In mid-January 2010, I approached my supervisor, *[Insert name of supervisor]*, for the second time and explained what had occurred between me and *[Insert name of harasser]*. *[Insert name of supervisor]* replied that this incident had happened before and that it would not be the last time it occurred.

On [date], *[Insert name of harasser]* stated to me that they should have "a nooner," inferring that they should go somewhere and have sex around the noon hour. *[Insert name of harasser]* mentioned that they should have a "nooner" because it was, in his words, convenient; I, who worked nights, could easily disappear during the day. I immediately told my supervisor, *[Insert name of supervisor]*, about this encounter and expressed to him my concerns about my job.

The next day, [date], [*Insert name of harasser*] again approached me and whispered to me, inquiring if he had a 50/50 or 60/40 chance of sleeping with me. I informed him, in no uncertain terms, that he had a zero chance of sleeping with me.

Ten days later, [date], [*Insert name of harasser*] again approached me and said that he would like to "fax" her. I took this to mean that he would like to have sex with her. This conversation happened within earshot and plain sight of my supervisor, [*Insert name of supervisor*]. [*Insert name of supervisor*], later that day, asked me if I was all right. I told him that I was not all right and explained what had occurred. [*Insert name of supervisor*] suggested that I contact Human Resources or set up an appointment with her harasser, [*Insert name of harasser*].

Four days later, on [date], [*Insert name of harasser*] approached me at work in an edit bay and proceeded to touch my rear end with his hand. I immediately went to my supervisor, [*Insert name of supervisor*], and told him everything that had just happened.

[*Insert company*] and [*Insert name of harasser*] were obligated to treat me in a manner which protected my civil rights. Instead, [*company*] and [*Insert name of harasser*] discriminated against and harassed me, physically and verbally assaulted and battered me, amongst other wrongs. Based on the above evidence, I can establish that [*Insert name of harasser*] and [*company*] are liable for sex discrimination and harassment, and failure to prevent discrimination and harassment, all in violation of the [*State/Federal Civil Rights Act*].

[Discuss recent comparable jury verdict in your jurisdiction. You can find them online. For example: According to data compiled by U.S. Equal Employment Opportunity Commission (EEOC) in the past 10 years, the average jury award for sexual harassment cases in the U.S. courts exceeded $250,000, not including legal fees, court costs and punitive damages.].

In order to settle my claims and thereby prevent the necessity of turning to a more formal and costly means of resolution, I request the following for settlement of all claims against [*Insert name of harasser*] and [*company*]:

1. Compensate me for pain and suffering in the amount of $100,000;

2. Provide me with a positive letter of recommendation;

3. Reimburse me for her attorneys' fees and costs incurred as a result of the drastic and upsetting course of events [if you have retained a lawyer already]; and

4. Agree to put [*Insert name of harasser*] through one year of psychotherapy and/or anger management to avoid the abuse of other employees.

Please be advised that if I am forced to file a civil action in this matter, my claim will be substantially greater.

There are several ways in which this matter can be resolved, including the following:

1. <u>Civil Litigation</u>. Litigation will be time consuming, extremely expensive for both parties and could result in adverse publicity. Note, of course, that the complaint filed in this matter will be a public document, and the press could show great interest in the facts of this case, something neither party is really interested in.

2. <u>Discussion</u>. The least expensive way to resolve this dispute is if [company]'s counsel and/or you and this office discuss the case through an exchange of correspondence, telephone calls, meetings, etc. Our experience is that if both parties are reasonable and act in good faith, they can settle matters such as these.

3. <u>Mediation</u>: The parties can agree to a private mediation with someone skilled in the employment area. This option works only if both sides are motivated to resolve the case.

4. <u>Government Complaint</u>: While less expensive than civil litigation, you will still incur attorney's fees as well as be under investigation by a government board which may result in detailed scrutiny and public proceedings.

This letter is written solely for the purpose of furthering settlement discussions. Therefore, neither this letter nor any of the information contained in it may be used for any purpose in any subsequent litigation.

Your immediate review of this matter is requested. I look forward to your reply on or before [*date*].

Very truly yours,

[*Insert your name*]

Sample Racial Discrimination Letter

[insert date]

[Insert Employer's Address]

Re: Complaint of Discrimination

[Complainant] v [Employer]

Dear Ms. *[Recipient]*:

Please allow this letter to serve as my complaint of discrimination against the *[Employer]*. I have contacted your office both by phone and in person and have received no response. Most recently, on October 16, 2010, I came to your office to file a complaint of discrimination and filled out an Information Inquiry Summary. Since that date, I have received no further communication from your office. I have therefore sought timely counseling but no representative has contacted me. Thirty days have passed and this is a Formal Complaint of Discrimination.

My complaint of discrimination includes the following:

- I am a 51 year old Asian female and I began working for *[Employer]*. As of today, I am still in the same position.

- There are 6 *[Position]* with same series and title. Every one of them, including 4 Caucasian females, is a *[level]* except for me. We all have the exact same job title, and have at times performed similar work. Yet, I have remained as a *[your level]*.

- I requested a desk audit at the same time as a Caucasian worker for the same work; she was promoted but I was not.

- I have requested, on a continuous basis, Flexiwork/work at home. I have been denied and a Caucasian co-worker was approved but it is not clear what, if any, work she does at home.

- Management has intentionally given the Caucasian employees better work assignments in order to promote them.

- I feel that I am being discriminated based on my race and age by management because I have been treated differently than other, Caucasian, *[Position]*.

- Secondly, I have been treated differently than other employees in that I have received a lower rating than all of the other employees. My lowered ratings are also discriminatory in nature. This has meant that I do not receive any monetary awards.

- I have also been subject to harassment and a hostile work environment by my supervisors including [*Insert name of harasser*], [*Insert harasser's title*]. He told me on several occasions that I should not speak to other supervisors about any problems I am having. He told me that he put my name on a list of people who were going to retire without having received my permission.

- Mr. [*Insert name of other person you spoke to*], Chief of [*Department*], told me to go find a job somewhere else. His actions were discrimination based on my age and race. [*Insert name of another supervisor who would not help*] also said that I would be sitting here in 10 years complaining about the same thing. These discriminatory remarks and the constant and severe harassment by my supervisors have lead to a hostile work environment.

- Lastly, on October 6, 2010, I was given a memorandum of counseling by [*Insert name of harasser*], which was unfair and discriminatory in nature.

- When [*Insert name of harasser*] became my supervisor in September 2010, he interviewed me and cancelled my company credit card which I had used for purchasing. No other employee had their credit card taken from them.

- [*Insert name of harasser*] then asked me to work on supplies and repeatedly harassed me regarding status reports. No other employees were subject to this behavior. I was then unfairly accused of not working fast enough.

In short, I am being subjected to disparate treatment and a hostile work environment based upon illegal factors such as my race.

Please be aware that I am being represented by counsel in the above referenced matter.

After reviewing the Complaint of Discrimination, please contact my attorney so the appropriate actions can be taken.

Sincerely,

_____ _____

Complainant Date

ATTORNEY CONTACT INFORMATION

Sample Letter Notice of Default

[insert date]

[Insert Employer's Address]

Dear *[Insert Employer]*:

Re: *[EMPLOYER]* and *[YOUR NAME]*

Severance Agreement dated March 1, 2011 NOTICE OF DEFAULT

By this letter, you are advised that *[Employer]* is in default of its obligations to me under my Severance Agreement in my employment contract with that company dated March 1, 2011. To be more precise, Paragraph 19 of our employment agreement provides that *[Employer]* will pay to me, mailed to my home address written above, a check for $9,772.50 every month for three consecutive months, to arrive no later than the second day of each calendar month. Though today is the ninth day of this month, I have not yet received my check for this month.

This obligation is a "material" obligation. The payment of monies under this agreement is a central obligation; it is not an insignificant one. This would make your default a material breach of the severance agreement, and entitle me to consider it null and void or to sue the company for the monies due me, as well as for other related "damages", including among others, interest on the monies owed and legal costs of enforcement and collection.

If I am mistaken in my belief that *[Employer]* has defaulted in its obligations to me, please let me know, in writing. If *[Employer]* has, indeed, defaulted, but the default is accidental and to be promptly corrected, or "cured", please also let me know in writing.

If you believe that *[Employer]* either has not defaulted or has not paid me with good reason, please also let me know, in writing.

If I do not hear from you within seven days of your receipt of this letter, I will have no choice but to initiate legal proceedings to protect all of my interests and rights. I sincerely hope that will not be necessary.

Very truly yours,

[Insert your name]

Sample Non-Acceptance Letter

[Insert date]

[Insert employer address]

Re: SEVERANCE DISCUSSIONS

Dear [*Name*]:

Following our recent talk about [*Company*]'s termination of my employment, I have carefully reviewed the details of the severance package presented. I have thought long and hard about my termination, discussed it extensively with my spouse, and have come to accept its inevitability. I have also consulted with my accountant as well as an attorney who specializes in severance packages. The latter suggests that I work out the basics with you, and that I reach him to finalize details after an agreement is reached.

Everyone I have talked with agrees that I have to be comfortable with the package, and that is why I am writing you. There are two aspects of my life that make this situation so very much more difficult; the needs created by my health, especially my heart condition, and the needs of my family. Both weight heavily on me; neither is very flexible.

I appreciate very sincerely the spirit of the overall package offered, but four certain elements are just not in keeping with my very real, urgent needs. As you can surely imagine, my utmost concern is how long I will remain unemployed, and what damage that delay and its stress may do to my finances, my health, and my insurance coverage. All of them are related.

A. Compensation

Severance: In the narrow sense of the term, the severance element of my package – two weeks for each year worked – seems short. Even middle-level management in the [*Company1*] /[*Company 2*] merger received, after their notice period, three weeks per year, while Managing Director level received four weeks per year, if not more. The just-announced four weeks per year from [*Other Company*] further recognizes the need for a material severance component in today's brutal employment market in financial services. This makes me question why I should deserve less than the increasingly standard four weeks per year of severance they and others are receiving, and I have real difficulty accepting less.

Notice/salary continuation: Each of these seems fair, at least at this time, though I'm certain that, as they come closer to being exhausted, the feeling of fairness will run thin. To address my very real concerns about the time it may take to achieve re-employment, I ask that [*Company*] permit combined notice, salary, and severance (with company benefits) to be paid to me as salary, and to run through December 2011 but to end as soon after June 30, 2011 if I am reemployed. This I would consider reasonable, and only, fair, under the circumstances of my termination.

Continuation of the combined compensation as salary through at least June 30, 2011, is absolutely critical to me: it gets me to the ten-year service level, and therefore allows for possible retirement at age fifty-five, an extremely important option considering my health; and it provides me for the approximate amount of time someone at my level could expect to need to find a comparable position.

B: Service Length and Calculations

In speaking to others who have gone through this before, I am told that the most common area of severance discussions these days is in pension "accommodations". Since I had planned to remain at [Company] and would have, except for this restructuring, I ask that, for pension calculation purposes, five years be added to my service length, especially in light of my very positive performance record and loyalty to the company. This would bring total service length to at least fifteen years, assuming I remain on the payroll until June 30, 2010.

C: Insurance Coverages

With my serious heart condition and, more recently, back problems, and my pressing financial needs – two kids fast approaching college age—these are crucial. I would hope and expect that all coverage be continued and paid through the period of my combined compensation, that is, through December 2011, but as early as June 2011, if I am reemployed. Expiration of any one or more of life insurance, disability insurance or health benefits could be disastrous, as replacement without my being reemployed may prove impossible because of requalification requirements. The prospect of no insurance is daunting, to say the least. The prospect of no insurance and no work, given my situation, is frightening.

The necessary minimum coverage would be achieved by continuation of compensation through June 2011, as I have requested above.

D. Outplacement

Along with the three basic concerns above, I would request as extension of coverage to eighteen months, that is, through June 2011, to cover the possible gap in employment. Of course, upon reemployment I would discontinue the service.

[Insert Supervisor's name], you have always been fair and straightforward with me, and I thank you for that. I've always been a team player at [Company] and am in position of need that requires that I ask the company to go the extra yard for me. These requests are surely not beyond the company's resources, nor precedent setting. As you know, I preferred to remain a contributing member of the Group rather than be in my current position, but that is no longer possible.

I would like you to know that your commitment to consider these requests for me is highly appreciated.

Sincerely

[Insert your name]

Sample Reprimand Protest Memo

[Insert date]

[Insert Employer's address]

Dear [*Name*]:

This letter serves as a formal protest to the letter of reprimand and case of corrective action unlawfully made against me, that I received regarding a formal yet unsubstantiated claim against me on January, 23rd, 2011.

Firstly, I whole-heartedly condemn the company's use of dishonorable methods of approaching me with unsubstantiated claims regarding the "supposed" formal complaint unjustly made against me by Genevieve Baxter. A proper "formal" complaint would firstly include a documented statement signed by the complainant and be submitted for review by management. Once management receives said complaint, they would then be accountable to substantiate whether the allegations have any merit. Once merit is determined through including the person the complaint is against (me in this case), through civilized discussion, a solution would be brokered for the two persons in conflict to agree to and the matter would then be dealt with, accordingly. What the complainant did further bolstered by the corporation's management team's lacking in affording me my undeniable rights to confront my accuser and deciding my culpability in these false claims without my proper inclusion in the clearly defined process as mandated by law, was a clear and malicious departure from the description of "formal" process, above.

Genevieve Baxter claims that she was privy to hearing information over her private telephone that inspired her to be offended and make her not-so-formal-after-all complaint against me. The law, as it stands, may not be clearly understood by the present management team and if that is the case, allow me to reference some highly applicable law in this regard so that there may indeed be absolute clarity. Under the Electronic Communications Privacy Act – Title 1; in short, this portion of the Act addresses the issue of interception of private oral communications. In summary, the applicable Act makes it illegal for the interception of private oral communications unless either authorized by a legal warrant or consented to by the alternate party involved in the communication. I am in no way substantiating that anything Genevieve reports to have occurred happened but what I am stating for the record quite clearly is that I have never consented to any communication between Genevieve Baxter and myself being recorded nor has Genevieve ever asked me for my consent. This and I highly doubt there was any legal warrant issued for any communications between Genevieve and myself. Hearsay (or "he-said, she-said") is absolutely inadmissible in a court of law for very specific and highly logical reasons. Violating this law results in the undue harassment of those finding themselves, like me, on the dark-hearted intentions of the Genevieves of the world.

Further, management has approached me with the letter of reprimand and demanded that I sign it, further violating my undeniable rights. Management does not have the right to demand any signature form me, at any time and I will never consent to the brow-beating tactics displayed regarding this matter. As stated above, the federal Electronic Communications Privacy Act prohibits the intentional interception of electronic communications at the workplace. Any surveillance can only be carried out if actual or implied consent or knowledge of the surveillance by the employee (myself). This did not occur in this situation and it is your obligation to provide evidence to the contrary.

As an American, I reserve my right to live my life, free of harassment from any legal entity, let alone any corporation both privately and in the work-place. The actions that Genevieve and subsequently the management team took in dealing with this unsubstantiated and ludicrous matter constitutes harassment and will not be tolerated.

Consider this letter my official and formal complaint against Genevieve Baxter for making false and unsubstantiated claims against me, tarnishing both my good-standing and respectable reputation, culpable as liable and slander against my name. This type of action will not be tolerated. I expect the management team to conduct themselves accordingly, sighting my concerns within the body of this letter's text as substantiated evidence to support my claim. I am available, in coordination with my lawyer's presence, to discuss the matter further and expect an invitation to do so at your convenience.

Further, consider this letter to serve as an official and formal complaint against Gary Smith for taking Genevieve Baxter's unsubstantiated claims, giving them merit without my inclusion in the rightful process to defend myself and show that Genevieve's intent is both dishonorable and without substance. Further, Gary Smith having played the role of judge, jury and executioner in the farce and façade called my due-process, has affected my ability to live "harassment free" and I intend to hold him accountable, to the fullest extent.

On the over-all matter at hand, it is unfortunate that this situation has spiraled out of control but it doing so is not within my range of accountability. It started with Genevieve lighting the fire and was fuelled by Gary pouring way too much gasoline all over it. I feel I have had no choice but to respond as I have.

Unless Genevieve's claims are substantiated and I believe they never will be, I will not tolerate any further undue harassment nor will I be addressing any further comments about this or any other matters unless my legal council is present. My distrust for management in these affairs, sighting the disgraceful methods applied to me so far, is warranted and is exercised out of self protection. If Genevieve and Gary realize that they have acted without honor and were out-of-order, in the interest of honor and peace, I will accept a written letter of apology from each of them and consider the matter closed. If not and they or the corporation for that matter continue to persist, I am fully capable and more than willing to protect my rights and will hold any offender fully accountable to the letter of the law.

Without ill-will, vexation or malice,

Your Name

Sample Tip Reduction Complaint Letter

[Insert date]

[Insert Employee's Address]

Dear [Name]:

I am writing you to file an official complaint against New Wave Day Spa's illegal practices of withholding customer tips from me, a licensed massage therapist at your business location since April of 2011. Further I have serious concerns about the method by which the tips in question are being taxed.

According to New Wave Day Spa's tip distribution and payment practices, every Monday all massage therapists that are tipped by New Wave Day Spa's clientele are informed of the amount of tips they have received via a tip information sheet generated by you based upon receipts of business from the previous week. Last Monday, the tip information sheet denoted that I was to expect the amount of $257.00.

On every Wednesday, all the massage therapists including myself submit our hours of work from the previous week for review, approval and signature by you. And on every Friday, we are paid out for our wages and tips. Last Friday I was paid out properly for my wages but not for my tips, as I was only paid $192.00 instead of $257, according to the "tips earned" column of my pay stub. After receiving the week in questions pay, I brought my concern to your attention personally and asked for you to review my claim. You have failed to do so in violation of Washington State's Labor and Industry Board, whereas no employer, manager or supervisor shall withhold tips from an employee.

I'd like to remind you of the fact that we do not having a tip pooling policy in place as there are no other providers of service in the chain of New Wave Day Spa's daily business and thus there is no justification for withholding monies put forward by clientele intended for me. Thus any discrepancies between the tips information sheet and the amount actually paid out for tips is unlawful and unacceptable.

Further, I have recently inquired with Washington State's Labor and Industry Board (L&I) about the taxation of tips as wages, as per the current practice with New Wave Day Spa. L&I agents had clearly informed me that tips were not considered a part of an employee's wages or income and should not be taxed. Each and every pay stub I have received from New Wave Day Spa for the entire duration of my tenure of employment has had my tips added to my wages and taxed. Further evidenced of this is reflected on my last W2 form where the "tips" section was left blank and the "total income" section reflected any wages I earned combined with my tips.

After having complained to you about this in person on the day I noticed the discrepancy you unlawfully fired me a mere 3 days later.

I hereby formally request that you pay me any and all outstanding monies owed to me through any and all withheld tips as well as return to me any and all monies unlawfully deducted through improper taxation within 10 business days of your receipt of this letter. If you fail to do so, I reserve all of my rights and will act accordingly and with legal authority to file suit against you and New Wave Day Spa where I will lawfully demand a full and impartial investigation by a third party into your unlawful accounting practices in the form of a detailed financial audit. I will further inform any and all remaining massage therapist employees at New Wave Day Spa as to your scrupulous practices and encourage them to do the same as I.

I most sincerely hope that you will see the error of your ways and make the appropriate actions to rectify your wrong doings and avoid costly and reputation damaging litigation.

Sincerely and in honor,

Your name

Sample Pregnancy Discrimination Complaint Letter

[Insert date]

[Insert Employee's Address]

Dear *[Name]*:

I am writing to you, the Director of Human Resources for Drift River Senior Living, with the intent to have this communiqué serve as an official complaint with you regarding my rights being violated under the United States Family and Medical Leave Act, here onwards referred to as FMLA, and the Pregnancy Discrimination Act, here onwards referred to as PDA, by Operations Manager Douglas Burns, in charge of my particular location of employment, and to serve you my notice of intent to pursue legal action if I cannot attain satisfactory justice with regards to the following claim.

I began working at Drift River Senior Homes as an Operations Coordinator in the month of June, 2011. I took to my responsibilities and have been successful at my job ever since. In the month of February of 2012, I informed my immediate superior, Mr. Douglas Burns of my learning of being in the early stages of pregnancy and my subsequent intention of taking leave following the birth of my child, as per the rights afforded to me under the FMLA. Mr. Burns acknowledged my notice verbally and wished me well. Since my job does not require much in terms of physical demands, I had no problem carrying out my responsibilities with the same high quality as I have always performed.

Since my announcement to Mr. Burns though, I have been subjected to being written up and harassed repeatedly for each and every occasion that I have had to take time off work to meet with my medical practitioner for the health and well being of myself and my unborn child. On each of these occasions of reprimand and harassment, I have repeatedly cited my rights under the FMLA and the PDA. Said rights have never been acknowledged, evidenced by each and every letter of reprimand I've received never being retracted. Further, since the onset of the letters of reprimand and the subsequent harassment, I have had to endure the unreasonable stress unduly caused by Mr. Burns, acting on behalf of Drift River Senior Living, which has had a medically documented affect on my personal health during my pregnancy and has further caused complications to my pregnancy.

It was in May of 2012, after having worked 11 months without any official or documented complaint about my abilities to competently perform my job duties that I was unjustly terminated from my position with Drift River Senior Living. I respectfully assume that Mr. Burns was not acting alone and was following direction given to him from the Human

Resources department and that you and or other Human Resources employees were aware of the above and willfully condoned the interactions I have experienced through dealing with Mr. Burns.

I hereby ask that you reconsider your position with regards to the matter expressed herein and do the honorable and righteous thing by re-instating me in my position, retracting all letters of reprimand, apologizing on the record for violating my undeniable rights afforded to me under the FMLA, the PDA and The Civil Rights Act and for all subsequent undue harassment and finally, compensating me fairly for wages lost to me while unlawfully dismissed due to your company's negligence.

If you cannot fulfill my reasonable requests listed above I will have no other choice but to bring this matter to the public courts with the guidance, experience and representation and resolve of seasoned legal counsel in order to uphold my clear and undeniable rights under the FMLA.

I hope that you will use wisdom to come to the conclusion that my claim is lawful and that I have acted and continue to act in honor and according to the law with regards to this matter; despite the hardship I have had to unlawfully endure throughout this regrettable and unnecessary experience.

I hereby give you 15 business days to lawfully respond to my claims. I remind you that If you fail to respond lawfully within this time or refuse to fulfill my reasonable requests listed above, I will have no other choice but to move forward with retaining legal counsel and filing suit against you, Mr. Burns and Drift River Senior Living.

Sincerely and without malice or ill-will,

Your Name

Sample Bullying Complaint Letter to Human Resources

[Insert date]

Dear *[Name]*:

I am writing this letter so that *[insert company name]* management is aware of my Personal Medical Situation and the events that transpired on Friday, March the 19th, 2011.

Effective immediately, my doctor has placed me on a medical leave of absence from my employment. His note in this regard is attached.

On March 19, 2011 at approximately 1:00 pm, *[name of harasser]*, *[title of harasser]*, was hanging around outside the *[office location of harassment e.g. your office, lunch room, etc.]* that I was working in. I found this to be odd because if *[harasser's name]* isn't using the photocopier outside of *[office location]*; located immediately next to *[office location of harassment]*, he isn't in the area. He was behaving overtly jovial and outside his normal self. When everyone had cleared away from the immediate work environment, *[harasser's name]* looked at me and saw me crying. *[Harasser's name]* said in a loud strong voice: "JIMBO" rather emphatically. Afterwards, *[harasser's name]* looked left, looked right, faced me and pointed at me and laughed over and over in my face while continuing to point at me the whole time. Then when he was done after 5 or 6 seconds, he walked away, went to his office and left the building for the remainder of the day.

[Harasser's name] was aware that I had experienced an emotional meltdown earlier in the day and that I was under severe mental distress due to a family crisis. Knowing that I was in an extremely vulnerable mental state, *[harasser's name]* targeted me for harassment. His unlawful actions were discriminatory. His unprovoked harassment was clearly designed to exacerbate my mental suffering and cause me to suffer further harm. Put another way, *[harasser's name]* deliberately set out to create a poisoned work environment.

On Monday March 22, 2011 I brought these allegations forward to management, specifically *[Manager's name]*. *[Manager's name]*, however, claimed not to have the time to deal with my complaint. As a result, I am contacting Human Resources.

I ask that *[company's name]* formally investigate the unlawful workplace bullying and harassment that occurred on March 19, 2011.

It is my intention to return to *[company name]* as soon as I have sufficiently recovered. When I return, I hope to continue to contribute to *[company name]*'s success. I genuinely love what I do for a living, the people that I work with and the over-all work environment.

Sincerely,

[Your name]

Sample Bullying Complaint Letter as follow-up to Human Resources Complaint

[Insert date]

[Insert Employee's Address]

Dear *[Name]*:

I am sending you this letter in response to your response to my harassment complaint letter dated March 22nd, 2011 as a result of an incident of harassment on March 19th, 2011.

In your March 28, 2011 email, you responded to my harassment complaint by stating that I am "*an at-will employee of [company name]*" and that I do not have any "*guarantees of continued employment*". Your March 30, 2011 set out the findings of your investigation stating that you were "*unable to verify [my] version of events of March 19th*"

I disagree with your interpretation of my employee contract with *[company name]* as set out in your March 28, 2011 email. Application of any of the common law employment tests would find that I am a protected employee of *[company name]* as inferred in my signed employment contract, despite *[company name]*'s attempt to classify the relationship as that of an at-will employee. Alternatively, at a minimum, I would be classified as an employee entitled to reasonable notice of dismissal as outlined in your employee policy manual. My employment is therefore protected by the Family Medical and Leave Act ("FMLA") as well as *[company's name]*'s policy on paid medical leave.

It is my researched opinion that the workplace "investigation" undertaken by *[company name]* fell far short of its legal obligation given the fact that my complaint included allegations that raised the possibility that both the FMLA and company policies and procedures had been breached. As a result, the results of the investigation must be questioned. It appears that your investigation into the complaint consisted simply of asking *[harasser's name]* if he engaged in the impugned activity. As would be expected, he denied it. Any thorough investigation would have interviewed other *[company's name]* employees and contractors to determine if my complaint was consistent with *[harasser's name]*'s managerial behavior and if *[harasser's name]* was aware of the emotional difficulties I was experiencing prior to the date when *[harasser's name]* reportedly harassed me. It is my understanding that *[harasser's name]* is widely viewed by the other employees of *[company's name]* as that of a workplace bully who regularly harasses his subordinate employees. That description, if accurate, describes an unlawful poisoned work environment at *[company's name]* that *[company's name]* has a legal obligation to rectify.

In addition, it is my respectful opinion that you are not the appropriate individual to investigate the workplace harassment complaint filed against *[harasser's name]*. He is a powerful senior individual within your organization and may be able to influence you career, either negatively or positively. As a result, there is a reasonable apprehension that the results of your investigation will be biased.

I have experienced serious compensable mental distress as a result *of [harasser's name]*'s unlawful actions. My physician is concerned that I am likely to suffer a relapse if I return to work under the current working conditions at *[company's name]* immediately. As a result, we ask that *[company's name]* assign an external independent investigator to immediately conduct a full, thorough, investigation into the allegations of harassment against *[harasser's name]*.

I look forward to receiving confirmation as to whether *[company's name]* is prepared to conduct an independent investigation into this matter by agreeable to the above-noted settlement proposal by Friday, May 18, 2011.

Yours very truly,

Your name

Appendix D: Case Studies

The following case studies outline real world examples in order to highlight how the labor laws can be applied as well as mistakes that the employee or employer may make. While some situations seem simple when they start out, the application of the law is usually dependent on the actions of the parties involved.

Allegation: Racial Discrimination

Employee's Basis for Allegation: David, a minority, feels that neither he nor other minorities in the company are receiving promotions in comparison to non-minorities.

Background: David has been working for Widget Inc. for a few years. David feels discriminated against due to his race because he feels that new job assignments and promotions are going to non-minorities. He wants to address the topic but does not want to do it directly for fear that he would be seen as a troublemaker.

David goes to see his supervisor and during the conversation, he mentions how hard it is for people to move up the ladder at Widget. David makes sure that he doesn't mention the word "race". He also mentions how he knows he performs well while other co-workers do not but they seem to be receiving the better job assignments and promotions.

As a result of the conversation, David's supervisor assumes that the plant manager is holding a grudge against David and they discuss some minor incidents that have occurred that may have tainted the plant manager's view. David knows that the plant manager might have similar issues with non-minorities who still get promotions and good assignments, but he doesn't mention that in the conversation.

At no point does David clarify that his complaint is based on racial discrimination. He is afraid that by raising this issue using the words "race" and "discrimination", he will jeopardize his job.

Within six months, David is fired. Widget does not look fondly on instigators as they feared that he was setting them up for a discrimination lawsuit.

Justification: After the discussion with David, his supervisor started monitoring David's work more closely. He recorded every incident, no matter how small, that would call into question David's performance on the job. Eventually, David was placed on formal discipline for poor performance, rule violations and attendance/tardiness issues even though some of these items may have been overlooked in the past. After another short period, David is terminated for violating the terms of his discipline by committing additional poor performance or rule violations.

Action: David contacted a lawyer as he felt that he had been wrongfully terminated because he got disciplined for infractions that others don't get disciplined for. He feels that he has a case for racial discrimination and retaliation. David tells the lawyer about the conversation that he had with his supervisor.

Resolution: David's case does not get very far as his lawyer advises him that he made several errors in his complaint to his supervisor:

- David did ***not*** say he felt discriminated against because of his race. It would have been to his advantage to openly state the legal category that might apply to his complaint that he was making rather than be evasive. As a result, the employer will argue that he did not in fact make a race discrimination complaint and therefore did not gain protection against retaliation.

- David did ***not*** state any facts in his complaint which directly show that discrimination might be occurring. He could have talked about non-minorities getting treated better, but he did not. It's not necessarily enough even if he had mentioned "race". A solid complaint that will hold up in court will mention "race" and will use race-related examples.

- David said damaging things during the complaint process about how he agreed that the plant manager might hold a grudge towards him due to some incidents in the past. This makes it look like David did not believe he was being discriminated against due to race but rather because of ongoing problems resulting from old events including ongoing personality conflicts.

- David did not complain to Human Resources or to some designated high-level manager. It's best to get the problem into the hands of Human Resources or people with more power to fix it than front-line supervisors, especially if front-line supervisors are the source of the problem.

- David did not complain in writing. It's best to make a written complaint using relevant facts. Verbal complaints allow the employer to dispute what he claims he said in his complaint, even though he is still allowed to testify to his own recollection, however, a written complaint would end any speculation about what David said. With a verbal complaint, it is easy to jeopardize your credibility in court if you testify with even the slightest differential from your original statements.

Those problems could cause the case to get tossed out of court on the technicality that David didn't say enough of the right issues and he said too much of the wrong issues in his complaint. So what could have been a thriving retaliation and discrimination case is now a more questionable case that may not be worthwhile pursuing.

Allegation: Sexual Harassment by a Superior

Employee's Basis for Allegation: Working in the Accounting department of XYZ Corp., Pam was a dedicated employee who got along with everyone in the department. After about one year on the job, Mark, who was the Controller and one of Pam's supervisors, started making inappropriate comments towards her and giving her "gifts" of a sexual nature. While there were currently no demands on Pam to get involved in a physical relationship with Mark, this ongoing unwanted attention impacted Pam's work performance as well as her comfort in the workplace. She also suffered from sleeplessness, headaches and chronic stomach pain from the stress.

Background: While the reporting structure of the Accounting department was relaxed in practice, the department had a hierarchy. It had one Manager (John) who ran the team, one Controller (Mark) who reported directly to the Manager. The staff reported to both the Manager and Controller. After about a year on the team, Pam noticed that Mark's behavior towards her changed. He would make comments to her such as "Let's hear about Pam's wild weekend with her boyfriend. I'll bet I know what she did" in a team meeting or "Only Pam makes me hot and sweaty" when he came back from a lunchtime run. He also gave Pam a deck of cards with scantily clad people on them as a Christmas gift. In addition, he would put newspaper articles that related to sexual studies on her keyboard when she wasn't at her desk.

While disgusted with suggestive nature of Mark's behavior, Pam collected the evidence by keeping the "gifts" and recording his inappropriate comments in a journal with dates and names of witnesses. It got to a point where Pam felt the need to put an end to the situation without jeopardizing her career at XYZ. She contemplated going to HR to file a complaint, however, she felt that in her best efforts to contain the situation, she would go to the team's Manager, John, to present her evidence. Besides, the HR Manager was usually travelling to conferences and it would be another week until she returned.

While meeting with John, she presented her evidence, detailed the circumstances and emphasized how this has impacted her emotionally, physically and professionally. When John asked Pam what she was anticipating the outcome to be, she said that she just wanted the harassment to stop. He agreed to speak to Mark and asked to keep the evidence to show Mark during their discussion. Pam reluctantly complied.

After John's discussion with Mark, the harassment ceased. However, when Pam requested the return of her evidence, John told her that he had destroyed it while stating that it was no longer necessary. While Pam was not pleased about this, she felt that there was nothing she could do at this point.

Months later, Pam decided that the atmosphere at XYZ was still uncomfortable for her and decided to take a job at another company. During her exit interview with HR, the HR Manager asked her questions about how well XYZ handled employee concerns. Pam told her the extent of her experience with Mark. Surprised, the HR Manager asked if she had any evidence available. Pam told her that she presented it to John who later destroyed it.

Justification: In hindsight, Pam should have gone directly to HR with her evidence but felt that the HR Manager was not accessible with her travelling schedule. However, Pam was still following company protocol by going to John as he was a department manager at a senior level and is in a position to deal with these matters. Pam did everything right by documenting the incidents and keeping any tangible proof. However, she could have strengthened her case by writing an email to John after their meeting outlining their discussion points and copying the HR Manager. She also could have offered John photocopies of her evidence instead of giving him the originals but Pam had every reason to trust John to not tamper with such important items.

Action: Under the Civil Rights Act, Pam had every right to pursue an alternative settlement rather than feeling that it was necessary for her to leave the company. She could have taken the company to court for damages or asked for Mark to be formally reprimanded or transferred. However, initially, Pam felt that getting the harassment to stop would be enough to go back to normal but soon after she realized that it was not enough. While she left XYZ on her own volition, she felt compelled to leave for her own emotional well-being.

Resolution: After the HR Manager spoke with Pam and then John, she realized that Mark has put the company at risk even though Pam had no intention to sue and even stated that to HR. However, this was not sufficient for XYZ regardless of Pam's departure from the company. Mark was formally reprimanded and was later terminated for additional performance issues. John's conduct was also questioned. He was warned about his inappropriate handling of this case and was sent on training to strengthen his people management skills. He left the company soon after.

Allegation: Attempted Dismissal Using Harassment

Employee's Basis for Allegation: Jane, a visible minority who had emigrated from Asia, felt harassed and intimidated by her employer and their attempts to bully her into signing their written justification to fire her for causes completely manufactured by both her counterpart and her manager.

Background: Jane had been working for 5 years as a manager of a consumer product distribution company with several outlets; one of which she had complete management control upon being hired. Jane was hired by another recently hired manager at the time by the name of Genevieve. Jane was hired to do the exact same job as Genevieve and that was to manage her own distribution outlet. Jane was trained by Genevieve at her respective location and she just so happened to be a very quick study and had completed her training in record time, impressing both Genevieve and Gary, the Regional Sales Manager. Upon Jane's completion of training, she was promptly assigned her own business location and began her managerial duties. In a short period of time, Jane began producing exceptional sales results, customer and employee satisfaction levels that her specific location had never seen before. In fact, Jane's numbers and over-all performance were on par with and trending towards surpassing Genevieve's.

Soon after Jane's performance exceeded Genevieve's, Genevieve started to exhibit behaviors that were indicative of her outright jealousy. She began speaking sarcastically and critically of Jane to both the Regional Manager and to Jane's own employees at every opportunity; nit-picking about mundane, irrelevant and trivial matters, at best. No matter how hard Genevieve tried to belittle Jane over the years, Jane's store continued to outperform Genevieve's as well as breaking its own previous sales and over-all performance records.

Throughout the company, it was generally understood that if an employee was "written up" for three violations of the company's rules, that the company was within its rights to immediately terminate the employee with just cause. Genevieve had approached Gary, the Regional Manager, and in a closed-door meeting accused Jane of violating three separate company rules. The first accusation related to Jane's alleged selling of merchandise at a heavily and unauthorized discount rate to her own employees. The second accusation was that Jane had allegedly returned said merchandise and provided a full refund on the item, well after 4 months from the time of the unauthorized sale. The third accusation was that Jane had allegedly spoken in an ill-intended and slanderous fashion about Genevieve to one of Jane's employees (Linda) in the workplace while that same employee was on the phone to Genevieve.

After having heard Genevieve's claims and accusations, Gary immediately wrote a letter of reprimand referencing the three accusations that Genevieve had put forth and that Jane should expect to receive "Corrective Action" in the very near future. The letter included an area at the bottom for Jane to sign, acknowledging the letter and its contents. Upon completing the letter,

Gary began to fax it over to Jane's location and proceeded to call Jane on her personal cell phone. Jane answered to hear Gary yelling at her with disgust, informing her of the three separate complaints having been made against her and that her fax machine should be receiving her letter of reprimand for these infractions. Gary then proceeded to demand that Jane sign the document immediately upon receipt and fax it back over immediately and that he would deal with her accordingly shortly thereafter. Jane, on at least two occasions of Gary's tantrum, tried to interject and inform Gary that he had things rather unfairly mixed up and attempted to discuss her side of the story. Gary yelling louder told Jane that he was not interested in hearing anything more from her about this and that the matter was not up for any discussion. Gary, still yelling and rather rudely reminded Jane to sign the letter or else. Gary then hung up the phone abruptly.

Jane received the fax and read Gary's letter in shock. With Jane being emotionally upset by the treatment she just endured and by what she felt were unfair accusations, Linda approached Jane and asked her why she was so upset. Jane explained that, among the other accusations, she was accused of slandering Genevieve during a recent and obviously secret phone call that Linda had made to Genevieve. Linda told Jane that she knew that Jane had never spoken ill of Genevieve nor did her character in the past five years ever show a single reflection of the accusations she was facing. Linda told Jane that she had usual cell phone contact with Genevieve for work purposes but at no time did she intentionally try to trick Jane into speaking ill of Genevieve while in contact with Genevieve via Bluetooth cell phone. Linda looked into her cell phone records with Jane and it was found that she there was a phone call made from her phone at the time Jane was accused of slander. Linda could only offer Jane the explanation that she may have accidentally dialed Genevieve's number (it was on speed dial) as she wore her phone on her hip and had regularly bumped into things resulting in unintended calls out. The phone call was found to have taken place over 12 minutes, something Linda never does, as her communication requirements with Genevieve require only a minute or two at a time; no more. Further, she does not recall Genevieve ever saying "hello" upon the receipt of the call in question. Linda told Jane that she was willing to stand by her side and tell Gary that she never participated in any secret calls and that at no time did Jane say anything ill-willed about Genevieve or anyone else. Jane appreciated Linda's support and retired to her office for a few minutes to determine her next course of action.

While trying to settle down, Gary had phoned Jane back demanding to know if the fax had come through and what was detaining her from signing it and returning it. Jane told Gary that she felt absolutely sick to her stomach about all of this and that she was headed home right away. She further informed Gary that she would have an answer to his letter upon her imminent return. She told Gary that she had nothing more to say and wasn't going to be taking phone calls from anyone until her return and calmly ended the conversation and went straight home.

Action: After arriving home and taking some time to calm down, Jane spoke of her issues with her husband over dinner that night. Jane's husband mentioned a friend that happened to be a labor lawyer and that she should contact him first thing in the morning and let him know all of the details. Jane indeed called and the lawyer mentioned that she had one heck of a case. He asked Jane what she really wanted at the end of the day and Jane replied that she really liked her job and that she was hoping to put this behind her and go back to doing a really good job and enjoying her career. The lawyer commended Jane for her positive attitude and offered to help her write a few letters in attempt to salvage the situation as he was currently working an numerous cases and did not have sufficient time to represent her right away. Jane agreed and they started immediately. Jane returned to work after two days of absence and had multiple copies of her letter of response ready for distribution. Jane was approached by Gary and she handed him an envelope with a copy of her letter, citing that an official copy was on its way to him, the President, Human Resources and the State Labor Commission and that she was not going to engage in any discussions until all parties had a chance to read what she had to say.

The letter that Jane and her lawyer had crafted was sent to each recipient through registered mail prior to her return. Jane's letter began by condemning the company's dishonorable method of approach regarding the unsubstantiated claims made against her and their threats of unwarranted corrective action. Jane, rather professionally, then criticized the management team for not allowing her any opportunity to speak to any of the alleged infractions that she was being accused of. Jane went on to address Genevieve's slander allegations by informing the letter's addressees of Part I of the Electronic Communications Privacy Act that addresses the issue of invasion of privacy, specifying its applicability to her situation as it is illegal to intercept her private communications without her consent. As well, the letter accused the company of undue harassment for taking this route with her. Jane asserted further acts of harassment by referencing Gary's pressure that Jane sign his letter of reprimand; something Jane knew she had no legal obligation to do. Jane continued by claiming her response to serve as a formal complaint against both Genevieve and Gary for making false accusations and tarnishing her good reputation in the workplace. Jane insisted that speaking in person about these issues would not occur unless both she and her lawyer were present and that she looked forward to hearing back from the management team to make an appointment to do so and that for their offenses against her, she was prepared to hold all parties accountable to the fullest extent that the law allowed.

Jane closed out her letter citing the unfortunate and no longer tolerable choices that management had made through Gary's actions. Jane warned the company that she was more than willing to hold all parties accountable if the company insisted on pursuing their questionable and dubious claims any further. However, Jane did offer a resolution to all involved citing that if Gary and Genevieve agreed to provide her with a written letter of apology acknowledging their wrongdoings, she would forgive them and move forward with continued success at her business location, putting the entire matter behind her.

A few days went by and Jane was invited to meet with Gary and the Human Resources department to discuss the issue. Jane attended but when questioned about anything to do with the alleged accusations, she reported that everything she had to say was in her letter and would not speak to any issues until her concerns with the violation of her rights were addressed. The Director of Human Resources repeatedly tried to coax Jane to talk about the unfounded allegations but Jane stood her ground. She told the Director that if she was to endure the same repeated questions over and over again, she would conclude the meeting and go back to her work. The Director instructed Jane to return back to her duties and that she would be in touch with her about the matters at hand soon.

Justification: Through the help of her lawyer, Jane understood that the company she worked for had no right to treat her in the fashion that they did. She fully understood that they were highly accountable for gross violations of her rights as an employee, her rights as afforded by the Civil Rights Act, as well as her rights as a human being. Her lawyer, knowing that all Jane wanted was to continue doing the great job she was known for, thought it appropriate for Jane to clearly communicate her knowledge of her rights and her willingness to defend them completely, if necessary. Jane left the matter in the company's hands and awaited their response.

Result: After some days of discussion amongst its representatives, the company including the President, the Director of HR and Gary, the Regional Manager, realized that their position was a very weak one and they requested a meeting with Jane to discuss their perspective and what they intended to do about the complaints at hand. At that meeting, the company's representatives informed Jane that they would like to consider the matter resolved and they expressed their hopes that they could all put this unfortunate incident behind them and move forward as per Jane's original desires. Being intimidated by Jane's inclusion of the State Labor Board, the company requested Jane write a letter to all of the original addressees, including the State Attorney General withdrawing her official complaint. Jane asked for a moment to call her lawyer and did so, explaining to him the proceedings and what the company was asking from her. Jane's lawyer was pleased to hear the news and advised her that he would draft the letter being requested of Jane and submit it to the Labor Board and the rest of the company representatives soon. Jane returned to the meeting after a few minutes and informed the group that her legal representative agreed and that a letter would be forthcoming. Under the instruction of management, Gary apologized verbally to Jane for his inappropriate behavior. Jane accepted and the meeting concluded. A few days later Jane's lawyer delivered, via registered mail the following letter, affirming Jean's good character and honorable intentions…

"This letter serves as a formal Notice to all addressed parties regarding my letter of protest to the letter of reprimand and case of corrective action unlawfully made against me that I received regarding a formal yet unsubstantiated claim against me on DATE of this year.

This Notice serves to inform you all that after face-to-face discussions with representatives from the Human Resources Department and the offending manager Gary, I was pleased to see the that the management team in question had come to recognise my inalienable rights and had realised that further pursuit of their unsubstantiated claims through clearly illegal, let alone immoral methods was neither in their best interest nor honourable. I was further pleased to hear that they considered any of their unlawful claims to no longer be of any issue and that they wished to continue operating in business with me, putting this unfortunate and ill-intended experience behind us, where it belongs. I am pleased to confirm to all parties addressed that I, acting in honour, was in agreement and wished the same.

This Notice further informs you that I have forgiven my wrongful accusers, my abusers of my inalienable rights and that I mean them no harm and that I wish for a continued peaceful and prosperous relationship as one of the company's highest performing employees, intending to be so for years and years to come.

This notice further informs you that in the interest of all parties' legal responsibilities with upholding my rights as a Human Being, as an American Citizen and as an employee of the corporation, it is advised that the corporation and its agents strictly adhere to the Equal Employment Opportunities Commission, The Civil Rights Act as well as the State Labor Code and that that strict adherence be in-tact at all times, never to deviate. With all clarity, be advised that if further repeated deviations from this strict adherence to lawful process on behalf of the corporation towards myself in any future regard, I reserve all of my rights afforded to me in the above mentioned Laws, Statutes and Acts and will hold all offending parties fully accountable to the maximum extent of the law.

For the public record, this specific matter has now come to a mutually agreed upon close and I personally look forward to experiencing a quick return to my normal, harmonious and harassment free working and personal life as well as a quick return to my sense of well being.

Sincerely, without ill-will, vexation or malice.

Jane"

Jane continues to work in her store with her employees and has continued to do so harassment-free. Jane's confidence grew tremendously with this experience, even though it came at an initial high emotional cost.

Allegation: Creating / Sustaining a Hostile Work Environment

Employee's Basis for Allegation: Jerry, although not an obvious visible minority, was a first generation born American of both Middle Eastern and European heritage and it was only his second day on the job in an I.T. department as an Advanced Computer Support Specialist assigned to support the Senior Executives of a major American banking firm. Jerry's manager demonstrated public displays of racism and bigotry towards Muslims and Arabs early on in his employment and held Jerry's background against him.

Background: The morning of his second day at the office, Jerry was hard at work getting familiar with the firm's technology platform when he was approached by his hiring manager, Donald, who asked him to join him in the boardroom as there was news of an aircraft flying into one of the World Trade Center's towers. Jerry's second day on the job ended up being the dreadful September 11th that the world would never forget. As Jerry entered the boardroom with Donald, he saw many of his new colleagues standing in front of a television watching the news and expressing their fears and concerns. Donald called for everyone's attention and said that efforts were underway to release employees for the day allowing them to return home to their families and loved ones. Donald further stated that the firm was going into a disaster recovery mode and that the Executive Team would be transferring to their designated recovery facility until further notice. Donald expressed regret over what was occurring in New York and called for prayers for the people who lost their lives. Donald then stated to the group that he didn't understand why we haven't "nuked" the Muslims and the Arabs off the face of the planet yet and that if we had done so already, we wouldn't be going through what we are today. He wished everyone a safe journey home and asked Jerry to stay behind. After everyone left, Donald approached Jerry and asked if he was able to stay to help the Executive Team transition to their operational protected location known as "The Bunker", advising Jerry that he didn't have to if he didn't want to. Before Jerry could say yes, Donald continued with his insults towards Muslims and Arabs, referring to the tragedies unfolding on the television before them. Jerry did eventually get a chance to answer and agreed to help out as much as he could. Donald thanked him and assigned tasks for him to perform.

Jerry finished his second day with rather mixed emotions. While he liked his new job and liked the people he works with, he was also seriously troubled at the racism and bigotry his hiring manager had for Muslims and Arabs in general. Jerry felt that if he didn't say anything, it would let Donald know that he was accepting of his behavior. But Jerry also worried that since he was a new employee and also on probation, his hiring manager Donald might terminate his employment.

Jerry deliberated and finally decided that the firm would not be a worthy place for him to work at if Donald was going to continue with his hostile demeanor, so he chose to speak with Donald about his concerns the very next day. Jerry asked Donald if he could spare a few moments to speak with him privately and Donald said yes. While in a closed door meeting, Jerry politely mentioned his concerns about Donald's offensive comments in the workplace. Jerry told Donald that, while he did not agree with Donald's statements, he could accept that he has these feelings, however, it did not excuse Donald's sharing of his hatred, racism and bigotry publicly in the workplace.

Donald acknowledged that his behavior may have been inappropriate and appreciated Jerry's bravery in bringing such concerns to his attention. Donald told Jerry that he never intended to make anyone feel uncomfortable and was going to make an extra effort not to share his personal opinions in the work environment. Jerry expressed his appreciation for Donald's understanding and thanked him for his time. Feeling better about the situation, Jerry returned to his job and enjoyed successfully accomplishing his responsibilities during his probation period. However, throughout those first three months Jerry had seen and heard on numerous occasions Donald speaking with hostility against Muslims and Arabs to his peers in public company locations such as the designated lunch room, the water cooler area and the hallways between the cubicles. Each time Donald would openly and loudly convey his general disdain for Muslims and Arabs, the instability of the Middle East, our need to limit immigration of "these types" and his support of President Bush's campaign to invade Afghanistan. Donald always went further and added that "they" should be wiped of the face of the earth and be done with already. Whenever Donald was aware that Jerry was within earshot, he would lower his voice and change the topic to something generic such as the weather. As soon as Donald thought that Jerry had left the area, he would carry on with his negative and discriminating rants. After some time, things became so bad that colleagues of Jerry spoke to him and mentioned Donald claiming that Jerry was "one of those dirty Arabs in disguise" and that "we have to keep an eye on him because we just can't trust him". They all revealed how uncomfortable they felt about the stress in the environment whenever Donald went off on another one of his tirades, but feared retaliation from him if they conveyed their feelings as he was their manager too. Many expressed concern that Jerry might come to the conclusion that when Donald voiced his opinions that their silence would be misinterpreted by Jerry as agreement. Jerry thanked his colleagues for sharing their thoughts. He reassured them that he would be patient and try to accept Donald for who he was and hope that he may change his biased opinions once he saw Jerry's strong work ethic and teamwork over time.

At the end of his probation period, Jerry was asked to fill out a probation review form, asking him to describe what his accomplishments so far and what he would work on to aspire further if chosen to continue with the firm. Since Jerry never received any criticism, formally or informally, of his work, he was confident that he would pass his probation with flying colors. Jerry completed the form and handed it in to his manager, Donald. Shortly thereafter, Jerry was called into Donald's office and was accused of doing less than satisfactory work and that numerous complaints had come in from the Executive Team about his inability to meet their technical needs. Jerry was shocked and asked why none of this was brought to his attention during his time with the firm so far. Donald said that he wasn't obligated to answer any of his questions and suggested that Jerry was going to lose his job. According to the company's policy, Donald must also fill out a probation review form and discuss it with the employee and compare differences. Jerry's and Donald's forms could not be more far apart. Jerry's was detail oriented and specific where Donald's was generic, accusatory and void of any examples. Jerry politely protested referencing his example-filled form of achievements where Donald's had none and Donald began to raise his voice in return accusing Jerry of insolence. The commotion caught the attention of Yufi, the Vice President of the I.T. department, who came out of his office and walked into Donald's office. Yufi was concerned about the yelling and asked what was going on. Jerry began to answer but was interrupted by further shouting from Donald, telling Yufi that Jerry was demonstrating a lack of respect he had never had to endure before and that he was in the midst of firing Jerry. Yufi asked both Donald and Jerry to enter his office to discuss the matter further.

Action: In Yufi's office, Jerry provided a detailed review of Donald's behavior on his second day, their subsequent discussion the next day, Donald's commitment to refrain from expressing his personal opinions at work and the repeated outbursts of bigotry towards Muslims and Arabs to colleagues in the work environment. Donald admitted to his comments on 9/11 and attributed them to his emotional frustrations at such a horrific incident but tried his very best to deny his repeated demonstrations of hatred since then. Yufi was concerned that Donald was a couple of years away from retiring and that he may have "old school" ideas about people outside his own "culture". Concerned about the sensitive nature of the matter, Yufi suspected that Donald was walking on very thin ice with regards to how he was handling himself and representing the company in this situation. He called for calm from both parties and invited Jerry to return to his work duties and expressed his happiness with Jerry's performance. Yufi investigate further by discreetly speaking to Donald's peers. Some had affirmed that he had been speaking negatively about Muslims and Arabs and that they were in open areas where other employees could hear. Yufi consulted with his HR division as per company policy and it was ultimately decided that Donald would benefit from attending cultural sensitivity training classes as well as other manager/employee relationship development courses with the hopes that they help him with his challenges. These training sessions would serve as a warning to Donald that his actions would not be tolerated anymore and continuing with this behavior would result in Donald's long-term employment with the company being terminated. He was soon enrolled in the classes and the educational institution reported that Donald completed the courses successfully.

Resolution: Donald, however, continued to publicly demonstrate his disdains, even though it was less frequent and with a smaller group of people. Jerry went on to complete his first year with the company having won the favor of his Executive Team and his colleagues for being an industrious and studious employee who took his job seriously and performed it to the maximum of his abilities. But Donald decided to write another poor performance review for Jerry that year. The situation was the same as before as Jerry's form was full of examples that backed up his claims of success and Donald's form on Jerry was full of accusatory one-liners that were unsubstantiated.

Jerry launched an official complaint to the Human Resources department, sighting Donald's discrimination and racism towards him, referencing his experiences starting from his second day on the job, and everything in between. After Human Resources investigated the issue and had interviewed several Executive Team members including Yufi, as well as Jerry's peers, it was found that Jerry's claims were substantiated. Further, Jerry's peers affirmed their own concerns and expressed complaints about Donald's unacceptable behavior through his constant display of hatred and racism. It was decided that Donald was a liability to the work environment in that the emotional well being of the employees was at risk and the reputation of the company was at stake overall. Thusly, Donald's employment with the bank was terminated immediately.

While Jerry had every right to be concerned about filing a complaint against Donald with HR while on probation, it might have been advantageous to review the company policies about employee's rights to a respectful environment as well as the complaint process. If Yufi had not been so intent on finding out the truth of the matter, this case may have gone a different way and Donald may have gotten away with dismissing Jerry.

Allegation: Discrimination for Disability/Racial & Retaliation

Employee's Basis for Allegation: Natasha worked as a clothes fitter for Jaxson's Department Store chain in Dallas before transferring to San Francisco in the mid- 1990s. She suffered from recurrent back and joint pain and was diagnosed with carpal tunnel syndrome and osteoarthritis. In November 2003, she commenced a requested family medical leave of absence, which was extended at least four times over the following nine months. By the time Jaxson's terminated Natasha's employment, after several leave extensions, she did not have a release from her doctor to perform her job duties, and she had exhausted her remaining sick and vacation benefits. After her termination, Natasha sued Jaxson's for disability discrimination under the California Fair Employment and Housing Act ("FEHA") and for wrongful termination in violation of public policy.

Background: Natasha began working as a clothes fitter for the Jaxson's Department Store chain, Inc. (Jaxson's), in Dallas, Texas, in April 1985. In the mid-1990's, she transferred to a fitter position in the San Francisco store. Between 1997 and 2003, Natasha had recurrent problems with back and joint pain. Dr. Black, her treating physician, informed Jaxson's that Natasha needed various accommodations, including time off work and a shortened work week, which Jaxson's provided. In December 2002, Dr. Black informed Jaxson's that Natasha had carpal tunnel syndrome in both hands and osteoarthritis in her fingers.

On November 7, 2003, Natasha requested family medical leave for about one month. Dr. Black signed a "Certification of Health Care Provider," which described her condition as pain in multiple joints, including the back, ankles, shoulders, and fingers. He wrote that the condition commenced in about July 2003 and the probable duration of the disability was until January 10, 2004. In response to the question "[I]s the employee unable to perform work of any kind?" Dr. Black responded "yes." When asked to list the essential functions of the job that Natasha was unable to perform, he wrote "all." Jaxson's granted Natasha's family medical leave until December 10, 2003.

In a letter dated January 21, 2004, Natasha informed Jaxson's that she could not return to her fitter job due to her disability, and she asked to be assigned to another position at Jaxson's. Dr. Black wrote Jaxson's a similar letter on January 25, confirming Natasha's disability and recommending she be reassigned to a position "that would not involve bending, standing, or kneeling."

This prompted Jaxson's San Francisco Human Resource Manager Kelly to enter into an extended dialogue with Natasha regarding her qualifications, restrictions and available positions within [Jaxson's]. Natasha acknowledged in her deposition that Kelly told her that she should call when she was released to return to work so that Kelly could look for other jobs in the store for her, and she acknowledged that she had agreed to do so.

In a letter dated February 16, 2004, Kelly wrote to Natasha, "Your FMLA approved leave is exhausted as of February 1, 2004. Your latest doctor's note indicates that you are unable to return to work prior to March 5, 2004. We are no longer able to hold your position open. Business needs dictate that we must make some staffing changes. You agreed to contact me when you are released to return to work so that we can assist you in exploring other opportunities within the store. . . . With proper medical updates, your sick pay benefits will continue unchanged until you are able to return to work, or your sick benefit hours are exhausted. If your situation changes and you are able to return to work prior to March 5, 2004, please get in touch with me so we can plan for your return."

In a letter dated February 24, 2004, Natasha acknowledged receipt of Kelly's February 16 letter and wrote, "According to my physician and specialists through examinations, I need to still be under their care for a little while longer before I can return to work. . . . I will be looking forward to contact you as soon as my physician let me know I can release from his care."

Dr. Black extended Natasha's medical leave four more times through August 16, 2004. The June 28, 2004 extension stated, "Natasha remains unable to return to work as she is having increasing pain. I am extending her disability for an additional 6 weeks. I believe she may be able to return to work on 8/16/04 but not in her previous position."

On July 14, 2004, Jaxson's terminated Natasha, who by that time had exhausted her remaining sick and vacation benefits. Kelly averred, "At the time, she did not have a release from her doctor to perform work of any kind. Even with a release, I concluded that given her existing (and continuing) restrictions, she was not qualified to fill any open and available position within [Jaxson's]. Moreover, Ms. Natasha utterly failed to provide me with any reason to believe that her condition was likely to change anytime in the near future. In fact, our conversations and correspondence (or the lack thereof) lead [*sic*] me to believe just the opposite."

Justification: Natasha did not receive any notice that she was going to be terminated. When she received the letter informing her she had been terminated, she was shocked and called Humphrey, the secretary in the human resources department. Humphrey simply told her the termination was a human resource decision. She felt that she was following the rules by providing doctor's authorization for extending medical leave under the FMLA. Her claim of disability was legitimate as she was unable to perform the job that she held at Jaxson's.

Action: Natasha sued Jaxson's for employment discrimination based on disability, national origin, and ethnicity in violation of the California Fair Employment and Housing Act, Government Code section 12940 et seq. (FEHA); for retaliation in violation of the FEHA; and for wrongful termination in violation of public policy. She also sued Kelly and Humphrey for retaliation. She later dismissed her claim against Humphrey.

Resolution: The court found that Natasha was not justified on her claims for disability discrimination, failure to accommodate, and failure to engage in the interactive process because the undisputed facts established that she was not able to perform the essential functions of her fitter position or any other available position at Jaxson's. Jaxson's reasonably accommodated Natasha by providing six months of leave beyond the requirements of the Family and Medical Leave Act of 1993 (FMLA) and it was not required to wait indefinitely for her medical condition to improve to the point where she could perform an available job. The court ruled in Jaxson's' favor on the retaliation claim because the termination decision was not unlawful and thus could not be retaliatory and because Natasha was not a qualified individual with a disability. Moreover, there was no evidence that Butler acted with a retaliatory motive. The court ruled in Jaxson's' favor on the national origin and ethnicity discrimination claim because Natasha failed to present admissible evidence to dispute defendants' evidence that their conduct was not discriminatory.

Allegation: Retaliation in the form of Constructive Dismissal

Employee's Basis for Allegation: After a higher ranking coworker (Paul) tried to kiss Lisa at a bikini contest that she was completing in, she told another coworker who mentioned it to another coworker, Kym, who later filed a DFEH complaint, claiming she was retaliated against for reporting the incident. Afterwards, Lisa was subsequently reprimanded for various performance deficiencies and misconduct. Eventually, Lisa resigned her employment but before she left, she was asked to and did sign statements denying the kissing incident and any inappropriate conduct on Paul's part. In her subsequent lawsuit, Lisa alleged she had been constructively terminated because she was a potential witness in Kim's retaliation case and because the YOPB wanted the DFEH investigators to rely exclusively on the (false) statements Lisa had been asked to sign before she quit.

Background: Lisa started working for the Youthful Offender Parole Board (YOPB) as an office assistant/receptionist. In October 2001, Lisa competed in three bikini contests held by a local radio station. On the day of the last contest, Pau , Chairman of the YOPB board, came up to Lisa at work and said he had heard she was doing bikini contests. He asked if she was going to do another one and Lisa told him there was one scheduled for that night. At his request, Lisa provided Paul directions to the contest. After the contest, Paul leaned in to kiss her on the mouth. Lisa turned her head so that she received the kiss on her cheek. Lisa was taken aback, but not offended.

Lisa and her boyfriend got into a physical altercation later that night and Lisa was injured. She called into work the next day and spoke to a coworker, Jeannie. Lisa told Jeannie she was not coming in and why. Lisa mentioned the kiss incident to Jeannie. Lisa also talked to her then supervisor Shelley and told her about the fight with her boyfriend.

Jeannie relayed the discussion with Lisa to another coworker, Kym.

Anthony, a manager at YOPB, heard about the kissing incident from Jeannie and subsequently interviewed Kym regarding her knowledge of what had happened at the bikini contest. Anthony told Kym to go back into the office and keep her mouth shut. Anthony told Kym that what she knew could get Paul fired, as well as get her into trouble. It could cost her job.

Anthony called Kym into his office again. Anthony told Kym she was no longer to have any contact with any of the board members or the Chairman (Paul). Peacock threatened Kym with adverse action if she said anything.

A few days later, Kym filed a complaint with the State Personnel Board in which she claimed, in part, unlawful retaliation by Anthony based on her disclosure of the kissing incident between Paul and Lisa. She said Peacock told her it could cost Paul and her their jobs.

A week later, Lisa met with her current supervisor. He criticized Lisa's work performance in the areas of her work schedule, her maintenance and organization of travel and attendance records, her need to notify him if she needed additional work, her conduct of personal business at her desk, and her installation of America Online (AOL) on her workstation computer in violation of state policy. These criticisms were memorialized in a three-page memorandum to Lisa dated November 7, 2001. Lisa was very upset by the memo. She believed it was inaccurate and contained numerous false accusations. Lisa prepared a written response addressing each area of criticism. On November 14, her supervisor sent another memo to Lisa criticizing both Lisa and her November 9th response to his first memo.

Lisa brought both of her supervisor's memos to the attention of Anthony, telling him they contained false accusations. Peacock agreed the memos were unfair, excessive and inappropriate. Anthony told Lisa that the memos did not constitute a performance issue or grounds for discipline. Anthony told Lisa he would speak to her supervisor about the matter and told Lisa he would get Lisa and him together to resolve their personality conflict. He did neither.

In early November 2001, Anthony told Lisa and Kym that there might be budget cuts in the future, and that it might be in their best interests to look for another job. Anthony did not warn any other YOPB employees to look for another job. He claimed he met with only Lisa and Kym because they were the least senior in the office.

On November 19, 2001, Lisa was given a "letter of instruction" for re-installing AOL on her computer. A letter of instruction is the first step in progressive discipline under state civil service. The letter of instruction was not placed in Lisa's personnel file, but kept by Anthony in his supervisor's file for future reference. According to Anthony, the steps for progressive discipline went from a letter of instruction to a formal letter of reprimand to suspension, short then long, to finally, termination. At each step of the process, the employee has a right to a hearing before an independent officer to review the discipline. Lisa did not request a hearing with respect to the letter of instruction.

In mid-January 2002, the YOPB transferred Kym to the Department of Corrections. Although Anthony disclaimed at trial any knowledge in January of Kym's State Personnel Board complaint, Lisa testified Anthony told her the department had decided to transfer Kym "due to a sexual harassment suit she had pending at the time."

On February 5, 2002, the YOPB received a complaint that Kym had filed with the Department of Fair Employment and Housing (DFEH) again claiming, in part, retaliation based on her report of the kissing incident.

On February 7, 2002, Anthony claimed that Lisa had once again re-installed AOL on her computer. According to Lisa, this accusation was false. She never re-installed the AOL program after receiving the letter of instruction. On February 8, 2002, Anthony told her she needed to seek employment elsewhere. He said, it "would be in my best interest to seek employment elsewhere, because I would make the office look bad if the investigators [for Kym's complaint] are there investigating and I was still there." Anthony warned Lisa that a suspension would be a huge black mark, making it harder to transfer to another state job. Anthony offered to give Lisa assistance in transferring to another state job. Anthony subsequently put four state job announcements on her chair.

On February 19, 2002, Lisa's supervisor sent Lisa an e-mail complaining that Lisa had left for the day before taking down the video conference equipment at the conclusion of the board hearings. The e-mail also criticized Lisa's handling of document disposal, forwarding of phone calls, reading of non-work related materials at her desk and time spent tending to personal telephone calls.

The email got to Anthony's superior who emailed him with directions to "[w]rite her [Lisa] up about this and other things that happen so we are in place we are [sic] with Kym, verbally dealing with it and no paper back up. Document it all." Anthony was also instructed to change Lisa's work hours "to make Lisa's job less desirable."

On February 26, 2002, Lisa told Anthony she wanted to resign from her position at the YOPB. Anthony told her to put it into writing, which Lisa did. Anthony then asked Lisa to draft another document describing the events of the bikini contest. Anthony edited the draft Lisa provided, adding his own comments and telling her to omit any mention of the kiss. Anthony also specifically directed Lisa to include a statement that Kym had made comments about Lisa's body, but that Lisa was not offended. With respect to Paul, the memo stated, in part, that Kym and Paul appeared to be on a friendly basis. Lisa "didn't notice [Paul] being more friendly to [Kym] over anyone else. Both seemed like they had a professional relationship, nothing out of the ordinary or anything I would perceive as sexual harassment." Lisa stated her "relationship with Paul was strictly on a friendly basis. He would acknowledge me in the office and that was the extent of it. Kym was just an acquaintance at work. I never observed Paul being inappropriate either inside or outside of the office to anyone."

Anthony then presented Lisa with an additional note handwritten by Anthony in his own words, which he asked Lisa to type up and sign as if she had written it out. The note stated: "Memo to File. Regarding the unfortunate `bikini contest' at McGee's, I need to clear up some misconceptions. First, Paul did not kiss me. Kym told Anthony that Paul tried to kiss me, which she just made up." Lisa typed the note up and signed it, although the statement was false. She did so because she was upset by the heavy pressure during these weeks and she was under the impression Anthony was going to assist her in transferring. She still wanted to retain a state job. She thought if she resigned, Anthony would give her a reference and help her. Anthony had been consistently friendly and Lisa did not feel he criticized her.

Lisa remained unemployed until January 2003 when she obtained a clerical job in the private sector.

Anthony provided Lisa's current contact information to the DFEH after Lisa left the YOPB's employment as part of the DFEH investigation into Kym's claims. Lisa told the DFEH that she had never seen anything indicating Paul had sexually harassed Kym. Lisa did, however, tell the DFEH about Paul kissing her.

Justification: In her subsequent lawsuit, Lisa alleged she had been constructively terminated because she was a potential witness in Kym's retaliation case and because the YOPB wanted the

DFEH investigators to rely exclusively on the (false) statements Lisa had been asked to sign before she quit.

Action: Lisa sued YOPB for retaliation based on grounds that FEHA (Fair Employment and Housing Act) makes it unlawful "[f]or any employer ... or person to discharge, expel, or otherwise discriminate against any person because the person has opposed any practices forbidden under [FEHA] or because the person has filed a complaint, testified, or assisted in any proceeding under [FEHA].

Resolution: The jury awarded Lisa $9,046 in lost wages and $146,705 in attorney's fees. The Court of Appeal affirmed the judgment, finding substantial evidence of constructive termination of Lisa's employment that was causally linked to her potential participation as a witness in Kym's DFEH proceeding.

Allegation: Retaliation for Verbal Complaint

Employee's Basis for Allegation: Plaintiff Kevin worked for SG Performance Plastics from October 2003 to December 2006. In order to receive their weekly paychecks, SG hourly employees must use a time card to swipe in and out of an on-sight Kronos time clock. Kevin alleged that from October through December, 2006, he verbally complained to his supervisors about the legality of the location of SG's time clocks. On December 11, 2006, Human Resources Manager Dennis Brown told Kevin over the phone that SG had decided to terminate his employment. Kevin filed suit under the FLSA, claiming that he had been terminated in retaliation for his verbal complaints regarding the location of the time clocks.

Background: Kevin worked in SG Performance Plastic's Portage, Wisconsin facility from October 2003 to December 2006. In order to receive their weekly paychecks, SG hourly employees must use a time card to swipe in and out of an on-sight Kronos time clock. On February 13, 2006, Kevin received a "Disciplinary Action Warning Notice - Verbal Counseling Warning" from SG because of several "issues" Kevin had with regard to punching in and out on the Kronos time clocks. The notice stated that "[i]f the same or any other violation occurs in the subsequent 12-month period from this date of verbal reminder, a written warning may be issued." Kevin signed the notice, acknowledging that he read and understood it.

On August 31, 2006, Kevin received a written warning from defendant, again related to swiping in and out on the Kronos clocks. The notice stated that "[i]f the same or any other violation occurs in the subsequent 12-month period from this date [sic] will result in further disciplinary action up to and including termination." Kevin signed the written warning, again acknowledging that he read and understood it.

On November 10, 2006, plaintiff received yet another written warning from SG for failure to swipe in and out, this time accompanied by a one day disciplinary suspension. The warning stated that "[t]his is the last step of the discipline process" and that if another violation occurred, further discipline, including termination, could result. Kevin signed the warning, again acknowledging that he read and understood it.

Kevin alleged that from October through December, 2006, he verbally complained to his supervisors about the legality of the location of SG's time clocks. Specifically, Kevin claims that he told his supervisors that the location of the Kronos clocks prevented employees from being paid for time spent donning and doffing their required protective gear. Regarding his complaints, Kevin alleged (1) that he told David (his shift supervisor) that he believed the location of defendant's time clocks was illegal; (2) that he told Lani (a Human Resources generalist) that the location of the time clocks was illegal; (3) that he told April (a "Lead Operator" and apparently another of Kevin's supervisors) that the location of the time clocks was illegal; and (4) that he told Luther that he was thinking of commencing a lawsuit regarding the location of defendant's time clocks.

SG denies that Kevin ever told any of his supervisors or any human resources personnel that he believed that the clock locations were illegal.

On December 6, 2006, SG suspended Kevin on the ground that he had violated its policy regarding time clock punching for the fourth time. Kevin claims that at a meeting regarding this suspension, he again verbally told his supervisors that he believed the location of the clocks was illegal and that if he challenged the company in court regarding the location of the clocks the company would lose. Saint-Grobain disputes that Kevin complained about the time clocks at this meeting. On December 11, 2006, Human Resources Manager Dennis

Brown told Kevin over the phone that SG had decided to terminate his employment.

Justification: Kevin states that his repeated oral complaints falls under the scope of the statutory term "filed any complaint" under the FLSA's anti-retaliation provision and was deemed protected activity. Therefore, he feels that his termination was based solely on retaliation instead of his performance issues.

Action: Kevin filed suit under the FLSA, claiming that he had protected status due to his repeated verbal complaints regarding the location of the time clocks.

Resolution: The key phrasing in the FLSA provision is "filing". It does not specify written or verbal. After the Wisconsin court ruled for SG, it was appealed to the Supreme Court. The Supreme Court determined that Congress intended the anti-retaliation provision to include oral complaints, observing that a contrary conclusion would undermine the Act's basic objectives and remove needed flexibility from those who enforce the Act. The Court also cited the Department of Labor's and other agencies' longstanding interpretations of this and similar provisions to include oral complaints. The Court concluded that oral complaints are generally permissible under the FLSA's anti-retaliation provision as long as an employee's oral complaint puts the employer on notice about a possible FLSA violation and is "sufficiently clear and detailed for a reasonable employer to understand it."

Glossary

Adoption Leave	A period of job-protected leave granted to adoptive parents to care for a newly adopted child.
Arbitration	A binding process used to resolve a particular dispute to an impartial third person. The parties involved agree, in advance, to abide by the arbitrator's award issued after a hearing at which both parties have an opportunity to be heard.
At Will	The employer is free to discharge individuals "for good cause, or bad cause, or no cause at all," and the employee is equally free to quit, strike, or otherwise cease work.
Bereavement Leave	Unpaid, job-protected leave upon death of a member of an employee's immediate family.
Common Law	Refers to outcome of cases ruled in a court of law.
Compassionate Care Leave	Leave that provides an employee with time off to provide care or support to a family member who has a serious medical condition with a significant risk of death within 26 weeks.
Complaint	Also known as a "petition." An action filed by the plaintiff in civil court, thus commencing the lawsuit.
Conduct	Personal behavior or way of acting.
Conflict of Interest	Occurs when an individual or organization is involved in multiple interests, one of which could *possibly* corrupt the motivation for an act in the other. For example, advising on a panel to regulate activities of the oil industry in the public's best interest while sitting on the Board of Directors of a large oil company. The interest of ensuring the oil company retains its profits through less government controls is in direct conflict with the needs of stricter controls for the benefit of the public. Therefore, objectivity as a panel member cannot be guaranteed due to the conflict of interest.
Constructive Dismissal	Occurs when employees resign because their employer's behavior has become so heinous or made life so difficult that they may consider themselves to have been fired.
De facto contract:	Latin term used to describe an implied contract when no

written contract exists.

Discrimination

Workplace discrimination means putting an employee at a disadvantage based on prohibited ground (Race, national or ethnic origin, color, religion, age, sex, sexual orientation, marital status, family status, disability or criminal conviction for which a pardon has been granted). Discrimination results in barriers to workplace equity because it blocks access to equal opportunities.

Dismissal

The termination of the employment relationship for cause at the direction of the employer.

Employment-at-will

Also known as "at-will employment," this term describes the mutual, voluntary entry into the working relationship by both employer and employee, with the understanding that either party may terminate the arrangement at any time and for any reason (or no reason at all) without legal ramifications, as long as there is no written contract. In this case, a contract is implied due to the nature of the employer-employee relationship.

Employment contract

Also known as a "contract of service," this is an agreement between employer and employee, which states each party's rights and responsibilities. Contains important information related, but not limited to, length of employment, salary, retirement and health insurance, vacation/holiday pay, performance expectations and much more.
Interrogatories: Process of discovery in which written questions are typed and sent to the opposing party for response. The party must sign a sworn statement attesting to the truthfulness of their responses.

Family Medical Leave

Unpaid, job-protected leave to provide care or support to certain family members who have a serious medical condition with a significant risk of death occurring within 26 weeks.

Family Responsibility Leave

Unpaid, job-protected leave that enables an employee to meet responsibilities related to care, health or education of child or care or health issues of immediate family member.

Grievance

A wrong or hardship suffered, which is the grounds of a complaint.

Group Termination	The simultaneous dismissal of a specified number of employees over a short period of time. This type of dismissal usually requires government approval beforehand.
Harassment	Engaging in a course of vexatious comment or conduct against a worker in a workplace that is known or ought reasonably to be known to be unwelcome. Workplace harassment may include bullying, intimidating or offensive jokes or innuendos, displaying or circulating offensive pictures or materials, or offensive or intimidating phone calls.
Inducement	An act, promise, threat or item that helps to persuade someone to do something.
Insolence	Condescendingly rude or disrespectful behavior or speech.
Insubordination	Misconduct where the employee refuses to recognize and submit to the authority of the employer.
Jurisdiction	The right and power to interpret and apply the law in regards to a specific territory or authority.
Jury Duty	Job-protected leave to allow employee to serve on trial jury.
Just Cause	A legally, sufficient reason to terminate an employment contract immediately and for which, no notice or severance pay is due to the employee.
Layoff	A temporary interruption of the employment relationship at the direction of the employer because of lack of work.
Malicious	Motivated by wrongful, vicious, or mischievous purposes.
Marriage Leave	Paid one day leave for wedding/civil union of employee or member of employee's immediate family. (Québec only)
Mass Termination	See "Group Termination"
Maternity Leave	Job-protected leave designed to give expectant mothers the possibility of withdrawing from work in the later stages of their pregnancy and to allow them some time to recuperate after childbirth.
Medical Leave	See "Family Medical Leave" and "Personal Emergency Leave"
Misconduct	Work related conduct that is in substantial disregard of an employer's interests. Such conduct may be willful or

intentional, but it may also be unintentional conduct that results from extreme carelessness, indifference, or lack of effort.

Mobbing	An extreme form of bullying where the victim is attacked by a group of co-workers on an almost daily basis for periods that can extend many months. This activity forces the victim to feel helpless and insecure.
Organ Donor Leave	Paid, job-protected leave of up to 30 days, for the purpose of undergoing surgery to donate all or part of certain organs to a person or 5 paid days off for bone marrow donation. (Currently in California only)
Overtime	For most employees, whether they work full-time, part-time, are students, temporary help agency assignment employees, or casual workers, overtime begins after they have worked 44 hours in a work week. After that time, they must receive overtime pay.
Parental Leave	Both new parents have the right to take parental leave of unpaid job-protected time off work.
Period Of Employment	The period of time from the last hiring of an employee by an employer to the termination of his/her employment, and includes any period of layoff or suspension of less than 12 consecutive months.
Personal Emergency Leave	Unpaid, job-protected leave due to illness, injury and certain other emergencies and urgent matters.
Plaintiff	A person, who starts, brings a case to court or who sues or who asks the Court for a trial against a person or organization.
Probation	A status given to new or poor performing employees of a company or business. This status allows a supervisor or other company manager to closely evaluate the progress and skills of the newly hired worker, determine appropriate assignments and monitor other aspects of the employee – such as how they interact with co-workers, supervisors or customers.
Probationary Period	Period allows an employer to terminate an employee on probationary status who is determined not to be doing well at their job or otherwise deemed not suitable for a particular position. Some jurisdictions have an *at will* policy, which allows

a company manager to terminate an employee at any point during the probationary period.

Reservist Leave

Job-protected leave for civilians serving as military reservist in the American Forces.

Retaliation

Penalizing conduct by an employer who cause or threaten to cause any harm to an individual on the basis that they have participated in any proceeding such as filing a complaint or refusing to act unethically to benefit the employer.

Revoke

To withdraw or cancel.

Severance

In some states, it is synonymous with termination. If specified in an employment contract or company manual, employees are entitled to severance pay which compensates for loss of seniority and job-related benefits and recognizes an employee's years of service.

Sick Leave

Leave for employees who need time off for their own illness.

Statutory Holiday

Also referred to as general or public holidays in many statutes, are days of special significance that have been established by governments to commemorate or celebrate certain events, usually of a religious or historical nature.

Suspension

A temporary interruption of the employment relationship other than a layoff at the direction of the employer.

Temporary Layoff

An employee is on temporary layoff when an employer cuts back or stops the employee's work without ending his or her employment (e.g., laying someone off at times when there is not enough work to do). An employer may put an employee on a temporary layoff without specifying a date on which the employee will be recalled to work.

Termination

The unilateral severance of the employment relationship at the direction of the employer.

Termination Notice

Written notification provided by an employer stating the date on which an employee's or employees' contract of employment will end.

Termination Pay

An employee who does not receive the written notice required by law must be given termination pay in lieu of notice. Termination pay is a lump sum payment equal to the regular *wages* for a regular work week plus benefits and vacation pay that an employee would otherwise have been entitled to during the written notice period.

Wages

All forms of remuneration. This definition includes salary, commissions, vacation pay, severance pay and bonuses. It also includes employer contributions to pension funds or plans, long-term disability plans and all forms of health insurance plans.

Wrongful Dismissal

Where an employer wishes to terminate employment, and no grounds exist for doing so, an employer is required to give reasonable notice of termination to an employee. Where reasonable notice is not given, an employer is required to provide termination pay (see above). Where an employer fails to provide such compensation, or seeks to provide inadequate compensation, an employee's legal rights may be enforced by proceeding with a claim for compensation for wrongful dismissal.

Index

A

Alcohol Testing..80

B

Breaks 13, 24
Bullying 135

C

Complaint Process 205, 291
Conduct Outside of Work 167
Conflict of Interest 166
Constructive Dismissal 118, 163

D

Disciplinary Action 149
Discrimination...................................123
    Age 130
    Disability......................................131
    Ethnicity 133
    National Origin 133
    Racial..126
    Religion 134
    Sex...129
    Sexual Harassment......................129
Dismissal 104
    Absenteeism 114
    Breach of Trust.............................113
    Constructive 118
    Dishonesty 111
    Incompetence 115
    Insubordination............................113
    Intoxication 116
    Just Cause...................................110
    Lateness 114
    Layoff 119
    Misrepresentation 115
    Poor Performance.........................115
    Probation 122
    Wrongful 104

Drug Testing 80
Duty to Accommodate 131

E

Employee
    Responsibilities..............................4
Employer
    Responsibilities..............................4
    Rights.......................................65
    Sells business 159
Employers
    Mistakes 147
Equal Pay 17
Evidence 145

G

Glossary.......................................399

H

Harassment
    Sexual Harassment 129
Holidays.......................................17
Hours of Work 13, 24
Human Resources...........................5

J

Jury Duty 25
Just Cause......................................110

L

Leave
    Adoption 29
    Maternity...................................29
    Parental 29
    Sick 48
    Voting 26
Legal Advice
    Checklist 177

Costs 185

Court Process 186

Hiring an attorney 173

Initial Consultation 175

M

Meals 13, 24

Minimum Wage 7

Mobbing 135

N

Negotiation

    Compensation 202

    How to 188

    Preparation 195

O

Overtime 13, 24

P

PIPs 150

Privacy

    Biometrics 98

    Credit Checks 87

    Emails 95

    Fingerprints 98

    GPS 95

    Lie Detector Tests 99

    Medical Information 92

    Personnel files 92

    References 92

    Search and Seizure 100

    Security Checks 89

    Spying 168

    Telephone 95

    Videotape Surveillance 93

    Websites 95

Probation 122

R

Reinstatement 169

Resignation 160

    Constructive Dismissal .... *See Constructive Dismissal*

S

Sample Letters 351

T

Temporary Layoff 119

Termination

    Cause After Firing 167

    Emotions 154

    Job Elimination 165

    Meeting 151

    Misrepresentation 167

    Release 153

    Reputation 168

    Signs of 138

    Targetted 141

Termination Law 165

V

Vacation Pay 19

W

Whistleblower Protection 52

Wrongful Dismissal 104

CPSIA information can be obtained at www.ICGtesting.com
Printed in the USA
BVOW050255060912

299706BV00001B/2/P

9 780986 668487